THE APOLOGIES
OF
JUSTIN MARTYR

THE APOLOGIES

OF

JUSTIN MARTYR

EDITED BY

A. W. F. BLUNT, M.A.,

VICAR OF CARRINGTON, SOMETIME FELLOW AND CLASSICAL LECTURER
OF EXETER COLLEGE, OXFORD

Wipf & Stock
PUBLISHERS
Eugene, Oregon

Ἕλληνές τινες...προσῆλθαν Φιλίππῳ...καὶ ἠρώτων αὐτὸν λέγοντες Κύριε, θέλομεν τὸν Ἰησοῦν ἰδεῖν...ὁ δὲ Ἰησοῦς ἀποκρίνεται...λέγων Ἐλήλυθεν ἡ ὥρα ἵνα δοξασθῇ ὁ υἱὸς τοῦ ἀνθρώπου.

S. JOHN xii. 20.

Ἕλλησίν τε καὶ βαρβάροις, σοφοῖς τε καὶ ἀνοήτοις ὀφειλέτης εἰμί.

ROMANS i. 14.

Wipf and Stock Publishers
199 W 8th Ave, Suite 3
Eugene, OR 97401

The Apologies of Justin Martyr
Edited by Blunt, A. W. F.
ISBN: 1-59752-603-7
Publication date 3/17/2006
Previously published by Cambridge University Press, 1911

PREFACE

THIS is sometimes said to be an age of new theologies. It is at any rate an age when the old formulae and phraseology of theology are on their defence. On all sides the appeal is made, explicitly and implicitly, for an interpretation or re-interpretation of theological dogmas, in order to show the real truths involved in them, the conventional expression of which has to some extent ceased to carry a vital significance to modern minds. No theological student can be absolved from the attempt to satisfy this appeal. And few things can be of more value for such an object than the study of the Patristic writings of the second century; for in them we find Christian theology still in solution, and Christian thinkers still feeling their way towards systematic dogma; and we are enabled to gather what were the realities, of which they were looking for a suitable formulation. Among such writings the Apologies of Justin Martyr must hold an important place, just because they are in no sense a technical or esoteric treatise, but a plain statement in popular terms of Christian truth, such as a plain man in that age understood it.

The present edition conforms to the general plan of the series, to which it belongs. It is primarily intended for theological students; and it does not aim at doing more than giving general guidance for the understanding of the author's meaning. In preparing it, I have received constant and most valuable help from Dr Mason, the general editor of the series; and I am also indebted to a former colleague, Dr L. R. Farnell, for supplying me with some references bearing upon passages, in which points of Pagan mythology and cultus were alluded to. To these I desire to express my cordial thanks.

A. W. F. BLUNT.

CARRINGTON VICARAGE.
October 18th, 1910.

CONTENTS

INTRODUCTION PAGE

§ 1. Justin's life ix
Justin's Apologies x
Place in history xii
Christianity and the State xvi

§ 2. Justin's theology xix
Angels and demons xxix
Ethics and Eschatology xxxi
Justin and the N.T. Canon xxxiii
The Sacraments xxxvi

§ 3. The number of the Apologies . . . xliv
Date of composition xlvii

§ 4. MSS lii
Chief editions liii
Bibliography liv
Analysis of the Apologies lv
Differences from Krüger's text . . . lviii

APOLOGY (I) 1
    " (II) 104

APPENDIX I 131
    " II 135

INDICES
  I. Subjects 137
  II. Scripture References 141
  III. Greek Words 145

INTRODUCTION.

I. *Justin's life.*

JUSTIN was a native of Flavia Neapolis (the ancient Sichem), and was probably of heathen descent[1]. The exact date of his birth is unknown, but it must have been near the end of the first century. He himself tells us[2] that he was in his youth a zealous student of philosophy, and that he was converted in mature life to Christianity. Eusebius, who calls him γνήσιος τῆς ἀληθοῦς φιλοσοφίας ἐραστής[3], states that after his conversion he continued to wear the philosopher's robe, and that he lived at Rome[4]; the latter fact is established by the evidence of the Apology itself. The details of his life are otherwise quite uncertain; but there is good reason for believing that he was martyred at Rome under the prefecture of Junius

---

[1] *Apol.* i 1. Cf. i 53.

[2] *Tryph.* 2 ff. Some suggest that this account is fictitious or at least trimmed up for artistic purposes. But we cannot be sure that it is not genuine. Events in life sometimes take place with artistic propriety. His conversion may have occurred at Ephesus, where (Eus. *H.E.* iv 18) the dialogue with Trypho is said to have taken place; but the claims of Flavia Neapolis, Corinth, or Alexandria have supporters.

[3] *H.E.* iv 8.

[4] *H.E.* iv 11. He is described there as πρεσβεύων τὸν θεῖον λόγον, which may mean that he acted as an itinerant evangelist.

x   INTRODUCTION

Rusticus (A.D. 163—167)[1], during the Principate of M. Aurelius[2]. Eusebius tells us that his death was due to the intrigues of Crescens, the Cynic; but the evidence adduced for this statement is very weak, consisting only of an ambiguous passage from Tatian[3], which may itself be due, so far as it relates to Justin, to the passage where Justin states that he is anticipating persecution owing to the hostility of Crescens[4]. It has been suggested[5] that a *loculus* in a gallery of the first floor of the catacomb of Priscilla may mark his burial-place, as it has painted on it the inscription M ZOYCTINOC, where M perhaps stands for Μάρτυς.

Justin's Apologies.

Justin must have been a prolific writer; but few of his works have survived, and many of those ascribed to him in the MSS are undoubtedly spurious. The Apologies and the Dialogue are certainly genuine;

[1] His martyrdom is attested by the title commonly given to him in Church literature. The *Acta S. Justini philosophi* (Ruinart, edition of 1859 p. 105) is now usually acknowledged to be an authentic account of the Apologist's fate, and it ascribes the event to the prefecture of Rusticus. The Paschal Chronicle gives the date as A.D. 165. Epiphanius (*Haer.* xlvi 1) says it occurred when Rusticus was ἡγεμών, though he is wrong in placing it under the Principate of Hadrian. His statement that Justin was 30 years old at the time is probably mistaken; but he may have meant that Justin had been a Christian for 30 years. Cf. Harnack *Chronol. Altchristl. Litt.* i p. 282 ff.

[2] Eus. *H.E.* iv 16.

[3] Eus. *l.c.* The passage (from Tat. *Or.* 19) runs in Eusebius Κρήσκης... οὕτως αὐτὸς ἐδεδίει τὸν θάνατον ὡς καὶ Ἰουστῖνον καθάπερ μεγάλῳ κακῷ τῷ θανάτῳ περιβαλεῖν πραγματεύσασθαι.

[4] *Apol.* ii 8 (3).

[5] Allard *Hist. des persécutions pendant les deux premiers siècles* (edition of 1903), p. 390 note.

INTRODUCTION

but there are no others which can be confidently accepted as his work. The Apologies are the type of apologetic literature, and had a distinct influence on the writings of subsequent Apologists (though there is little to show that they were much read after Eusebius' time, if we except the citations in the *Sacra Parallela* of John of Damascus). In these Justin gives no formal or logical exposition, scarcely even an outline, of a complete Christian system. His purpose is merely to collect arguments to justify fair and equitable treatment of the Christians by the authorities, and to support his demand that they should not be condemned unheard. With this object he seeks to refute the popular calumnies against the Christians, he insists on the excellence and truth of the Christian teaching and on the effects which it produces, and he struggles to prove the claims of Christ, especially by the argument from the fulfilment of prophecy[1]. Thus, although he is dogmatic to a degree exceptional among Apologists, owing to the fact that he concentrates his argument round the Person of Christ, yet it is futile to seek in the Apologies for a formulated system of Christian theology.

His style has no artistic greatness, except a certain vein of sarcasm[2]; though he can sometimes rise to an occasion[3]. In general the style is, though fluent, yet careless and diffuse; his reasoning is sometimes rambling and fanciful, abounding in digressions, repetitions, and parentheses, which confuse the argument; and the construction of his sentences is often clumsy. His merits as a writer are due to moral rather than artistic qualities.

---

[1] The popular belief in daemonic miracles and magic probably induced him to avoid using the argument from miracles; and he only mentions miracles of exorcism.

[2] e.g. i 9 : 21 : ii 12.   [3] e.g. i 14.

The straightforward boldness of his language is remarkable; he gives a decided impression of earnestness, candour, and thoughtfulness; and his Christianity is tinged with a liberality of mind that produces in him a reverence for truth and nobility of character, wherever they are found. He is, however, not a deep thinker; he betrays many symptoms of an uncritical disposition[1], though possibly he was not in this respect behind the standard of his age; nor is he entirely free from clear errors of fact[2]. In general he appears as a man of respectable rather than remarkable talent, well-read and well-educated (though far inferior in learning and scholarship to Clement of Alexandria), but with very few claims to be considered an original thinker, standing, as regards power and independence of mind, at a much lower level than his disciple Tatian.

Place in history.

The importance and interest of Justin's writings are due to his historical position in the development of Christian thought. His writings were well known to and freely used by later authors such as Tatian, Athenagoras, Irenaeus, Tertullian. He was one of the first who tried to reconcile Christian theology with philosophy, and to justify Christianity to the ordinary world of Greek culture. He represents therefore the fusion of Christianity with the Greek spirit. He sees foreshadowings of the truth in the old mythology, and does not shirk the argument from comparative religion[3]; his treatment of heathenism is not bigoted, though he

---

[1] e.g. in i 20 : 44 : 59, and in his treatment of O.T. prophecy.
[2] e.g. in i 31 : 62, possibly also in i 26.
[3] Cf. i 21 : 22.

holds that its immoralities and corruption show it to be a trick of the demons. He is to some extent influenced, on the ethical side, by Stoicism, but he insists upon the doctrine of free-will in opposition to the Stoic fatalism[1]. He disliked the Epicureans as licentious[2], and the Cynics as unprincipled[3]. His chief mental prepossessions are Platonic. He was, by his philosophical training, an enthusiastic Platonist[4]. He probably did not get from Plato his Trinitarianism or his general conception of a personal God, though he often puts it in Platonic form; and he is not incapable of unwittingly parodying Platonic thought, as he parodies Old Testament prophecies[5]. His Platonism is therefore not more profound than his general thought; but it shows itself in constant reminiscences, in frequent comparisons between Platonic and Christian doctrine, and in an open and whole-hearted admiration of Socrates[6]. He assumes that, so far as Christianity and philosophy are both true, they cannot be opposed to one another, but must be the product of the same *Logos*. But he considers that Christianity possesses the whole truth, whereas Greek philosophy possesses only a part, and a debased part, of the truth[7].

It is a great mistake to represent Justin's theology as little more than popularized heathen philosophy[8], or to lay equal stress upon the heathen and Christian elements in it[9], just as it is a mistake to treat him as a Jewish Christian of the Ebionitic type[10], or as a Vatican Romanist of the most developed orthodoxy[11].

---

[1] Cf. ii 6 (7). [2] Cf. ii 15. [3] Cf. ii 8 (3).
[4] Cf. ii 13. [5] Cf. i 60. [6] Cf. i 5.
[7] Cf. ii 13. And see Bardenhewer *Altkirchl. Litt.* § 18, 10.
[8] As is done by Aubé. [9] This is what Engelhardt does.
[10] This was the theory of Credner and the Tübingen critics.
[11] The view adopted in Maran's edition.

He is rather a type of the 'plain man,' firmly believing in Christ, and yet at the same time reluctant to abandon the principles of secular philosophy, and attempting to find a formula which shall allow the two to be harmonized. Many of the subjects of later controversy do not come at all within his purview, and some of his language certainly contains potentialities of theories which were later condemned by the Church[1]. But his general standpoint is that of common-sense orthodoxy of the primitive type, combined with a distinct liberality and tolerance for imperfect approximations to Christian belief in pre-Christian systems, such as is a creditable characteristic in many of the early Fathers. At the same time his view of Christianity is not entirely the same as that which is most prominent in the Apostolic writings; at least the emphasis is different. Justin has but small concern with doctrinal ideas. He makes little of Atonement and Redemption, compared to the function of Christianity as an attestation of rational truth. This may be partly due to the purpose which the Apologies were intended to serve; but it must also be due to the temper of the author's mind. He was rather a philosopher and a moralist than a theologian or a mystic; and so the chief interest which Christianity possessed for him was as the true philosophy theoretically, and the right law of life practically. In this respect he is representative of his age. As Dorner points out[2], for all the early Christian writers Christianity is the philosophy $\kappa\alpha\tau'$ $\dot{\epsilon}\xi o\chi\acute{\eta}\nu$, and was only saved from evaporation in vague spiritual emotion by the growth of a Canon giving an objective representation of Christian truth (as contrasted with the *gnôsis* and with Montanism, which

---

[1] See later, p. xxii.
[2] *Person of Christ.* Period i, Epoch 2, § 1.

INTRODUCTION

are definitely anti-historical). And so, while Justin is of little importance in the development of scientific Christian theology (his only notable contribution being the theory of the spermatic *Logos*), yet his writings are of abiding interest, as showing us the manner in which liberally-minded men of ordinary talent and culture were seeking, in the second century, to express the fundamentals of the Christian faith in terms which should commend themselves according to the canons of current philosophical thought. As an Apologist he was compelled to lay small stress upon the technical doctrines of Christian theology, and to present Christianity rather as a system of philosophy[1] (philosophy being then treated as a rule of life and not as a mere intellectual system), than as a method of Redemption. But Justin was undoubtedly predisposed to this apologetic standpoint, not only by the general tendencies of his time, but also by the special quality of his own mental habit. The conditions, under which apologetic treatises had to be written, suited his own bent, and the bent of his time. His works therefore are not to be estimated so much by their anticipations of points of subsequent theological controversy, as by the picture, which they give, of the attitude of ordinary Christians of the second century towards the Christian faith, and of the method in which they approached the problem of reconciling Christian doctrine with secular thought. It was necessary to prove that Christianity was 'rational,' before the heathen world could accept it; and not till that point had been disposed of, could Christian thinkers proceed to examine technically the dogmatic implications contained in the simple statements of the New Testament.

[1] Cf. i 4 : 7.

Christianity and the State.

The broad plea of the Apologies is that Christianity should be treated on the same lines as any other philosophy. It was not likely that this suggestion should be favourably received by the authorities. Christianity was the first system which was definitely antagonistic to the State religion. Other philosophers had acquiesced in the State gods as a political expedient, without necessarily believing in them. Christianity flouted them. It is true that Judaism had been similarly opposed to the State worship. But, though Jews were not averse from proselytism, yet their religion was exclusive rather than, like Christianity, aggressive. Moreover Judaism was a national religion[1] and, as such, a fit subject for Roman toleration (which was a matter of high politics), whilst the Christians represented no particular nation. Thus we find that, despite occasional Jew-baiting, the Jews were on the whole tolerated in the East (though not to the same extent in the West) under the early Emperors, partly because the kings of Judaea were closely connected with the Imperial family, partly because Rome conceived herself to be carrying on what had been the general policy (with the exception of the interlude during the reign of Antiochus Epiphanes) of the Seleucid kings. Even after A.D. 70, when the Jewish State came to an end and the centralization of worship at Jerusalem was suppressed, and after the risings of A.D. 116 and 130 had been crushed, the Jews were still released from such civil and military duties as were incompatible with their faith. But the growth of Judaism in the West, and of

---

[1] Cf. Mommsen *Roman provinces* Bk viii, c. xi.

Christianity regarded as a Jewish sect, awoke the watchfulness of the authorities. Hadrian made circumcision penal, and Pius allowed it only to children of Jewish descent, i.e. conversion to Judaism was penalized, obviously as being an attack on the State religion. Christianity therefore stood in a different position from Judaism. Nevertheless the government, as such, was not on the whole bitterly hostile to the Christians in the early days of the Empire; as a rule it did not institute persecution against them, and tried to secure to them a fair trial. Where persecution arose, it was usually due either to considerations of political expediency or to popular clamour. Thus the Apologists' work was likely to do good among the people, by protesting the moral innocence of the Christians, by spreading a knowledge of the Christian position, and by refuting popular calumnies.

At the same time Christianity was legally a *religio illicita*, and the confession of Christianity was a legal ground for punishment, being tantamount to a secession from the State cult; and this position of affairs was bound to continue, so long as the Emperors conceived it to be a part of their policy to maintain the State religion as revived by Augustus. Hence, though the practice of individual Emperors might vary, and though some might attempt to make the conditions more equitable to the Christians, the theoretical policy was always the same towards them. The Apologists ignore the existence of this political necessity; indeed, from their point of view, they had no option but to do so. But, so long as the necessity was an acknowledged maxim of State policy, Apologies could effect no amelioration in the legal position of the Christian religion.

Antoninus Pius and Marcus Aurelius, the two

INTRODUCTION

Emperors to whom the Apologies are addressed (Verus may be neglected as of subordinate importance), were among the best of the Roman Emperors. Antoninus was a man of simple and temperate life, of estimable and honourable character, and personally religious in temperament. It is to his credit that he infused a stronger spirit of equity and humanity into Roman law, and endeavoured to facilitate the enfranchisement of slaves. Though he did not discountenance the laying of informations against Christians, he was disposed to be tolerant towards them; he did not encourage official inquisition for them, and at the end of his reign he intervened to stop persecution of them in the cities of Asia and Greece. In short, he discouraged the practical exercise of the law against Christianity. M. Aurelius is one of the best types of the neo-Stoicism of Rome; he was animated with a sincere desire for moral perfection, regulated by the Stoic principle of obedience to duty; and he had an earnest zeal for the service of mankind, based upon the principles of brotherly love and forgiveness. He continued the policy of Antoninus in legislation and in the administration of justice. But his *doctrinaire* sense of duty to society caused him to countenance the persecution of Christians, and to regard their refusal to worship the State gods as sheer obstinacy ($\psi\iota\lambda\grave{\eta}$ $\pi\alpha\rho\acute{\alpha}\tau\alpha\xi\iota\varsigma$[1]). The rescript, which he issued in A.D. 177, providing for the punishment of new sects which excited popular feeling, led to an outbreak of popular animosity against the Christians at Lugdunum.

---

[1] *Med.* xi 3. The sole reference to Christianity in the *Meditations*.

II. *Justin's theology.*

Although, as has been said, the Apologies are not intended to give a complete or systematic exposition of Christian doctrine, yet they contain in solution most of Justin's main ideas; and the indications, which they afford, of his notions of Christian truth are numerous enough to enable us, by piecing them together, to make a general outline of his theological position.

The Father. Like the majority of early Christians, Justin is fundamentally and primarily a monotheist. The conception of One God is with him an axiom; he does not argue in its favour, but merely assumes it as the basis of faith. In this point his Platonic training and his Christian belief are entirely at one. He is lavish of epithets to express the unique transcendence of the Only God. He is $\dot{a}\gamma\acute{\epsilon}\nu\nu\eta\tau\sigma_{S}$ (i 14, 1: ii 5 (6), 1 etc.), $\ddot{a}\rho\rho\eta\tau\sigma_{S}$ (i 9, 3: 61, 11: ii 10, 8), $\dot{a}\nu\omega\nu\acute{o}\mu\alpha\sigma\tau\sigma_{S}$ (i 63, 1: cf. i 10, 1: 61, 11: ii 5 (6), 1), $\dot{a}\epsilon\grave{\iota} \, \ddot{\omega}\nu$ (i 13, 4), $\ddot{a}\tau\rho\epsilon\pi\tau\sigma_{S}$ (ib.), $\dot{a}\pi a\theta\acute{\eta}_{S}$ (i 25, 2), $\gamma\epsilon\nu\nu\acute{\eta}\tau\omega\rho \, \tau\hat{\omega}\nu \, \dot{a}\pi\acute{a}\nu\tau\omega\nu$ (i 13, 4), $\pi a\tau\grave{\eta}\rho \, \pi\acute{a}\nu\tau\omega\nu$ (i 8, 1 etc.), $\delta\epsilon\sigma\pi\acute{o}\tau\eta_{S} \, \pi\acute{a}\nu\tau\omega\nu$ (i 12, 9: 32, 10 etc.), $\pi\acute{a}\nu\tau\omega\nu \, \delta\eta\mu\iota o\nu\rho\gamma\acute{o}_{S}$ (i 8, 2 etc.), $\kappa\tau\acute{\iota}\sigma\tau\eta_{S}$ (ii 5 (6), 2), $\pi o\iota\eta\tau\grave{\eta}_{S} \, \pi\acute{a}\nu\tau\omega\nu$ (i 20, 2: cf. 26, 5: 58, 1: 67, 2). It is difficult to decide whether Justin did or did not reject the belief in the eternity of matter. The passage in i 10, 2 is certainly ambiguous (see note *ad loc.*). And it is possible that the influence of Plato might have affected his ideas on the subject (cf. i 59, 1), though the problem of Plato's theory of matter is by no means an easy one. It is probable, however, that the distinction between a world made by God out of matter which He had not made, and a world made by God out of matter which He had made, scarcely suggested itself with any definiteness to Justin. And there can be no question that in his view God was transcendently and uniquely supreme, unbegotten Himself and the begetter of all things. At the same time he does not treat God as abstractly or metaphysically simple and without attributes. God is metaphysically incomprehensible, but Justin does not fail to emphasize His moral personality and His personal interest in the affairs of mankind. He calls Him πατὴρ δικαιοσύνης καὶ σωφροσύνης καὶ τῶν ἄλλων ἀρετῶν, ἀνεπίμικτός τε κακίας (i 6, 1), he speaks of σωφροσύνη and δικαιοσύνη and φιλανθρωπία as οἰκεῖα θεῷ, τὰ προσόντα αὐτῷ ἀγαθά (i 10, 1). Similarly God is termed τῶν πάντων ἐπόπτης δίκαιος (ii 12, 6), and His concern in human conduct is asserted (ii 3 (4), 2 : 7, 1).

The Logos. So far then Justin's monotheism is quite simple to understand. It is a theory of One Supreme God, who transcends human comprehension, but nevertheless possesses a moral Will and exercises it in the supervision of terrestrial events. The problem, therefore, that lay before the Apologist was that of finding room in his monotheistic system for a second Divine Person, without falling into Ditheism on the one hand, or into materialistic views of a Son of God on the other, such as had been characteristic of heathen mythology. This difficulty Justin attempted to overcome by the theory of the *Logos*, which is the central pivot of his theology. He uses the word in a double sense[1]; the *Logos* is both the Creative Word, the agent in creation (i 64, 5: ii 5 (6), 3), and also the Divine Reason, the sum of Divine truth (ii 10, 1). In this respect Justin's

[1] Cf. Dorner *Person of Christ*, Period i, Epoch ii, § 1, who refers us to *Tryph.* 61.

conception is not quite the same as that of St John's Gospel, where the *Logos* is rather considered in the former aspect. It bears more analogies to Philo's use of the term. But there is no proof that Justin was consciously borrowing his ideas from Philo. He uses the *Logos* doctrine as if it were not novel, but fully naturalized in the Church, and a prevalent method of interpretation. It may be doubted whether he derived it from the fourth Gospel, though it is possible that that Gospel was held to sanction the use of the term in the thought of the Church[1]. But Justin's version of the *Logos* doctrine seems, in the process of exposition at any rate, to start from a general philosophic conception, such as was current in the schools of the time, especially among the Stoics.

It was a maxim of current philosophy that Reason, λόγος, is what unites God and man, and allows man to know God; and here probably can be found Justin's starting-point. A very slight effort of personification was needed in order to avoid the pantheism to which this theory, when crudely stated, easily led. And the means for this was provided by the Church doctrine of Christ as the Incarnate *Logos*. According to this, the *Logos* represented a distinction in the Divine essence. He was diverse ἀριθμῷ, though not γνωμῇ, from the Father (cf. ii 5 (6), 3). But nevertheless He proceeded from the Father, and His mission in all ages had been to interpret the Father to man. Thus the Old Testament manifestations were given by the *Logos* (i 63, 10); and indeed all approximations to the truth, of which any man in any age had been capable, had been due to

---

[1] On the point whether Justin was acquainted with the fourth Gospel, see later, p. xxxv.

His work (i 5, 4: ii 7 (8), 1). In fact it is not always easy to decide whether Justin is using the word λόγος in the abstract sense, or as a title for a definitely-conceived Person (e.g. in i 10, 6: 64, 5: ii 9, 4). And so Justin arrives at his great theory of the λόγος σπερματικός. Previously to the advent of Christ, men had possessed seeds of the *Logos*, and so had been enabled to arrive at such fragments of truth as they could grasp (i 32, 8: 46, 3: ii 8, 1: 10, 2: 13, 3; cf. i 28, 3). The *Logos* was thus the eternal and universal source of all goodness and all truth, and in every age ὁ νουνεχής, as such, would obey His commands (i 12, 8), and to that extent could even be called a Christian (i 46, 3).

And now this *Logos*, formerly apprehended only in fragmentary fashion, had in entirety become incarnate in the historical Christ. The dispensation of the λόγος σπερματικός had now yielded to that of the λόγος μορφωθείς (i 5, 4). In Christ was embodied τὸ λογικὸν τὸ ὅλον (ii 10, 1; cf. i 46, 2). Thus, though a quantitative distinction could be drawn between the Persons of the Father and the *Logos*, yet the doctrine of their absolute and necessary moral unity precluded any ditheistic inferences. Father and Son were not separate parts of the Godhead. The *Logos* was the *Logos* of God, and not an unbegotten subsistence like the Father. Indeed Justin was so anxious to lay stress upon this point that he has been accused of subordinationist tendencies. So far as the Apologies are concerned, there are only four passages which give the slightest ground for such an accusation. Of one, viz. i 13, 3, it is possible to say at once that it may be dismissed as irrelevant. The assertion, which is there made, that Christ is honoured ἐν δευτέρᾳ χώρᾳ, refers to the position of the Incarnate Word in liturgical worship, and not to His position absolutely as a Person in the Godhead. The same is probably the case with regard to the passage in ii 13, 4. The phrase in i 32, 10 denotes logical precedence rather than the absolute subordination of the Son to the Father[1]. But the words used in i 12, 7 are less susceptible of being explained in a Nicene sense, though they are not so strongly tinged with subordinationist ideas as the passage in *Tryph.* 128. And there can be little doubt that Justin, in his anxiety to avoid any danger of representing God as qualitatively distinct from the *Logos*, or as suffering change by the procession of the *Logos*, tended to fall into an opposite error. He was so eager to escape all appearance of Ditheism that he can scarcely be held to lay sufficient stress upon the equality of Son and Father, as touching their Godhead. But it needed a longer process of reflexion and controversy, before the Christology of the Church could be properly formulated. And it is undeniable that Justin held firmly the doctrine, which is ultimately incompatible with strict Subordinationism, viz. that the *Logos* is of the essence of God and not parallel to a creature. This essential Divinity of the Son is unceasingly asserted in the Apologies. Justin calls Him ὁ παρ' αὐτοῦ (τοῦ θεοῦ) υἱός (i 6, 2), θεῖος (i 10, 6), υἱὸς τοῦ θεοῦ (i 12, 9), or τοῦ ὄντως θεοῦ (i 13, 3). And other phrases are less vague; He is πρῶτον γέννημα τοῦ θεοῦ, born ἄνευ ἐπιμιξίας (i 21, 1), μόνος ἰδίως υἱὸς τῷ θεῷ, λόγος αὐτοῦ ὑπάρχων καὶ πρωτότοκος καὶ δύναμις (i 23, 2; cf. also i 46, 2), or again λόγος καὶ πρωτότοκος ὢν τοῦ θεοῦ καὶ θεὸς ὑπάρχει (i 63, 15), or lastly He is μόνος λεγόμενος κυρίως υἱός, ὁ λόγος πρὸ τῶν ποιημάτων

---

[1] Cf. Dorner *op. cit.* Div. i, vol. i, note TTTT, and his discussion in the text, to which the note refers.

καὶ συνὼν καὶ γεννώμενος κτλ. (ii 5 (6), 3). These passages make it clear that Justin did not regard the *Logos* as inferior in essential Divinity to the Father, although some occasional phrases, which he uses, show that he had not firmly grasped the complete implications of his own view.

The *Logos* therefore, according to Justin's theology, is God's Creative Word and the Divine Reason, the first-begotten of God, God's agent in creation and His instrument in pre-Christian theophanies, the source of all human truth and goodness; He is quantitatively diverse from the Father, and is sometimes represented as subordinate to Him; but at the same time He is regarded as the only and absolute Son of God, in a sense in which that title can be applied to no other person, for He is begotten, not created. In short the *Logos* 'was with God and was God.' It is open to doubt, however, whether Justin also believed that the *Logos* was 'in the beginning,' or whether he was inclined to actualize Him only as related to the world. The crucial passage bearing on this point in the Apologies is ii 5 (6), 3 ὁ δὲ υἱὸς ἐκείνου, ὁ μόνος λεγόμενος κυρίως υἱός, ὁ λόγος πρὸ τῶν ποιημάτων καὶ συνὼν καὶ γεννώμενος, ὅτε τὴν ἀρχὴν δι' αὐτοῦ πάντα ἔκτισε καὶ ἐκόσμησε, χριστὸς μὲν κατὰ τὸ κεχρῖσθαι καὶ κοσμῆσαι τὰ πάντα δι' αὐτοῦ τὸν θεὸν λέγεται, ὄνομα καὶ αὐτὸ περιέχον ἄγνωστον σημασίαν, ὃν τρόπον καὶ τὸ θεὸς προσαγόρευμα οὐκ ὄνομά ἐστιν. The usual interpretation of this passage, which conjoins the clause ὅτε...ἐκόσμησε with γεννώμενος, has appeared to some to present a difficulty of theology, by making, apparently, the statement that the *Logos* was not begotten, until the world was created as a κόσμος; He had existed before in some sense, πρὸ τ. π. συνών, where συνών can scarcely imply mere existence as an attribute[1], but rather union in a common life or conception; but His begotten existence, i.e. in diversity from the Father, began at the creation. This view appears to Dorner[2] so inconsistent with the many passages, in which Justin asserts the begetting of the Son before the creation of the world, that, to avoid the inconsistency, he suggests the textual alteration of ὅτε to ὅτι. And Donaldson[3] suggests that the clause ὅτε... ἐκόσμησε should be taken in conjunction with χριστὸς λέγεται, the meaning then being that the Son was entitled χριστός at the creation. But this reading of the words seems somewhat unnatural. And it may be questioned whether the difficulty of theology suspected in the other method of interpretation is not fictitious. It is scarcely conceivable that Justin could ever have thought the generation of the Son to be coincident with the act of creation; nor could this passage be taken to have that meaning, which could only be given if Justin had written γεννηθείς instead of γεννώμενος. The ὅτε clause must be attached, moreover, not only to γεννώμενος but also and equally to συνών; it simply interprets and develops πρὸ τῶν ποιημάτων. The phrase καὶ συνὼν καὶ γεννώμενος expresses the same idea as was later expressed by Origen's phrase 'eternal generation.' It implies that He who 'is with' the Father is nevertheless in process of 'being begotten,' and that this was the state of things 'before the creatures were made,' 'when at the beginning God through Him created and ordered (*or* beautified) the universe.' It is plain that, though Justin may not have definitely put to himself the question how long the *Logos* had been with the Father, yet he

---

[1] Cf. Dorner *loc. cit.* Donaldson *Hist. of Chr. lit. and doctr.* Vol. ii, c. 3, p. 221.
[2] *loc. cit.*   [3] *loc. cit.*

regarded Him as essentially Divine, begotten not made, and therefore holding a position quite unique and distinct from any creature. No doubt his Christology is not very clear, nor his view of the *Logos* free from confusion[1]. He was struggling with the difficulty of a conception, which the Church had not yet had time to discuss fully. No phrase of his is so definitely Arian as Tertullian's *Fuit tempus cum filius non fuit* (*adu. Hermog.* c. 3). He allows for a state of pre-existence of the *Logos*, though he tends to regard it rather as a potentiality until the creation[2]; and he seems to regard this state as having endured 'from the beginning.' But it is not wonderful that he could not clearly understand all the difficulties of Christological doctrine, nor anticipate all possible points of future controversy. At least he is firm to the great Christian doctrine that the *Logos* is essentially God, not a creature but a $\gamma\acute{\epsilon}\nu\nu\eta\mu a$, and so unique in the universe. And thus he saves his Christianity from Ditheism, by representing the *Logos* as always with God, quantitatively separated from the Father by process of begetting, but one in nature and will with Him, causing no break in the unity of the Godhead.

The Incarnation. And this *Logos* became incarnate in Jesus Christ (ii 10, 8)[3], by the will of God (i 23. 2: 46 5: 63, 10: ii 5 (6), 5). His birth was miraculous (i 32, 11: 33, 4: 46, 5), but His life was fully human (i 31, 7). The purposes of the Incarnation are not systematically explained, but they are broadly alluded to as being (1) the salvation, transformation, purification, and restoration of the human race (i 23, 2: 32, 7: 63, 16); (2) the conquest of death (i 63, 16); (3) the defeat of the

---

[1] Other symptoms of confusion are noted later, p. xxviii.
[2] Cf. Dorner *loc. cit.*   [3] Cf. ii 10, 1 note.

demons (ii 5 (6), 5); (4) the revelation of the unnameable God (i 63, 5). And this the *Logos* achieved by His teaching (i 6, 2 : 23, 2 : 63, 5 : ii 10, 8), and by His sufferings (i 32, 7: 63, 10, 16: ii 13, 4). He is now reigning over the world and helping those who believe in Him (i 41, 1 : 42, 4 : 50, 12); and He shall come again to judge mankind (i 52, 3). Justin's doctrine of the Incarnation, as stated in the Apologies, lays most stress upon its didactic purpose, and upon Redemption mainly as effected by its 'subjective' influence, as a redemption from sin rather than from guilt and punishment. There is no systematic treatment of the doctrine of the Atonement, no hint of a ransom to Satan, and scarcely any trace of a theory of 'satisfaction.' In this respect Justin is as primitive as he is in his Christology. But, as has been said, he was the creature of his age; his bent was not so much to theological speculation as to the highly practical philosophy of his time[1]; and the interest of his writings is due not so much to any expert discussion on points of controversial theology, as to the revelation of the ordinary attitude of a right-minded and well-educated Christian of the second century towards the fundamentals of the Christian faith.

The Holy Spirit. Justin has very little to say about the Holy Spirit as defined by scientific theology. In his language concerning Him he seems to vacillate between treating Him as a Person and as a mere attribute. He never speaks of Him, in the Apologies, as God, nor alludes to His mode of existence. He appears to have accepted Him as a distinct object of liturgical worship (i 6, 2 : 13, 3 : 60, 7 : 61, 3, 13 : 67, 2), but not

[1] E.g. it was a commonplace with Roman writers on education that women ought to study philosophy as an aid to virtue and to the proper conduct of household affairs.

to have concerned himself with speculations as to His being or distinct personality. Furthermore he scarcely draws any distinction, or at least draws it very unsteadily, between the *Logos* and the Spirit. Thus he commonly regards the Spirit as the instrument in Old Testament prophecy, the προφητικὸν πνεῦμα, subordinate to God and under God's control (i 33, 2: 44, 11); and yet in i 36, 1: ii 10, 8 this function is ascribed to the *Logos*. Similarly the ἅγιον πνεῦμα is spoken of in i 33, 5 as the agent in the Incarnation; but in § 6 of the same chapter (and again in i 46, 5: 66, 2) the *Logos* is described as performing this work (and so the Incarnation is not only due to the Father's will, but is also a voluntary act on the part of the *Logos*). This can be explained as a mere confusion of functions[1], though it looks remarkably like a real confusion of Persons. But the fact is that the early Church was very slow in grasping the full meaning of the idea of the Holy Spirit, and Justin himself plainly did not know, or had not considered, what to make of the conception. The Trinitarianism of the Apologies is therefore crude and unsettled. So far as the Third Person in the Trinity is concerned, Justin seems to have accepted Him on the authority of the Church's liturgical formulae, without thinking it necessary to speculate upon His relation to the Father and the Son or His distinct sphere of operation. It might even be possible, on the evidence of i 6, 2, to maintain that the Holy Spirit stood for Justin in no higher position than that of the angels. But that supposition is scarcely consistent with the place which he elsewhere assigns to Him, as next to the Father and the Son, in the baptismal and eucharistic formulae. The passage

---

[1] Cf. Semisch *Justin der Märtyrer* ii 303 ff.

quoted should not be strained to bear too definite a meaning. In that chapter Justin is seeking to show that the Christians are not atheists; he does so by simply enumerating the objects of their worship and reverence; and though he names the Holy Spirit after the angels, it is yet an extreme inference that he therefore considered Him to be no more than, or even inferior to, the angels. Maran suggests that in that passage Justin intends the word $\sigma\epsilon\beta\acute{o}\mu\epsilon\theta a$ alone to refer to the angels, and $\sigma\epsilon\beta\acute{o}\mu\epsilon\theta a\ \kappa a\grave{\iota}\ \pi\rho o\sigma\kappa\upsilon\nu o\hat{\upsilon}\mu\epsilon\nu$ to refer to the Three Persons of the Godhead. This is not an impossible theory. But even if it be correct we must admit that Justin's expression is somewhat loose and untechnical, and it seems clear that he had not attained to any scientific conception of the Trinity, such as was the outcome of later theological controversy. The *Logos* doctrine occupied all his attention; and the doctrine of the $\mathring{a}\gamma\iota o\nu\ \pi\nu\epsilon\hat{\upsilon}\mu a$ had to wait for its formulation by later theologians.

Angels and demons.

It is scarcely disputable that St Paul, following the common Jewish view of his time, believed in a hierarchy of angels, though in the Epistle to the Colossians he makes a protest against angelolatry. In the Church of the second century the belief in angels was quite general; but Justin's Apologies say very little concerning them. He mentions in i 33, 5 the angel of the Annunciation, and asserts in ii 6 (7), 5 that the angels were endowed with free-will. In ii 4 (5), 2 he states that the government of the world had been entrusted by God to angels, but that these had been unfaithful to their trust. He does not speak of prayers to or invocations of angels, but in i 6, 2 he states that the Christians reverence and worship (σεβόμεθα καὶ προσκυνοῦμεν) the Father, the Son, the angels, and the prophetic Spirit. The bearing of this passage upon the subject of Justin's view of the Holy Spirit has been already considered[1]. As regards the mention of the angels, it seems a natural, though not an inevitable interpretation, that Justin is giving to them a place in ordinary Christian worship; and the worship of angels was not unknown in certain districts of early Christendom[2]. At the same time the expression is, as has been said, careless and unscientific; and it is scarcely to be supposed that Justin put the angels upon a plane at all level with that of the Father and the *Logos*, nor probably with that of the Spirit.

Justin has not an elaborate demonology, as Origen has; but a theory of demons is fundamental in him, as in most of the Church Fathers. It cannot be ascertained whether Justin derived his views on the subject from the demonology of Plutarch and the philosophical schools of his time. At least we may be sure that his conception of δαίμονες would not have appeared singular to any contemporary thinker. All the evil in the world is ascribed to their agency. Their work is a general opposition to the *Logos* and all His works (i 10, 6: ii 8, 2), their object is to enslave men to evil and falsehood (i 14, 1: 58, 3: ii 4 (5), 4: 9, 4). They were responsible for the heathen mythology (i 5, 2), and the idols were copies of their shapes (i 9, 1). They had tried to forestall the New Testament and the rites of the Church (i 23, 3: 62: 64: 66, 4), though their attempts

---

[1] See p. xxviii.
[2] See Lightfoot's edition of Colossians, *Introd.*

often showed an entire misunderstanding of the true meaning of the Old Testament prophecies (i 54). They had caused the human sufferings of Christ (i 44, 12); and they were the authors of calumny and violence against the Christians (i 10, 6: 23, 3: 57, 1: ii 1, 2: 13, 1), the opponents of Christian knowledge (i 44, 12), the instigators of heretics (i 26: 56: 58). They would undergo eternal punishment (i 28, 1). This is not the place to enter upon a full discussion of demonology in general or of Justin's views in particular. It is sufficient to notice that the theory of the Apologies possesses a primitive crudity; but it is quite in line with the contemporary theory of the cause of evil, and it is a natural outcome of the views which are set forward in the Old Testament (perhaps under Oriental and Greek influences), and in the uncanonical literature such as the book of Enoch, and which were current in New Testament times.

Justin occasionally distinguishes between the evil angels and the demons. Thus in ii 4 (5), 2 he adopts the view that the angels fell by unnatural union with women, and that their offspring were the demons[1]. Similarly in ii 6 (7), 1 the same distinction is drawn. But usually the term δαίμονες seems to include all the powers of evil. In the only reference in the Apologies to Satan, the Serpent, or the Devil (i 28, 1), he is called the leader of the evil demons.

Ethics and Eschatology.

Though Justin was much interested in the moral power and results of Christianity (i 14, 2: ii 10, 8), yet he gives no systematic theory of Christian ethics

[1] See note *ad loc.*

in the Apologies, nor, as might be expected, does he touch on such delicate subjects as the morality of slavery. His chief ethical doctrine is that of human free-will (i 10, 4: 28, 3: 43: 44, 11: ii 6 (7), 3), which he attempts to reconcile with the belief in God's foreknowledge (i 43). Ethically considered, Christ's work is to effect a conversion of the will, to supplement free-will by imparting a bias towards good (i 61, 10). Thus we are saved ἐκ μετανοίας (i 28, 2), and Gehenna is the punishment of immorality and unbelief in Christ's teaching (i 19, 8); Christian faith results in goodness of life (i 65, 1: 66, 1: ii 3 (4), 2). Isolated details of conduct are touched upon; e.g. marriage and continence in i 15: 29; divorce in i 15, 5: ii 2, 5; the exposure of children in i 27: 29; obedience to constituted authority in i 17. Suicide is condemned in ii 3 (4). The passage in ii 12, 2 has been taken to imply a certain sympathy with the self-advertising desire for martyrdom, but it seems too vague to justify such an inference. It probably refers only to the public profession of Christian faith or the public championship of Christians, which entailed capital punishment. Justin does not attribute any special merit to virginity. In i 15, 6 ἄφθοροι may mean 'virgins' (though it may simply mean 'chaste,' which would probably include legally married people), but even so virginity is not exalted to a higher position than wedlock.

Justin's eschatology is no more scientifically expounded than his ethical views. He believes that souls will possess perception after death (i 18, 2: 20, 4: 52, 3), and states that men will rise with the same bodies as they had on earth (i 8, 5: 18, 6: 19, 4: 52, 3). His language is quite uncritical, but, so far as it goes, it seems to express a belief in the resurrection of the natural body. Any theorizing on the subject would however have been quite out of place in the Apologies. After the Resurrection comes the judgment (i 12, 1 : 17, 4 : 44, 11). The good will inherit eternal life and become indestructible and free from pain (i 8, 2 : 10, 2 : 12, 2 : 21, 6 : 52, 3), the wicked will suffer the pains of fire (i 44, 5 : 19, 8). This fire seems to be quite materially understood, and to be connected with the eventual conflagration of the world (i 20, 4 : 57, 1 : ii 6 (7), 1). No definition of eternity or eternal punishment is attempted, but it is stated to be an $αἰωνία$ $κόλασις$, and not merely punishment for a period of a thousand years (i 8, 4 : 45, 6), the $πῦρ$ is $αἰώνιον$ (i 21, 6 etc.), and the punishment will last $τὸν$ $ἀπέραντον$ $αἰῶνα$ (i 28, 1). It is also hinted that there will be no possibility of repentance after the judgment (i 28, 2 : 40, 7).

Justin and the N.T. Canon[1].

In Justin's time there was no fixed Canon of the New Testament, corresponding to that of the Old Testament. That there were Christian writings in existence is of course unquestionable, but the Church had not as yet compiled an official list of the books which best embodied its tradition. The process of selection of the fittest was not yet completed or approaching completion, and no doubt there were in use many Christian books (and probably many orally transmitted narratives) which varied both in text and in subject-matter from the books which eventually were

[1] The whole subject is fully discussed in Westcott *N.T. Canon*, and in Stanton *The Gospels as Historical Documents* i p. 76 foll., to which the student is referred.

included in the Canon. It is quite possible that Justin was acquainted with such writings; but there are very few passages in the Apologies that give any clear indications of such an acquaintance. As a rule they are more naturally susceptible of a different explanation. (See notes on the separate passages i 16, 5: 35, 6: 50, 12: 60, 3: 61, 4, 9.) There can be little question that Justin was acquainted with the chief books of the New Testament. Though he nowhere mentions St Paul, he must have known most of his epistles; for not only do many passages in his works justify the supposition (see Index of Scripture quotations), but also the fact that he engaged in controversy with Marcion makes it incredible that he had not studied the Pauline literature. So far as the Synoptic Gospels are concerned, Justin quotes freely from them (though less, so far as can be traced, from St Mark than from the two others) in the Apologies; and he speaks of the ἀπομνημονεύματα τῶν ἀποστόλων, ἃ καλεῖται εὐαγγέλια[1] in i 66, 3, and states that they were read at the Eucharistic meetings (i 67, 3). It seems impossible that these 'memoirs' should be any other than the Synoptic Gospels, from which Justin cites with such frequency, though it is not incredible that other writings, which did not at last obtain a place in the Canon, were still used in the public services of Churches in some places. Justin nowhere calls these writings inspired or quotes them as from God or the Spirit, and he supports the credibility of the New Testament by pointing to its accord with Old Testament prophecy (i 33, 5); but he had no doubts of the Divine mission of the Apostles (i 39, 3: 50, 12), and he calls the Christian documents 'our writings' (i 28, 1). Their

[1] See note *ad loc.*

liturgical use, alternative to or in company with the use of the prophetic Scriptures (i 67, 3), would naturally produce, or be produced by, a belief in their inspiration.

Justin is, like most ancient authors, very careless in quotation. He misquotes, adapts, introduces glosses, combines passages, to suit his requirements; many of his variations from the text of the New Testament can also be explained as sheer lapses of memory, or as due to a variant text or to a divergence of oral tradition, or as influenced by a liturgical formula which differed from the Biblical text. But such phenomena are very frequent in ancient literature, and afford no proof that Justin possessed no text of the Synoptic Gospels. They appear similarly in his quotations from the Old Testament[1] and from classical authors[2].

The question whether he was acquainted with the Fourth Gospel can scarcely be answered with any certainty. The passages in i 6, 2: 35, 6: 52, 12: 60, 3 suggest reminiscences of that Gospel, but the inference in their case is exceedingly doubtful (see notes). In i 14, 5 he says that Christ's sayings were $βραχεῖς καὶ σύντομοι$, which seems scarcely true of the teaching in the Fourth Gospel, and Veil argues therefore that Justin could not have known that Gospel. The argument however is not entirely convincing. Justin might have special reasons for quoting only from the Synoptists in his Apologies[3].

---

[1] He even ascribes passages to their wrong authors in i 35, 10: 51, 8: 53, 10. His quotations bear most resemblance to the LXX version, but Credner (*Beiträge z. Einleit. in die bibl. Schriften*) suggests that he is quoting from a sort of *Ur-evangelium*, consisting of a corpus of O.T. prophecies about Christ, in which the oldest parts depended on the Hebrew version, though it followed principally the LXX.

[2] E.g. he misquotes Plato in i 3, 3: 60, 1.

[3] As Westcott (*op. cit.*) puts it, Justin is only laying a foundation, and not building up the Christian faith.

And it would be quite possible to argue that even in the Fourth Gospel the teaching, though more continuous than it is in the Synoptic Gospels, is yet essentially gnomic in character. The passage in i 61, 4, 5 seems to be an unquestionable, though inexact, citation from John iii 3—5 (see note *ad loc.*), but it is not outside the bounds of possibility that the phrase was a common formula in use at baptisms. If, leaving isolated passages, we turn to consider the *Logos* doctrine of Justin, we are met by a similar uncertainty. The phraseology, in which that doctrine is stated, is Johannine, and yet the underlying idea is not quite that of the Fourth Gospel. Furthermore it is quite possible that Justin is only expressing and developing views which had become the common property of the Church, or which were based upon the current philosophical teaching of the schools[1]. It cannot be confidently affirmed that Justin's theory must have been derived from a knowledge of the Fourth Gospel. When all the evidence is accumulated, the balance of probability may seem to incline in the direction of supposing that Justin was acquainted with this Gospel, but the supposition must be made tentatively, and the possibility of alternative explanations must be admitted.

The Sacraments.

The Apologies give very little evidence for the system of Church organization with which Justin was acquainted. There is no mention of presbyters, and it is not stated whether the 'president' (ὁ προεστώς

---

[1] Paul (*Jahrb. f. prot. Theol.*, 1886, 690, and 1891, 147) concludes that Justin is not dependent on the Fourth Gospel, but that he is philosophizing on parallel lines to it, being however more closely related to the philosophic ideas of his time than is the author of the Gospel.

i 65, 3: 67, 4) at the Eucharistic service is a temporary or a regular official. But the 'deacons' of i 65, 5: 67, 5 certainly seem to be permanent ministers. Justin however gives us exceedingly valuable descriptions of the Baptismal and Eucharistic services, and his account deserves detailed consideration.

Holy Baptism. No formulated creed is quoted, though it is not inconceivable that fragments of some such creed are found in i 13, 3: 21, 1: 31, 7; and it is admitted that the Roman Church had a Greek baptismal creed by the year 150. Nor is any definite allusion made to the custom of Infant Baptism. The passage in i 15, 6 is often quoted as being such an allusion[1], but it can, by itself, hardly be pressed to bear such a meaning. Οἳ ἐκ παίδων ἐμαθητεύθησαν is far too vague a phrase to be invoked as definite evidence for the practice of Infant Baptism, though it is not hereby implied that the practice did not exist. But Justin's detailed description in i 61 is obviously meant to refer to the baptism of converts. So far as the form of administration is concerned, the following points should be noted; it is preceded by instruction, profession of faith (πεισθῶσι), and promise of obedience, by prayer and fasting in company with the converts' Christian instructors (2); the baptism is administered in the threefold Name (3, 10, 13), and Justin seems to speak only of immersion, using regularly the term 'bath' in reference to it[2]; nothing is said as to the person by whom the sacrament was administered, and it is not stated to be the privilege of any official person to perform the rite (cf. 10); after baptism the baptized person is introduced to the assembly of brethren, prayer

[1] E.g. in Gibson *XXXIX Articles*. Article 27.
[2] Whereas the *Didaché* (c. 7) allows affusion, where immersion is impossible.

is offered, and the worshippers kiss one another; the celebration of the Eucharist follows (i 65, 1—3). There is no mention of unction, or signing with the cross, or imposition of hands (though some suggest that the last ceremony may be implied in the mention of the prayers after baptism, and the coming to the $\pi\rho o\epsilon\sigma\tau\dot{\omega}\varsigma$ very naturally falls in with this view[1]); and it is not made clear whether the kiss is the last baptismal or the first Eucharistic action. Warren (*Ante-Nicene Liturgy* p. 61) points out that in the Clementine liturgy the kiss of peace occurs at the beginning, as well as just before the offertory.

Justin's doctrine of the Sacrament is very simply stated, without any technical discussion of the various questions of later controversy. His statements may be summed up as follows: Baptism is firstly the completion of conversion (i 61, 2), involving self-dedication (1), public profession, repentance (2), and conscious recognition of a new ideal (i 65, 1). Secondly it is regeneration (i 61, 3, 10) and the beginning of a new life ($\kappa\alpha\iota\nu\sigma\pi\sigma\iota\eta\theta\dot{\epsilon}\nu\tau\epsilon\varsigma$, i 61, 1). Those born in sin, the $\tau\dot{\epsilon}\kappa\nu\alpha$ $\dot{\alpha}\nu\dot{\alpha}\gamma\kappa\eta\varsigma$ and $\dot{\alpha}\gamma\nu oi\alpha\varsigma$, become children $\pi\rho o\alpha\iota\rho\dot{\epsilon}\sigma\epsilon\omega\varsigma$ $\kappa\alpha\dot{\iota}$ $\dot{\epsilon}\pi\iota\sigma\tau\dot{\eta}\mu\eta\varsigma$ (i 61, 10). Thirdly it brings remission of sins (i 61, 2, 10). Fourthly it is an 'illumination' (i 61, 12), the seal of the enlightenment of those who have been taught the Christian faith. But Justin does not discuss in the Apologies the question whether the sacrament is merely symbolical or actually efficacious. His language is quite naive and untechnical, and could hardly have been otherwise in the conditions under which the Apologies were written, addressed as they are to heathen readers, and for the purpose of showing that the Christian rites are at any rate harmless.

---

[1] Cf. Mason *Confirmation and Baptism* p. 319.

The Eucharist. We have two descriptions of this service in the Apologies, one (i 65) giving the procedure after the baptism of converts, perhaps the Easter celebration, the other (i 67) describing the ordinary Sunday Eucharist. The reasons for the observance of Sunday are stated in i 67, 8; they are that on this day God dispelled darkness and created the world, and Christ rose from the dead; there is no allusion to the Fourth Commandment.

The outline of the service is as follows: A reading from the 'memoirs' of the Apostles or the writings of the prophets is given (i 67, 3: this is the first reference to the liturgical use of Christian writings); the president delivers a homily (*ib.* 4); all stand up and pray in common (though no formulae of prayer are cited); then bread, wine, and water are brought to the president, who delivers over them a prayer (obviously not from a book), to which the congregation responds Amen (i 65, 3: 67, 5); then the elements are distributed to the worshippers, and taken to the absent by the deacons (i 65, 5: 67, 5); the free-will offerings are presented to the president, who uses them to help those who are in need (i 67, 6). This service is restricted to those who believe and have been baptized, and are living good lives (i 66, 1); but Justin specifies no distinction between a *missa catechumenorum* and a *missa fidelium*. There is no mention of the use of the words of institution, though they are quoted in i 66, 3; nor are the words of administration given. Furthermore there is no mention of singing or of a benediction; though these ceremonies may have been in use at the time[1].

---

[1] Thus the antiphonal singing of the Christians is mentioned by Pliny *Ep.* x 96 and a formula of blessing is given in the *Apostolic Constitutions.* Cf. Warren *op. cit.* p. 310.

The carrying of the elements to the absent does not involve Reservation in the modern sense, nor is it suggested that the absent were only absent on grounds of sickness. It is perhaps a case of coincident administration; or possibly the worshippers reserved for later use all or part of that which they received, and the absent similarly reserved for a convenient opportunity the consecrated elements brought to them[1].

It is difficult to discover the precise nature of Justin's views on the Eucharistic sacrament, so far as they are stated in the Apologies; and it seems to be a mistake to extract the dogmatic theories of later Sacramentalism from his vague and unscientific language. It is obvious that he regarded the Eucharist primarily as a service of praise (cf. i 13, 2 : 10, 1), a sacrifice[2] of praise and thanksgiving; his term for the elements is $εὐχαριστία$ (i 66, 1). And so he lays more stress upon it as an opportunity for corporate thanksgiving than as a memorial of Christ's death, a mystery, or a sacrament, or a social meal[3]. The crucial passage, in which he attempts to define the nature of the elements after consecration, is i 66, 2; and unfortunately the language of that passage is extraordinarily obscure, and admits of various interpretations. According to Otto's view, it means 'Just as by the word of God Christ became flesh, so by the word of prayer proceeding from Him the food is made the body and blood of the Incarnate Christ.' The 'word of prayer' is supposed by some to mean the Lord's Prayer[4], which may have been thus used in the

[1] Cf. Bethune-Baker *Hist. of Chr. Doctr.* p. 420.

[2] The Apologies say nothing about the Eucharist as a sacrifice in the technical sense.

[3] On the question whether Justin understood the words $ποιεῖτε τοῦτο$ in a sacrificial sense, see Gore *Body of Christ* Appended note 20.

[4] E.g. Wordsworth *Holy Communion* p. 62.

Eucharist; Otto takes it to refer to Christ's words of institution, whilst Bishop Gore[1] admits that 'any form of benediction of the elements, believed by the Church to be substantially what Christ used, or any form of prayer repeating His words of institution, would answer sufficiently to Justin's description.' This is also Donaldson's view[2], though he translates δι' εὐχῆς λόγου 'by the prayer of reason,' i.e. any Christian prayer.

Another interpretation[3] of the words, however, takes λόγου as objective genitive; 'by prayer to (i.e. invocation of) the *Logos* which comes from God' (which may be identified with the Holy Spirit, cf. i 33, 6). This is a possible construction, for we find εὐχαὶ θεῶν in classical Greek (cf. Luke vi 12). And it is perhaps impossible to decide which of the two renderings is the more plausible. In either case the phrase refers to the consecration of the elements by prayer. (See note *ad loc.*)

But what does Justin mean when he says that from these consecrated elements αἷμα καὶ σάρκες κατὰ μεταβολὴν τρέφονται ἡμῶν? The phrase has been taken to involve Transubstantiation in the fullest sense, but it is very dangerous to draw such definite inferences from the words of Justin. The general idea certainly seems to be that of a mysterious change in the elements, whereby they become more than κοινὸς ἄρτος or κοινὸν πόμα. And this change is compared to the Incarnation. Just as the Divine word effected the union of Divine and human in Christ, so the word of consecration effects a similar union in the elements. And this consecrated food operates upon our human nature (αἷμα καὶ σάρκες is used in that general meaning, just as σάρκα καὶ αἷμα

---

[1] *Body of Christ* Appended note 1.
[2] *op. cit.* p. 314.   [3] Bethune-Baker *op. cit.* p. 399.

has been used of the nature which Christ assumed) κατὰ μεταβολήν, i.e. by process of assimilation. It seems obvious that Justin's language expresses a confused notion of Sacramental grace. The physical operation and the spiritual operation are both present in his thought, but he is not yet quite clear as to their relation. He explains the Eucharist by the Incarnation; Christ became incarnate by the Word of God; so His incarnate nature is imparted in the Eucharist. But it is very doubtful whether he fully understood his own language. There is the germ of a Sacramental theory in his words, and his language may be taken to foreshadow later developments of such theory; but the time was not yet ripe for a full discussion of the methods by which Sacramental grace operated upon the recipient of the consecrated elements. Justin plainly believed that the bread and wine became Christ's body and blood, and by assimilation nourished the recipients; but it is very questionable whether he had considered the method of that change or the meaning of the 'assimilation' of which he speaks. He was, however, clearly convinced that the power of Christ's incarnate life was, through the medium of the consecrated elements, conveyed to the recipients, and he does not seem to have realized that the method of this communication was a point of difficulty, needing elucidation.

It has been suggested that the mention of wine as one of the Eucharistic elements is a later interpolation in Justin's works, and that he only knew of the use of bread and water. Harnack[1], after emending οἶνον to ὄνον in i 54, 6, *Tryph.* 69, argues that there is no other mention of wine in Justin except in *Apol.* i 65: 67. He

---

[1] *Texte und Untersuch.* vii 2, 1891.

points out that in i 66 Justin does not quote the passage 'I will not drink of the fruit of the vine'; further, that the phrase ποτήριον ὕδατος καὶ κράματος in i 65, 3 is very suspicious, and that the words καὶ κράματος are absent in Cod. Ottob.; that therefore κράματος is to be regarded as a later correction for ὕδατος, which eventually got incorporated into the text. He then proceeds to excise the mention of wine in i 65, 4: 67, 5, pointing out also that in the reference to the Mithras-cult in i 66, 4 water alone is spoken of. He thus arrives at the conclusion that the early Church used indifferently water or wine in the Eucharist, and attached the promise not to the specific elements but to the general act of eating and drinking in Christ's name. This theory is highly ingenious; but it seems dangerous thus to controvert the universal Church tradition, whereby bread and wine were regarded as the characteristic elements of the Eucharistic celebration. And Harnack's methods of dealing with the MS text are uncomfortably drastic. The references to the use of wine are too plain and simple to be thus ruthlessly deleted. The phrase ὕδατος καὶ κράματος is no doubt strange; but is it likely that the scribe, who *ex hypothesi* first corrupted the text into this form, would not have been conscious of its singularity? It is equally possible that Justin makes such special and repeated mention of water in order to refute the popular charge of drunkenness. The analogy of the Mithras-cult proves nothing. Justin has already pointed out that many anticipations of Christian usage showed plainly the ignorance of the demons who prompted them; and this might seem to him but another example of the same fact. The omissions of Cod. Ottob. are so numerous that it can scarcely be taken as a sufficiently authoritative guide in this matter. Nor can much be inferred from Justin's omission to quote the passage referring to the 'fruit of the vine.' He might have quoted it, but he was under no necessity to do so. On the whole it may therefore be said that Harnack's arguments are more ingenious than convincing. Nor even is the emendation of οἶνον to ὄνον to be accepted without hesitation[1].

III. *The number of the Apologies.*

So far the Apologies, which we possess, have been spoken of in the plural number. But it is now necessary to discuss the question whether they are not really one single Apology. On this question authorities are divided in opinion. Thus Krüger[2] declares that there are no grounds to suppose that these two Apologies were originally one. Cramer[3] agrees with this view, but supposes them to have been united before the time of Eusebius. Harnack[4] believes them to have been one, the second being an appendix to the first, and thinks it probable that Justin never wrote a second Apology, and that Eusebius, who says that he did, was attributing the work of Athenagoras to Justin. Similarly Bardenhewer[5] points out that there is no evidence in later literature for another Apology by Justin. Finally Veil[6] holds the extreme view that the two Apologies were always and organically one.—The external evidence is derived

---

[1] See note *ad loc.* The most complete refutation of Harnack's theory is provided by Zahn *Brod und Wein im Abendmahl der alten Kirche.*

[2] *Theol. Lit. Zeit.* xvii, 1892, p. 298; *Die Apologieen J. d. M.* p. xiv.

[3] *Theol. Stud.*, 1892.

[4] *Altchristl. Litt. Chronol.* i p. 274.

[5] *Altkirchl. Litt.* p. 202.

[6] *Justinus Rechtfertigung des Christentums.*

INTRODUCTION

entirely from Eusebius. (The MSS place the second Apology first and call the first ἀπολογία δευτέρα.) Eusebius tells us[1] that Justin wrote λόγους ἀπολογίαν ἔχοντας, addressed to Antoninus Pius and the Senate; again[2], that he wrote a λόγος to Pius and his sons and the Senate, and a second ἀπολογία to Antoninus Verus; again[3], that he addressed a δεύτερον βιβλίον to Aurelius and L. Verus. These statements are by themselves somewhat vague and discrepant. But the confusion becomes worse, when we proceed to examine Eusebius' quotations from the Apologies. Thus in ii 13 he quotes *Apol.* i 26 as found ἐν τῇ προτέρᾳ πρὸς Ἀντωνῖνον ἀπολογίᾳ; in iv 8 he quotes i 29, 31 as ἐν τῇ πρὸς Ἀντωνῖνον ἀπολογίᾳ, but immediately afterwards quotes ii 12 as ἐν ταὐτῷ; in iv 16 he quotes ii 8 (3) as ἐν τῇ δεδηλωμένῃ ἀπολογίᾳ, which might mean the first Apology or the δεύτερον βιβλίον which he has just mentioned. In iv 17 he quotes ii 2 as ἐν τῇ προτέρᾳ ἀπολογίᾳ.

The inference seems obvious, that Eusebius' evidence is wholly untrustworthy. Perhaps he derived his quotations merely from a book of excerpts. But it is noteworthy that none of his quotations (with the doubtful exception of that in iv 16) is stated to come from the second Apology, and also that his statements in iv 16 and 18 as to the persons, to whom the second Apology was addressed, are almost certainly incorrect.—When we turn to the internal evidence of the Apologies themselves, we are faced with difficulties connected with the text. Thus in three passages of the second Apology there are references back to the first[4]; but Krüger

---

[1] *H.E.* iv 11. [2] *ib.* iv 18.
[3] *ib.* iv 16 (cf. iv 15).
[4] ii 3 (4), 2 to i 10, 1; ii 5 (6), 5 to i 23, 2: 63, 10, 16; and ii 7 (8), 1 to i 46, 3, 4. See notes *ad loc.*

supposes two of these, and possibly all three, to be later glosses, and Cramer suggests that they were inserted by the man who put the two Apologies together. It is however a perilous habit to be too ready to discover glosses. Similarly the text in i 1 is doubtful; but at least it seems clear from i 3, 2 that the first Apology is addressed especially to a pious Caesar and to a philosophic Caesar; and the same seems to be the case with the second Apology (ii 2, 16: 15, 5). Finally it is possible to maintain that the opening of the second Apology is strangely abrupt[1], taking as it does the tone of an appeal to the Romans, whereas later the Apology is seen to be addressed to the Caesars. No doubt a certain amount of rhetorical licence might be allowed to Justin; but it seems incredible that in a formal document, addressed to the heads of the Roman State, he should begin in the tone of the opening words of ii 1.—The internal evidence is thus seen to be somewhat deficient in amount and strength[2]. And it is possible that complete agreement upon the point at issue will never be reached. But to the present writer it appears that the cumulative effect of the internal evidence, conjoined with the phenomena of Eusebius' quotations, and with a general feeling as to the line of argument pursued in the work, inclines the scale towards a belief in the unity of the two Apologies. It is possible that they were not originally one, and that the second Apology was added as an Appendix, when the event recorded in ii 2 occurred to excite Justin to a renewed effort; and that he then took the opportunity to answer certain

[1] But see note *ad loc*.

[2] Veil would see in i 46, 5 a hint of a future discussion of the subject there mentioned, such a discussion being found in ii 5 (6) and 10. But certainly the hint is far from clear; and the suggestion seems over-fanciful.

objections and to round off his arguments. This may be the explanation of the confusion visible in Eusebius' quotations. But it seems quite improbable that the two Apologies, which we possess, were wholly separate works. The probability in favour of the contrary view seems so strong that in the present edition the two have been printed as one continuous treatise. The disruption of the two may be explained as due to accident, or to the fact that the second was a later Appendix to the first; the two editions (of the first separately, and of the first and second together) might have co-existed and thus caused confusion.

Date of composition.

The date, at which this work was composed, is a matter of dispute. The question rests entirely upon internal evidence, and in order to understand the bearing of that evidence it is essential to be acquainted with the facts of Imperial adoptions under the Antonine Emperors.—In A.D. 136 Hadrian adopted L. Ceionius Commodus Verus and gave to him the name of Caesar; he thus became L. Aelius Verus Caesar. He died in A.D. 138 and Hadrian adopted T. Aurelius Fulvus Boionius Antoninus (later known as Antoninus Pius); at Hadrian's command Antoninus adopted M. Annius Verus or Verissimus, born A.D. 121 (who thus became M. Aurelius Antoninus), and the son of L. Verus, born A.D. 130, who thus became L. Aelius Aurelius Commodus. On Hadrian's death in 138 Antoninus Pius became Emperor. In 139 M. Aurelius was given the title of Caesar, and he became co-regent in 147. L. Verus was received into the Senate in 153[1]. In 161 Pius died and

[1] Capitolinus *Verus* 3.

M. Aurelius became Emperor; he immediately made L. Verus *Augustus* and *Princeps*, i.e. fully equal to himself. In 162 L. Verus departed to the Parthian war.

If now we turn to the dedication of the 'first' Apology (i 1), we find that it is addressed to the Emperor Antoninus Pius, to his son Verissimus the philosopher, and to Lucius the philosopher, son of Caesar (i.e. of L. Aelius Verus Caesar) and adopted son of Pius. The text is probably corrupt. Thus υἱῷ by itself seems suspicious, and the insertion of Σεβαστοῦ before it would be an improvement. Some also would insert Καίσαρι with Οὐηρισσίμῳ, or insert Καίσαρι after Αὐτοκράτορι and read later Σεβαστῷ καὶ Καίσαρι Οὐηρισσίμῳ. The emendation of Λουκίῳ φιλοσόφῳ to Λουκίῳ φιλοσόφου (omitting the subsequent comma) is also possible, as Spartian[1] tells us that Lucius' father was *eruditus in litteris*. Veil suggests that the word φιλοσόφου (if accepted) is a mistaken gloss to designate Aurelius, L. Verus being confused with L. Commodus, Aurelius' own son. None, however, of these emendations affects the evidence as to the date, except the suggested insertion of Καίσαρι.

At first glance it certainly seems as if the date must be taken to be 138/139, on the simple ground that Aurelius is called Verissimus, a name which he ceased to bear on his adoption, and is not called Caesar, a title which he received in 139. This evidence appears decisive to various authors[2]. And, though the omission of the title Caesar might certainly be due to textual corruption[3], it may be admitted that the name Verissimus

---

[1] *Ael. Ver.* 5.
[2] Dorner, Ramsay, Otto, Krüger (*Theol. Lit. Zeit.*, xvii, 1892, p. 298), Cramer (*Theol. Stud.*, 1892).
[3] Cf. Harnack *op. cit.* p. 275.

is not such as could readily be supposed to be a later insertion, nor is it very probable that Justin was wrong in his nomenclature for the rulers whom he was addressing. At the same time it is fair to remark that the name Verissimus is in itself a species of nickname, such as might have clung to Aurelius all through life, as the epithet Pius clung to Antoninus.

And there are certain difficulties in the way of accepting this early date. Too much should not be made of the fact that in 139 Aurelius was only 18, and Lucius 9 years old, and therefore that the title of 'philosopher' is scarcely fitting to them. For we hear of Aurelius[1] that *philosophiae operam uehementer dedit et quidem adhuc puer. Nam duodecimum annum ingressus habitum philosophi sumpsit*. Thus Lucius might be called *philosophus* even at the age of 9 (a point which does not need making, if φιλοσόφου be the right reading). But it is worth remarking that L. Verus was not taken into the Senate till 153, and yet is here addressed as if he were in public position and authority.

Hence many authors[2] prefer to favour a later date than 139 for the composition of the first Apology, and certain other passages agree with that theory. Thus in i 26 Justin says that he has already written a σύνταγμα against Marcion. The chronology of the Marcionite heresy is very uncertain, but it seems probable that Marcion came to Rome circ. A.D. 139. At first he was an orthodox Christian; and he stood forward as an independent heresiarch only after some time, i.e. perhaps circ. A.D. 144. And Justin's words attest the fact that he had attained some influence. Again in i 29, 3 the mention of Felix

[1] Capitol. *Marc.* 2.
[2] Bury (*Student's Roman Empire* c. 30) suggests 148. Harnack (*Theol. Lit. Zeit.* xxii p. 77) 150—153. Veil 153—155.

INTRODUCTION

naturally leads to the supposition that hereby is meant C. Munatius Felix, who, according to a papyrus, was prefect of Egypt A.D. 148—154. So too in i 46, 1 Justin tells us that he is writing about 150 years after Christ. No doubt that number is a round one, but it need not be entirely vague; and, if we adopt the chronology of St Luke, we should again have 147—154 as the date of the first Apology.

There are therefore many indications which favour the later date; and, apart from the use of Οὐηρισσίμῳ in i 1, there is nothing which conflicts with that date. It is true that in i 31, 6 Justin refers to the revolt of Barcochba as ἐν τῷ νῦν γεγενημένῳ πολέμῳ (the revolt having taken place in A.D. 132—135). But it is clear that his use of νῦν is quite loose. Thus in i 29, 4 he uses it with regard to Antinous, who was drowned A.D. 130; in i 42, 4 he speaks of Christ as having been crucified καθ' ἡμᾶς, and in i 63, 16 of Christ's advent as having been νῦν. Thus also in *Tryph*. 1 and 9 (which was written after the Apology, for he refers to it in c. 120) he speaks of the Judaic wars as only just over.

If the two Apologies are really one, they were probably (though not necessarily, if the second was an Appendix) written at the same or nearly the same time. And we find in ii 1, 1 that the events narrated in ii 2 took place when Urbicus was prefect of the city. He is known to have held that office from A.D. 144—160. It has however been supposed, on the authority of Eusebius[1], that the second Apology was addressed to Aurelius and L. Verus. But the internal evidence seems clearly against this view. Thus in ii 2, 16 it seems inevitable to suppose that the reference is to Pius and

---

[1] *H.E.* iv 16.

INTRODUCTION   li

Aurelius. It is certainly strange that Verus should not be mentioned; but here again there is some insecurity of text, and Valesius, in his edition of Eusebius, suggests the reading φιλοσόφῳ Καίσαρι οὐδὲ φιλοσόφου Καίσαρος παιδί, which Harnack and Schwartz accept. A more definite point is found in ii 2, 8, which presupposes the existence of only one autocrat, whereas in Aurelius' reign there were two *Augusti*. These arguments can be answered; thus Ruinart and Otto, arguing for a date in Aurelius' reign, point out that Verus might have been absent at the Parthian war, to which he went in A.D. 162, and that therefore there would only have been one autocrat in Rome; again they suggest that Urbicus may have held office in Rome twice, and that the εὐσεβὴς αὐτοκράτωρ of ii 2, 16 might be Aurelius (in which case the 'philosophic son of Caesar' of the same passage would have to be Commodus, who was not born till A.D. 161). But these arguments are obviously unconvincing, and Eusebius' statement is scarcely worth the trouble of defending. It seems inevitable to believe that the second Apology was written in Pius' reign, and probably after 152, for Crescens, according to Eusebius, did not become influential till that date, and in Apol. ii 8 (3) he is represented as a dangerous enemy to Justin. The balance of evidence seems to be in favour of uniting the two Apologies; and the internal evidence of the first Apology is mainly on the side of a date about A.D. 150—153. The only alternative is to place the date of the first Apology about A.D. 139; in which case the second must have been written many years after the first, though even so there would be no impossibility in the way of supposing that Justin re-published the first, with the second added as an Appendix. But the bulk of the evidence is almost irreconcilable with the theory of so early a date as A.D. 139 for the first, and any date in Aurelius' reign for the second Apology. Nearly every indication is in the direction of bringing the dates of their composition closer to one another, and fixing them in a period very near to the year 153.

IV. MSS.

The text of the Apologies principally depends upon one MS, *Codex Regius Parisinus CDL*, of the year A.D. 1364, in the National Library at Paris. It contains, besides other works, the Dialogue with Trypho and the Apologies, the so-called second Apology preceding the first. This text has been suspected of containing deliberate interpolations, as well as casual mistakes or additions; but it is our only guide of authority. This MS is symbolized in this edition, as in Otto's, by the letter A.

The *Codex Claromontanus (LXXXII)* or *Fenwickianus* (noted as B in Otto), of the year A.D. 1541, is an inferior copy of A, and is very seldom of any use for the correction of the text. It contains the Dialogue and the Apologies in the same order as A. According to Otto, this MS came into the possession of the Rev. J. A. Fenwick, of Cheltenham, in 1872.

Codex Ottobonianus graecus CCLXXIV, of the 15th century, containing Apology i 65—67, seems to represent a different tradition to that of A, but is very faulty. (Rome, Vatican Library.)

Codex Parisinus supplementi graeci CXC, of the 17th century, contains excerpts. (Paris. National Library.)

Besides these, two MSS, *Codex Ambrosianus H.* 142 *infer.* (Milan) of the year 1564, and *Codex Monacensis*

CXXXII (Royal Library, Munich) of the year 1565, contain in Latin version i 65—67. Occasional help for the establishment of the text is also derived from the quotations in Eusebius *Hist. Eccl.*; the text of these has been taken from the edition of E. Schwartz (Leipzig, 1908). The quotations in John of Damascus' *Sacra Parallela* are valueless for critical purposes; they are collected in K. Holl *Fragmente vornicänischer Kirchenväter aus den Sacra Parallela*.

Chief editions.

Stephanus. Paris, 1551.
Perionius. Paris, 1554.
Sylburgius. Heidelberg, 1593.
    Paris, 1615, 1636.
Grabius (Apol. i). Oxford, 1700.
Hutchin (Apol. ii). Oxford, 1703.
Thirlby. London, 1722.
Maran. Paris, 1742.
    Re-edited by Migne, 1857, 1884.
Thalemann. Leipzig, 1755.
Ashton. Cambridge, 1768.
Braun. Bonn, 1830.
    Re-edited by Gutberlet. Limburg, 1890.
Otto. Jena, 1842, 1875. (This edition is a work of monumental accuracy and erudition, and practically supersedes all previous editions, though additional help can still be obtained by consulting the latest editions of Braun's and Maran's commentaries.)
Trollope. Cambridge, 1845.
Veil. Strassburg, 1894. (A German translation, with notes, some of great value.)

Krüger. Leipzig, 1904. (A text based on Otto, but occasionally varying from it.)

Pautigny. Paris, 1994. (A French translation, not always accurate, and an introduction, which gives a full list of the literature dealing with the Apologies.)

The present edition follows mainly, though not entirely, the text of Krüger.

Bibliography.

GENERAL.

Harnack, *Die Ueberlieferung der griechischen Apologeten des zweiten Jahrhunderts.* Leipzig, 1882.

Harnack, *Geschichte der altchristlichen Litteratur.* Leipzig, 1897.

Bardenhewer, *Geschichte der altkirchlichen Litteratur.* Freiburg, 1902.

Krüger, *Early Christian Literature.* New York, 1897.

Allard, *Histoire des persécutions.* Paris, 1903.

Duchesne, *Origines du culte chrétien.* Paris, 1903.

Warren, *Liturgy of the ante-Nicene Church.* London, 1897.

Turmel, *Histoire de la théologie positive.* Paris, 1904.

Westcott, *History of the Canon of the New Testament.* London, 1896.

Zahn, *Brod und Wein im Abendmahl der alten Kirche.* Erlangen, 1892.

Scheiwiler, *Die Elemente der Eucharistie in den ersten Jahrhunderten.* Mainz, 1903.

Dorner, *Doctrine of the Person of Christ.* Edinburgh, 1861.

Bethune-Baker, *Early history of Christian doctrine.* London, 1903.

SPECIAL.

Donaldson, *History of Christian literature and dogma*, Vol. ii. London, 1866.

Aubé, *S. Justin philosophe et martyr.* Paris, 1875.

Purves, *Testimony of Justin Martyr to early Christianity.* New York, 1889.

Semisch, *Justin der Märtyrer.* Breslau, 1840.
Otto, *De Justini martyris scriptis et doctrina.* Jena, 1841.
Thümer, *Ueber den Platonismus in den Schriften des Justinus Martyr.* Glauchau, 1880.
Steeg, *Exposé de la doctrine de Justin Martyr sur la personne et l'œuvre de Jésus-Christ.* Strassburg, 1859.
Schaller, *Les deux apologies de Justin Martyr au point de vue dogmatique.* Strassburg, 1861.
Engelhardt, *Das Christentum Justins des Märtyrers.* Erlangen, 1878.
Stählin, *Justin der Märtyrer und sein neuester Beurtheiler.* Leipzig, 1880.
Clemen, *Die religions-philosophische Bedeutung des stoisch-christlichen Eudämonismus in Justins Apologie.* Leipzig, 1890.
Flemming, *Zur Beurtheilung des Christentums Justins des Märtyrers.* Leipzig, 1893.
Rivière, *S. Justin et les apologistes du deuxième siècle.* Paris, 1907.
Ruinart, *Acta martyrum.* Ratisbon, 1859.

PERIODICAL.

Études de critique et d'histoire, 2me série, 1896, 169—187.
Revue d'histoire et de littérature religieuses, iii 1898, 289 ff.; viii 1903, 152 ff.
Texte und Untersuchungen, vii 2, 1891.
Zeitschrift für Kirchengeschichte, viii 1886, 16—84.
Theologische Literaturzeitung, xvii 1892, 297—300; xxii 1897, 77.
Jahrbücher für protestantische Theologie, xii 1886, 661—690; xvi 1890, 550—593; xvii 1891, 124—148.
Modern Review, July and October, 1882.

Analysis of the Apologies.

i 1—5. *Introductory.* I claim for the Christians justice and a fair trial. The mere name of Christian is not a sufficient ground of punishment; it is the conduct of Christians that should be investigated. The ordinary procedure against us is due to the influence of the demons, who have always been opposed to the *Logos*.

6—12. *Examination of popular complaints against the Christians.* (*a*) Atheism. We are not atheists (6); some of us may indeed be malefactors, and if so, should be punished as such (7). Our doctrine has analogies with that of Plato (8). True, we do not worship idols (9), nor offer material oblations (10), but we believe in a God who desires moral conduct on the part of men. (*b*) Treason. The kingdom we look forward to is not one of this world. We are obedient to your authority (11), and are really your best allies in the cause of peace and virtue (12).

13—67. *Explanation of Christianity.*

(*a*) The Christian faith is perfectly rational (13), and produces purity of life (14), in obedience to Christ's injunctions (15—17), and in accordance with our belief in immortality (18, 19). And this belief has its parallels in heathen writings (20), even as our doctrine of Christ is not dissimilar to, though it is more moral than, heathen mythology (21). But we believe Christ to be the Son of God in a unique way (22). The truth of this shall now be proved (23).

(*b*) i. Christianity alone is true. For the Christians alone are persecuted (24), and yet persist in their faith (25). Even heretical Christians suffer immunity (26), and therefore it is plain that the opposition to us is the work of the demons. Moreover our lives are pure (27—29).

ii. Christ is really the Son of God. This is proved by the fulfilment of prophecy (30—53).

iii. The disbelief in Christ is due to the demons, who attempted to forestall His coming by propagating heathen myths (54, 55), and since that time have instigated magicians and heretics (56—58). Other anticipations of Christian doctrines can be found in the philosophers, who borrowed their ideas from the Bible (59, 60).

(*c*) The Christian cultus must be described, viz. Baptism (61), a rite which has also been anticipated by the demons (62) [Cap. 63 is a digression], as they anticipated other Christian ideas (64), and the Eucharist (65—67).

68—ii 2. *Appeal.* I claim fair treatment. Hadrian's rescript shows that this would be no reversal of previous policy (68). And the necessity for such an appeal is proved by the persecutions of Christians at the hands of the demons' tools (ii 1), of which I can give you a recent example (2).

3 (4)—9. I may briefly *answer certain objections*: (*a*) Why Christians may not commit suicide, and must not deny their faith (3). (*b*) Why God allows persecution. It is due to the abuse of free-will by fallen angels (4), and the only power which enables men to use their free-will rightly is the power of Christ (5). But God's final judgment on life will come in time (6). All champions of righteousness have been persecuted (7), and I am anticipating a similar fate (8). (*c*) The doctrine of Divine retribution is not degrading, but true and moral (9).

10. *Summary.* The superiority of Christian doctrine is due to the very nature of Christ.

11—13. *Personal challenge.* We do not fear death (11), and this shows the nobility of our belief (12), and our right to take a pride in it (13).

14, 15. *Conclusion.*

lviii *INTRODUCTION*

Differences from Krüger's text.

page	line		K.
10	8	προελεγχθέντας	προλεχθέντας
16	13	οἱ γὰρ διά...ἀδικοῦσιν, εἰ ἔμαθον	οὐ γὰρ διά...ἀδικοῦσιν, εἰ δ' ἔμαθον
40	1	ἐν ταφαῖς	ἐν γραφαῖς
40	2	ὅτι γὰρ οὖν	ὅτι γὰρ οὐ
42	10	ἐνεργηθέντα καὶ αὐτὸν	ἐνεργηθέντα καὶ
43	7	πέπεικε	πεποίηκε
43	12	οἱ οὐ κοινωνοῦντες τῶν αὐτῶν δογμάτων ἐν τοῖς φιλοσόφοις τὸ ἐπικατηγορούμενον ὄνομα τῆς φιλοσοφίας κοινὸν ἔχουσιν	οὐ κοινῶν ὄντων δογμάτων τοῖς φιλοσόφοις τὸ ἐπικαλούμενον ὄνομα τῆς φιλοσοφίας κοινόν ἐστιν
47	4	ἐνεκρατευόμεθα	ἐνεγκρατευόμεθα
47	14	διὰ φόβου	διὰ φόβον
57	16	ἀπὸ τοῦ	ἀπὸ προσώπου τοῦ
58	6	ἀπὸ τοῦ	ἀπὸ προσώπου τοῦ
66	8	ἀπὸ τοῦ	ἀπὸ προσώπου τοῦ
73	9	Χριστὸν παραγενησόμενον, παραγενόμενον	Χριστόν, παραγενόμενον
76	15	ἀποδείκνυμεν	ἀπεδείκνυμεν
85	1	θεὸς	θεὸν
91	4	γενομένους	γεννωμένους
92	6	ἁμαρτιῶν ὧν	ἁμαρτιῶν [ὑπὲρ] ὧν
105	8	συγγενέσθαι	συγγενήσεσθαι
106	16	ἐπειδὴ	ἐπεὶ
107	7	ἀνέδωκεν	ἀναδέδωκε
107	12	[ὃν Οὔρβικος ἐκολάσατο]	ὃν Οὔρβικος ἐκολάσατο
107	15	[εἰς δεσμὰ ἐμβαλόντα τὸν Πτολεμαῖον]	εἰς δεσμὰ ἐμβαλόντα τὸν Πτολεμαῖον
107	17	εἰ αὐτὸ τοῦτο μόνον	αὐτὸ τοῦτο μόνον, εἰ
108	3	διδασκαλεῖον	διδασκάλιον
109	4	MS Caps. 3—8	MS Caps. 4—8, 3
118	14	ὁμοίως Σωκράτει	om.
120	13	διὰ τοῦ τὸ λ.	διὰ τὸ λ.
124	12	ἀνθρωπίνων	ἀνθρωπείων

ΤΟΥ ΑΓΙΟΥ ΙΟΥΣΤΙΝΟΥ ΦΙΛΟΣΟΦΟΥ ΚΑΙ
ΜΑΡΤΥΡΟΣ ΑΠΟΛΟΓΙΑ ΥΠΕΡ ΧΡΙΣΤΙΑΝΩΝ
ΠΡΟΣ ΑΝΤΩΝΙΝΟΝ ΤΟΝ ΕΥΣΕΒΗ.

1. 1. Αὐτοκράτορι Τίτῳ Αἰλίῳ Ἀδριανῷ Ἀντωνίνῳ Εὐσεβεῖ Σεβαστῷ Καίσαρι, καὶ Οὐηρισσίμῳ υἱῷ φιλοσόφῳ, καὶ Λουκίῳ φιλοσόφῳ, Καίσαρος φύσει υἱῷ καὶ Εὐσεβοῦς εἰσποιητῷ, ἐραστῇ παιδείας, ἱερᾷ τε συγκλήτῳ καὶ δήμῳ παντὶ Ῥωμαίων, ὑπὲρ τῶν ἐκ παντὸς γένους ἀνθρώπων ἀδίκως μισουμένων καὶ ἐπηρεαζομένων, Ἰουστῖνος Πρίσκου τοῦ Βακχείου, τῶν ἀπὸ Φλαουΐας Νέας πόλεως τῆς Συρίας Παλαιστίνης, εἷς αὐτῶν ὤν, τὴν προσφώνησιν καὶ ἔντευξιν πεποίημαι.

ΑΤΤΟΥ ΑΓΙΟΥ...ΑΠΟΛΟΓΙΑ ΔΕΥΤΕΡΑ A ‖ 2 Καίσαρι Σεβαστῷ Eus *H E* iv 12 ‖ 3 Λουκίῳ φιλοσόφου plur Eus MSS ‖ 5 παντὶ Δήμῳ Eus ‖ 8 ὤν Otto om A Eus

1. *Dedication.* See *Intr.* p. xlvii.
4. ἐραστῇ παιδ.] '*lover of letters.*' Cf. 2, 2. In Plato we find ἐραστὴς νοῦ, ἐπιστήμης, περὶ τὸ καλόν, ἐπὶ σοφίᾳ. Παιδεία is the Platonic word for mental culture and accomplishments, fairly equivalent to the Latin *humanitas*.
ib. ἱερᾷ τε συγκ.] Cf. Cic. *de Divin.* i 12 'sanctus Senatus.' Also in Verg. *Aen.* i 426. Juv. xi 29 has 'sacri Senatus.' Justin repeats the phrase i 56, 2, ii 2, 16.
5. ἐκ παντὸς γένους] possibly '*hated by every race*' (cf. Matt. x 22, and for a similar use of ἐκ Thuc. iii 69); but far more probably '*out of every race*,' alluding to the wide spread of Christianity. Cf. *Tryph.* 52, 131, *Ap.* i 25, 1.

6. μισουμένων κ. ἐπηρ.] Cf. Luke vi 27, 28; *Ep. ad Diogn.* 5.
7. Πρίσκου κτλ.]. The father's name is Latin, the grandfather's is Greek. Flavia Neapolis was near the old Sichem, and was organized as a Greek city in A.D. 70; now called Nablous. The Roman province lost its name of Judaea after the rebellion in Hadrian's reign and was officially called Syria Palaestina. This was the old name found in Herodotus Συρίη ἡ Παλαιστίνη i 105, ii 106, iii 91, iv 39. The article with Παλαιστίνη is sometimes omitted on coins of Neapolis, according to Otto.
8. αὐτῶν] i.e. τῶν μισουμένων κτλ.
9. προσφώνησιν καὶ ἔντευξιν] The

2. 1. Τοὺς κατὰ ἀλήθειαν εὐσεβεῖς καὶ φιλοσόφους μόνον τἀληθὲς τιμᾶν καὶ στέργειν ὁ λόγος ὑπαγορεύει, παραιτουμένους δόξαις παλαιῶν ἐξακολουθεῖν, ἂν φαῦλαι ὦσιν· οὐ γὰρ μόνον μὴ ἕπεσθαι τοῖς ἀδίκως τι πράξασιν
5 ἢ δογματίσασιν ὁ σώφρων λόγος ὑπαγορεύει, ἀλλ' ἐκ παντὸς τρόπου καὶ πρὸ τῆς ἑαυτοῦ ψυχῆς τὸν φιλαλήθη, κἂν θάνατος ἀπειλῆται, τὰ δίκαια λέγειν τε καὶ πράττειν αἱρεῖσθαι δεῖ. 2. ὑμεῖς μὲν οὖν ὅτι λέγεσθε εὐσεβεῖς καὶ φιλόσοφοι καὶ φύλακες δικαιοσύνης καὶ ἐρασταὶ παι-
10 δείας, ἀκούετε πανταχοῦ· εἰ δὲ καὶ ὑπάρχετε, δειχθήσεται. 3. οὐ γὰρ κολακεύσοντες ὑμᾶς διὰ τῶνδε τῶν γραμμάτων οὐδὲ πρὸς χάριν ὁμιλήσοντες, ἀλλ' ἀπαιτήσοντες κατὰ τὸν ἀκριβῆ καὶ ἐξεταστικὸν λόγον τὴν κρίσιν ποιήσασθαι προσεληλύθαμεν, μὴ προλήψει μηδ' ἀνθρωπαρεσκείᾳ τῇ

3 παλαιῶν ἐξακ. Α πολλῶν ἀκολουθεῖν Sacr Parall Holl 94 ‖ 8 ὅτι λέγεσθε A om Steph λέγεσθε ὅτι Trollope ‖ 14 προσεληλύθαμεν Otto προσεληλύθειμεν A

former word is used meaning 'an address,' Lat. *oratio*. Ἔντευξις is a technical word for a '*petition*.' It is found in Böckh's *C.I.*, 2829. 11. (See Liddell and Scott.)

2. *Do not be led astray by bad precedent, prejudice, rumour, or superstition to prefer anything to truth. Be true to your reputation. We ask for a fair and diligent examination; do not condemn yourselves by refusing it. We at any rate can suffer no hurt, even if you kill us, unless we be proved to be evildoers.*

2. ὁ λόγος] '*reason*' in general, the sense of right, feeling for truth. A Platonic use. It is caught up by ὁ σώφρων λ. just below.

3. παραιτουμένους] The word means '*to excuse oneself, decline*.' Cf. Luke xiv 18, and, with infinitive, Heb. xii 19, Acts xxv 11.

5. ὁ σώφρων λόγ.] Cf. ὁ ἀληθὴς λόγος in 3, 1. The distinction between the two adjectives is not very definite. The phrase here could be Latinized into *sana ratio* and the second phrase into *uera ratio*.

ib. ἐκ παντὸς τρόπ.] The phrase is found in Xen. *An.* iii 1, 43 and elsewhere.

6. πρό] '*in preference to*,' Lat. *prae*. For a similar sentiment cf. Plat. *Ap*. 28 B.

8. ὅτι λέγεσθε] If retained, the sentence is pleonastic; '*you have the reputation that you are called.*' It is tempting to excise these two words as a gloss or to alter them so as to avoid the pleonasm. Otto suggests οἶδα instead of οὖν, but does not admit the conjecture into his text.

12. πρὸς χάριν ὁμιλ.] '*speaking to win your favour.*'

14. μὴ προλήψει κτλ.] '*asking you to judge us, not with prejudice, nor in obedience to a desire of pleasing the superstitious, not with unreasonable impetuosity, nor by (reference to) the popular disfavour*

APOLOGIA

δεισιδαιμόνων κατεχομένους ἢ ἀλόγῳ ὁρμῇ καὶ χρονίᾳ
προκατεσχηκυίᾳ φήμῃ κακῇ τὴν καθ᾽ ἑαυτῶν ψῆφον
φέροντας. 4. ἡμεῖς μὲν γὰρ πρὸς οὐδενὸς πείσεσθαί
τι κακὸν δύνασθαι λελογίσμεθα, ἢν μὴ κακίας ἐργάται
ἐλεγχώμεθα ἢ πονηροὶ διεγνώσμεθα· ὑμεῖς δ᾽ ἀποκτεῖναι 5
μὲν δύνασθε, βλάψαι δ᾽ οὔ.

3. 1. Ἀλλ᾽ ἵνα μὴ ἄλογον φωνὴν καὶ τολμηρὰν δόξῃ
τις ταῦτα εἶναι, ἀξιοῦμεν τὰ κατηγορούμενα αὐτῶν ἐξετάζεσθαι, καί, ἐὰν οὕτως ἔχοντα ἀποδεικνύωνται, κολάζεσθαι
ὡς πρέπον ἐστί, †μᾶλλον δὲ κολάζειν†· εἰ δὲ μηδὲν ἔχοι 10
τις ἐλέγχειν, οὐχ ὑπαγορεύει ὁ ἀληθὴς λόγος διὰ φήμην
πονηρὰν ἀναιτίους ἀνθρώπους ἀδικεῖν, μᾶλλον δὲ ἑαυτούς,
οἳ οὐ κρίσει ἀλλὰ πάθει τὰ πράγματα ἐπάγειν ἀξιοῦτε.

10 μᾶλλον δὲ κολ. A om mult μᾶλλον δὲ κολάζεσθαι πικρότερον Sylburg
ἄλλον δὲ κολ. Maran (δὴ vice δὲ Nolt γε Beckmann) ἁλόντας κολάζειν
Bellios Otto

which has for a long time prejudiced our case; for so you will be condemning yourselves.' A somewhat slipshod sentence even if (as is not certain) all the datives depend on κατεχομένους. The change from μηδὲ to ἢ suggests that ὁρμῇ and φήμῃ should be taken with φέροντας. Προκατέχω means 'to preoccupy' and so literally here 'which has preoccupied your minds, or the public mind.' The idea in τὴν καθ᾽ ἑαυτῶν ψῆφον φέροντας is a favourite one with Justin (e.g. c. 3, 1; 4, 2). Cf. also Plat. Ap. 30 c.

3. ἡμεῖς μὲν γάρ] γὰρ justifies καθ᾽ ἑαυτῶν. 'The sentence will be against yourselves, not us; for we cannot be hurt.'

4. ἢν μή] Cf. 1 Pet. iv 15.

5. ἀποκτεῖναι] Cf. Plat. loc. cit.

3. We ask for a fair inquiry and agree to punishment, if any charges are proved against us. But if we are guiltless, it is irrational to punish us; if you judge from passion, you are wronging yourselves. As subjects should be able to account for their lives, so rulers should obey the dictates of piety and philosophy; this is for the public good and is in accordance with old maxims. So we must explain our case; you must listen and judge fairly.

8. αὐτῶν] i.e. τῶν χριστιανῶν. Ἐξετάζεσθαι and κολάζεσθαι are both passive; with the latter word αὐτούς would strictly be required.

9. ἀποδεικνύωνται] Note the plural verb with a neuter plural subject; an exceptional use, generally found with nouns denoting persons.

10. μᾶλλον δὲ κολ.] It may conceivably be intended to mean 'we would feel called upon to punish ourselves.' But the phrase seems dubious; it probably comes from the μᾶλλον δὲ ἑαυτούς below, to which some one has added κολάζειν as an explanation.

14. τὰ πράγματα ἐπάγ.] Otto translates lites intendere, 'to set up proceedings.' Cf. ἐπάγειν δίκην,

2. καλὴν δὲ καὶ μόνην δικαίαν πρόκλησιν ταύτην πᾶς ὁ σωφρονῶν ἀποφανεῖται, τὸ τοὺς ἀρχομένους τὴν εὐθύνην τοῦ ἑαυτῶν βίου καὶ λόγου ἄληπτον παρέχειν, ὁμοίως δ᾽ αὖ καὶ τοὺς ἄρχοντας μὴ βίᾳ μηδὲ τυραννίδι ἀλλ᾽ εὐσεβείᾳ 5 καὶ φιλοσοφίᾳ ἀκολουθοῦντας τὴν ψῆφον τίθεσθαι· οὕτως γὰρ ἂν καὶ οἱ ἄρχοντες καὶ οἱ ἀρχόμενοι ἀπολαύοιεν τοῦ ἀγαθοῦ. 3. ἔφη γάρ που καί τις τῶν παλαιῶν· Ἂν μὴ οἱ ἄρχοντες φιλοσοφήσωσι καὶ οἱ ἀρχόμενοι, οὐκ ἂν εἴη τὰς πόλεις εὐδαιμονῆσαι. 4. ἡμέτερον οὖν ἔργον καὶ 10 βίου καὶ μαθημάτων τὴν ἐπίσκεψιν πᾶσι παρέχειν, ὅπως μὴ ὑπὲρ τῶν ἀγνοεῖν τὰ ἡμέτερα νομιζόντων τὴν τιμωρίαν,

1 πρόκλησιν A πρόσκλησιν Thirlb ‖ 2 τὸ...ἄληπτον A τοῦ...ἀμεμπτον Sacr Par Holl 95 ‖ 7 που καί τις κτλ A τίς που τῶν παλαιῶν· ἢν μὴ οἱ ἄρχοντες φιλοσοφήσωσιν, οἱ ἀρχόμενοι οὐκ ἂν εἶεν εὐδαίμονες Sacr Par ib ‖ 10 ὅπως μὴ κτλ Otto ὅπως ὑπὲρ...αὐτῶν αὐτοῖς A

αἰτίαν Dem. 277, 12; 275, 4; πράγματα ἐπάγεσθαι id. 1256, 11. Otto cites Xen. *Mem.* ii 9, 1; Joseph. *Antiq.* xiv 10, 7; 1 Cor. vi 1. It is perhaps more simple to translate '*to bring on us the trouble we mention*' (this being the force of τά), referring to ἀναιτίους ἀδικεῖν. Cf. the common phrases πράγματα παρέχειν, ἐπάγειν κινδύνους.

1. πρόκλησιν] '*a legal challenge*.' Πρόσκλησις means '*a judicial summons or citation*.'

2. εὐθύνην]. A legal word meaning strictly '*an examination of accounts*' at the expiration of a term of office. So εὐθύνειν (4, 6) means '*to audit accounts, to call to account*.'

3. λόγου] '*doctrine*.' Thus we have later βίου καὶ μαθημάτων ἐπίσκεψιν.

ib. ἄληπτον '*not to be laid hold of*,' and so here '*offering no handle for reproof*.' The comparative is used in the sense of '*impregnable*,' Thuc. i 37, 143.

4. εὐσεβείᾳ καὶ φιλ.] used with special reference to the description of Antoninus and Marcus.

7. ἂν μὴ κτλ.] An inaccurate reminiscence of Plat. *Rep.* 473 D, E, ἐὰν μὴ οἱ φιλόσοφοι βασιλεύσωσιν ἐν ταῖς πόλεσιν ἢ οἱ βασιλῆς...φιλοσοφήσωσι...οὐκ ἔστι κακῶν παῦλα. We hear (Capit. *Marc.* 27) that one of Aurelius' favourite maxims was '*florere ciuitates si aut philosophi imperarent aut imperatores philosopharentur*.'

10. ὅπως μὴ κτλ.] The idea is that it would be the Christians' own fault if they allowed people to remain in ignorance of the principles of the Christian religion, and so suffered; if they did not speak for themselves, they were morally responsible for the injustice committed against them. The MS text is impossible. Otto's reading gives excellent sense. He translates ὑπὲρ by *eorum causa* '*on account of them*.' But its sense here perhaps is rather '*in place of*.' (So Veil has *an Stelle derer*. This sense is not unknown or uncommon in Attic. See Liddell and Scott.) The sentence is not thoroughly lucid, but can be translated '*so that we may not—in place of those who live in ignorance* (νομιζόντων ἀγνοεῖν *are*

ὧν ἂν πλημμελῶσι τυφλώττοντες, αὐτοὶ ἑαυτοῖς ὀφλήσωμεν· ὑμέτερον δέ, ὡς αἱρεῖ λόγος, ἀκούοντας ἀγαθοὺς εὑρίσκεσθαι κριτάς. 5. ἀναπολόγητον γὰρ λοιπὸν μαθοῦσιν, ἢν μὴ τὰ δίκαια ποιήσητε, ὑπάρξει πρὸς θεόν.

4. 1. Ὀνόματος μὲν οὖν προσωνυμία οὔτε ἀγαθὸν οὔτε κακὸν κρίνεται ἄνευ τῶν ὑποπιπτουσῶν τῷ ὀνόματι πράξεων· ἐπεί, ὅσον γε ἐκ τοῦ κατηγορουμένου ἡμῶν ὀνόματος, χρηστότατοι ὑπάρχομεν. 2. ἀλλ' ἐπεὶ οὐ τοῦτο

5 προσωνυμία Grab προσωνυμίᾳ A ‖ 7 ὅσον γε Otto ὅσον τε A

in the habit of ignorance) of our life and doctrines—bring on ourselves the punishment for the errors they commit in blindness,' i.e. ' if we do not enlighten them, we shall suffer in their place, on their behalf; for we shall be accountable for their ignorance.' A good principle of missionary enterprise.

2. ὡς αἱρεῖ λόγ.] '*it stands to reason.*' The phrase is common in Herodotus.

3. ἀναπολόγητον κτλ.] '*When once you have learnt the truth, if you do not act justly, you will have no excuse for the future before God.*' The impersonal turn of the sentence is distinctly curious.

4. *A name by itself is insignificant; it is the conduct accompanying it which matters. You punish others for proved ill-deeds, but us merely for our name. Perhaps some of us are evildoers, but it is unfair to treat us all on an equality. All philosophers have not the same theories, and some live very unworthily; some also teach atheism or degrade the moral character of the gods; and yet you do not punish them.*

5. ὀνόματος κτλ.] Cf. 1 Pet. iv 14—16; Tert. *Apol.* 2 'illud solum expectatur quod odio publico necessarium est, confessio nominis non examinatio criminis.' Here is the regular distinction between the *nomen ipsum* and the *flagitia cohaerentia nomini*, about which Pliny had inquired in his famous letter to Trajan (x 96). Trajan (*ib.* 97) had replied 'Conquirendi non sunt; si deferantur et arguantur, puniendi sunt, ita tamen ut qui negauerit se Christianum esse idque re ipsa manifestum fecerit, id est supplicando diis nostris, quamuis suspectus in praeteritum, ueniam ex paenitentia impetret. Sine auctore uero propositi libelli in nullo crimine locum habere debent.' Tertullian *Ap.* 2 criticises this 'O sententiam necessitate confusam; negat inquirendos ut innocentes et mandat puniri ut nocentes.' This criticism is unfair. It was the ordinary Roman procedure to require an accuser; the Christians were not *conquirendi*, because they were not malefactors, and so inquisition for them by the State was unnecessary. But if they were accused and refused to abjure their faith, they were to be punished as Christians, i.e. for the mere name. Pius on the whole followed Trajan's policy.

8. χρηστότατοι] It is hardly necessary to point out that Justin knew the real meaning of Christ's name. Cf. ii 5 (6), 3. The play upon words here is such as the ancients were fond of. It seems to have been made possible by popular mispronunciation of the word. Cf. Suet. *Claud.* 25 'impulsore Chresto' (unless the Chrestus there named is some other person than Christ). Lact. iv 7, 5 'ex-

δίκαιον ἡγούμεθα, διὰ τὸ ὄνομα, ἐὰν κακοὶ ἐλεγχώμεθα, αἰτεῖν ἀφίεσθαι, πάλιν, εἰ μηδὲν διά τε τὴν προσηγορίαν τοῦ ὀνόματος καὶ διὰ τὴν πολιτείαν εὑρισκόμεθα ἀδικοῦντες, ὑμέτερον ἀγωνιᾶσαί ἐστι, μὴ ἀδίκως κολάζοντες
5 τοὺς μὴ ἐλεγχομένους τῇ δίκῃ κόλασιν ὀφλήσητε. 3. ἐξ ὀνόματος μὲν γὰρ ἢ ἔπαινος ἢ κόλασις οὐκ ἂν εὐλόγως γένοιτο, ἢν μή τι ἐνάρετον ἢ φαῦλον δι' ἔργων ἀποδείκνυσθαι δύνηται. 4. καὶ γὰρ τοὺς κατηγορουμένους ἐφ' ὑμῶν πάντας πρὶν ἐλεγχθῆναι οὐ τιμωρεῖτε· ἐφ' ἡμῶν
10 δὲ τὸ ὄνομα ὡς ἔλεγχον λαμβάνετε, καίπερ, ὅσον γε ἐκ τοῦ ὀνόματος, τοὺς κατηγοροῦντας μᾶλλον κολάζειν ὀφείλετε.
5. Χριστιανοὶ γὰρ εἶναι κατηγορούμεθα· τὸ δὲ χρηστὸν μισεῖσθαι οὐ δίκαιον. 6. καὶ πάλιν, ἐὰν μέν τις τῶν κατηγορουμένων ἔξαρνος γένηται τῇ φωνῇ μὴ εἶναι φήσας,
15 ἀφίετε αὐτὸν ὡς μηδὲν ἐλέγχειν ἔχοντες ἁμαρτάνοντα, ἐὰν δέ τις ὁμολογήσῃ εἶναι, διὰ τὴν ὁμολογίαν κολάζετε· δέον καὶ τὸν τοῦ ὁμολογοῦντος βίον εὐθύνειν καὶ τὸν τοῦ ἀρνουμένου, ὅπως διὰ τῶν πράξεων ὁποῖός ἐστιν ἕκαστος φαίνηται. 7. ὃν γὰρ τρόπον παραλαβόντες τινὲς παρὰ
20 τοῦ διδασκάλου Χριστοῦ μὴ ἀρνεῖσθαι ἐξεταζόμενοι παρα-

9 ἐφ' ὑμῶν A ὑφ' ὑμῶν Sacr Par Holl 96 ‖ οὐ τιμωρεῖτε A οὐ δίκαιον τιμωρηθῆναι Sacr Par ib ‖ 16 τις ὁμολογήσῃ Otto τι ὁμολ A

ponenda huius nominis ratio est propter ignorantium errorem qui eum immutata littera Chrestum solent dicere.' Tert. *ad Nat.* 3 'A uobis Chrestiani pronuntiamur, nam ne nominis quidem ipsius liquido certi estis.'

3. πολιτείαν] *ratio uitae ciuilis.* Cf. Dem. 399, 6 οἷς ἐστ' ἐν λόγοις ἡ πολιτεία = *qui in oratione uersantur.* Pautigny neatly translates here '*S'il est prouvé que notre genre de vie n'est pas plus coupable que notre nom.*'

4. ἀγωνιᾶσαι] A strong word, '*to be exceedingly anxious*'; perhaps it might be rendered in Latin by *laborare.*

7. ἐνάρετον] '*virtuous.*'
9. ἐφ' ὑμῶν] probably not '*in your presence*' (though that is a possible rendering), but '*in relation to yourselves,*' i.e. non-Christians, parallel to the subsequent ἐφ' ἡμῶν '*in relation to us.*'

16. διὰ τὴν ὁμολογίαν] Cf. the vivacious passage in Tert. *Ap.* 2.

17. εὐθύνειν] Cf. note on εὐθύνη 3, 2.

19. παραλαβόντες κτλ.] Cf. Matt. x 33 where ἀρνεῖσθαι is used; in Mark viii 38, Luke ix 26 we find ἐπαισχύνεσθαι.

20. παρακελεύονται] middle, '*en-*

κελεύονται, τὸν αὐτὸν τρόπον κακῶς ζῶντες ἴσως ἀφορμὰς παρέχουσι τοῖς ἄλλως καταλέγειν τῶν πάντων Χριστιανῶν ἀσέβειαν καὶ ἀδικίαν αἱρουμένοις. 8. οὐκ ὀρθῶς μὲν οὐδὲ τοῦτο πράττεται· καὶ γάρ τοι φιλοσοφίας ὄνομα καὶ σχῆμα ἐπιγράφονταί τινες, οἳ οὐδὲν ἄξιον τῆς ὑποσχέσεως 5 πράττουσι· γινώσκετε δ᾽ ὅτι καὶ οἱ τὰ ἐναντία δοξάσαντες καὶ δογματίσαντες τῶν παλαιῶν, τῷ ἑνὶ ὀνόματι προσαγορεύονται φιλόσοφοι. 9. καὶ τούτων τινὲς ἀθεότητα ἐδίδαξαν, καὶ τὸν Δία ἀσελγῆ ἅμα τοῖς αὐτοῦ παισὶν οἱ γενόμενοι ποιηταὶ καταγγέλλουσι· κἀκείνων τὰ διδάγματα 10 οἱ μετερχόμενοι οὐκ εἴργονται πρὸς ὑμῶν, ἆθλα δὲ καὶ τιμὰς τοῖς εὐφώνως ὑβρίζουσι τούτους τίθετε.

5. 1. Τί δὴ οὖν τοῦτ᾽ ἂν εἴη; ἐφ᾽ ἡμῶν, ὑπισχνου-

2 ἄλλως A ἄλλοις mult

courage one another' to follow Christ; or, better, passive '*are encouraged*,' as the omission of an object after παρακ. (if middle) is harsh.

1. κακῶς ζῶντες] A general statement, perhaps with a special reference to the immoral Christian sects of the time, such as the Carpocratians.

2. ἄλλως] '*anyhow*,' *alioquin* (Otto), *auch ohnedem* (Veil).

ib. καταλέγειν] properly '*to tell at length, reckon up*.' Here it seems used as equivalent to κατηγορεῖν, and takes a genit. of the person accused, and an accus. of the crime alleged.

5. ὑποσχέσεως] properly '*promise*,' so here '*profession*.' Cf. ὑπισχνουμένων in 5, 1. Ἐπαγγέλλεσθαι occurs in the same sense, e.g. in 1 Tim. ii 10.

8. ἀθεότητα] Under the early Empire Epicureanism and Cynicism grew in influence, especially among the educated, though the populace still preserved much of its old religious feeling. In the 2nd century the educated classes underwent a reaction towards religion, reaching often to childish and fanatical superstition. Of this reaction Fronto and Plutarch are striking instances; Lucian and Galen are exceptions. Ἀθεότης was one of the main charges brought against the Christians.

9. Δία ἀσελγῆ] Cf. the strictures of Heraclitus, Xenophanes, and Plato.

11. οἱ μετερχόμενοι] '*those who attend to, pursue, follow after*.'

12. τούτους] i.e. Zeus and his children.

5. *You are really urged on by evil demons, who in ages past committed abominations and frightened men into calling them gods, each with a special name. Socrates tried to recall men from this belief, but the demons procured his death; and similarly they are causing us too to be attacked as atheists and impious. Just as Socrates, by λόγος, refuted the belief in the so-called gods, so the Λόγος incarnate in Christ teaches us that these are evil demons.*

13. τί δὴ οὖν κτλ.] A rhetorical question. '*Why should this be? what is the meaning of it?*'

ib. ἐφ᾽ ἡμῶν] '*in our case.*'

μένων μηδὲν ἀδικεῖν μηδὲ τὰ ἄθεα ταῦτα δοξάζειν, οὐ
κρίσεις ἐξετάζετε, ἀλλὰ ἀλόγῳ πάθει καὶ μάστιγι δαιμόνων φαύλων ἐξελαυνόμενοι ἀκρίτως κολάζετε μὴ φροντί-
ζοντες. 2. εἰρήσεται γὰρ τἀληθές· ἐπεὶ τὸ παλαιὸν
5 δαίμονες φαῦλοι, ἐπιφανείας ποιησάμενοι, καὶ γυναῖκας
ἐμοίχευσαν καὶ παῖδας διέφθειραν καὶ φόβητρα ἀνθρώποις
ἔδειξαν, ὡς καταπλαγῆναι τοὺς οἳ λόγῳ τὰς γινομένας
πράξεις οὐκ ἔκρινον, ἀλλὰ δέει συνηρπασμένοι καὶ μὴ
ἐπιστάμενοι δαίμονας εἶναι φαύλους θεοὺς προσωνόμαζον,
10 καὶ ὀνόματι ἕκαστον προσηγόρευον, ὅπερ ἕκαστος ἑαυτῷ
τῶν δαιμόνων ἐτίθετο. 3. ὅτε δὲ Σωκράτης λόγῳ ἀληθεῖ
καὶ ἐξεταστικῶς ταῦτα εἰς φανερὸν ἐπειρᾶτο φέρειν καὶ
ἀπάγειν τῶν δαιμόνων τοὺς ἀνθρώπους, καὶ αὐτοὶ οἱ δαίμονες διὰ τῶν χαιρόντων τῇ κακίᾳ ἀνθρώπων ἐνήργησαν
15 ὡς ἄθεον καὶ ἀσεβῆ ἀποκτείνεσθαι, λέγοντες καινὰ εἰσφέρειν αὐτὸν δαιμόνια· καὶ ὁμοίως ἐφ' ἡμῶν τὸ αὐτὸ

10 ἑαυτῷ Asht Otto αὐτῷ A ‖ 13 αὐτοί A αὐτὸν Otto ‖ 15 ἀποκτείνεσθαι
Otto ἀποκτεῖναι A

1. δοξάζειν] 'to hold an opinion';
so occasionally in Plato.
ib. οὐ κρίσεις ἐξετ.] 'you do not
investigate disputes.' This sense of
κρίσις is a direct derivative from
κρίνεσθαι. Cf. Plat. Rep. 379 E,
where commentators cite in comparison Pind. Olymp. vii 80 κρίσις
ἀμφ' ἀέθλοις and Nem. x 23 ἀέθλων
κρίσιν. Cf. also Plato Legg. 876 B
τὰς κρίσεις διαδικάζειν.

2. μάστιγι δαιμ.] Justin's demonology is treated Introd. p. xxx.

3. ἀκρίτως] 'without trial.' Cf.
Dion. Halic. xi 43 ἀκρίτως ἀποκτεί-
νειν.

5. ἐπιφανείας] The reference
here is to the Greek myths, which
Justin seems to accept as true records
of daemonic manifestations, perhaps
combined with Genesis vi.

7. τοὺς οἵ] A rare, mainly Ionic,
use of the definite article. Cf. Tryph.
47 τὰ ὅσα, 67 τῶν ὅσα.

10. ὀνόματι κτλ.] Cf. ii 4 (5), 6
where the fallen angels are represented as having given names to
themselves and their children the
demons.

11. Σωκράτης] Harnack (Reden
und Aufsätze, Socrates und die alte
Kirche) points out that Justin, in his
reverence for Socrates, set an example
which the later Greek apologists,
with the exception of Theophilus,
generally followed. They regarded
Christianity not as a, but as the
religion, and so treated the condemnation of Christians as a con-
tinuation of Socrates' condemnation.
Christianity was superior to Socra-
ticism in purity, universality, compre-
hensibility, power; Socrates was only
a tool of the Logos, whereas Christ
was the Logos; but Socrates was on
the side of Christ, because he was
on the side of truth.

15. καινὰ εἰσφ. δαιμ.] One of the

ἐνεργοῦσιν. 4. οὐ γὰρ μόνον ἐν Ἕλλησι διὰ Σωκράτους ὑπὸ λόγου ἠλέγχθη ταῦτα, ἀλλὰ καὶ ἐν βαρβάροις ὑπ' αὐτοῦ τοῦ λόγου μορφωθέντος καὶ ἀνθρώπου γενομένου καὶ Ἰησοῦ Χριστοῦ κληθέντος, ᾧ πεισθέντες ἡμεῖς τοὺς ταῦτα πράξαντας δαίμονας οὐ μόνον μὴ ὀρθοὺς εἶναί 5 φαμεν, ἀλλὰ κακοὺς καὶ ἀνοσίους δαίμονας, οἳ οὐδὲ τοῖς ἀρετὴν ποθοῦσιν ἀνθρώποις τὰς πράξεις ὁμοίας ἔχουσιν.

6. 1. Ἔνθεν δὲ καὶ ἄθεοι κεκλήμεθα· καὶ ὁμολογοῦμεν τῶν τοιούτων νομιζομένων θεῶν ἄθεοι εἶναι, ἀλλ' οὐχὶ τοῦ ἀληθεστάτου καὶ πατρὸς δικαιοσύνης καὶ σωφροσύνης 10 καὶ τῶν ἄλλων ἀρετῶν, ἀνεπιμίκτου τε κακίας θεοῦ· 2. ἀλλ' ἐκεῖνόν τε καὶ τὸν παρ' αὐτοῦ υἱὸν ἐλθόντα καὶ διδάξαντα ἡμᾶς ταῦτα, καὶ τὸν τῶν ἄλλων ἑπομένων καὶ

1 ἐν Ἕλλησι Otto ἐν om A ‖ 5 ὀρθοὺς A θεοὺς Thirlb Braun

formal charges in Socrates' indictment. Cf. Xen. *Mem.* i 1, Plat. *Ap.* 24 B.

1. ἐν Ἕλλησι] ἐν is not indispensable to the grammar, but the parallelism with ἐν βαρβάροις perhaps justifies its insertion.

2. ὑπὸ λόγου] A hint of the Spermatic *Logos*. See *Introd.* p. xxii.

ib. ἐν βαρβάροις] This is the usual opposition between Greeks and non-Greeks. Cf. i 7, 3; 46, 3. See also Tat. *Or.* i μὴ πάνυ φιλέχθρως διατίθεσθε πρὸς τοὺς βαρβάρους, ὦ ἄνδρες Ἕλληνες.

5. ὀρθούς] Braun insists that δαίμονες in the Church fathers is always used in a bad sense, that therefore ὀρθοὺς δαίμονας is an impossible expression here, and that θεούς must be substituted for ὀρθούς. Braun's generalization may apply to later fathers, but Justin's use seems less definite; sometimes he uses δαίμονες by itself for the evil demons (cf. ἀπάγειν τῶν δαιμόνων just above), sometimes he joins adjectives to the word, which, if his use were constant, would be otiose (cf. δαίμονες φαῦλοι above, κακοὺς δαίμονας i 23, 3). In this context the reminiscence of Socrates (whose δαιμόνιον Justin would doubtless have in mind and recognize as ὀρθόν) would influence Justin's use of the word.

6. *We are called atheists, because we do not worship such immoral gods. But we worship and revere the true God, father of all virtues, and His Son who came from Him and taught us our belief, the angels His followers, and the prophetic Spirit.*

9. θεῶν ἄθεοι] A grammatical genitive of separation.

11. ἀνεπιμίκτου κακ.] '*unmixed with evil*,' '*purum a uitiositate*' (Otto). Another genitive of separation.

13. ταῦτα] The reference is general, to the body of Christian truth.

ib. τὸν τῶν ἄλλων κτλ.] '*The army of angels also, who follow Him and are like Him.*' Τῶν ἄλλων is probably used in the idiomatic sense of '*also.*' This passage seems to put the angels, if not on an equality

ἐξομοιουμένων ἀγαθῶν ἀγγέλων στρατόν, πνεῦμά τε τὸ προφητικὸν σεβόμεθα καὶ προσκυνοῦμεν, λόγῳ καὶ ἀληθείᾳ τιμῶντες, καὶ παντὶ βουλομένῳ μαθεῖν, ὡς ἐδιδάχθημεν, ἀφθόνως παραδιδόντες.

7. 1. Ἀλλά, φήσει τις, ἤδη τινὲς ληφθέντες ἠλέγχθησαν κακοῦργοι. 2. καὶ γὰρ πολλοὺς πολλάκις, ὅταν ἑκάστοτε τῶν κατηγορουμένων τὸν βίον ἐξετάζητε, ἀλλ᾽ οὐ διὰ τοὺς προελεγχθέντας καταδικάζετε. 3. καθόλου

1 στρατόν A στρατηγόν Keil alii ‖ 8 προελεγχθέντας Perion Maran προλεχθέντας A Otto

with Christ, at any rate in precedence to the Holy Spirit. In consequence hopeless efforts have been made to take στρατόν as the object of διδάξαντα, either parallel to ἡμᾶς (*who taught us, and taught the angels*'), or parallel to ταῦτα (*who taught us these beliefs, and (the belief in) the army of angels*'). The emendation στρατηγόν is intended to avoid the difficulty by transferring the reference to Christ as the '*chief of the angels.*' See *Intr.* p. xxviii. Ἐξομοιουμένων seems to imply the view that the angels are advancing towards a fuller likeness to Christ. No doubt the reason why Justin mentions the angels here is because of the foregoing passage about good and bad demons.

2. λόγῳ καὶ ἀληθ. τιμ.] Cf. John iv 24, v 23.

4. παραδιδόντες] The object may be ὡς ἐδιδάχθημεν, used substantively as equivalent to μάθησιν or διδαχήν. So Otto, but the construction may be quite normal—sc. ἐκεῖνόν τε κτλ.

7. *Some Christians have been condemned as malefactors; but that is no reason why all Christians should be condemned. All Christians have not the same views, any more than all philosophers have. You must differentiate, and punish wrongdoers as such, and not as Christians.*

8. διὰ τ. προελεγχθέντας] Otto retains the MS προλεχθέντας and explains it '*you condemn many Christians for their crimes, but not by reason of those I have mentioned* (viz. sincere Christians)' i.e. they who do no wrong are not the cause of the condemnation of others; bad Christians are condemned for their lives and not for their Christianity; therefore it is not the name that matters. The explanation is unconvincing. '*You do not condemn criminal Christians by reason of true Christians*' is not equivalent to '*you do not condemn criminal Christians because their Christianity is the same as that of true Christians.*' Nor is it easy to find a preceding passage to which τοὺς προλεχθέντας might plainly refer. The emendation προελεγχθέντας makes excellent sense and the argument of the passage becomes simple and intelligible. '*Some Christians, you say, have been condemned as malefactors. True; but you often condemn many people, when at any time you inquire into the lives of those who are being accused* (the reference of πολλούς is thus general, and not to Christians specially), *but you do not do so because others have been condemned before.* (Therefore the fact that some Christians have been condemned is no reason for condemning all Christians.) *As a general fact*

APOLOGIA

μὲν οὖν κἀκεῖνο ὁμολογοῦμεν, ὅτι ὃν τρόπον οἱ ἐν Ἕλλησι τὰ αὐτοῖς ἀρεστὰ δογματίσαντες ἐκ παντὸς τῷ ἑνὶ ὀνόματι φιλοσοφίας προσαγορεύονται, καίπερ τῶν δογμάτων ἐναντίων ὄντων, οὕτως καὶ τῶν ἐν βαρβάροις γενομένων καὶ δοξάντων σοφῶν τὸ ἐπικατηγορούμενον ὄνομα κοινόν ἐστι· 5 Χριστιανοὶ γὰρ πάντες προσαγορεύονται. 4. ὅθεν πάντων τῶν καταγγελλομένων ὑμῖν τὰς πράξεις κρίνεσθαι ἀξιοῦμεν, ἵνα ὁ ἐλεγχθεὶς ὡς ἄδικος κολάζηται, ἀλλὰ μὴ ὡς Χριστιανός· ἐὰν δέ τις ἀνέλεγκτος φάνηται, ἀπολύηται ὡς Χριστιανὸς οὐδὲν ἀδικῶν. 5. οὐ γὰρ τοὺς κατη- 10 γοροῦντας κολάζειν ὑμᾶς ἀξιώσομεν· ἀρκοῦνται γὰρ τῇ προσούσῃ πονηρίᾳ καὶ τῇ τῶν καλῶν ἀγνοίᾳ.

8. 1. Λογίσασθε δ' ὅτι ὑπὲρ ὑμῶν ταῦτα ἔφημεν ἐκ τοῦ ἐφ' ἡμῖν εἶναι ἀρνεῖσθαι ἐξεταζομένους. 2. ἀλλ' οὐ βουλόμεθα ζῆν ψευδολογοῦντες· τοῦ γὰρ αἰωνίου καὶ 15 καθαροῦ βίου ἐπιθυμοῦντες τῆς μετὰ θεοῦ τοῦ πάντων πατρὸς καὶ δημιουργοῦ διαγωγῆς ἀντιποιούμεθα, καὶ σπεύ-

---

we allow that "Christian" is a generic name applied to different people. (You must therefore differentiate.)'

2. ἐκ παντὸς τ.ἑ.ὀ.] *Uno omnino nomine* Otto. I can find no other example of this use; but διὰ παντὸς (= *altogether*) occurs in classical Greek. Cf. ἐκ π. τρόπου above, 2, 1.

4. ἐν βαρβάροις] Cf. i 5, 4. The argument from the analogy of philosophy has been alluded to in c. 4. See *Introd.* p. xiv.

5. τὸ ἐπικατηγορούμενον] 'the name which is made a charge against them' (so Otto) or 'the name applied to them' (Maran). Cf. c. 26, 6.

10. οὐ γὰρ τοὺς κατηγ. κτλ.] There may be a reference to the concluding phrase of Hadrian's rescript, quoted by Justin at the end of c. 68.

8. *We defend ourselves in order to save you from error, and because we will not utter falsehood; for we desire the eternal life with God, and* believe that to confess our faith is a sign that we follow God and desire to be with Him. This teaching of Christ has analogies in some of Plato's doctrines. You may think it absurd; but, if it is a mistake, it hurts only ourselves, so long as we do no wrong.

13. ὑπὲρ ὑμῶν] Cf. Plat. *Apol.* 30 D πολλοῦ δέω ἐγὼ ὑπὲρ ἐμαυτοῦ ἀπολογεῖσθαι ἀλλ' ὑπὲρ ὑμῶν μή τι ἐξαμάρτητε.

14. ἐφ' ἡμῖν] '*in our power.*'

17. δημιουργοῦ] '*Maker*,' a Platonic word; cf. Plat. *Rep.* 530 A. In neo-Platonic language it means the fabricator ἐξ ὄντων, as opposed to κτίστης, the Creator ἐξ οὐκ ὄντων. In the Gnostic systems the Demiurge was the maker of the world and either the power opposed to God or a rebellious servant. Neither the neo-Platonic nor the Gnostic implications of the word can fairly be read into Justin's use of it.

ib. ἀντιποιούμεθα] '*We seek after*,

δομεν επι το ομολογειν, οι πεπεισμένοι και πιστεύοντες τυχείν τούτων δύνασθαι τους τον θεον δι' έργων πείσαντας, ότι αυτώ είποντο και της παρ' αυτώ διαγωγής ήρων, ένθα κακία ουκ αντιτυπεί. 3. ως μεν ουν δια βραχέων 5 ειπείν, ά τε προσδοκώμεν και μεμαθήκαμεν δια του Χριστού και διδάσκομεν ταυτά εστι. 4. Πλάτων δ' ομοίως έφη Ραδάμανθυν και Μίνω κολάσειν τους αδίκους παρ' αυτούς ελθόντας· ημείς δε το αυτό πράγμα φαμεν γενήσεσθαι, αλλ' υπό του Χριστού, καν τοις αυτοίς σώμασι μετά των 10 ψυχών γινομένων και αιωνίαν κόλασιν κολασθησομένων, αλλ' ουχί χιλιονταετή περίοδον, ως εκείνος έφη, μόνον. 5. ει μεν ουν άπιστον η αδύνατον τούτο φήσει τις, προς ημάς ήδε η πλάνη εστιν αλλ' ου προς έτερον, μέχρις ου έργω μηδέν αδικούντες ελεγχόμεθα.

15 **9.** 1. Αλλ' ουδέ θυσίαις πολλαίς και πλοκαίς ανθών τιμώμεν ους άνθρωποι μορφώσαντες και εν ναοίς ιδρύσαντες θεούς προσωνόμασαν, επεί άψυχα και νεκρά ταύτα γινώσκομεν και θεού μορφήν μη έχοντα (ου γαρ τοιαύτην ηγούμεθα τον θεον έχειν την μορφήν, ην φασί τινες εις 20 τιμήν μεμιμήσθαι), αλλ' εκείνων των φανέντων κακών

9 κἄν τοῖς αὐτοῖς Otto καὶ τ.α. A ‖ 12 φήσει τις κτλ Thirlb φήσει τις πρὸς ἡμᾶς, ἥδε ἡ πλάνη ἐστὶν ἄλλου A

exert ourselves for the life with God.' Διαγωγή absolutely or διαγωγή βίου is a Platonic phrase, equivalent to *ratio uitae.*

4. ἀντιτυπεῖ] 'resists, opposes.'
6. Πλάτων] For Rhadamanthys and Minos cf. *Gorg.* 523 E. For the χιλιονταετὴς περίοδος cf. also *Phaedr.* 249 A.
9. κἄν τοῖς αὐτοῖς κτλ.] With γινομένων must be supplied αὐτῶν as a genitive absolute.
12. πρὸς ἡμᾶς κτλ.] '*This error concerns us and nobody else.*' For similar statements cf. Tert. *Apol.* 38, Arnob. *adu. Nat.* ii 53, Athenag. *Suppl.* 36.

9. *We do not worship idols, for they are merely images representing demons in shape and name. God's form is not so; His ineffable likeness cannot be copied in destructible articles which need man's care. And the very men who make these articles and are their guardians are immoral.* Cf. Isaiah xliv 9—17, Acts xvii 24, 25.
18. θεοῦ μορφήν] Cf. Phil. ii 6.
19. ἥν φασί τινες κτλ.] '*which some say is fashioned to His honour,*' or *for the purpose of worship.*
20. ἐκείνων τῶν φ.] refers to c. 5 above.

δαιμόνων καὶ ὀνόματα καὶ σχήματα ἔχειν.   2. τί γὰρ δεῖ εἰδόσιν ὑμῖν λέγειν, ἃ τὴν ὕλην οἱ τεχνῖται διατιθέασι ξέοντες καὶ τέμνοντες καὶ χωνεύοντες καὶ τύπτοντες; καὶ ἐξ ἀτίμων πολλάκις σκευῶν διὰ τέχνης τὸ σχῆμα μόνον ἀλλάξαντες καὶ μορφοποιήσαντες θεοὺς ἐπονομάζουσιν. 3. ὅπερ οὐ μόνον ἄλογον ἡγούμεθα, ἀλλὰ καὶ ἐφ' ὕβρει τοῦ θεοῦ γίνεσθαι, ὃς ἄρρητον δόξαν καὶ μορφὴν ἔχων ἐπὶ φθαρτοῖς καὶ δεομένοις θεραπείας πράγμασιν ἐπονομάζεται.   4. καὶ ὅτι οἱ τούτων τεχνῖται ἀσελγεῖς εἰσὶ καὶ πᾶσαν κακίαν, ἵνα μὴ καταριθμῶμεν, ἔχουσιν, ἀκριβῶς ἐπίστασθε· καὶ τὰς ἑαυτῶν παιδίσκας συνεργαζομένας φθείρουσιν.   5. ὢ τῆς ἐμβροντησίας, ἀνθρώπους ἀκολάστους θεοὺς εἰς τὸ προσκυνεῖσθαι πλάσσειν λέγεσθαι καὶ μεταποιεῖν, καὶ τῶν ἱερῶν, ἔνθα ἀνατίθενται, φύλακας τοιούτους καθιστάναι, μὴ συνορῶντας ἀθέμιτον καὶ τὸ νοεῖν ἢ λέγειν ἀνθρώπους θεῶν εἶναι φύλακας.

10. 1. Ἀλλ' οὐ δέεσθαι τῆς παρὰ ἀνθρώπων ὑλικῆς προσφορᾶς παρειλήφαμεν τὸν θεόν, αὐτὸν παρέχοντα πάντα, ὁρῶντες· ἐκείνους δὲ προσδέχεσθαι αὐτὸν μόνον

9 εἰσὶ καὶ Otto εἰσί τε καὶ A ‖ 13 λέγεσθαι Stephan λέγεσθε A ‖ 18 παρειλήφαμεν Thalem Otto προσειλήφαμεν A (et infr) προειλήφαμεν Stephan

2. ἃ τὴν ὕλην] a double accusative. 'What workmen fashion their material into, by planing and cutting and casting and hammering.'
4. ἀτίμων σκευῶν] Cf. Rom. ix 21.
7. ὃς ἄρρητον κτλ.] 'Who, though of ineffable glory and form, yet has His name set upon articles which are corruptible and need to be cared for.' Plato Tim. 28 C tells us that God cannot be named. Cf. i 61, 11; ii 5 (6), 1.
9. ἀσελγεῖς εἰσί] Cf. Orig. Cels. i 5.
12. ἐμβροντησίας] 'stupidity.' The adjective ἐμβρόντητος is found in classical Greek.
14. μεταποιεῖν] 'transform.' Ashton suggests μορφοποιεῖν.
15. ἀθέμιτον] 'nefas.'
10. We do not believe that God requires material oblations, since He gives all; but He receives those who try to be like Him in character. He created the world for men's sake, and those who act worthily in His sight live and reign with Him. We had no choice as to birth, but for the choice of our future we can use the rational powers He has given us. Human laws cannot incline men to do this, but the Divine reason could, were it not opposed by the demons.
18. προσφορᾶς] 'offering' or 'oblation.' It is used in the sense of 'present' in Theophrastus Char. xvii (xxx) ad fin. Cf. Acts xvii 25.

δεδιδάγμεθα καὶ πεπείσμεθα καὶ πιστεύομεν, τοὺς τὰ προσόντα αὐτῷ ἀγαθὰ μιμουμένους, σωφροσύνην καὶ δικαιοσύνην καὶ φιλανθρωπίαν καὶ ὅσα οἰκεῖα θεῷ ἐστι, τῷ μηδενὶ ὀνόματι θετῷ καλουμένῳ. 2. καὶ πάντα τὴν
5 ἀρχὴν ἀγαθὸν ὄντα δημιουργῆσαι αὐτὸν ἐξ ἀμόρφου ὕλης δι' ἀνθρώπους δεδιδάγμεθα· οἳ ἐὰν ἀξίους τῷ ἐκείνου βουλεύματι ἑαυτοὺς δι' ἔργων δείξωσι, τῆς μετ' αὐτοῦ ἀναστροφῆς καταξιωθῆναι παρειλήφαμεν συμβασιλεύοντας, ἀφθάρτους καὶ ἀπαθεῖς γενομένους. 3. ὃν τρόπον γὰρ
10 τὴν ἀρχὴν οὐκ ὄντας ἐποίησε, τὸν αὐτὸν ἡγούμεθα τρόπον, διὰ τὸ ἑλέσθαι τοὺς αἱρουμένους τὰ αὐτῷ ἀρεστὰ, καὶ ἀφθαρσίας καὶ συνουσίας καταξιωθῆναι. 4. τὸ μὲν γὰρ τὴν ἀρχὴν γενέσθαι οὐχ ἡμέτερον ἦν· τὸ δ' ἐξακολουθῆσαι οἷς φίλον αὐτῷ, αἱρουμένους δι' ὧν αὐτὸς ἐδωρήσατο
15 λογικῶν δυνάμεων, πείθει τε καὶ εἰς πίστιν ἄγει ἡμᾶς.

1. τὰ προσόντα...ἀγ.] 'essential good qualities.'
4. θετῷ] 'imposed.'
ib. τὴν ἀρχήν] probably 'in the beginning' (as in § 3 infr.), though Braun translates omnino. Cf. i 59, 1.
5. ἀγαθὸν ὄντα κτλ.] Cf. Plat. Tim. 29 D. The apparent dualism of language is found in the Timaeus, but it would be rash to infer that Justin held a theory of the eternity of matter. His point here is merely that God made the world out of matter, which is the common view of philosophers, though Justin adds the Christian touch that it was δι' ἀνθρώπους. Ἐξ ἀμ. ὕλης represents Gen. i 2.
6. ἀξίους] with dative, either 'worthy in relation to His counsel,' or possibly 'show themselves by His counsel worthy'; cf. δι' ὧν αὐτὸς ἐδωρήσατο κτλ. below.
8. συμβασιλεύοντας] e.g. 2 Tim. ii 12.
13. τὸ δ' ἐξακολ. κτλ.] The sense required is 'We had no choice as to birth, but we have a choice as to

our life.' Otto translates 'ea uero sectari quae ipsi placent persuasionem generat et ad fidem nos ducit' and compares c. 53, 12, the idea being that to obey God generates confidence in us about the future. This seems scarcely to be the sense required. Maran translates 'ut sequamur...id ipse nobis persuadet et ad fidem nos adducit'; i.e. 'God gave us no choice about being born, but He tries to persuade us (He gives us a choice) to do His will, and leads us to faith.' This is nearer the required sense, but the last clause comes in somewhat clumsily. Veil translates 'streben wir aber dem nach, was ihm lieb ist, so machen wir (ihn) uns gewogen und gewinnen (sein) Vertrauen.' But it seems scarcely possible that εἰς πίστιν ἄγει ἡμᾶς could mean 'leads us into being trusted by God,' nor, again, is the needed antithesis thus established. On the other hand cf. 8, 2 τοὺς τὸν θ. δι' ἔργων πείσαντας.
15. λογικῶν δυνάμεων] Note that Justin regards the exercise of free-

5. καὶ ὑπὲρ πάντων ἀνθρώπων ἡγούμεθα εἶναι τὸ μὴ εἴργεσθαι ταῦτα μανθάνειν, ἀλλὰ καὶ προτρέπεσθαι ἐπὶ ταῦτα. 6. ὅπερ γὰρ οὐκ ἠδυνήθησαν οἱ ἀνθρώπειοι νόμοι πρᾶξαι, ταῦτα ὁ λόγος θεῖος ὢν εἰργάσατο, εἰ μὴ οἱ φαῦλοι δαίμονες κατεσκέδασαν πολλὰ ψευδῆ καὶ ἄθεα κατηγορήματα, σύμμαχον λαβόντες τὴν ἐν ἑκάστῳ κακὴν πρὸς πάντα καὶ ποικίλην φύσει ἐπιθυμίαν, ὧν οὐδὲν πρόσεστιν ἡμῖν.

11. 1. Καὶ ὑμεῖς, ἀκούσαντες βασιλείαν προσδοκῶντας ἡμᾶς, ἀκρίτως ἀνθρώπινον λέγειν ἡμᾶς ὑπειλήφατε, ἡμῶν τὴν μετὰ θεοῦ λεγόντων, ὡς καὶ ἐκ τοῦ ἀνεταζομένους ὑφ' ὑμῶν ὁμολογεῖν εἶναι Χριστιανούς, γινώσκοντες τῷ ὁμολογοῦντι θάνατον τὴν ζημίαν κεῖσθαι, φαίνεται. 2. εἰ γὰρ ἀνθρώπινον βασιλείαν προσεδοκῶμεν, κἂν ἠρνούμεθα, ὅπως μὴ ἀναιρώμεθα, καὶ λανθάνειν ἐπειρώμεθα, ὅπως τῶν προσδοκωμένων τύχωμεν· ἀλλ' ἐπεὶ οὐκ εἰς τὸ νῦν τὰς ἐλπίδας ἔχομεν, ἀναιρούντων

1 τὸ μὴ εἴργεσθαι Sylburg τῷ μὴ εἰ A

will for good as due to the use of the rational powers, i.e. the sanctified reason, which is the sphere of the Divine *Logos*' operation.

1. ὑπέρ] '*We consider it to be for the benefit of all men.*'

4. ὁ λόγος κτλ.] According to Otto this is a reference to the *Logos diuinus*, i.e. Christ. In that case οἱ ἀ. νόμοι might include the Jewish law (Rom. viii 3). But it may rather be a general reference to the Divine λόγος in life, of which Christ is the incarnate manifestation. Εἰργάσατο is conditional in its force, without ἄν.

6. κατηγορήματα]. This refers to the well-known charges of cannibalism and promiscuity, which were commonly levelled at the Christians. Cf. i 26; 27; ii 12. Tac. *Ann.* xv 44 'Christianos per flagitia inuisos.' Suet. *Nero* 16 'Christiani, genus hominum superstitionis nouae ac maleficae.' Eus. *Hist. Eccl.* v 1, 14.

7. ὧν] refers back to κατηγορήματα.

11. *We look forward to a kingdom; but it is not a human one; if it were such, we should deny or conceal our faith, so that we might not lose by death what we hoped for. But our hope is not for this world, and therefore, since death is the lot of all, we care nothing for execution.*

10. ἀκρίτως] '*without exercising judgment,*' '*uncritically.*' Cf. above, 5, 1. Parallel uses of ἄκριτος are quoted by Liddell and Scott.

12. γινώσκοντες] ought in strict grammar to be accusative. A similar anacoluthon is found in i 55, 6 δι' ὧν αἵ τε πρόοδοι ὑμῶν γίνονται, δεικνύντες. For the sentiment here expressed cf. John xviii 36.

17. ἀναιρούντων οὐ π.] '*we do not heed our executioners.*' A common construction with φροντίζω.

οὐ πεφροντίκαμεν τοῦ καὶ πάντως ἀποθανεῖν ὀφειλομένου.

12. 1. Ἀρωγοὶ δ' ὑμῖν καὶ σύμμαχοι πρὸς εἰρήνην ἐσμὲν πάντων μᾶλλον ἀνθρώπων, οἳ ταῦτα δοξάζομεν, ὡς λαθεῖν θεὸν κακόεργον ἢ πλεονέκτην ἢ ἐπίβουλον ἢ ἐνάρετον ἀδύνατον εἶναι, καὶ ἕκαστον ἐπ' αἰωνίαν κόλασιν ἢ σωτηρίαν κατ' ἀξίαν τῶν πράξεων πορεύεσθαι. 2. εἰ γὰρ οἱ πάντες ἄνθρωποι ταῦτα ἐγίνωσκον, οὐκ ἄν τις τὴν κακίαν πρὸς ὀλίγον ᾑρεῖτο, γινώσκων πορεύεσθαι ἐπ' αἰωνίαν διὰ πυρὸς καταδίκην, ἀλλ' ἐκ παντὸς τρόπου ἑαυτὸν συνεῖχε καὶ ἐκόσμει ἀρετῇ, ὅπως τῶν παρὰ τοῦ θεοῦ τύχοι ἀγαθῶν καὶ τῶν κολαστηρίων ἀπηλλαγμένος εἴη. 3. οἱ γὰρ διὰ τοὺς ὑφ' ὑμῶν κειμένους νόμους καὶ

12 τύχοι Otto τύχῃ A || 13 οἱ γὰρ...εἰ ἔμαθον Thirlb al οὐ γὰρ...εἰ ἔμαθον A οὐ γὰρ...εἰ δ' ἔμαθον Otto Krüger

Cf. i 39; 57, for similar expressions of fearlessness.

1. τοῦ καὶ πάντως κτλ.] '*since death is in any case the debt of nature.*' Similar phrases are found in i 57, 2; ii 11, 1. Otto suggests that Justin may have in mind the common Euripidean phrase κατθανεῖν ὀφείλεται, which occurs for instance in Eur. *Alc.* 419, 782, *Androm.* 1272.

12. *We are your allies in the cause of peace. For we teach that no acts can escape the judgment of God. If all men knew this, they would be virtuous; human laws only cause them to conceal their crimes. Are you afraid that crime may cease to exist, and the supply of criminals for you to punish run short? Such a fear is irrational, the inspiration of demons, unbecoming to pious and philosophic rulers. But if you still neglect the truth, you may do your worst, but you will not succeed; for rational men will not do what reason forbids. Christ prophesied persecution for us; and His foresight shows His Divinity.*

4. ὡς εἶναι] A mixed construction, combining ὡς ἐστί and the infinitive without ὡς. It can be paralleled from classical Greek. Cf. Xen. *Cyr.* viii 1, 25 ἐλογίζετο ὡς ἧττον ἂν αὐτοὺς ἐθέλειν: id. *Hellen.* vi 5, 42 ἐλπίζειν ὡς ἄνδρας ἀγαθοὺς αὐτοὺς γενήσεσθαι: Soph. *O. C.* 385 ἔσχες ἐλπίδ' ὡς ἐμοῦ θεοὺς Ὥραν τιν' ἕξειν.

5. ἢ ἐνάρετον] It is a little odd to throw this alternative in with simple ἤ. Hence some emend to ἀναιρέτην.

9. πρὸς ὀλίγον] '*for a little while.*' This use of πρός is found in Plutarch and Lucian.

10. καταδίκην] '*sentence*'; properly of the damages awarded.

12. κολαστηρίων] '*punishments.*'

13. οἱ γὰρ διὰ κτλ.] The sense is '*men now seek to conceal their crimes because of the laws, and they know they can do so; if they were to learn that they cannot evade God, they would not commit crimes.*' This is a simple and logical statement, and the alteration of the MS οὐ to οἱ is a trivial change. Otto adopts Maran's explanation of the

κολάσεις πειρῶνται λανθάνειν ἀδικοῦντες, ἀνθρώπους δ᾽
ὄντας λανθάνειν ὑμᾶς δυνατὸν ἐπιστάμενοι ἀδικοῦσιν, εἰ
ἔμαθον καὶ ἐπείσθησαν θεὸν ἀδύνατον εἶναι λαθεῖν τι, οὐ
μόνον πραττόμενον ἀλλὰ καὶ βουλευόμενον, κἂν διὰ τὰ
ἐπικείμενα ἐκ παντὸς τρόπου κόσμιοι ἦσαν, ὡς καὶ ὑμεῖς 5
συμφήσετε. 4. ἀλλ᾽ ἐοίκατε δεδιέναι μὴ πάντες δικαιοπραγήσωσι, καὶ ὑμεῖς οὓς κολάζητε ἔτι οὐχ ἕξετε· δημίων
δ᾽ ἂν εἴη τὸ τοιοῦτον ἔργον, ἀλλ᾽ οὐκ ἀρχόντων ἀγαθῶν.
5. πεπείσμεθα δ᾽ ἐκ δαιμόνων φαύλων, οἳ καὶ παρὰ τῶν
ἀλόγως βιούντων αἰτοῦσι θύματα καὶ θεραπείας, καὶ 10
ταῦτα, ὡς προέφημεν, ἐνεργεῖσθαι· ἀλλ᾽ οὐχ ὑμᾶς, οἵ γε
εὐσεβείας καὶ φιλοσοφίας ὀρέγεσθε, ἄλογόν τι πρᾶξαι
ὑπειλήφαμεν. 6. εἰ δὲ καὶ ὑμεῖς ὁμοίως τοῖς ἀνοήτοις
τὰ ἔθη πρὸ τῆς ἀληθείας τιμᾶτε, πράττετε ὃ δύνασθε·
τοσοῦτον δὲ δύνανται καὶ ἄρχοντες πρὸ τῆς ἀληθείας 15

7 κολάζητε Sylburg al κολάζετε A κολάσετε Thirlb

reading which he prefers; 'Justin is showing the superiority of Christianity to human laws; there is hope of evading the laws, no hope of evading God. The desire to evade does not show the power of the laws but their weakness; men seek secrecy for crime, not through fear of the laws, but through hope of concealing their crime; take that hope away and crime will cease.' The objections to this argument are (1) it is not true to human nature; the normal reason for seeking to conceal crime is fear of the laws; (2) it seems perilously like nonsense to say 'men seek secrecy for crime because they hope they can conceal their crime.' The question still remains, why men should trouble about secrecy at all, if it be not for fear of the laws. For the sentiment, Otto cites as parallels Tert. *Ap.* 45, Lact. *Inst.* v 8.

4. κἂν διὰ τὰ ἐπικ.] '*at least because of the impending penalties*' (if for no more noble reason). Cf. i 18, 6 οἷς κἂν ὁμοίως ἡμᾶς ἀποδέ-

ξασθε: i 26, 7; ii 7 (8), 1. This limiting use of κἄν is elliptical in nature. Cf. Soph. *Electr.* 1482 ἀλλά μοι πάρες κἂν σμικρὸν εἰπεῖν. Jebb (Appendix *ad loc.*) says that 'in such instances κἄν can usually be resolved into καὶ ἐάν, with a subjunctive verb understood.' So here we may insert ὦσιν '*if they be so only because of the penalties.*'

6. δικαιοπραγήσωσι, ἕξετε] Cf. ἀλλ᾽ ὅπως μὴ λήσεις αὐτὸν ἐξαπατῶν καὶ ὕστερον μεταγνῷς. Two possible constructions are thus combined for the sake of variety, though sometimes a faint shade of difference in meaning may be distinguished between them.

11. ὡς προέφημεν] c. 5.
ib. οἵ γε κτλ.] referring to the epithets of the dedication in c. 1.

14. τὰ ἔθη] '*the custom*,' i.e. of persecuting Christians. Or it may mean that conservatism was against the novelty of Christianity.

15. τοσοῦτον...ὅσον] i.e. to kill us and no more. Cf. Luke xii 4.

δόξαν τιμῶντες, ὅσον καὶ λῃσταὶ ἐν ἐρημίᾳ. 7. ὅτι δ᾽ οὐ καλλιερήσετε, ὁ λόγος ἀποδείκνυσιν, οὗ βασιλικώτατον καὶ δικαιότατον ἄρχοντα μετὰ τὸν γεννήσαντα θεὸν οὐδένα οἴδαμεν ὄντα. 8. ὃν γὰρ τρόπον διαδέχεσθαι πενίας ἢ
5 πάθη ἢ ἀδοξίας πατρικὰς ὑφαιροῦνται πάντες, οὕτως καὶ ὅσα ἂν ὑπαγορεύσῃ ὁ λόγος μὴ δεῖν αἱρεῖσθαι, ὁ νουνεχὴς οὐχ αἱρήσεται. 9. γενήσεσθαι ταῦτα πάντα προεῖπε, φημί, ὁ ἡμέτερος διδάσκαλος καὶ τοῦ πατρὸς πάντων καὶ δεσπότου θεοῦ υἱὸς καὶ ἀπόστολος ὢν Ἰησοῦς Χριστός,
10 ἀφ᾽ οὗ καὶ τὸ Χριστιανοὶ ἐπονομάζεσθαι ἐσχήκαμεν. 10. ὅθεν καὶ βέβαιοι γινόμεθα πρὸς τὰ δεδιδαγμένα ὑπ᾽ αὐτοῦ πάντα, ἐπειδὴ ἔργῳ φαίνεται γινόμενα ὅσα φθάσας γενέσθαι προεῖπεν· ὅπερ θεοῦ ἔργον ἐστί, πρὶν ἢ γενέσθαι εἰπεῖν καὶ οὕτως δειχθῆναι γινόμενον ὡς προείρηται.
15 11. ἦν μὲν οὖν καὶ ἐπὶ τούτοις παυσαμένους μηδὲν προστιθέναι, λογισαμένους ὅτι δίκαιά τε καὶ ἀληθῆ ἀξιοῦμεν· ἀλλ᾽ ἐπεὶ γνωρίζομεν οὐ ῥᾷον ἀγνοίᾳ κατεχομένην ψυχὴν συντόμως μεταβάλλειν, ὑπὲρ τοῦ πεῖσαι τοὺς φιλαληθεῖς

13 πρὶν ἢ γενέσθαι A πρὸ τοῦ γενέσθαι Sacr Par Holl 97 ‖ 14 εἰπεῖν Otto εἶπε A

2. καλλιερήσετε] 'you will prosper.'
ib. ὁ λόγος] Here undoubtedly Christ. Semisch and Pautigny see a trace of Subordinationism in the phrase μετὰ τὸν γεννήσαντα θεόν. See *Introd.* p. xxii. Note that in the next sentence ὁ νουνεχής is identified as the doer of what ὁ λόγος (reason or Christ) commands.
ib. οὗ βασιλικώτατον κτλ.] A genitive of comparison with a superlative. This is found in classical Greek with plural words, e.g. Thuc. i 1 ἀξιολογώτατον τῶν προγεγενημένων, where the genitive approximates to one of class. Here it is probably a symptom of the confusion between comparative and superlative, which is a feature of late Greek. Cf. John i. 15 πρῶτός μου.

5. ὑφαιροῦνται] '*refugiunt*' Otto. The word means '*to purloin*' and so here, '*to filch oneself away from.*'
7. ταῦτα] i.e. persecution and its failure.
ib. προεῖπε] Cf. Matt. x 26, xxiv 9.
9. ἀπόστολος] Cf. i 63, 5, and Heb. iii. 1, the only place in the New Testament where the term is applied to Christ.
11. ὅθεν καὶ β.] Cf. Matt. xxiv 25, John xvi 4.
13. θεοῦ ἔργον] Cf. Is. xli 22 f.
17. ῥᾷον] This may be the comparative of ῥᾴδιος, meaning '*particularly easy*'; or it may be from an erroneous collateral form of ῥᾴδιος, found in grammarians. See Liddell and Scott.
18. μεταβάλλειν] probably in the

APOLOGIA

μικρὰ προσθεῖναι προεθυμήθημεν, εἰδότες ὅτι οὐκ ἀδύνατον ἀληθείας παρατεθείσης ἄγνοιαν φυγεῖν.

13. 1. Ἄθεοι μὲν οὖν ὡς οὔκ ἐσμεν, τὸν δημιουργὸν τοῦδε τοῦ παντὸς σεβόμενοι, ἀνενδεῆ αἱμάτων καὶ σπονδῶν καὶ θυμιαμάτων, ὡς ἐδιδάχθημεν, λέγοντες, λόγῳ εὐχῆς καὶ εὐχαριστίας ἐφ᾿ οἷς προσφερόμεθα πᾶσιν, ὅση δύναμις, αἰνοῦντες, μόνην ἀξίαν αὐτοῦ τιμὴν ταύτην παραλαβόντες, τὸ τὰ ὑπ᾿ ἐκείνου εἰς διατροφὴν γενόμενα οὐ πυρὶ δαπανᾶν, ἀλλ᾿ ἑαυτοῖς καὶ τοῖς δεομένοις προσφέρειν, 2. ἐκείνῳ δὲ εὐχαρίστους ὄντας διὰ λόγου πομπὰς καὶ ὕμνους πέμπειν ὑπέρ τε τοῦ γεγονέναι καὶ τῶν εἰς εὐρωστίαν πόρων πάντων, ποιοτήτων μὲν γενῶν καὶ μεταβολῶν ὡρῶν, καὶ τοῦ πάλιν ἐν ἀφθαρσίᾳ γενέσθαι διὰ πίστιν τὴν ἐν

neuter sense. '*It is not easy for a soul enchained by ignorance to change quickly, but yet ignorance may be escaped from, if the truth is set over against it.*' Quoted by Irenaeus iii 2, 3.

13. We are not atheists, for we worship God the Creator, though not with sacrifices, praising Him and praying to Him. Second to Him we hold Christ in reverence, and the prophetic Spirit in the third place. We shall show that this is perfectly rational.

4. ἀνενδεῆ] Cf. Acts xvii. 25. Braun cites Clem. Rom. *ad Corinth.* 52 ἀπροσδεής, ἀδελφοί, δεσπότης ὑπάρχει τῶν ἁπάντων, and other passages. The sentiment is a commonplace in Church writers, and is found in some heathen works, e.g. Eurip. *H. F.* 1348 δεῖται γὰρ ὁ θεὸς εἴπερ ἔστ᾿ ὄντως θεὸς Οὐδενός (cited by Braun).

5. λόγῳ εὐχῆς] Cf. i 66 δι᾿ εὐχῆς λόγου.

6. ἐφ᾿ οἷς προσφερόμεθα] Some translate '*at all our offerings*'; but more probably it is a genuine middle '*for all that we receive*.' So again in i 67, 2. Cf. also Liddell and Scott.

ib. ὅση δύναμις] Cf. i 55; 67.

8. διατροφήν] '*sustenance*.' Οὐ πυρὶ δαπανᾶν of course refers to the sacrifices.

9. προσφέρειν] '*contribute*.' There may be an allusion to the Eucharistic distributions to the poor.

10. διὰ λόγου κτλ.] Maran translates *rationalibus pompis=a reasonable service*. Διὰ λόγου is better taken as='*in speech*,' cf. i 55, 8; i 67, 4. Πομπή nearly always means '*a solemn procession*,' often in connexion with a religious ceremony. In this passage a contrast with the solemnities of heathen ritual is obviously intended. There could scarcely be any Christian processions in Justin's time. The phrase πομπὰς καὶ ὕμνους should probably be regarded as zeugmatic; '*We celebrate our solemnities, with hymns, in speech*' (and not by ceremonial processions). There seems to be an allusion to the Eucharistic service.

11. τῶν εἰς εὐρωστίαν π. π.] '*all the means of health*.'

12. ποιοτήτων γενῶν] '*the qualities of things*.'

13. τοῦ πάλιν] The genitive is dependent upon αἰτήσεις.

2—2

αὐτῷ αἰτήσεις πέμποντες,— τίς σωφρονῶν οὐχ ὁμολογήσει; 3. τὸν διδάσκαλόν τε τούτων γενόμενον ἡμῖν καὶ εἰς τοῦτο γεννηθέντα Ἰησοῦν Χριστόν, τὸν σταυρωθέντα ἐπὶ Ποντίου Πιλάτου, τοῦ γενομένου ἐν Ἰουδαίᾳ ἐπὶ
5 χρόνοις Τιβερίου Καίσαρος ἐπιτρόπου, υἱὸν αὐτὸν τοῦ ὄντως θεοῦ μαθόντες καὶ ἐν δευτέρᾳ χώρᾳ ἔχοντες, πνεῦμά τε προφητικὸν ἐν τρίτῃ τάξει ὅτι (μετὰ λόγου τιμῶμεν) ἀποδείξομεν. 4. ἐνταῦθα γὰρ μανίαν ἡμῶν καταφαίνονται, δευτέραν χώραν μετὰ τὸν ἄτρεπτον καὶ ἀεὶ ὄντα
10 θεὸν καὶ γεννήτορα τῶν ἁπάντων ἀνθρώπῳ σταυρωθέντι διδόναι ἡμᾶς λέγοντες, ἀγνοοῦντες τὸ ἐν τούτῳ μυστήριον, ᾧ προσέχειν ὑμᾶς ἐξηγουμένων ἡμῶν) προτρεπόμεθα.

14. 1. Προλέγομεν γὰρ ὑμῖν φυλάξασθαι, μὴ οἱ προδιαβεβλημένοι ὑφ᾽ ἡμῶν δαίμονες ἐξαπατήσωσιν ὑμᾶς καὶ
15 ἀποτρέψωσι τοῦ ὅλως ἐντυχεῖν καὶ συνεῖναι τὰ λεγόμενα (ἀγωνίζονται γὰρ ἔχειν ὑμᾶς δούλους καὶ ὑπηρέτας, καὶ ποτὲ μὲν δι᾽ ὀνείρων ἐπιφανείας, ποτὲ δ᾽ αὖ διὰ μαγικῶν

5 υἱὸν αὐτὸν Otto al υἱὸν αὐτοῦ A ‖ 10 τῶν ἁπάντων Otto al τὸν ἁπάντων A

1. τίς οὐχ ὁμολογήσει] Here at last we get the principal verb, upon which all that preceded, introduced by ὡς, depends.

5. ἐπιτρόπου] The regular Greek equivalent for the Latin *procurator*. Pilate is called *procurator* of Judaea, Tac. *Ann.* xv 44. Luke iii 1 has ἡγεμονεύοντος Ποντίου Πειλάτου τῆς Ἰουδαίας, where D and other authorities read ἐπιτροπεύοντος, a correction made in order to mark Pilate's office with more precision. (So Plummer, St Luke, note *ad loc.*)

6. ἐν δευτέρᾳ χ.] See *Introd.* p. xxii.

7. μετὰ λόγου] '*rationally*'; this phrase leads on at once to ἐνταῦθα γὰρ μανίαν ἡμῶν καταφαίνονται. Probably not '*with the Word*,' as it is translated by Bethune-Baker *Early Hist. of Chr. Doctr.* p. 199 note 4.

9. ἄτρεπτον] '*immutable.*'

11. μυστήριον] in the sense of '*mystery*,' '*secret above human intelligence.*'

14. Do not be deceived by the demons and hindered from reading our pleas. We have shaken off their despotism, and the reformation of our life proves the virtue of our new belief. To show that this is truly what we have learnt and teach, we will quote you some of Christ's sayings.

13. προδιαβεβλημένοι] '*previously accused.*'

15. ἐντυχεῖν] '*read.*' This use of the word is mentioned in Liddell and Scott from Lucian, Plutarch, etc.

ib. συνεῖναι] 2 aor. from συνίημι.

στροφῶν χειροῦνται πάντας τοὺς (οὐκ ἔσθ' ὅπως) ὑπὲρ τῆς
αὐτῶν σωτηρίας ἀγωνιζομένους), ὃν τρόπον καὶ ἡμεῖς μετὰ
τὸ τῷ λόγῳ πεισθῆναι ἐκείνων μὲν ἀπέστημεν, θεῷ δὲ μόνῳ
τῷ ἀγεννήτῳ διὰ τοῦ υἱοῦ ἑπόμεθα· 2. οἱ πάλαι μὲν
πορνείαις χαίροντες, νῦν δὲ σωφροσύνην μόνην ἀσπαζό- 5
μενοι· οἱ δὲ καὶ μαγικαῖς τέχναις χρώμενοι, νῦν ἀγαθῷ
καὶ ἀγεννήτῳ θεῷ ἑαυτοὺς ἀνατεθεικότες· χρημάτων δὲ
καὶ κτημάτων οἱ πόρους παντὸς μᾶλλον στέργοντες, νῦν
καὶ ἃ ἔχομεν εἰς κοινὸν φέροντες καὶ παντὶ δεομένῳ
κοινωνοῦντες· 3. οἱ μισάλληλοι δὲ καὶ ἀλληλοφόνοι 10
καὶ πρὸς τοὺς οὐχ ὁμοφύλους (διὰ τὰ ἔθη) καὶ ἑστίας κοινὰς
μὴ ποιούμενοι, νῦν μετὰ τὴν ἐπιφάνειαν τοῦ Χριστοῦ ὁμοδί-
αιτοι γινόμενοι, καὶ ὑπὲρ τῶν ἐχθρῶν εὐχόμενοι, καὶ τοὺς
ἀδίκως μισοῦντας πείθειν πειρώμενοι, ὅπως οἱ κατὰ τὰς
τοῦ Χριστοῦ καλὰς ὑποθημοσύνας βιώσαντες εὐέλπιδες 15

6 νῦν ἀγαθῷ Otto al ἀγαθῷ A

1. στροφῶν] 'dodges, tricks.'
ib. οὐκ ἔσθ' ὅπως] 'plane non'
Otto.
2. ὃν τρόπον] refers back to
φυλάξασθαι.
3. τῷ λόγῳ] perhaps 'the Divine
Logos' i.e. Christ.
4. ἀγεννήτῳ] 'unbegotten.' Ashton and others insist that here
ἀγενήτῳ 'uncreated' should be
substituted, as also in all similar
passages; and that, in like reference,
γεγενῆσθαι should be substituted for
γεγεννῆσθαι. No doubt the two
words could easily be confused in
the MSS. But Justin might reason-
ably call God 'unbegotten' in opposition to the heathen myths about
Zeus or Jupiter, or to distinguish
Him from the Son, who was begotten. Change of the text is
therefore scarcely indispensable.
ib. οἱ πάλαι κτλ.] Here Justin
brings forward, as a proof of the
power of Christianity, its efficacy
in the reformation of individual
character. Cf. i 16, 4.
7. θεῷ ἑαυτοὺς ἀνατ.] As Otto
says, this seems to have been a
regular formula. It recurs in i 25,
2; 49, 5; 61, 1. Cf. Const. Apost.
viii 6 ἑαυτοὺς τῷ μόνῳ ἀγεννήτῳ
θεῷ διὰ τοῦ Χριστοῦ αὐτοῦ παράθεσθε
(the formula for dismissing catechumens after a baptism).
10. κοινωνοῦντες] implying not
communism, but general philanthropy.
11. διὰ τὰ ἔθη] 'because of
(difference in) customs.' Cf. 12, 6.
13. ὑπὲρ τῶν ἐχθρῶν εὐχ.] Cf.
i 15, 9.
14. ὅπως οἱ] Maran would delete
οἱ, and Otto suggests αὐτοί, in order
that the reference may be more
directly to τοὺς μισοῦντας. This
is attractive but not absolutely
necessary. The reference must in
any case include τοὺς μισοῦντας.
15. ὑποθημοσύνας] 'suggestions,
advice.'

ὦσι σὺν ἡμῖν τῶν αὐτῶν παρὰ τοῦ πάντων δεσπόζοντος
θεοῦ τυχεῖν. 4. ἵνα δὲ μὴ σοφίζεσθαι ὑμᾶς δόξωμεν,
ὀλίγων τινῶν τῶν παρ' αὐτοῦ τοῦ Χριστοῦ διδαγμάτων
ἐπιμνησθῆναι καλῶς ἔχειν πρὸ τῆς ἀποδείξεως ἡγησάμεθα,
5 καὶ ὑμέτερον ἔστω ὡς δυνατῶν βασιλέων ἐξετάσαι εἰ
ἀληθῶς ταῦτα δεδιδάγμεθα καὶ διδάσκομεν. 5. βραχεῖς
δὲ καὶ σύντομοι παρ' αὐτοῦ λόγοι γεγόνασιν· οὐ γὰρ
σοφιστὴς ὑπῆρχεν, ἀλλὰ δύναμις θεοῦ ὁ λόγος αὐτοῦ ἦν.
15. 1. Περὶ μὲν οὖν σωφροσύνης τοσοῦτον εἶπεν·
10 Ὃς ἂν ἐμβλέψῃ γυναικὶ πρὸς τὸ ἐπιθυμῆσαι αὐτῆς ἤδη
ἐμοίχευσε τῇ καρδίᾳ παρὰ τῷ θεῷ. 2. καί· Εἰ ὁ
ὀφθαλμός σου ὁ δεξιὸς σκανδαλίζει σε, ἔκκοψον αὐτόν·
συμφέρει γάρ σοι μονόφθαλμον εἰσελθεῖν εἰς τὴν βασιλείαν
τῶν οὐρανῶν, ἢ μετὰ τῶν δύο πεμφθῆναι εἰς τὸ αἰώνιον πῦρ.
15 3. καί· Ὃς γαμεῖ ἀπολελυμένην ἀφ' ἑτέρου ἀνδρὸς
μοιχᾶται. 4. καί· Εἰσί τινες οἵτινες εὐνουχίσθησαν
ὑπὸ τῶν ἀνθρώπων, εἰσὶ δὲ οἳ ἐγεννήθησαν εὐνοῦχοι,
εἰσὶ δὲ οἳ εὐνούχισαν ἑαυτοὺς διὰ τὴν βασιλείαν τῶν
οὐρανῶν· πλὴν οὐ πάντες τοῦτο χωροῦσιν. 5. ὥσπερ
20 καὶ οἱ νόμῳ ἀνθρωπίνῳ διγαμίας ποιούμενοι ἁμαρτωλοὶ

5 ὡς δυνατῶν A ὡς δὴ συνετῶν Stephan || 18 εὐνούχισαν B edd εὐνούχησαν A

2. σοφίζεσθαι] with accusative 'to deceive.' Liddell and Scott quote only two parallels, one from Anth. P. xii 25, the other from Aretae. Caus. M. Diut. i 15.

4. πρὸ τῆς ἀποδείξεως] 'before we embark on our promised demonstration' (c. 13) i.e. that it is reasonable to worship Christ.

5. δυνατῶν] 'Since you have the power, it is your duty to find out whether this is in truth our doctrine.'

6. βραχεῖς] See Introd. p. xxxv. 'Nota Sophistarum loquacitas,' Otto.

8. δύναμις κτλ.] 'His word was the power of God.' Cf. Matt. vii 29, 1 Cor. i 24.

15. Quotations to show Christ's teaching on chastity, philanthropy, unworldliness. On Justin's quotations see Introd. p. xxxiv.

10. ὃς ἂν ἐμβλέψῃ] Cf. Matt. v 28.

11. εἰ ὁ ὀφθαλμός] Cf. Matt. v 29, 30; xviii 9; Mark ix 47. Αἰώνιον πῦρ is probably substituted as a Gentile equivalent for γέενναν τοῦ πυρός.

15. ὃς γαμεῖ] Cf. Matt. v 32; Luke xvi 18.

16. εἰσί τινες] Cf. Matt. xix 12, 11.

20. διγαμίας] 'second marriages.' This might refer to (1) bigamy, (2) successive second marriage,

παρὰ τῷ ἡμετέρῳ διδασκάλῳ εἰσί, καὶ οἱ προσβλέποντες
γυναικὶ πρὸς τὸ ἐπιθυμῆσαι αὐτῆς· οὐ γὰρ μόνον ὁ μοι-
χεύων ἔργῳ ἐκβέβληται παρ' αὐτῷ, ἀλλὰ καὶ ὁ μοιχεῦσαι
βουλόμενος, ὡς οὐ τῶν ἔργων φανερῶν μόνον τῷ θεῷ ἀλλὰ
καὶ τῶν ἐνθυμημάτων.   6. καὶ πολλοί τινες καὶ πολλαὶ 5
ἐξηκοντοῦται καὶ ἑβδομηκοντοῦται, οἳ ἐκ παίδων ἐμαθητεύθησαν τῷ Χριστῷ, ἄφθοροι διαμένουσι· καὶ εὔχομαι κατὰ
πᾶν γένος ἀνθρώπων τοιούτους δεῖξαι.   7. τί γὰρ καὶ
λέγομεν τὸ ἀναρίθμητον πλῆθος τῶν ἐξ ἀκολασίας μετα-
βαλόντων καὶ ταῦτα μαθόντων; οὐ γὰρ τοὺς δικαίους οὐδὲ 10
τοὺς σώφρονας εἰς μετάνοιαν ἐκάλεσεν ὁ Χριστός, ἀλλὰ
τοὺς ἀσεβεῖς καὶ ἀκολάστους καὶ ἀδίκους.   8. εἶπε δὲ
οὕτως· Οὐκ ἦλθον καλέσαι δικαίους, ἀλλὰ ἁμαρτωλοὺς

(3) marriage after divorce. (1) Bigamy however can hardly be said to be permissible νόμῳ ἀνθρωπίνῳ (which must presumably refer to Roman law); and the MS text can hardly be taken in any way except '*as those who, by human law, contract second marriages are sinners in the eyes of our teacher.*' (2) Marriage after the death of a first wife was permitted by Roman law, and discouraged by some Church fathers on the authority of certain expressions of St Paul, e.g. by Athenagoras (*Leg.* 33), Origen, Theophilus, Tertullian (cf. Schaff *Hist. of Ante-Nicene Christianity* § 99). But no such view is found elsewhere in Justin, and the judgment of the Church never acquiesced in such a theory. (3) It seems then as if the reference here must probably be to marriage after divorce (so Thirlb., Otto); and so the three instances of unchastity mentioned are (1) looking on a woman lustfully, (2) marrying a divorced woman, (3) marrying a second wife after divorcing a first. Donaldson (*Hist. of Christ. Lit. and Doctr.* vol. ii, chap. iii, § 14 *ad fin.*, his whole discussion of this passage is worth reading) suggests with some force that διγαμίας, to Justin's readers, would mean nothing but *bigamy*; and he proposes the reading ὡς παρὰ τῷ νόμῳ ἀνθ. διγ. ποι. ἁμαρτωλοί, παρὰ τ. ἡμ. διδ. εἰσὶ καὶ οἱ προσβλέποντες κτλ. This gives the most obvious meaning to διγαμίας, and excellent sense to the passage. If the MS reading be retained, we must assume Justin to be using διγαμίας ecclesiastically, in the second or third sense, forgetting what meaning his Roman readers would attach to it, and that he means, '*Who avail themselves of human law to commit what is really bigamy.*'

2. οὐ γὰρ μόνον] Otto compares Iren. *c. Haer.* ii 32, 1 'non solum qui moechatur expellitur sed et qui moechari uult.'

5. ἐνθυμημάτων] '*thoughts.*' Heb. iv 12 has ἐνθυμήσεων in the same sense.

6. ἐκ παίδων] See *Int.* p. xxxvii.

7. ἄφθοροι] may mean '*virgins*' or, more simply, '*chaste.*'

ib. εὔχομαι] '*declare.*'

13. οὐκ ἦλθον] Cf. Matt. ix 13, Mark ii 17, Luke v 32.

εἰς μετάνοιαν. θέλει γὰρ ὁ πατὴρ ὁ οὐράνιος τὴν μετάνοιαν τοῦ ἁμαρτωλοῦ ἢ τὴν κόλασιν αὐτοῦ. 9. περὶ δὲ τοῦ στέργειν ἅπαντας ταῦτα ἐδίδαξεν· Εἰ ἀγαπᾶτε τοὺς ἀγαπῶντας ὑμᾶς, τί καινὸν ποιεῖτε; καὶ γὰρ οἱ
5 πόρνοι τοῦτο ποιοῦσιν. ἐγὼ δὲ ὑμῖν λέγω· Εὔχεσθε ὑπὲρ τῶν ἐχθρῶν ὑμῶν καὶ ἀγαπᾶτε τοὺς μισοῦντας ὑμᾶς καὶ εὐλογεῖτε τοὺς καταρωμένους ὑμῖν καὶ εὔχεσθε ὑπὲρ τῶν ἐπηρεαζόντων ὑμᾶς. 10. εἰς δὲ τὸ κοινωνεῖν τοῖς δεομένοις καὶ μηδὲν πρὸς δόξαν ποιεῖν ταῦτα ἔφη· Παντὶ τῷ
10 αἰτοῦντι δίδοτε καὶ τὸν βουλόμενον δανείσασθαι μὴ ἀποστραφῆτε. εἰ γὰρ δανείζετε παρ᾽ ὧν ἐλπίζετε λαβεῖν, τί καινὸν ποιεῖτε; τοῦτο καὶ οἱ τελῶναι ποιοῦσιν.
11. ὑμεῖς δὲ μὴ θησαυρίζητε ἑαυτοῖς ἐπὶ τῆς γῆς, ὅπου σὴς καὶ βρῶσις ἀφανίζει καὶ λῃσταὶ διορύσσουσι· θη-
15 σαυρίζετε δὲ ἑαυτοῖς ἐν τοῖς οὐρανοῖς, ὅπου οὔτε σὴς οὔτε βρῶσις ἀφανίζει. 12. τί γὰρ ὠφελεῖται ἄνθρωπος, ἂν τὸν κόσμον ὅλον κερδήσῃ, τὴν δὲ ψυχὴν αὐτοῦ ἀπολέσῃ; ἢ τί δώσει αὐτῆς ἀντάλλαγμα; θησαυρίζετε οὖν ἐν τοῖς οὐρανοῖς, ὅπου οὔτε σὴς οὔτε βρῶσις ἀφανίζει. 13. καί·
20 Γίνεσθε δὲ χρηστοὶ καὶ οἰκτίρμονες, ὡς καὶ ὁ πατὴρ ὑμῶν

---

1. θέλει γάρ] Cf. Ezek. xviii 23, xxxiii 11 'nolo mortem impii sed ut conuertatur impius a uia sua et uiuat.' Similar ideas are expressed in 2 Pet. iii 9; 1 Tim. ii 4. Justin's phraseology here may be his own, based on Bible reminiscence;· but he may possibly be quoting a traditional logion of Christ. Ὁ π. ὁ οὐράνιος is clearly an echo of N.T. language, especially of St Matthew. Ἤ = ' *rather than*.'

3. εἰ ἀγαπᾶτε] Cf. Matt. v 46, 47; Luke vi 32. Τί καινὸν ποιεῖτε is substituted for Matthew's τίνα μισθὸν ἔχετε or τί περισσὸν ποιεῖτε, and Luke's ποία ὑμῖν χάρις ἐστίν. Cf. Plat. *Rep.* 599 E οὐδέν γε καινὸν ποιοῦμεν. In place of Justin's πόρνοι Matthew has τελῶναι, Luke ἁμαρτωλοί (hence Thirlb. suggests πονηροί in place of πόρνοι here).

5. ἐγὼ δὲ ὑμῖν] Cf. Matt. v 44; Luke vi 27, 28. It is variously quoted in various passages, e.g. Just. *Tryph.* 96 ἀγαπᾶτε τοὺς ἐχθροὺς ὑμῶν : Tert. *Ap.* 31 'Praeceptum est nobis etiam pro inimicis Deum orare et persecutoribus nostris bona precari'; Iren. *c. Haer.* iii 18, 5 'Diligite inimicos uestros et orate pro eis qui uos oderunt.'

9. παντὶ τῷ αἰτοῦντι] Cf. Matt. v 42, 46; Luke vi 30, 34.

13. ὑμεῖς δὲ μή] Cf. Matt. vi 19, 20.

16. τί γὰρ ὠφελεῖται] Cf. Matt. xvi 26, vi 20.

20. γίνεσθε δέ] Cf. Matt. v 48, 45; Luke vi 35, 36. Justin *Tryph.*

χρηστός ἐστι καὶ οἰκτίρμων, καὶ τὸν ἥλιον αὐτοῦ ἀνατέλλει
ἐπὶ ἁρματωλοὺς καὶ δικαίους καὶ πονηρούς. 14. μὴ
μεριμνᾶτε δὲ τί φάγητε ἢ τί ἐνδύσησθε. οὐχ ὑμεῖς τῶν
πετεινῶν καὶ τῶν θηρίων διαφέρετε; καὶ ὁ θεὸς τρέφει
αὐτά. 15. μὴ οὖν μεριμνήσητε τί φάγητε ἢ τί ἐν- 5
δύσησθε· οἶδε γὰρ ὁ πατὴρ ὑμῶν ὁ οὐράνιος ὅτι τούτων
χρείαν ἔχετε. 16. ζητεῖτε δὲ τὴν βασιλείαν τῶν οὐρανῶν, καὶ ταῦτα πάντα προστεθήσεται ὑμῖν. ὅπου γὰρ ὁ
θησαυρός ἐστιν, ἐκεῖ καὶ ὁ νοῦς τοῦ ἀνθρώπου. 17. καί·
Μὴ ποιῆτε ταῦτα πρὸς τὸ θεαθῆναι ὑπὸ τῶν ἀνθρώπων· 10
εἰ δὲ μή γε, μισθὸν οὐκ ἔχετε παρὰ τοῦ πατρὸς ὑμῶν τοῦ
ἐν τοῖς οὐρανοῖς.

16. 1. Περὶ δὲ τοῦ ἀνεξικάκους εἶναι καὶ ὑπηρετικοὺς
πᾶσι καὶ ἀοργήτους ἃ ἔφη ταῦτά ἐστι· Τῷ τύπτοντί σου
τὴν σιαγόνα πάρεχε καὶ τὴν ἄλλην, καὶ τὸν αἴροντά σου 15
τὸν χιτῶνα ἢ τὸ ἱμάτιον, μὴ κωλύσῃς. 2. ὃς δ' ἂν
ὀργισθῇ, ἔνοχός ἐστιν εἰς τὸ πῦρ. παντὶ δὲ ἀγγαρεύοντί
σε μίλιον, ἀκολούθησον δύο. λαμψάτω δὲ ὑμῶν τὰ καλὰ
ἔργα ἔμπροσθεν τῶν ἀνθρώπων, ἵνα βλέποντες θαυμάζωσι
τὸν πατέρα ὑμῶν τὸν ἐν τοῖς οὐρανοῖς. 3. οὐ γὰρ 20

17 ἀγγαρεύοντί σε Otto ἀγγ. σοί A Post μίλιον nescio an ἕν (ob anteced lit
ν) exciderit Otto

96 has γίνεσθε χρηστοὶ καὶ οἰκτίρμονες
ὡς καὶ ὁ πατὴρ ὑμῶν ὁ οὐράνιος. καὶ
γὰρ τὸν παντοκράτορα θεὸν χρηστὸν
καὶ οἰκτίρμονα ὁρῶμεν, τὸν ἥλιον
αὐτοῦ ἀνατέλλοντα ἐπὶ ἀχαρίστους
καὶ δικαίους καὶ βρέχοντα ἐπὶ ὁσίους
καὶ πονηρούς. Hence Thirlb. would
read here ἁμαρτωλοὺς καὶ <ἀγαθοὺς
καὶ βρέχει ἐπὶ> δικαίους. And Otto
καὶ δικαίους <καὶ βρέχει ἐπὶ ὁσίους>
καὶ πονηρούς. The triplet of the
MS text is certainly very clumsy.

2. μὴ μεριμνᾶτε] Cf. Matt. vi
25 ff. 31—33; Luke xii 22 ff. 29—31,
34; Matt. vi 21.

10. μὴ ποιῆτε] Cf. Matt. vi 1.
This answers to the πρὸς δόξαν
ποιεῖν above.

16. *Quotations to show Christ's
teaching on patience, readiness to
help others, freedom from wrath,
truth-speaking, worship of God,
practice of religion.*

14. τῷ τύπτοντι] Cf. Luke vi
29, Matt. v 39. Σιαγόνα literally
'jaw.'

16. ὃς δ' ἂν ὀργισθῇ] Cf. Matt.
v 22; the phrase γέενναν τοῦ πυρός
is again simplified as in c. 15, 2.
Τὸ πῦρ = τὸ αἰώνιον πῦρ.

17. παντὶ δὲ ἀγγαρ.] Cf. Matt.
v 41. Ἀγγαρεύω literally 'to press
into service as a courier.'

18. λαμψάτω δέ] Cf. Matt. v 16.

20. οὐ γὰρ ἀνταίρειν] Cf. Matt.
v 39. Ἀνταίρειν = 'withstand.'

ἀνταίρειν δεῖ· οὐδὲ μιμητὰς εἶναι τῶν φαύλων βεβούληται ἡμᾶς, ἀλλὰ διὰ τῆς ὑπομονῆς καὶ πραότητος ἐξ αἰσχύνης καὶ ἐπιθυμίας τῶν κακῶν ἄγειν πάντας προετρέψατο. 4. ὃ γὰρ καὶ ἐπὶ πολλῶν τῶν παρ᾽ ὑμῖν γεγενημένων 5 ἀποδεῖξαι ἔχομεν· ἐκ βιαίων καὶ τυράννων μετέβαλον, ἡττηθέντες ἢ γειτόνων καρτερίαν βίου παρακολουθήσαντες ἢ συνοδοιπόρων πλεονεκτουμένων ὑπομονὴν ξένην κατανοήσαντες ἢ συμπραγματευομένων πειραθέντες. 5. περὶ δὲ τοῦ μὴ ὀμνύναι ὅλως, τἀληθῆ δὲ λέγειν ἀεί, οὕτως παρε-10 κελεύσατο· Μὴ ὀμόσητε ὅλως· ἔστω δὲ ὑμῶν τὸ ναὶ ναί, καὶ τὸ οὒ οὔ· τὸ δὲ περισσὸν τούτων ἐκ τοῦ πονηροῦ. 6. ὡς δὲ καὶ τὸν θεὸν μόνον δεῖ προσκυνεῖν, οὕτως ἔπεισεν εἰπών· Μεγίστη ἐντολή ἐστι· Κύριον τὸν θεόν σου προσκυνήσεις καὶ αὐτῷ μόνῳ λατρεύσεις ἐξ ὅλης τῆς καρδίας 15 σου καὶ ἐξ ὅλης τῆς ἰσχύος σου, κύριον τὸν θεὸν τὸν ποιήσαντά σε. 7. καὶ προσελθόντος αὐτῷ τινος καὶ

4 ὑμῖν γεγενημένων Otto ἡμῖν γεγενημένων A

1. βεβούληται ... προετρέψατο] The subject is Christ, understood.
4. ὃ γὰρ καί] γάρ=γε ἄρα. Τῶν παρ᾽ ὑμῖν γεγενημένων=' those who were of your side,' i.e. heathens. 'Ἐπί='in the case of.'
6. ἡττηθέντες κτλ.] 'conquered, either by the constancy of life which they traced in (Christian) neighbours, or by the strange endurance which they noticed in defrauded fellow-travellers or experienced in those with whom they had dealings.' Πλεονεκτουμένων is a pure passive, and is found in classical Greek. Here again Justin supports Christianity by an appeal to its ethical influence as in c. 14, 2.
10. μὴ ὀμόσητε] Cf. Matt. v 34, 37; James v 12. In Clem. Hom., xix 2, the quotation occurs in the same form as here: ἔστω ὑμῶν τὸ ναὶ ναὶ καὶ τὸ οὒ οὔ. Probably the form was traditional; it is that found in James, loc. cit. (with ἤτω instead of ἔστω), and, as Westcott points out (N.T. Canon, ad loc.), in Clem. Strom. v 14, 100; Epiph. adu. Haer. i 20, 6.
13. μεγίστη ἐντολή] Cf. Mark xii 29, 30; Luke x 27; though Justin's phraseology differs considerably from that of the two Evangelists. The last clause κύριον τὸν θεὸν τὸν ποιήσαντά σε may perhaps be added to combat the Gnostic distinction between the Creator of Judaism and the God of Christianity. Justin Tryph. 93 cites the same passage more in accordance with the N.T. text; ἀγαπήσεις κύριον τὸν θεόν σου ἐξ ὅλης τῆς καρδίας σου καὶ ἐξ ὅλης τῆς ἰσχύος σου, καὶ τὸν πλησίον σου ὡς σεαυτόν.
16. καὶ προσελθόντος] Cf. Mark x 17, 18; Luke xviii 18, 19; Matt. xix 17. Ὁ ποιήσας τὰ πάντα is again an addition. Clem. Hom. xviii 3 has μή με λέγε ἀγαθόν· ὁ γὰρ ἀγαθὸς εἷς ἐστίν, ὁ πατὴρ ὁ ἐν τοῖς

εἰπόντος· Διδάσκαλε ἀγαθέ, ἀπεκρίνατο λέγων· Οὐδεὶς ἀγαθὸς εἰ μὴ μόνος ὁ θεός, ὁ ποιήσας τὰ πάντα.   8. οἳ δ' ἂν μὴ εὑρίσκωνται βιοῦντες, ὡς ἐδίδαξε, γνωριζέσθωσαν μὴ ὄντες Χριστιανοί, κἂν λέγωσιν διὰ γλώττης τὰ τοῦ Χριστοῦ διδάγματα· οὐ γὰρ τοὺς μόνον λέγοντας, ἀλλὰ τοὺς καὶ τὰ ἔργα πράττοντας σωθήσεσθαι ἔφη.   9. εἶπε γὰρ οὕτως· Οὐχὶ πᾶς ὁ λέγων μοι Κύριε κύριε εἰσελεύσεται εἰς τὴν βασιλείαν τῶν οὐρανῶν, ἀλλ' ὁ ποιῶν τὸ θέλημα τοῦ πατρός μου τοῦ ἐν τοῖς οὐρανοῖς.   10. ὃς γὰρ ἀκούει μου καὶ ποιεῖ ἃ λέγω ἀκούει τοῦ ἀποστείλαντός με.   11. πολλοὶ δὲ ἐροῦσί μοι· Κύριε κύριε, οὐ τῷ σῷ ὀνόματι ἐφάγομεν καὶ ἐπίομεν καὶ δυνάμεις ἐποιήσαμεν; καὶ τότε ἐρῶ αὐτοῖς· Ἀποχωρεῖτε ἀπ' ἐμοῦ, ἐργάται τῆς ἀνομίας.   12. τότε κλαυθμὸς ἔσται καὶ βρυγμὸς τῶν ὀδόντων, ὅταν οἱ μὲν δίκαιοι λάμψωσιν ὡς ὁ ἥλιος, οἱ δὲ ἄδικοι πέμψωνται εἰς τὸ αἰώνιον πῦρ.   13. πολλοὶ γὰρ ἥξουσιν ἐπὶ τῷ ὀνόματί μου, ἔξωθεν μὲν ἐνδεδυμένοι δέρματα προβάτων, ἔσωθεν δὲ ὄντες λύκοι ἅρπαγες· ἐκ τῶν ἔργων αὐτῶν ἐπιγνώσεσθε αὐτούς. πᾶν δὲ δένδρον, μὴ ποιοῦν καρπὸν καλόν, ἐκκόπτεται καὶ εἰς πῦρ βάλλεται.   14. κολάζεσθαι δὲ τοὺς οὐκ ἀκολούθως τοῖς διδάγμασιν αὐτοῦ βιοῦντας, λεγομένους δὲ μόνον Χριστιανούς, καὶ ὑφ' ὑμῶν ἀξιοῦμεν.

16 πέμψωνται Otto πέμπωνται A

οὐρανοῖς. Justin *Tryph*. 101 quotes it as τί με λέγεις ἀγαθόν; εἷς ἐστὶν ἀγαθός, ὁ πατήρ μου ὁ ἐν τοῖς οὐρανοῖς.

7. οὐχὶ πᾶς ὁ λέγ.] Cf. Matt. vii 21.

9. ὃς γὰρ ἀκούει] Cf. Matt. vii 24; Luke x 16; Matt. x 40; John xiv 24. Justin's phrase may be from an unwritten logion of Christ or may be a rough synopsis, composed by himself, of Christian precepts.

11. πολλοὶ δὲ ἐροῦσι] Cf. Matt. vii 22, 23; xiii 42, 43; Luke xiii 26-28. Justin *Tryph*. 76 has πολλοὶ ἐροῦσί μοι τῇ ἡμέρᾳ ἐκείνῃ· Κύριε κύριε, οὐ τῷ σῷ ὀνόματι ἐφάγομεν καὶ ἐπίομεν καὶ προεφητεύσαμεν καὶ δαιμόνια ἐξεβάλομεν; καὶ ἐρῶ αὐτοῖς, Ἀναχωρεῖτε ἀπ' ἐμοῦ.

16. πέμψωνται] a middle aorist, used in a passive sense, parallel to λάμψωσιν.

ib. πολλοὶ γὰρ ἥξ.] Cp. Matt. vii 15, 16, 19; xxiv 5. Justin *Tryph*. 35 has πολλοὶ ἐλεύσονται ἐπὶ τῷ ὀνόματί μου, ἔξωθεν ἐνδεδυμένοι δέρματα προβάτων, ἔσωθεν δέ εἰσι λύκοι ἅρπαγες.

23. ἀξιοῦμεν] Cf. c. 3, 1; 7, 4.

17. 1. Φόρους δὲ καὶ εἰσφορὰς τοῖς ὑφ' ὑμῶν τεταγμένοις πανταχοῦ πρὸ πάντων πειρώμεθα φέρειν, ὡς ἐδιδάχθημεν παρ' αὐτοῦ. 2. κατ' ἐκεῖνο γὰρ τοῦ καιροῦ προσελθόντες τινὲς ἠρώτων αὐτόν, εἰ δεῖ Καίσαρι φόρους τελεῖν. καὶ ἀπεκρίνατο· Εἴπατέ μοι, τίνος εἰκόνα τὸ νόμισμα ἔχει; οἱ δὲ ἔφασαν· Καίσαρος. καὶ πάλιν ἀνταπεκρίνατο αὐτοῖς· Ἀπόδοτε οὖν τὰ Καίσαρος τῷ Καίσαρι καὶ τὰ τοῦ θεοῦ τῷ θεῷ. 3. ὅθεν θεὸν μὲν μόνον προσκυνοῦμεν, ὑμῖν δὲ πρὸς τὰ ἄλλα χαίροντες ὑπηρετοῦμεν, βασιλεῖς καὶ ἄρχοντας ἀνθρώπων ὁμολογοῦντες καὶ εὐχόμενοι μετὰ τῆς βασιλικῆς δυνάμεως καὶ σώφρονα τὸν λογισμὸν ἔχοντας ὑμᾶς εὑρεθῆναι. 4. εἰ δὲ καὶ ἡμῶν εὐχομένων καὶ πάντα εἰς φανερὸν τιθέντων ἀφροντιστήσετε, οὐδὲν ἡμεῖς βλαβησόμεθα, πιστεύοντες μᾶλλον δὲ καὶ πεπεισμένοι, κατ' ἀξίαν τῶν πράξεων ἕκαστον τίσειν διὰ πυρὸς αἰωνίου δίκας, καὶ πρὸς ἀναλογίαν ὧν ἔλαβε δυνάμεων παρὰ θεοῦ τὸν λόγον ἀπαιτη-

17. *Christ taught us to be obedient citizens; we pay all taxes, and, though we worship God alone, we pray for our rulers. However, if you will not listen to us, yours is the responsibility, in proportion to the greatness of the powers entrusted to you.*

The early Christians certainly acknowledged the claims of civil law and government to their obedience; but they were reluctant to take an active share in politics. They were peaceable subjects, and some served in the legions, though others refused to do so; but they were indifferent to, and partially averse from, the civil government of an 'idolatrous' state. They obeyed the laws, except in regard to religion, but they did not seek for office in a state, whose political ceremonial was closely connected with a religion which they repudiated. Cf. Tert. *Apol.* 38 'Nec ulla res aliena magis quam publica.'
This followed necessarily from the intimate union of religion and politics which the Augustan system had established.

1. φόρους...εἰσφοράς] The former word refers to the regular taxation usually assessed on the census; the latter to special taxes.

3. παρ' αὐτοῦ] i.e. Christ. Justin makes no reference to Rom. xiii 1—7, because he is only quoting Christ's words.

ib. κατ' ἐκεῖνο] Cf. Matt. xxii 17—21; Luke xx 21—25.

8. θεὸν μόνον προσκυνοῦμεν] The great test of the Christians on trial was the order to sacrifice to the Emperor.

11. εὐχόμενοι μετὰ κτλ.] Cf. 1.Tim. ii 1, 2, and the prayer in Clem. Rom. *ad Corinth.* c. 61, quoted by Schaff, *Hist. of ante-Nic. Christianity*, § 66, note *ad fin.*

16. πρὸς ἀναλογίαν] Cf. Matt. xxv 15.

θήσεσθαι, ὡς ὁ Χριστὸς ἐμήνυσεν εἰπών· ᾯ πλέον ἔδωκεν ὁ θεός, πλέον καὶ ἀπαιτηθήσεται παρ' αὐτοῦ.

18. 1. Ἀποβλέψατε γὰρ πρὸς τὸ τέλος ἑκάστου τῶν γενομένων βασιλέων, ὅτι τὸν κοινὸν πᾶσι θάνατον ἀπέθανον· ὅπερ εἰ εἰς ἀναισθησίαν ἐχώρει, ἕρμαιον ἂν ἦν τοῖς ἀδίκοις πᾶσιν. 2. ἀλλ' ἐπεὶ καὶ αἴσθησις πᾶσι γενομένοις μένει καὶ κόλασις αἰωνία ἀπόκειται, μὴ ἀμελήσητε πεισθῆναί τε καὶ πιστεῦσαι ὅτι ἀληθῆ ταῦτά ἐστι. 3. νεκυομαντεῖαι μὲν γὰρ καὶ αἱ ἀδιαφθόρων παίδων ἐποπτεύσεις καὶ ψυχῶν ἀνθρωπίνων κλήσεις καὶ οἱ λεγόμενοι παρὰ τοῖς μάγοις ὀνειροπομποὶ καὶ πάρεδροι καὶ τὰ

9 ἀδιαφθόρων marg A διαφθόρων A

1. ᾧ πλέον] Cf. Luke xii 48. Otto refers to Clem. *Strom.* ii, p. 507, ᾧ πλεῖον ἐδόθη, οὗτος καὶ πλεῖον ἀπαιτηθήσεται.

18. *Life is eternal; extinction would indeed be a boon to the wicked; but sense remains and punishment awaits. The customs of Gentile religions and the teaching of your philosophers and poets would attest this for you. Listen then to our teaching, as you do to theirs. We believe in a God, no less than others believe; we even hold that He will be able to effect a resurrection of bodies.*

5. ὅπερ εἰ κτλ.] A reminiscence of Plato *Phaedo* 107 C εἰ μὲν γὰρ ἦν ὁ θάνατος τοῦ παντὸς ἀπαλλαγή, ἕρμαιον ἂν ἦν τοῖς κακοῖς ἀποθανοῦσι. Id. *Apol.* 40 εἴτε μηδεμία αἴσθησίς ἐστιν, ἀλλ' οἷον ὕπνος, θαυμάσιον κέρδος ἂν εἴη ὁ θάνατος. Justin *Tryph.* 5 οὐδὲ ἀποθνήσκειν φημὶ πάσας τὰς ψυχὰς ἐγώ· ἕρμαιον γὰρ ἦν ὡς ἀληθῶς τοῖς κακοῖς. Ἕρμαιον properly '*a gift of Hermes*,' i.e. '*a godsend*.'

6. πᾶσι γενομένοις] '*all men that have been*.'

9. νεκυομαντεῖαι κτλ.] The 2nd century after Christ saw a general return to religion; superstition prevailed and miracles were fashionable, as the story of Apollonius of Tyana shows; astrology was encouraged, as can be seen from Tacitus' reference to the *mathematici* in *Hist.* i 22, 'genus hominum quod in ciuitate nostra et uetabitur semper et retinebitur.' Νεκυομαντεῖαι are '*oracles of the dead*,' like that near lake Aornos in Thesprotia. Cf. Herod. v 92, § 7.

ib. αἱ ἀδιαφθόρων π. ἐ.] According to Socrates *H. E.* iii 13, this refers to the sacrifice of innocent children and the inspection of their entrails. Presumably this was a way of taking special omens. Cf. Dion. Al. apud Euseb. *H. E.* vii 10 (of Valerian) ὑποτιθέμενος παῖδας ἀθλίους ἀποσφάττειν καὶ τέκνα δυστήνων πατέρων καταθύειν καὶ σπλάγχνα νεογενῆ διαιρεῖν, and Eus. viii 14 (of Maxentius) μαγικαῖς ἐπινοίαις ποτὲ μὲν γυναῖκας ἐγκύμονας ἀνασχίζοντος, ποτὲ δὲ νεογνῶν σπλάγχνα βρεφῶν διερευνωμένου. Cic. *in Vat.* 6, 14 'cum puerorum extis deos manis mactare soleas.'

10. ψυχῶν ἀνθρ. κλ.] Necromancy. '*Summonings of human souls*.'

11. ὀνειροπομποί] A general

γινόμενα ὑπὸ τῶν ταῦτα εἰδότων πεισάτωσαν ὑμᾶς, ὅτι
καὶ μετὰ θάνατον ἐν αἰσθήσει εἰσὶν αἱ ψυχαί, 4. καὶ
οἱ ψυχαῖς ἀποθανόντων λαμβανόμενοι καὶ ῥιπτούμενοι
ἄνθρωποι, οὓς δαιμονιολήπτους καὶ μαινομένους καλοῦσι
5 πάντες, καὶ τὰ παρ' ὑμῖν λεγόμενα μαντεῖα Ἀμφιλόχου
καὶ Δωδώνης καὶ Πυθοῦς, καὶ ὅσα ἄλλα τοιαῦτά ἐστι,
5. καὶ τὰ τῶν συγγραφέων διδάγματα, Ἐμπεδοκλέους
καὶ Πυθαγόρου, Πλάτωνός τε καὶ Σωκράτους, καὶ ὁ παρ'
Ὁμήρῳ βόθρος καὶ ἡ κάθοδος Ὀδυσσέως εἰς τὴν τούτων
10 ἐπίσκεψιν, καὶ τῶν τὰ αὐτὰ τούτοις εἰπόντων· 6. οἷς
κἂν ὁμοίως ἡμᾶς ἀποδέξασθε, οὐχ ἧττον ἐκείνων θεῷ
πιστεύοντας ἀλλὰ μᾶλλον, οἳ καὶ τὰ νεκρούμενα καὶ εἰς

term for spirits which send dreams. Πάρεδροι, familiar spirits in particular. The same collocation (doubtless with reference to this passage) occurs in Iren. i 23, 4. See also Eus. *Hist. Eccl.* iv 7.

1. πεισάτωσαν] Justin does not commit himself to any positive assertion about the genuineness of these oracular deliverances. He merely asks that his readers should believe that there is a survival after death on the authority of their own religious customs, and so be ready to listen to Christian teaching on the subject.

4. δαιμονιολήπτους] Cf. ii 5 (6), 6. Joseph. *Bell. Iud.* vii 6, 3 mentions a herb, supposed to be efficacious for driving away demons 'which are no other than the spirits of the wicked, that enter into men that are alive and kill them, unless they can obtain some help against them' (Whiston's translation).

5. Ἀμφιλόχου] son of Amphiaraus. His oracle at Mallos in Cilicia was famous in Pausanias' time, circ. A.D. 180.

6. Δωδώνης] oracle of Zeus, where omens were given from the groves of oak and beech-trees.

ib. Πυθοῦς] oracle of Apollo at Delphi, where the prophetess sat on a tripod over a chasm whence fumes arose.

7. Ἐμπεδοκλέους] circ. 450 B.C. He taught that all living souls had once been divine spirits, who had been banished to earth for some crime, but could be restored by abstinence and expiatory rites.

8. Πυθαγόρου] 6th century B.C. He taught that souls are embodied because of sin, and after death will go into Kosmos or Tartarus according to their deserts, or have to pass through life again as men or animals.

ib. Πλάτωνός τ. κ. Σωκρ.] Socrates regards a future life as probable. Plato seems on the whole to believe in it, and in an eventual incorporeal immortality. Probably the reference here is to the myth which closes the *de Republica*.

ib. ὁ παρ' Ὁμήρῳ βόθρ.] Homer *Od.* xi 25 etc.

9. εἰς τὴν τούτων ἐπίσκ.] 'to view the things in Hades.'

10. τῶν εἰπόντων] refers back to διδάγματα. Καὶ ὁ παρ' Ὁμ. β. κ. ἡ κ. Ὀδ. εἰς τ. τ. ἐπίσκ. is, somewhat awkwardly, inserted as a parenthesis.

11. κἂν ὁμοίως] Cf. c. 12, 3, note *ad loc.*, and 2 Cor. xi 16 κἂν ὡς ἄφρονα δέξασθέ με. So here it is '*receive us, even if you receive us only on an equality with them.*'

γῆν βαλλόμενα,πάλιν ἀπολήψεσθαι ἑαυτῶν σώματα προσδοκῶμεν, ἀδύνατον μηδὲν εἶναι θεῷ λέγοντες.

19. 1. Καὶ κατανοοῦντι τί ἀπιστότερον ἂν μᾶλλον δόξαι, ἢ εἰ ἐν σώματι μὴ ὑπήρχομεν καί τις ἔλεγεν, ἐκ μικρᾶς τινος ῥανίδος τῆς τοῦ ἀνθρωπείου σπέρματος δυνα- τὸν ὀστέα τε καὶ νεῦρα καὶ σάρκας εἰκονοποιηθέντα, οἷα ὁρῶμεν, γενέσθαι; 2. ἔστω γὰρ νῦν ἐφ᾽ ὑποθέσεως λεγόμενον· εἴ τις ὑμῖν μὴ οὖσι τοιούτοις μηδὲ τοιούτων ἔλεγε, τὸ σπέρμα τὸ ἀνθρώπειον δεικνὺς καὶ εἰκόνα γραπτήν, ἐκ τοῦ τοιοῦδε οἷόν τε γενέσθαι,διαβεβαιούμενος, πρὶν ἰδεῖν γενόμενον ἐπιστεύσατε; οὐκ ἄν τις τολμήσειεν ἀντειπεῖν. 3. τὸν αὐτὸν οὖν τρόπον,διὰ τὸ μήπω ἑωρακέναι ὑμᾶς ἀναστάντα νεκρὸν,ἀπιστία ἔχει. 4. ἀλλ᾽ ὃν τρό-

3 κατανοοῦντι τί Otto om τί A ‖ 10 τοιοῦδε οἷόν τε A fortasse ἐκ (τοῦ) τοιοῦδε τοιόνδε οἷόν τε Otto

1. σώματα] A clear profession of belief in a resurrection of the body. See *Introd.*, p. xxxii. Cf. Justin *Apol.* i 52, 3; *Tryph.* 80 καὶ σαρκὸς ἀνάστασιν γενήσεσθαι ἐπιστάμεθα: *Vet. Eccl. Rom. Symb.* σαρκὸς ἀνάστασιν.

19. *Without evidence, we should find the process of human generation incredible. Similarly, resurrection is difficult for you to believe in, because you have never seen a dead man come to life again. But the processes may be considered analogous. It is dishonouring to God to say that He cannot raise the dead; and Christ has taught us that God can do what man cannot.*

5. ῥανίδος] 'drop.' A similar argument is found in Tat. *Or.* 6, Athenag. *de Resurr.* 17.

7. ἐφ᾽ ὑποθέσεως] 'by way of supposition.'

8. μὴ οὖσι τοιούτοις μ. τ.] 'not being such nor sprung from such (as you are).' Τοιούτων is genitive of origin. Perion. inserts ἐκ.

11. οὐκ ἄν τις τολμ. ἀντ.] 'Would you believe? No one would dare to contradict (and say that you would disbelieve).' Such a confusion of elliptical phraseology seems to be due to the negative assertion involved in the question : 'You would not believe, would you? Nor will anyone dare to contradict me and say you would.' Similar confusions are found in Plato, e.g. *Rep.* 336 E μὴ γὰρ δὴ οἵου ἡμᾶς οὐ σπουδάζειν· οἵου γέ σὺ, ὦ φίλε (Stallbaum emends to μὴ οἵου σύ), where the affirmative σπουδάζειν has to be understood with οἵου γε. *Phaedo* 68 B οὐκ ἀσμένως εἶσιν αὐτόσε; οἴεσθαί γε χρή. A fairly parallel case is seen in Justin *Tryph.* 33 ἱερεὺς δὲ ὅτι οὔτε γέγονεν Ἐξεκίας οὐδὲ ὑμεῖς ἀντειπεῖν τολμήσετε, 'That Hezekiah was not a priest, you will not be able to contradict (and say that he was).' Otto also quotes *Tryph.* 95 οὐδεὶς ἀκριβῶς πάντα ἐποίησεν, οὐδὲ ὑμεῖς τολμήσετε ἀντειπεῖν. But that is a perfectly normal use of two paratactic sentences.

πον τὴν ἀρχὴν οὐκ ἂν ἐπιστεύσατε ἐκ τῆς μικρᾶς ῥανίδος δυνατὸν τοιούτους γενέσθαι, καὶ ὁρᾶτε γινομένους, τὸν αὐτὸν τρόπον λογίσασθε, ὅτι διαλυθέντα καὶ δίκην σπερμάτων εἰς γῆν διαχυθέντα τὰ ἀνθρώπεια σώματα κατὰ 5 καιρὸν προστάξει θεοῦ ἀναστῆναι καὶ ἀφθαρσίαν ἐνδύσασθαι οὐκ ἀδύνατον. 5. ποίαν γὰρ ἀξίαν θεοῦ δύναμιν λέγουσιν οἱ φάσκοντες εἰς ἐκεῖνο χωρεῖν ἕκαστον ἐξ οὗπερ ἐγένετο, καὶ παρὰ ταῦτα μηδὲν ἄλλο δύνασθαι μηδὲ τὸν θεόν, οὐκ ἔχομεν λέγειν· ἀλλ' ἐκεῖνο συνορῶμεν, ὅτι οὐκ
10 ἂν ἐπίστευσαν δυνατὸν εἶναι τοιούτους ποτὲ γενέσθαι, ὁποίους καὶ ἑαυτοὺς καὶ τὸν σύμπαντα κόσμον καὶ ἐξ ὁποίων γεγενημένα ὁρῶσι. 6. κρεῖττον δὲ πιστεύειν καὶ τὰ τῇ ἑαυτῶν φύσει καὶ ἀνθρώποις ἀδύνατα, ἢ ὁμοίως τοῖς ἄλλοις ἀπιστεῖν, παρειλήφαμεν, ἐπειδὴ καὶ τὸν ἡμέ-
15 τερον διδάσκαλον Ἰησοῦν Χριστὸν ἔγνωμεν εἰπόντα· Τὰ ἀδύνατα παρὰ ἀνθρώποις δυνατὰ παρὰ θεῷ. 7. καί·

4 διαχυθέντα Davis Otto διαλυθέντα A ǁ 14 παρειλήφαμεν Otto προειλήφαμεν A

5. ἀφθαρσίαν ἐνδύσ.] Cf. 1 Cor. xv 53. The δίκην σπερμάτων makes it the more probable that this text was in Justin's mind.
7. οἱ φάσκοντες] This is the Stoic theory of orthodox Pantheism, according to which the whole universe is permeated by the *anima mundi*, into which the nature of human beings, after purgation, is eventually resolved. Cf. Virg. *Georg.* iv 219 ff.; *Aen.* vi 724 ff.
8. παρὰ ταῦτα] '*beyond this*.'
13. τὰ τῇ ἑαυτῶν φύσει κτλ.] Otto translates '*quae et sua natura et hominibus sunt impossibilia.*' This seems an impossible rendering; even in an uncritical age, the belief in things, which are *by their nature* impossible, is scarcely widespread; nor did Christ urge such credulity. Maran translates with more regard to natural probability, '*Quae et nostrae naturae et aliorum hominum uires superant.*' So too Veil, '*Dinge die unserer eigenen Natur und überhaupt den Menschen unmöglich sind.*'
15. τὰ ἀδύνατα] Cf. Luke xviii 27; Matt. xix 26; Mark x 27. Otto quotes here Celsus' objection, ap. Orig. v 14, οὐδὲν ἔχοντες ἀποκρίνασθαι καταφεύγουσιν εἰς ἀτοπωτάτην ἀναχώρησιν ὅτι πᾶν δυνατὸν τῷ θεῷ· ἀλλ' οὔτι γε τὰ αἰσχρὰ ὁ θεὸς δύναται οὐδὲ τὰ παρὰ φύσιν βούλεται. Both of Celsus' limitations are perfectly valid. God cannot be false to His own moral character; nor does He act in defiance of His own natural laws. But the force of this second limitation depends on (1) our knowledge of natural law; (2) the extent to which we must presume our knowledge to be defective, as, for instance, in cases postulated to be unique.

Μὴ φοβεῖσθε τοὺς ἀναιροῦντας ὑμᾶς καὶ μετὰ ταῦτα μὴ δυναμένους τι ποιῆσαι, εἶπε, φοβήθητε δὲ τὸν μετὰ τὸ ἀποθανεῖν δυνάμενον καὶ ψυχὴν καὶ σῶμα εἰς γέενναν ἐμβαλεῖν. 8. ἡ δὲ γέεννά ἐστι τόπος, ἔνθα κολάζεσθαι μέλλουσιν οἱ ἀδίκως βιώσαντες καὶ μὴ πιστεύοντες 5 ταῦτα γενήσεσθαι ὅσα ὁ θεὸς διὰ τοῦ Χριστοῦ ἐδίδαξε.

20. 1. Καὶ Σίβυλλα δὲ καὶ Ὑστάσπης γενήσεσθαι τῶν φθαρτῶν ἀνάλωσιν διὰ πυρὸς ἔφασαν. 2. οἱ λεγόμενοι δὲ Στωϊκοὶ φιλόσοφοι καὶ αὐτὸν τὸν θεὸν εἰς πῦρ

7 Ὑστάσπης Otto Ὑστάσπις A

1. μὴ φοβεῖσθε] Cf. Luke xii 4, 5; Matt. x 28.
4. γέεννα] See Hastings *Dict. of the Bib.* s.v. 'Gehenna.'
20. *Your own oracles and philosophers foretell a fiery end to the world. And many of our views resemble those of poets and others whom you honour, or only differ from them in being nobler and more divine, and demonstratively proved.*
7. Σίβυλλα] The Sibylline oracles are a medley of Jewish and Christian fictions about a golden age, the future of Rome, the end of the world. They are the work of various authors in various centuries, and were arranged in a connected series in the Middle Ages. (Cf. Hastings *Dict. Bibl.* s.v.; Milman *Hist. of Christ.* ii 7, Geffcken's edition; *Texte und Untersuchungen* Bd xxiii.) They are quoted by many of the early Christian fathers. The passages here alluded to may be *Orac. Sibyll.* ii 196 ff.
καὶ τότε δὴ ποταμός τε μέγας πυρὸς αἰθομένοιο
ῥεύσει ἀπ' οὐρανόθεν καὶ πάντα τόπον δαπανήσει
(unless Bk ii is rightly supposed to date from the 3rd cent.); or iv 172 ff. πῦρ ἔσται κατὰ γαῖαν κτλ. (Bk iv is said to be of the reign of Titus.)
ib. Ὑστάσπης] A Persian Magus, supposed to have lived in Zoroaster's time and to have issued oracles. He is quoted by Clem. Alex. and Lactant. Ἀνάλωσιν = 'consumption.'
9. Στωϊκοί] Cf. ii 6 (7), 3. Many Stoics regarded the κόσμος as immortal, and Justin's statement here does not give what is generally supposed to have been the orthodox Stoic idea, though the Stoics did assert the ultimate resolution of the world into fire. Yet Justin can hardly have misconceived entirely the Stoic position, nor have falsified it in a treatise addressed to M. Aurelius. It is possible that, as Stoicism was based on Pantheism and identified God with the universe, it might go further and identify this God with fire, borrowing the Heraclitean notion of fire as the primal element of the universe. Cf. August. *de Ciu. D.* viii 5 'Stoici in igne causam principiumque rerum esse dixerunt'; and he adds that they call this principle ' uiuens et sapiens et mundi fabricator'; Plut. *de Placit. Philos.* 1, 6 (p. 879 c) ὁρίζονται τὴν τοῦ θείου οὐσίαν οἱ Στωϊκοὶ οὕτω· πνεῦμα νοερὸν καὶ πυρῶδες, οὐκ ἔχον μὲν μορφήν, μεταβάλλον δὲ εἰς ἃ βούλεται: *ib.* 7, 17 οἱ Στωϊκοὶ κοινότερον θεὸν ἀποφαίνονται πῦρ τεχνικὸν ὁδῷ βαδίζον ἐπὶ γενέσει κόσμου.

ἀναλύεσθαι δογματίζουσι καὶ αὖ πάλιν κατὰ μεταβολὴν τὸν κόσμον γενέσθαι λέγουσιν· ἡμεῖς δὲ κρεῖττόν τι τῶν μεταβαλλομένων νοοῦμεν τὸν πάντων ποιητὴν θεόν. 3. εἰ οὖν καὶ ὁμοίως τινὰ τοῖς παρ' ὑμῖν τιμωμένοις 5 ποιηταῖς καὶ φιλοσόφοις λέγομεν, ἔνια δὲ καὶ μειζόνως καὶ θείως, καὶ μόνοι μετ' ἀποδείξεως, τί παρὰ πάντας ἀδίκως μισούμεθα; 4. τῷ γὰρ λέγειν ἡμᾶς, ὑπὸ θεοῦ πάντα κεκοσμῆσθαι καὶ γεγενῆσθαι Πλάτωνος δόξομεν λέγειν δόγμα· τῷ δὲ ἐκπύρωσιν γενέσθαι Στωϊκῶν· τῷ δὲ κολά-
10 ζεσθαι ἐν αἰσθήσει καὶ μετὰ θάνατον οὔσας τὰς τῶν ἀδίκων ψυχάς, τὰς δὲ τῶν σπουδαίων ἀπηλλαγμένας τῶν τιμωριῶν εὖ διάγειν, ποιηταῖς καὶ φιλοσόφοις τὰ αὐτὰ λέγειν δόξομεν· 5. τῷ δὲ καὶ μὴ δεῖν χειρῶν ἀνθρωπίνων ἔργοις προσκυνεῖν, Μενάνδρῳ τῷ κωμικῷ καὶ τοῖς
15 ταῦτα φήσασι ταὐτὰ φράζομεν· μείζονα γὰρ τὸν δημιουργὸν τοῦ σκευαζομένου ἀπεφήναντο.

21. 1. Τῷ δὲ καὶ τὸν λόγον, ὅ ἐστι πρῶτον γέννημα τοῦ θεοῦ, ἄνευ ἐπιμιξίας φάσκειν ἡμᾶς γεγεννῆσθαι, Ἰησοῦν

13 χειρῶν ἀνθρωπίνων ἔργοις Sylburg χειρῶν ἀνθρώποις A χειρῶν ἔργοις ἀνθρώπους Stephan χειρονὶ ἀνθρώπους Maran

6. θείως] i.e. 'suitably to God.'
ib. μόνοι μετ' ἀποδείξεως] Christianity alone can prove its dogmas about God, by the revelation of Christ.
ib. παρὰ πάντας] 'beyond all others.'
8. Πλάτωνος] Certainly this is the general idea of Plato's philosophy.
10. ἐν αἰσθήσει] 'to be sensibly punished.'
14. προσκυνεῖν] with dative. This is found in late Greek. Cf. Matt. ii 2, 11; John iv 23. Justin uses it with the accusative also; cf. c. 17, 3, and many other passages.
ib. Μενάνδρῳ] He is quoted in pseudo-Justin *de Monarch.* 5, and these or similar passages may be in mind here: (quoted as from the *Hiereia*)
εἰ γὰρ ἕλκει τινὰ θεὸν
τοῖς κυμβάλοις ἄνθρωπος εἰς ὃ βούλεται
ὁ τοῦτο ποιῶν ἐστὶ μείζων τοῦ θεοῦ:
and (quoted as from the *Diphilus*)
διότι τὸν ὄντα κύριον πάντων ἀεὶ
καὶ πατέρα, τοῦτον διὰ τέλους τιμᾶν μόνον
ἀγαθῶν τοσούτων εὑρετὴν καὶ κτίστορα.

21. *Our story of Christ is in many respects analogous to heathen stories about Zeus' various sons, and to your own belief in deified Emperors. Of course the immoralities of Zeus and others are the work of evil demons. Only the good are immortal, as we teach; the wicked are punished in eternal fire.*

Justin's argument in this chapter is perhaps partly *ad captandum*; partly however it arises from his view of the Divine preparation for Christ in heathendom, the work of the Spermatic *Logos*.

APOLOGIA

Χριστὸν τὸν διδάσκαλον ἡμῶν, καὶ τοῦτον σταυρωθέντα καὶ ἀποθανόντα καὶ ἀναστάντα ἀνεληλυθέναι εἰς τὸν οὐρανόν, οὐ παρὰ τοὺς παρ' ὑμῖν λεγομένους υἱοὺς τῷ Διΐ καινόν τι φέρομεν. 2. πόσους γὰρ υἱοὺς φάσκουσι τοῦ Διὸς οἱ παρ' ὑμῖν τιμώμενοι συγγραφεῖς, ἐπίστασθε· 5 Ἑρμῆν μέν, λόγον τὸν ἑρμηνευτικὸν καὶ πάντων διδάσκαλον, Ἀσκληπιὸν δέ, καὶ θεραπευτὴν γενόμενον, κεραυνωθέντα ἀνεληλυθέναι εἰς οὐρανόν, Διόνυσον δὲ διασπαραχθέντα, Ἡρακλέα δὲ φυγῇ πόνων ἑαυτὸν πυρὶ δόντα, τοὺς ἐκ Λήδας δὲ Διοσκούρους, καὶ τὸν ἐκ Δανάης Περσέα, καὶ 10 τὸν ἐξ ἀνθρώπων δὲ ἐφ' ἵππου Πηγάσου Βελλεροφόντην. 3. τί γὰρ λέγομεν τὴν Ἀριάδνην καὶ τοὺς ὁμοίως αὐτῇ κατηστερίσθαι λεγομένους; καὶ τί γάρ, τοὺς ἀποθνῄσκοντας παρ' ὑμῖν αὐτοκράτορας, οὓς ἀεὶ ἀπαθανατίζεσθαι ἀξι-

12 ὁμοίως Otto ὁμοίους A ‖ 14 αὐτοκράτορας οὓς Thirlb om οὓς A

3. οὐ παρὰ τοὺς κτλ.] 'We bring forward nothing new, as compared with those whom you call sons of Zeus.' The dative τῷ Διΐ is influenced by λεγομένους, 'ascribed to Zeus as sons.'

6. Ἑρμῆν] The symbolical explanation of Hermes as the interpretative word, and teacher of all, was the work of the later Rationalistic school. Cf. i 22, 2; Clem. Al. Strom. vi 15.

7. Ἀσκληπιόν] Asclepius was traditionally held to have been struck with thunder by Zeus, because he had been bribed to recall a dead man to life. Cf. Pind. Pyth. iii 55; Plat. Rep. 408 B; Eur. Alc. 3; Virg. Aen. vii 770. His most famous shrine was at Epidaurus.

8. Διόνυσον] This refers to the myth of Dionysus Zagreus, which originated in Crete (Diod. Sic. v 75, 4) and was connected with Orphism; we hear of it mainly in late authors. The myth was that Dionysus was lured from the charge of the Kouretes by the Titans, who tore him in pieces. Zeus punished

them and restored him to life. Cf. Harrison Proleg. to Gk Relig. c. 10.

9. Ἡρακλέα] Herakles burnt himself to put an end to the pains caused by Nessus' shirt (Soph. Trachin.). Πόνων here probably = dolores (Otto). Most however take it as = labours. The dative φυγῇ is a little strange.

10. Διοσκούρους] Castor and Pollux.

ib. Περσέα] Cf. i 54, 8. Justin is probably thinking of the story that Perseus and Andromeda were placed among the stars after death.

11. Βελλεροφόντην] ἐφ' ἵππου Πηγάσου goes with ἀνεληλυθέναι εἰς οὐρανόν, which must be supplied throughout. According to Hor. Od. iv 11, 26, Pind. Isthm. vi 44, his ride to heaven on Pegasus failed. Either Justin knew some other myth on the subject, or his memory is here at fault.

13. κατηστερίσθαι] 'to have been placed among the stars.'

ib. καὶ τί γάρ] λέγομεν must be understood.

14. ἀπαθανατίζεσθαι ἀξ.] Either

3—2

οὖντες καὶ ὀμνύντα τινὰ προάγετε ἑωρακέναι ἐκ τῆς πυρᾶς ἀνερχόμενον εἰς τὸν οὐρανὸν τὸν κατακαέντα Καίσαρα; 4. καὶ ὁποῖαι ἑκάστου τῶν λεγομένων υἱῶν τοῦ Διὸς ἱστοροῦνται αἱ πράξεις, πρὸς εἰδότας λέγειν οὐκ ἀνάγκη, 5 πλὴν ὅτι εἰς διαφορὰν καὶ προτροπὴν τῶν ἐκπαιδευομένων ταῦτα γέγραπται· μιμητὰς γὰρ θεῶν καλὸν εἶναι πάντες ἡγοῦνται. 5. ἀπείη δὲ σωφρονούσης ψυχῆς ἔννοια τοιαύτη περὶ θεῶν, ὡς καὶ αὐτὸν τὸν ἡγεμόνα καὶ γεννήτορα πάντων κατ' αὐτοὺς Δία πατροφόντην τε καὶ πατρὸς 10 τοιούτου γεγονέναι, ἔρωτί τε κακῶν καὶ αἰσχρῶν ἡδονῶν ἥττω γενόμενον ἐπὶ Γανυμήδην καὶ τὰς πολλὰς μοιχευθείσας γυναῖκας ἐλθεῖν, καὶ τοὺς αὐτοῦ παῖδας τὰ ὅμοια πράξαντας παραδέξασθαι. 6. ἀλλ', ὡς προέφημεν, οἱ φαῦλοι δαίμονες ταῦτα ἔπραξαν· ἀπαθανατίζεσθαι δὲ 15 ἡμεῖς μόνους δεδιδάγμεθα τοὺς ὁσίως καὶ ἐναρέτως ἐγγὺς θεῷ βιοῦντας, κολάζεσθαι δὲ τοὺς ἀδίκως καὶ μὴ μεταβάλλοντας ἐν αἰωνίῳ πυρὶ πιστεύομεν.

22. 1. Υἱὸς δὲ θεοῦ, ὁ Ἰησοῦς λεγόμενος, εἰ καὶ

'*claiming that they are immortal*' or '*thinking right to deify.*'

1. ὀμνύντα τινά] This is known to have happened in the cases of Romulus and Julius Caesar; and at the funeral of Augustus 'nec defuit uir praetorius qui se effigiem cremati euntem in caelum uidisse iuraret' (Suet. *Aug.* 100). The idea is burlesqued in the *Apocolocyntosis*.

5. διαφοράν] '*advantage, profit.*' Προτροπήν '*instruction.*' The context here is presumably ironical.

8. ὡς καὶ ... παραδέξασθαι] '*as to believe that he, who is according to them* (κατ' αὐτούς) *the head and father of all*,' etc.

9. πατροφόντην κτλ.] The usual story was that Zeus mutilated and deposed Kronos, as Kronos had treated Uranus. There was no story of successive murder; the word πατροφόντης only applies roughly. The same condemnation of Greek mythology as Justin here expresses is found in Plato *Rep.* ii, iii.

13. ὡς προέφημεν] c. 5.

14. ἀπαθανατίζεσθαι] is used of a *happy* immortality. There is no hint here of conditional immortality, for the wicked are said to suffer eternal punishment.

16. τοὺς ἀδίκως] sc. βιοῦντας.

22. *If Christ were mere man, He would be worthy of being called 'Son of God' because of His wisdom. But we say that He was the Word of God born in a special way, like your legend of Hermes;—He was crucified; and many of your sons of Zeus suffered;—He was born of a virgin; so was Perseus;—He healed the sick and raised the dead; so did Asclepius.*

Justin has no fear of the 'argument from comparative religion.' The heathen fables, according to

κοινῶς μόνον ἄνθρωπος, διὰ σοφίαν ἄξιος υἱὸς θεοῦ λέγεσθαι· πατέρα γὰρ ἀνδρῶν τε θεῶν τε πάντες συγγραφεῖς τὸν θεὸν καλοῦσιν. 2. εἰ δὲ καὶ ἰδίως, παρὰ τὴν κοινὴν γένεσιν, γεγεννῆσθαι αὐτὸν ἐκ θεοῦ λέγομεν λόγον θεοῦ, ὡς προέφημεν, κοινὸν τοῦτο ἔστω ὑμῖν τοῖς τὸν Ἑρμῆν λόγον τὸν παρὰ θεοῦ ἀγγελτικὸν λέγουσιν. 3. εἰ δὲ αἰτιάσαιτό τις ἐσταυρῶσθαι αὐτόν, καὶ τοῦτο κοινὸν τοῖς προκατηριθμημένοις παθοῦσιν υἱοῖς καθ' ὑμᾶς τοῦ Διὸς ὑπάρχει. 4. ἐκείνων τε γὰρ οὐχ ὅμοια τὰ πάθη τοῦ θανάτου ἀλλὰ διάφορα ἱστορεῖται· ὥστε μηδὲ τὸ ἴδιον τοῦ πάθους ἥττονα δοκεῖν εἶναι τοῦτον, ἀλλ', ὡς ὑπεσχόμεθα, προϊόντος τοῦ λόγου καὶ κρείττονα ἀποδείξομεν, μᾶλλον δὲ καὶ ἀποδέδεικται· ὁ γὰρ κρείττων ἐκ τῶν πράξεων φαίνεται. 5. εἰ δὲ καὶ διὰ παρθένου γεγεννῆσθαι φέρομεν, κοινὸν καὶ τοῦτο πρὸς τὸν Περσέα ἔστω ὑμῖν. 6. ᾧ

him, are the work of the demons' cunning (cf. c. 54, etc.). But they ought at any rate to predispose the heathen to find nothing ridiculous in the Christian creed.

1. κοινῶς] contrasted with ἰδίως later.

2. πατέρα γάρ] i.e. it is not incongruous to call a man 'the son of God.'

3. παρὰ τὴν κοινὴν γένεσιν] 'contrasted with, different from, the ordinary method of birth.' The reference is probably to the eternal generation of the Logos, as indicated by the comparison with Hermes. The Virgin-birth is later compared with the Perseus-myth.

5. ὡς προέφημεν] Cf. ἄνευ ἐπιμιξίας c. 21, 1.

ib. Ἑρμῆν] Cf. i 21, 2.

8. προκατηριθμημένοις] In c. 21.—Υἱοῖς καθ' ὑμᾶς τοῦ Διός is a single phrase 'those whom you call sons of Zeus.'

9. οὐχ ὅμοια] They did not all suffer the same death; therefore Christ is not inferior to them, because His death was of a special nature.

10. τὸ ἴδιον τ. π.] The accusative of that in respect of which he might be thought ἥττων.

11. ὡς ὑπεσχόμεθα] Cf. c. 13.

13. ἀποδέδεικται] This may refer, as Otto suggests, to the quotations from Christ's teaching in cc. 15—17; but perhaps better to the πράξεις of Christ, i.e. His miracles, and the moral effects of Christianity. The sentence ὁ γὰρ κρείττων κτλ. is caught up again by Iren. ii 30, 5.

14. διὰ παρθένου] Jerome objected to this use of διὰ as tainted with Valentinian heresy. The Valentinians denied the ἐκ παρθένου. According to them, as Tertullian puts it, Christ was born *transmeatorio potius quam generatorio more*, i.e. He was not very man of the substance of His mother. But Jerome's criticism is too subtle. The Church fathers use διά or *per* in no heretical sense, and Justin uses διά, ἐκ, or ἀπὸ παρθένου without distinction of significance.

15. Περσέα] Son of Jupiter and Danae.

δὲ λέγομεν χωλοὺς καὶ παραλυτικοὺς καὶ ἐκ γενετῆς πονηροὺς ὑγιεῖς πεποιηκέναι αὐτὸν καὶ νεκροὺς ἀνεγεῖραι, ὅμοια τοῖς ὑπὸ Ἀσκληπιοῦ γεγενῆσθαι λεγομένοις καὶ ταῦτα φάσκειν δόξομεν.

23. 1. Ἵνα δὲ ἤδη καὶ τοῦτο φανερὸν ὑμῖν γένηται, ὅτι ὁπόσα λέγομεν μαθόντες παρὰ τοῦ Χριστοῦ καὶ τῶν προελθόντων αὐτοῦ προφητῶν μόνα ἀληθῆ ἐστι καὶ πρεσβύτερα πάντων τῶν γεγενημένων συγγραφέων, καὶ οὐχὶ διὰ τὸ ταὐτὰ λέγειν αὐτοῖς παραδεχθῆναι ἀξιοῦμεν, ἀλλ' ὅτι τὸ ἀληθὲς λέγομεν· 2. καὶ Ἰησοῦς Χριστὸς μόνος ἰδίως υἱὸς τῷ θεῷ γεγέννηται, λόγος αὐτοῦ ὑπάρχων καὶ πρωτότοκος καὶ δύναμις, καὶ τῇ βουλῇ αὐτοῦ γενόμενος ἄνθρωπος ταῦτα ἡμᾶς ἐδίδαξεν ἐπ' ἀλλαγῇ καὶ ἐπαναγωγῇ τοῦ ἀνθρωπείου γένους· 3. καὶ πρὶν ἢ ἐν ἀνθρώποις αὐτὸν γενέσθαι ἄνθρωπον φθάσαντές τινες διὰ τοὺς

---

1 πονηροὺς A πηροὺς Steph ‖ 3 καὶ ταῦτα Otto καὶ ταὐτὰ A ‖ 14 καὶ πρὶν Fabric Otto om καὶ A πρὶν δὲ Maran ‖ 15 φθάσαντές τινες διὰ τοὺς...διὰ τῶν π....εἶπον A φθάσαντές τινες, λέγω δὲ τοὺς...διὰ τῶν π....εἶπον Maran φθάσαντές τινες διὰ τοὺς...τὰ τῶν π....εἶπον Otto φθάσαντας τοὺς...διὰ τῶν π. ...εἰπεῖν Veil

1. πονηρούς] if genuine, must mean '*infirm*'; but perhaps we should read πηρούς. Cf. *Tryph.* 69. For the confusion between the two words, see Robinson *Ep. to the Ephes.* p. 272. Παραλυτικός is a N.T. word, found in Matthew and Mark. Luke has the more technical παραλελυμένος.

23. *I shall...prove* (1) *that Christianity is alone true and its creed anterior to heathen myths;* (2) *that Jesus Christ was the Son of God in a unique sense;* (3) *that the heathen myths are due to demons.*

This order is not strictly adhered to in the following chapters; Justin's method is not carefully systematic; but his three arguments may be roughly arranged as follows: (1) cc. 24–29; (2) cc. 30–53; (3) cc. 54–60.

6. τῶν προελθ. αὐτοῦ προφ.] 'The prophets who preceded Him.' Αὐτοῦ is genitive after προ in composition. Liddell and Scott quote Xen. *Cyr.* ii 2, 7, as a case of a similar usage. Προέρχεσθαι is found with the accusative in N.T., e.g. Mark vi 33.

9. αὐτοῖς] refers to τῶν συγγραφέων.

10. καὶ Ἰησοῦς] ὅτι is understood. Ὑπάρχων = '*being beforehand*.'

12. πρωτότοκος] Cf. 33, 6; 53, 2; 63, 15; Col. i 15; and Lightfoot's note *ad loc.*

ib. δύναμις] Cf. 1 Cor. i 24.

ib. τῇ βουλῇ αὐτοῦ] Christ was incarnate by the will of God. See *Introd.*, p. xxvi.

13. ἐπ' ἀλλαγῇ κτλ.] '*for the conversion and restoration of the human race.*' See *Introd.*, p. xxvi.

15. φθάσαντές τ. κτλ.] This sen-

προειρημένους κακοὺς δαίμονας διὰ τῶν ποιητῶν ὡς γενόμενα εἶπον ἃ μυθοποιήσαντες ἔφησαν, ὃν τρόπον καὶ τὰ
καθ' ἡμῶν λεγόμενα δύσφημα καὶ ἀσεβῆ ἔργα ἐνήργησαν,
ὧν οὐδεὶς μάρτυς οὐδὲ ἀπόδειξίς ἐστι,—τοῦτον ἔλεγχον
ποιησόμεθα. 5

24. 1. Πρῶτον μὲν ὅτι τὰ ὅμοια τοῖς "Ελλησι λέγοντες, μόνοι μισούμεθα δι' ὄνομα τοῦ Χριστοῦ, καὶ μηδὲν
ἀδικοῦντες ὡς ἁμαρτωλοὶ ἀναιρούμεθα, ἄλλων ἀλλαχοῦ
καὶ δένδρα σεβομένων καὶ ποταμοὺς καὶ μῦς καὶ αἰλούρους
καὶ κροκοδείλους καὶ τῶν ἀλόγων ζῴων τὰ πολλά, καὶ οὐ 10
τῶν αὐτῶν ὑπὸ πάντων τιμωμένων ἀλλ' ἄλλων ἀλλοχόσε,
ὥστ' εἶναι ἀσεβεῖς ἀλλήλοις πάντας διὰ τὸ μὴ τὰ αὐτὰ
σέβειν. 2. ὅπερ μόνον ἐγκαλεῖν ἡμῖν ἔχετε, ὅτι μὴ
τοὺς αὐτοὺς ὑμῖν σέβομεν θεούς, μηδὲ τοῖς ἀποθανοῦσι χοὰς

tence is exceedingly confused. The subject of ἐνήργησαν must be the demons, in which case it seems natural to make them also the subject of εἶπον; but this is forbidden by the διὰ τ....δαίμονας. Who then are the τινες? Otto explains the reference as being to the *mythologi*, and compares ii 4 (5), 5 and i 54, 1; though in the first of these parallels no distinction is drawn between poets and mythologists, and the second has no reference to mythologists at all. Still it is possible that Justin regards the myth-makers as being prior to the poets (by whom he especially means Homer), and therefore one step nearer to the demons, the original influences, the poets being thus in a rough sense the prophets of the myth-makers (Otto's alteration of διὰ τῶν to τὰ τῶν is unnecessary). Τινες therefore would be the original makers of the myths, the direct mouthpieces of the demons; but in the second half of the sentence the demons come into more prominence, and they are the subjects of ἐνήργησαν. Maran's reading avoids the difficulty, but it seems to give an unnatural turn of expression. The simplest emendation, if any is required, would be to omit the second διά, making τῶν ποιητῶν depend upon τινες. Veil considers the whole sentence to have been originally in the accus. and infin., and to have been corrected into nomin. and indic., the two readings being subsequently contaminated by an unintelligent scribe.

1. προειρημένους] Cf. cc. 5; 21.

3. ἐνήργησαν] 'they brought about the slanderous impieties which are alleged against us,' i.e. caused the slanderous allegation of impiety. Justin may have had in mind the N.T. conception of ἐνεργεῖν as meaning spiritual influence within men, cf. 26, 1; Mark vi 14; 1 Cor. xii 6, 11, etc.

24. *Firstly; though various people worship various gods, yet we alone are persecuted for our particular form of worship.*

This is Justin's first proof that Christianity is alone true.

8. ἄλλων ἀλλαχοῦ] There seems to be an especial reference here to Egyptian cultus.

13. μὴ τοὺς αὐτούς] The use of μή instead of οὐ in indirect quotation

καὶ κνίσας καὶ ἐν ταφαῖς στεφάνους καὶ θυσίας φέρομεν. 3. ὅτι γὰρ οὖν τὰ αὐτὰ παρ' οἷς μὲν θεοί, παρ' οἷς δὲ θηρία, παρ' οἷς δὲ ἱερεῖα ⸢νενομισμένα ἐστίν⸣ ⸢ἀκριβῶς ἐπίστασθε.⸣

25. 1. Δεύτερον δ' ὅτι ἐκ παντὸς γένους ἀνθρώπων οἱ πάλαι σεβόμενοι Διόνυσον τὸν Σεμέλης καὶ Ἀπόλλωνα τὸν Λητοΐδην, οἳ δι' ἔρωτας ἀρσένων ὅσα ἔπραξαν αἶσχος καὶ λέγειν, καὶ οἱ Περσεφόνην καὶ Ἀφροδίτην, τὰς διὰ τὸν Ἄδωνιν οἰστρηθείσας, ὧν καὶ τὰ μυστήρια ἄγετε, ἢ Ἀσκληπιὸν ἤ τινα τῶν ἄλλων ὀνομαζομένων θεῶν, καίπερ θανάτου ἀπειλουμένου διὰ Ἰησοῦ Χριστοῦ τούτων μὲν κατεφρονήσαμεν, 2. θεῷ δὲ τῷ ἀγεννήτῳ καὶ ἀπαθεῖ ἑαυτοὺς ἀνεθήκαμεν, ὃν οὔτε ἐπ' Ἀντιόπην καὶ τὰς ἄλλας ὁμοίως οὐδὲ ἐπὶ Γανυμήδην δι' οἶστρον ἐληλυθέναι πειθό-

---

1 ἐν ταφαῖς Fabric Cleric Otto ἐν γραφαῖς A Krüger ǁ 2 οὖν Otto οὐ A Krüger ǁ 6 οἱ πάλαι Otto οἱ παλαιοὶ A

---

after verbs of saying and thinking is common in late Greek.

1. ἐν ταφαῖς] This emendation seems almost inevitable. Maran urges the retention of γραφαῖς, which, he maintains, might mean 'statues,' though the parallels which he quotes hardly prove his case. But, whether the word could be so translated here, or would have to be taken in its usual sense of 'pictures,' the preposition ἐν seems very objectionable.

2. ὅτι γὰρ οὖν] The MS reading could give a conceivable sense, if οὐ τὰ αὐτά were taken together as equivalent to 'different, various things.' But the emendation οὖν is a very slight alteration and greatly improves the sentence. An alternative would be to omit οὐ altogether.

3. ἱερεῖα] 'victims.'

25. Secondly; in spite of the danger of death we have turned aside from your impure gods to the unbegotten, impassible, pure God.

This is the second proof that Christianity is alone true.

5. ἐκ παντὸς γένους] Cf. c. 1.

8. Περσεφόνην] There is no reference here to the rape of Proserpine by Pluto. The story here alluded to, told by Apollodorus, is that Aphrodite gave the infant Adonis to Persephone to keep in safety. She admired him and refused to give him up. The consequent dispute between the two goddesses was appeased by Zeus, who decided that Adonis should remain for one-third of each year by himself, and should spend the rest of the year in equal portions with Aphrodite and Persephone.

9. οἰστρηθείσας] 'stung to madness.' Οἶστρος literally = 'gadfly.'

12. ἀγεννήτῳ, ἀπαθεῖ] As Otto remarks, the former epithet is to be contrasted with τὸν Σεμέλης and τὸν Λητοΐδην, the latter with τὰς οἰστρηθείσας.

13. ἑαυτοὺς ἀνεθ.] Cf. c. 14, 2.

APOLOGIA

μεθα, οὐδὲ λυθῆναι βοηθείας τυχόντα διὰ Θέτιδος ὑπὸ τοῦ ἑκατοντάχειρος ἐκείνου, οὐδὲ μεριμνῶντα διὰ τοῦτο τὸν τῆς Θέτιδος Ἀχιλλέα διὰ τὴν παλλακίδα Βρισηΐδα ὀλέσαι πολλοὺς τῶν Ἑλλήνων. 3. καὶ τοὺς πειθομένους ἐλεοῦμεν· τοὺς δὲ τούτων αἰτίους δαίμονας γνωρίζομεν. 5

26. 1. Τρίτον δ' ὅτι καὶ μετὰ τὴν ἀνέλευσιν τοῦ Χριστοῦ εἰς οὐρανὸν προεβάλλοντο οἱ δαίμονες ἀνθρώπους τινὰς λέγοντας ἑαυτοὺς εἶναι θεούς, οἳ οὐ μόνον οὐκ ἐδιώχθησαν ὑφ' ὑμῶν, ἀλλὰ καὶ τιμῶν κατηξιώθησαν· 2. Σίμωνα μέν τινα Σαμαρέα, τὸν ἀπὸ κώμης λεγομένης 10 Γιττῶν, ὃς ἐπὶ Κλαυδίου Καίσαρος διὰ τῆς τῶν ἐνεργούντων δαιμόνων τέχνης δυνάμεις ποιήσας μαγικὰς ἐν τῇ πόλει ὑμῶν βασιλίδι Ῥώμῃ θεὸς ἐνομίσθη καὶ ἀνδριάντι

6 ἀνέλευσιν τοῦ χριστοῦ A ἀνάληψιν τοῦ κυρίου Eus *H E* II 13 ‖ 9 κατηξιώθησαν A ἠξιώθησαν Eus ‖ 11 Γιττῶν Eus τρίτον A ‖ 12 ποιήσας μαγικὰς A μαγικὰς ποιήσας Eus ‖ 13 βασιλίδι A τῇ βασιλίδι Eus

1. τοῦ ἑκατοντάχειρος] i.e. Briareus.

2. μεριμνῶντα κτλ.] 'nor because of this (i.e. of Thetis' assistance) was anxious that Achilles should destroy many of the Greeks.' Μεριμνῶντα should be in the infinitive, but may be considered to be influenced by the preceding τυχόντα. In any case the grammar is slovenly. The passage in Hom. *Il.* ii 3, 4 runs

ἀλλ' ὅ γε (Zeus) μερμήριζε κατὰ φρένα ὡς Ἀχιλῆα
τιμήσει· ὀλέσαι δὲ πολέας ἐπὶ νηυσὶν Ἀχαιῶν.

Hence Ashton proffers the emendation here οὐδὲ μεριμνῶντα τιμῆσαι τὸν τ. Θ. Ἀχ. καὶ διὰ κτλ. Certainly the MS text appears suspicious; but διὰ τοῦτο should probably be retained.

5. γνωρίζομεν] 'we recognize.'

26. *Thirdly; the demons have inspired men who claim to be gods; their followers are called 'Christians'; and perhaps it is through them that the slanders against us arise. And* yet *you do not punish them for their doctrines.*

The third proof that Christianity is true is that those who at the demons' bidding corrupt Christianity are not punished for their doctrines (whilst true Christians are); therefore plainly the demons, the enemies of truth, are the authors of the persecutions.

The following passage is quoted by Eus. *H. E.* ii 13.

11. Γιττῶν] The name was Gitta or Gittae, not far from Flavia Neapolis, Justin's own birthplace.—Simon appears to have come forward, in Claudius' reign, as a magician, and to have propounded a system mixed up of Jewish and Syro-Babylonian elements; he apparently represented himself as a kind of emanation of the deity, and may have been honoured (in Samaria, if nowhere else) as an embodiment of God's highest power. A woman named Helena appeared in his system as the world-creating

παρ' ὑμῶν ὡς θεὸς τετίμηται, ὃς ἀνδριὰς ἀνεγήγερται ἐν τῷ Τίβερι ποταμῷ μεταξὺ τῶν δύο γεφυρῶν, ἔχων ἐπιγραφὴν ῥωμαϊκὴν ταύτην· SIMONI DEO SANCTO.

3. καὶ σχεδὸν πάντες μὲν Σαμαρεῖς, ὀλίγοι δὲ καὶ ἐν ἄλλοις ἔθνεσιν, ὡς τὸν πρῶτον θεὸν ἐκεῖνον ὁμολογοῦντες προσκυνοῦσι· καὶ Ἑλένην τινά, τὴν περινοστήσασαν αὐτῷ κατ' ἐκεῖνο τοῦ καιροῦ, πρότερον ἐπὶ τέγους σταθεῖσαν,)τὴν ὑπ' αὐτοῦ ἔννοιαν πρώτην γενομένην λέγουσι.

4. Μένανδρον δέ τινα, καὶ αὐτὸν Σαμαρέα, τὸν ἀπὸ κώμης Καππαρεταίας, γενόμενον μαθητὴν τοῦ Σίμωνος, ἐνεργηθέντα καὶ αὐτὸν ὑπὸ τῶν δαιμονίων καὶ ἐν Ἀντιοχείᾳ

1 ὃς ἀνδριὰς ἀνεγήγερται A desunt ap Eus ‖ 3 Simoni Deo Sancto (ὅπερ ἐστὶν Σίμωνι θεῷ ἁγίῳ) Eus σίμωνι δεῷ σάγκτῳ A ‖ 4 πάντες μὲν A μὲν πάντες Eus ‖ 6 περινοστήσασαν A συμπεριυοστήσασαν Eus ‖ 7 σταθεῖσαν A ἐν Τύρῳ τῆς Φοινίκης add Eus ‖ 8 ὑπ' αὐτοῦ ἔνν. πρώτ. γεν. A ἀπ' αὐτοῦ πρώ. ἔνν. Eus ‖ 10 ἐνεργηθέντα καὶ (om αὐτὸν) A οἰστρηθέντα καὶ αὐτὸν Eus *H E* III 26

thought of God. But it is difficult to know how far Simon's doctrines and the history of his life have not been elaborated and garnished by the later heretics (there was a sect of Simonians in Justin's time) and by Catholics who treated Simon as the first heresiarch. The account in Acts viii 4 ff. seems to justify the belief that there was at least some tinge of rudimentary Gnosticism in his system (especially verse 10). It is not certain that Simon ever came to Rome.

1. *ἐν τῷ Τίβερι κτλ.*] '*In insula Tiberina*.'

3. Simoni Deo Sancto] Subsequent authors, probably deriving their information from Justin, mention this statue, e.g. Iren. *c. Haer.* i 23, Tert. *Ap.* 13, Augustin. *de Haer.* 1, and it is possible that statues in Simon's honour may have been erected at Samaria, and at Rome. This would not be singular, for Lucian describes extravagant honours that were paid to a similar charlatan called Alexander. But it is, at the least, a curious coincidence that in the island of the Tiber was found the base of a statue inscribed *Semoni Sanco Deo Fidio*. Such dedications to the Sabine god *Semo Sancus* have been found elsewhere. And it is possible that Justin was deceived by such an inscription, and read it as a dedication *Simoni Sancto Deo Filio*. The ignorance of Latin on his part, which is thus supposed, would not be at all incredible. But we need not therefore doubt Justin's accuracy in respect of the honours paid to Simon at Samaria.

7. *ἐπὶ τέγους σ.*] According to Eusebius, she had been a prostitute at Tyre.

8. *ἔννοιαν*] '*thought*' or '*conception*.'

9. *Μένανδρον*] A follower of Simon, he baptized in his own name, professing to confer a resurrection to eternal life and youth.

10. *ἐνεργηθ. κ.*] Αὐτὸν is almost

γενόμενον πολλοὺς ἐξαπατῆσαι διὰ μαγικῆς τέχνης οἴδαμεν, ὃς καὶ τοὺς αὐτῷ ἑπομένους ὡς μηδὲ ἀποθνήσκοιεν ἔπεισε· καὶ νῦν εἰσί τινες ἀπ' ἐκείνου τοῦτο ὁμολογοῦντες. 5. Μαρκίωνα δέ τινα Ποντικόν, ὃς καὶ νῦν ἔτι ἐστὶ διδάσκων τοὺς πειθομένους, ἄλλον τινὰ νομίζειν μείζονα 5 τοῦ δημιουργοῦ θεόν· ὃς κατὰ πᾶν γένος ἀνθρώπων διὰ τῆς τῶν δαιμόνων συλλήψεως πολλοὺς πέπεικε βλασφημίας λέγειν καὶ ἀρνεῖσθαι τὸν ποιητὴν τοῦδε τοῦ παντὸς θεόν, ἄλλον δέ τινα, ὡς ὄντα μείζονα, τὰ μείζονα παρὰ τοῦτον ὁμολογεῖν πεποιηκέναι. 6. πάντες οἱ ἀπὸ τού- 10 των ὁρμώμενοι, ὡς ἔφημεν, Χριστιανοὶ καλοῦνται, ὃν τρόπον καὶ οἱ οὐ κοινωνοῦντες τῶν αὐτῶν δογμάτων ἐν τοῖς φιλοσόφοις τὸ ἐπικατηγορούμενον ὄνομα τῆς φιλοσοφίας

2 ὡς μηδὲ A ὡς μὴ Eus ‖ 3 εἰσί τινες A τινές εἰσιν Eus ‖ 6 ὃς κατὰ πᾶν A ὃς καὶ κατὰ πᾶν Eus *H E* IV 11 ‖ 7 πέπεικε βλάσφημα Eus πεποίηκε βλασφημίας A ‖ 9 θεόν A πατέρα εἶναι τοῦ χριστοῦ Eus ‖ τὰ μείζονα A om Eus ‖ 10 πάντες οἱ A καὶ πάντες οἱ Eus ‖ 11 ἔφημεν A ἔφαμεν Eus ‖ 12 ἐν τοῖς φιλοσόφοις Otto ἐν om A ‖ 13 τὸ ἐπικατηγορούμενον A τὸ ἐπικαλούμενον Otto ὃν τρόπον καὶ οὐ κοινῶν ὄντων δογμάτων τοῖς φιλοσόφοις τὸ ἐπικαλούμενον ὄνομα τῆς φιλοσοφίας κοινόν ἐστιν Eus Krüger

unavoidably necessary after καί, and is supported by the reading in Eusebius.

3. ὁμολογοῦντες] '*professing*.'

4. Μαρκίωνα] Also governed by προεβάλλοντο. Marcion's system conceived of two gods: one, the demiurge, was the God of the O.T., which Marcion rejected together with all Judaism: the other was the First God, who was found in the N.T., especially in the Pauline writings.

Cramer (*Theol. Stud.*) believes this passage and c. 58 to be later insertions: this one, he says, breaks the connexion, and Marcion did not call himself a god, as did Simon and Menander. But such a theory is doubtful. Justin would not be unlikely to take a chance of attacking Marcion, nor reluctant to bracket him with other heresiarchs.

7. συλλήψεως] '*assistance*.'

11. ὡς ἔφημεν] c. 7, 3.

ib. ὃν τρόπον οἱ] '*even as those philosophers* (accepting Otto's insertion of ἐν) *who do not share the same views are yet all called by one common name*.' Otto, following Eusebius, alters ἐπικατηγ. to ἐπικαλούμενον, regarding the former word as being inserted from c. 7, where, in his opinion, it means '*adduced as an accusation*.' But the word can mean, and normally does mean, simply '*predicated of somebody or something*.' The Eusebian version of this passage is certainly more fluent, and may be correct. But it looks rather like a correction of an already corrupted text.

κοινὸν ἔχουσιν.   7. εἰ δὲ καὶ τὰ δύσφημα ἐκεῖνα μυθολογούμενα ἔργα πράττουσι, λυχνίας μὲν ἀνατροπὴν καὶ τὰς ἀνέδην μίξεις καὶ ἀνθρωπείων σαρκῶν βοράς, οὐ γινώσκομεν· ἀλλ' ὅτι μὴ διώκονται μηδὲ φονεύονται ὑφ' ὑμῶν, 5 κἂν διὰ τὰ δόγματα, ἐπιστάμεθα.   8. ἔστι δὲ ἡμῖν καὶ σύνταγμα κατὰ πασῶν τῶν γεγενημένων αἱρέσεων συντεταγμένον, ᾧ εἰ βούλεσθε ἐντυχεῖν, δώσομεν.

27. 1. Ἡμεῖς δέ, ἵνα μηδὲν ἀδικῶμεν μηδὲ ἀσεβῶμεν, ἐκτιθέναι καὶ τὰ γεννώμενα πονηρῶν εἶναι δεδι-
10 δάγμεθα· πρῶτον μέν, ὅτι τοὺς πάντας σχεδὸν ὁρῶμεν ἐπὶ πορνείᾳ προάγοντας, οὐ μόνον τὰς κόρας ἀλλὰ καὶ τοὺς ἄρσενας, καὶ ὃν τρόπον λέγονται οἱ παλαιοὶ ἀγέλας βοῶν

6 συντεταγμένον A om Eus ‖ 8 μηδὲν ἀδικῶμεν Stephan Otto μηδένα διώκωμεν A

1. τὰ δύσφημα] especially promiscuity and cannibalism. Λυχνίας ἀνατροπήν refers to the scandal that, at Christian meetings, a dog was tied to the lamp and excited. The lamp being thus overturned and extinguished, chance concubinage ensued. Cf. Min. Fel. *Octau.* p. 87.
3. ἀνέδην] '*promiscuously, without restraint.*'
4. ὅτι μή] for ὅτι οὐ. Cf. c. 24, 2, ii 8 (3), 2.
5. κἂν διὰ τ. δ.] '*at least for their opinions,*' i.e. if they are punished at all, it is for their crimes. Christians alone are punished for their opinions. On κἂν cf. c. 12, 3 note.
6. σύνταγμα] This work was probably known to Irenaeus. It is now lost.
7. ἐντυχεῖν] '*read*' as in c. 14, 1.
27. *We prohibit the exposure of children;* (1) *because such children are taken for vile uses, such as are practised commonly and openly among you, and even under the sanction of religion; whilst you falsely accuse us of practising them in secret.*

Justin does not make clear the connexion of cc. 27—29 with the preceding arguments. Possibly he inserted this point with regard to the exposure of children, because it seemed to him important, without making any definite attempt to connect it with his general argument. But the point strengthens his argument for the unique truth of Christianity, by showing the moral purity of Christian practice in one notable example.

The exposure of children is denounced by many Church writers. Emperors like Trajan, Pius, Septimius Severus, tried to diminish this and similar evils, and to provide for the education of poor children. Constantine promulgated in A.D. 315 a law to restrain the practice in Italy.

9. πονηρῶν εἶναι] Cf. *Didache* ii οὐ φονεύσεις τέκνον ἐν φθορᾷ οὐδὲ γεννηθέντα ἀποκτενεῖς.
11. προάγοντας] Intransitive, '*growing up.*'

ἢ αἰγῶν ἢ προβάτων τρέφειν ἢ ἵππων φορβάδων, οὕτως
νῦν καὶ παῖδας εἰς τὸ αἰσχρῶς χρῆσθαι μόνον· καὶ ὁμοίως
θηλειῶν καὶ ἀνδρογύνων καὶ ἀρρητοποιῶν πλῆθος κατὰ
πᾶν ἔθνος ἐπὶ τούτου τοῦ ἄγους ἔστηκε.   2. καὶ τούτων
μισθοὺς καὶ εἰσφορὰς καὶ τέλη λαμβάνετε δέον ἐκκόψαι 5
ἀπὸ τῆς ὑμετέρας οἰκουμένης.   3. καὶ τῶν τούτοις χρω-
μένων τις, πρὸς τῇ ἀθέῳ καὶ ἀσεβεῖ καὶ ἀκρατεῖ μίξει, εἰ
τύχοι, τέκνῳ ἢ συγγενεῖ ἢ ἀδελφῷ μίγνυται.   4. οἱ δὲ
καὶ τὰ ἑαυτῶν τέκνα καὶ τὰς ὁμοζύγους προαγωγεύονται,
καὶ φανερῶς εἰς κιναιδίαν ἀποκόπτονταί τινες καὶ εἰς 10
μητέρα θεῶν τὰ μυστήρια ἀναφέρουσι, καὶ παρὰ παντὶ
τῶν νομιζομένων παρ' ὑμῖν θεῶν ὄφις σύμβολον μέγα
καὶ μυστήριον ἀναγράφεται.   5. καὶ τὰ φανερῶς ὑμῖν
πραττόμενα καὶ τιμώμενα, ὡς ἀνατετραμμένου καὶ οὐ
παρόντος φωτὸς θείου ἡμῖν προσγράφετε· ὅπερ ἀπηλλαγ- 15
μένοις ἡμῖν τοῦ πράττειν τι τούτων οὐ βλάβην φέρει, ἀλλὰ
τοῖς πράττουσι καὶ ψευδομαρτυροῦσι μᾶλλον.

28. 1. Παρ' ἡμῖν μὲν γὰρ ὁ ἀρχηγέτης τῶν κακῶν

11 παρὰ παντὶ τ. νομ. παρ' ὑμ. θεῶν Sylburg παρὰ παντὶ τ. νομ. παρ' ὑμ. θεῷ A

1. φορβάδων] 'grazing with the herd.'
ib. οὕτως ν. κ. παῖδας] τρέφεσθαι understood.
4. ἐπὶ τούτου τοῦ ἄγους] 'with a view to this abomination.'
5. μισθούς] Cf. Suet. Calig. 40. These were abolished by Justinian.
9. προαγωγεύονται] 'prostitute.'
10. εἰς κιναιδίαν κτλ.] Referring to the worship of the Asiatic mother of the gods and the eunuch priests of that cult.
12. ὄφις] This hint is taken up in the next chapter. The snake played a prominent part in paganism, as the familiar genius of heroes and demigods, as the guardian of shrines, and in connexion with the cult of the dead.
15. φωτὸς θείου] Pautigny brackets θείου, and it certainly seems out of place and unnecessary, if the phrase goes with ἡμῖν προσγράφ. It is possible however that the clause ὡς...θείου ought to go with πραττ. κ. τιμώμ. and that the sense is that the heathen commit these sins openly, because the Divine light (i.e. of the Spirit) is perverted and absent in them. In that case there would be a sarcastic play upon words in ἀνατετραμμένου, which bears an allusion to the charge made against the Christians of λυχνίας ἀνατροπή (26, 7). The Christians are charged with overturning the material lamp for purposes of sin; but the heathen sin openly, because the spiritual light is overturned in their case.

28. *The snake which you rever-*

δαιμόνων ὄφις καλεῖται καὶ σατανᾶς καὶ διάβολος, ὡς
καὶ ἐκ τῶν ἡμετέρων συγγραμμάτων ἐρευνήσαντες μαθεῖν
δύνασθε· ὃν εἰς τὸ πῦρ πεμφθήσεσθαι μετὰ τῆς αὐτοῦ
στρατιᾶς καὶ τῶν ἑπομένων ἀνθρώπων κολασθησομένους
5 τὸν ἀπέραντον αἰῶνα, προεμήνυσεν ὁ Χριστός. 2. καὶ
γὰρ ἡ ἐπιμονὴ τοῦ μηδέπω τοῦτο πρᾶξαι τὸν θεὸν διὰ
τὸ ἀνθρώπινον γένος γεγένηται· προγινώσκει γάρ τινας ἐκ
μετανοίας σωθήσεσθαι μέλλοντας καί τινας μηδέπω ἴσως
γεννηθέντας. 3. καὶ τὴν ἀρχὴν νοερὸν καὶ δυνάμενον
10 αἱρεῖσθαι τἀληθῆ καὶ εὖ πράττειν τὸ γένος τὸ ἀνθρώπινον
πεποίηκεν, ὥστ' ἀναπολόγητον εἶναι τοῖς πᾶσιν ἀνθρώποις
παρὰ τῷ θεῷ· λογικοὶ γὰρ καὶ θεωρητικοὶ γεγένηνται.
4. εἰ δέ τις ἀπιστεῖ μέλειν τούτων τῷ θεῷ, ἢ μὴ εἶναι
αὐτὸν διὰ τέχνης ὁμολογήσει, ἢ ὄντα χαίρειν κακίᾳ φήσει
15 ἢ λίθῳ ἐοικότα μένειν, καὶ μηδὲν εἶναι ἀρετὴν μηδὲ κακίαν,
δόξῃ δὲ μόνον τοὺς ἀνθρώπους ἢ ἀγαθὰ ἢ κακὰ ταῦτα
ἡγεῖσθαι· ἥπερ μεγίστη ἀσέβεια καὶ ἀδικία ἐστί.

ence is with us the leader of the evil demons, who shall be punished eternally. This event is postponed at present so as to give man a chance of repentance; for we have reason and intelligence and therefore no excuse for sin. To deny that God cares for man is equivalent to denying His existence, His character, or His nature, and removes any absoluteness of distinction between good and evil.

1. ὄφις] Cf. Revel. xii 9 ὁ δράκων ὁ μέγας, ὁ ὄφις ὁ ἀρχαῖος ὁ καλούμενος Διάβολος καὶ ὁ Σατανᾶς. *ib.* xx. 2; Genes. iii 1. The first trace of an explicit identification of Satan with the Serpent of the Fall narrative is found in Wisd. ii 24.

2. ἡμετέρων] i.e. Christian.

4. κολασθησομένους] A not uncommon *constructio ad sensum*.

5. προεμήνυσεν] Cf. Matt. xxv 41.

6. ἡ ἐπιμονὴ κτλ.] The same idea recurs in ii 6 (7).

9. τὴν ἀρχήν] 'originally.' The same notion as in c. 10, 4.

10. εὖ πράττειν] may mean, as Otto takes it, 'to act rightly,' or 'to fare well,' καὶ having the sense of 'and so.'

11. ἀναπολόγητον] Cf. Rom. i 20, 21. For the construction cf. c. 3, 5.

12. λογικοί, θεωρητικοί] '*capable of exercising reason and intelligence.*'

13. μέλειν τούτων] i.e. τῶν ἀνθρώπων.

ib. ἢ μὴ εἶναι κτλ.] The apodosis begins at ἤ. '*If he denies God's care for men, either he will by some artifice deny His existence, or, while allowing His existence, he will assert that He rejoices in evil, or that He remains unmoved like a stone, and etc.*'

15. μηδὲν εἶναι κτλ.] This is the Sophistic view, which Socrates and Plato attacked. Justin main-

29. 1. Καὶ πάλιν, μὴ τῶν ἐκτεθέντων τις μὴ ἀναληφθεὶς θανατωθῇ, καὶ ὦμεν ἀνδροφόνοι· ἀλλ' ἢ τὴν ἀρχὴν οὐκ ἐγαμοῦμεν εἰ μὴ ἐπὶ παίδων ἀνατροφῇ, ἢ παραιτούμενοι τὸ γήμασθαι τέλεον ἐνεκρατευόμεθα. 2. καὶ ἤδη τις τῶν ἡμετέρων, ὑπὲρ τοῦ πεῖσαι ὑμᾶς ὅτι οὐκ ἔστιν ἡμῖν μυστήριον ἡ ἀνέδην μίξις, βιβλίδιον ἀνέδωκεν ἐν Ἀλεξανδρείᾳ Φήλικι ἡγεμονεύοντι, ἀξιῶν ἐπιτρέψαι ἰατρῷ τοὺς διδύμους αὐτοῦ ἀφελεῖν· ἄνευ γὰρ τῆς τοῦ ἡγεμόνος ἐπιτροπῆς τοῦτο πράττειν ἀπειρῆσθαι οἱ ἐκεῖ ἰατροὶ ἔλεγον. 3. καὶ μηδόλως βουληθέντος Φήλικος ὑπογράψαι, ἐφ' ἑαυτοῦ μείνας ὁ νεανίσκος ἠρκέσθη τῇ ἑαυτοῦ καὶ τῶν ὁμογνωμόνων συνειδήσει. 4. οὐκ ἄτοπον δὲ ἐπιμνησθῆναι ἐν τούτοις ἡγησάμεθα καὶ Ἀντινόου τοῦ νῦν γεγενημένου, ὃν καὶ πάντες ὡς θεὸν διὰ φόβου

4 ἐνεκρατευόμεθα Otto ἐνεγκρατευόμεθα A ‖ 7 Φήλικι (*infr* Φήλικος) Sylburg Φίληκι (Φίληκος) A ‖ 13 ἡγησάμεθα A ἡγούμεθα Eus *H E* IV 8 ‖ 14 γεγενημένου A γενομένου Eus ‖ διὰ φόβου A διὰ φόβον Eus Otto

tains that to deny God's interest in human affairs removes the only absolute sanction for the distinction between good and evil.

29. *We do not expose children* (2) *for fear they may consequently die. In fact, we marry to bring up children, or we do not marry and are continent. Contrast with our purity your deification of the profligate Antinous.*

The first reason for not exposing children was given in c. 27.

6. ἡ ἀνέδην μίξις] Cf. c. 26, 7.
ib. βιβλίδιον ἀνέδωκεν] *libellum obtulit* (Otto).

7. Φήλικι] Felix was *Praefectus Augustalis* in Egypt. A papyrus records one C. Munatius Felix as prefect of Egypt in A.D. 148—154. For the bearing of this fact on the date of the Apology, see *Introd.* p. l.

9. ἐπιτροπῆς] '*permission.*' Castration was forbidden by Roman law in the times of Nerva, Hadrian, and Domitian.

10. ὑπογράψαι] '*to subscribe,*' i.e. to approve the request by his signature.

11. ἠρκέσθη κτλ.] '*was satisfied with the testimony of his own conscience and that of his fellow-believers.*'

13. Ἀντινόου] was a favourite of Hadrian, drowned in the Nile A.D. 130 (νῦν). Hadrian deified him.

14. διὰ φόβου] Eusebius' reading, διὰ φόβον, is supported by Athanas. *c. Gent.* 9, who says men honour Antinous διὰ φόβον τοῦ προστάξαντος. Athenagoras however (*Leg.* 30, addressed to Aurelius and Commodus) says it was done φιλανθρωπίᾳ τῶν ὑμετέρων προγόνων. The difference of reading here is not important, but διὰ φόβου can stand as = '*with fear,*' i.e. '*they feared and reverenced*' Antinous. Cf. δι' αἰδοῦς '*respectfully.*' After all, too, it would not be specially to Justin's purpose to assert that

σέβειν ὥρμηντο, ἐπιστάμενοι τίς τε ἦν καὶ πόθεν ὑπῆρχεν.

30. 1. Ὅπως δὲ μή τις εἴπῃ ἀντιτιθεὶς ἡμῖν, τί κωλύει καὶ τὸν παρ' ἡμῖν λεγόμενον Χριστόν, ἄνθρωπον ἐξ ἀνθρώπων ὄντα, μαγικῇ τέχνῃ ἃς λέγομεν δυνάμεις πεποιηκέναι, καὶ δόξαι διὰ τοῦτο υἱὸν θεοῦ εἶναι, τὴν ἀπόδειξιν ἤδη ποιησόμεθα, οὐ τοῖς λέγουσι πιστεύοντες, ἀλλὰ τοῖς προφητεύουσι πρὶν ἢ γενέσθαι κατ' ἀνάγκην πειθόμενοι, διὰ τὸ καὶ ὄψει ὡς προεφητεύθη ὁρᾶν γενόμενα καὶ γινόμενα· ἥπερ μεγίστη καὶ ἀληθεστάτη ἀπόδειξις καὶ ὑμῖν, ὡς νομίζομεν, φανήσεται.

31. 1. Ἄνθρωποι οὖν τινες ἐν Ἰουδαίοις γεγένηνται θεοῦ προφῆται, δι' ὧν τὸ προφητικὸν πνεῦμα προεκήρυξε τὰ γενήσεσθαι μέλλοντα πρὶν ἢ γενέσθαι· καὶ τούτων οἱ ἐν Ἰουδαίοις κατὰ καιροὺς γενόμενοι βασιλεῖς τὰς προφητείας, ὡς ἐλέχθησαν ὅτε προεφητεύοντο, τῇ ἰδίᾳ αὐτῶν ἑβραΐδι φωνῇ ἐν βιβλίοις ὑπ' αὐτῶν τῶν προφητῶν συντεταγμένας κτώμενοι περιεῖπον. 2. ὅτε δὲ Πτολεμαῖος,

3 εἴπῃ Otto om A

Antinous was reverenced only out of fear of Hadrian.

1. τίς τε ἦν] So Athanas. *loc. cit.* εἰδότες ἄνθρωπον καὶ ἄνθρωπον οὐ σεμνὸν ἀλλ' ἀσελγείας ἔμπλεω.

30. *You may say that Christ was a mere man, and a magician, but the argument from prophecy will disprove that theory.*

Here Justin passes to the second subject announced in c. 23, viz. that Christ Jesus is the Son of God.

7. τοῖς λέγουσι] i.e. not trusting to those who tell about Christ Himself.

8. τοῖς προφητεύουσι] This is the argument from prophecy in the most literal sense, which points to the correspondence between forecast and event. Note that Justin does not refer to Christ's miracles as a proof of His Divinity, because it was possible to retort that miraculous works could be the product of magic; but true prophecy was admitted by the pagans to be a sure sign of Divine inspiration.

31. *A short sketch of Hebrew prophecy and of the LXX translation. In these prophecies are plain foretellings of Christ's life and of the Christian Church's expansion.*

18. περιεῖπον] 'treated with great heed,' from περιέπω.

ib. Πτολεμαῖος] Ptolemy Philadelphus B.C. 285—247. The insertion of Herod's name is a plain anachronism. Attempts have been made to exempt Justin from the charge of error by altering the text, or by treating Ἡρώδη and Ἡρώδης as the glosses of an ignorant annotator (in which case ὁ βασιλεύς would be the high-priest); it has also been sug-

ὁ Αἰγυπτίων βασιλεύς, βιβλιοθήκην κατεσκεύαζε καὶ τὰ πάντων ἀνθρώπων συγγράμματα συνάγειν ἐπειράθη, πυθόμενος καὶ περὶ τῶν προφητειῶν τούτων, προσέπεμψε τῷ τῶν Ἰουδαίων τότε βασιλεύοντι Ἡρώδῃ ἀξιῶν διαπεμφθῆναι αὐτῷ τὰς βίβλους τῶν προφητειῶν. 3. καὶ ὁ μὲν βασιλεὺς Ἡρώδης τῇ προειρημένῃ Ἑβραΐδι αὐτῶν φωνῇ γεγραμμένας διεπέμψατο. 4. ἐπειδὴ δὲ οὐκ ἦν γνώριμα τὰ ἐν αὐταῖς γεγραμμένα τοῖς Αἰγυπτίοις, πάλιν αὐτὸν ἠξίωσε πέμψας τοὺς μεταβαλοῦντας αὐτὰς εἰς τὴν ἑλλάδα φωνὴν ἀνθρώπους ἀποστεῖλαι. 5. καὶ τούτου γενομένου, ἔμειναν αἱ βίβλοι καὶ παρ' Αἰγυπτίοις μέχρι τοῦ δεῦρο, καὶ πανταχοῦ παρὰ πᾶσίν εἰσιν Ἰουδαίοις, οἳ καὶ ἀναγινώσκοντες οὐ συνιᾶσι τὰ εἰρημένα, ἀλλ' ἐχθροὺς ἡμᾶς καὶ πολεμίους ἡγοῦνται, ὁμοίως ὑμῖν, ἀναιροῦντες καὶ κολάζοντες ἡμᾶς ὁπόταν δύνωνται, ὡς καὶ πεισθῆναι δύνασθε. 6. καὶ γὰρ ἐν τῷ νῦν γεγενημένῳ ἰουδαϊκῷ πολέμῳ, Βαρχωχέβας, ὁ τῆς Ἰουδαίων ἀποστάσεως ἀρχηγέτης, Χριστιανοὺς μόνους εἰς τιμωρίας δεινάς, εἰ μὴ ἀρνοῖντο Ἰησοῦν τὸν Χριστὸν καὶ βλασφημοῖεν, ἐκέλευεν ἀπάγεσθαι. 7. ἐν δὴ ταῖς τῶν προφητῶν βίβλοις εὕρομεν προκηρυσσόμενον παραγινόμενον, γεννώμενον διὰ παρθένου, καὶ ἀνδρούμενον, καὶ θεραπεύοντα πᾶσαν νόσον καὶ

16 γεγενημένῳ A γενομένῳ Eus *H E* IV 8 ∥ 17 Βαρχωχέβας Eus Βαρχοχέβας A ∥ 20 ἀπάγεσθαι A ἄγεσθαι Eus

gested that Justin has confused Ptolemy's foundation of the library with Cleopatra's restoration of it in the Serapeum. Perhaps it is most simple to suppose Justin to be guilty either of ignorance or of a lapse of memory. Justin's account of the LXX translation (excluding the reference to Herod) seems based upon the well-known story of Aristeas, though he does not mention the romantic and miraculous details which formed part of the usual version.

17. Βαρχωχέβας] The revolt of Barcochba took place A.D. 132–135. Justin's use of νῦν is quite loose. Cf. 29, 4 Ἀντινόου τοῦ νῦν γεγενημένου, and 42, 4 ὁ καθ' ἡμᾶς Ἰησοῦς Χριστὸς σταυρωθείς, 63, 10 νῦν ἄνθρωπος γενόμενος.

20. εὕρομεν] '*we have found.*' The aorist is not easy to account for.

21. προκηρυσσόμενον παραγινόμενον] '*foretold as coming.*'

22. θεραπεύοντα κτλ.] Cf. Matt. iv 23; ix 35; x 1.

πᾶσαν μαλακίαν καὶ νεκροὺς ἀνεγείροντα, καὶ φθονού-
μενον καὶ ἀγνοούμενον καὶ σταυρούμενον Ἰησοῦν τὸν
ἡμέτερον Χριστόν, καὶ ἀποθνήσκοντα καὶ ἀνεγειρόμενον
καὶ εἰς οὐρανοὺς ἀνερχόμενον, καὶ υἱὸν θεοῦ ὄντα καὶ
5 κεκλημένον, καί τινας πεμπομένους ὑπ' αὐτοῦ εἰς πᾶν
γένος ἀνθρώπων κηρύξοντας ταῦτα, καὶ τοὺς ἐξ ἐθνῶν
ἀνθρώπους μᾶλλον αὐτῷ πιστεύειν. 8. προεφητεύθη
δέ, πρὶν ἢ φανῆναι αὐτόν, ἔτεσι ποτὲ μὲν πεντακισχιλίοις,
ποτὲ δὲ τρισχιλίοις, ποτὲ δὲ δισχιλίοις, καὶ πάλιν χιλίοις
10 καὶ ἄλλοτε ὀκτακοσίοις· κατὰ γὰρ τὰς διαδοχὰς τῶν
γενῶν ἕτεροι καὶ ἕτεροι ἐγένοντο προφῆται.

32. 1. Μωϋσῆς μὲν οὖν, πρῶτος τῶν προφητῶν γενόμενος, εἶπεν αὐτολεξεὶ οὕτως· Οὐκ ἐκλείψει ἄρχων ἐξ
Ἰούδα οὐδὲ ἡγούμενος ἐκ τῶν μηρῶν αὐτοῦ, ἕως ἂν ἔλθῃ ᾧ
15 ἀπόκειται· καὶ αὐτὸς ἔσται προσδοκία ἐθνῶν, δεσμεύων
πρὸς ἄμπελον τὸν πῶλον αὐτοῦ, πλύνων ἐν αἵματι σταφυλῆς τὴν στολὴν αὐτοῦ. 2. ὑμέτερον οὖν ἐστιν ἀκριβῶς
ἐξετάσαι καὶ μαθεῖν, μέχρι τίνος ἦν ἄρχων καὶ βασιλεὺς
ἐν Ἰουδαίοις ἴδιος αὐτῶν· μέχρι τῆς φανερώσεως Ἰησοῦ
20 Χριστοῦ, τοῦ ἡμετέρου διδασκάλου καὶ τῶν ἀγνοουμένων
προφητειῶν ἐξηγητοῦ, ὡς προερρέθη ὑπὸ τοῦ θείου ἁγίου
προφητικοῦ πνεύματος διὰ τοῦ Μωϋσέως μὴ ἐκλείψειν

12 Μωϋσῆς edd Μωσῆς A (et infr) || 14 ᾧ ἀπόκειται edd ὃ ἀπόκειται A

7. μᾶλλον αὐτῷ πιστεύειν] 'more,'
i.e. than the Jews.
8. ἔτεσι ποτὲ μὲν κτλ.] The
dates are obviously intended to be
merely approximate. The earliest
may be intended for Moses (whom
Justin calls the first of the prophets
in c. 32, 1) or Adam. It is not
worth while to attempt to fix the
reference of the later dates to any
particular prophets.
10. κατὰ γὰρ τὰς διαδ.] '*in successive generations.*'
32. O.T. passages prophetic of
Christ.

13. αὐτολεξεί] '*in express terms*.'
The quotation is from Gen. xlix
10, 11.
14. ᾧ ἀπόκειται] sc. τὸ βασίλειον,
as Justin subsequently explains.
Cf. *Tryph.* 120, where he insists
that this is the correct reading, as
opposed to the normal LXX text
τὰ ἀποκειμένα αὐτῷ.
19. μέχρι τῆς φαν.] Justin traces
a providential connexion between
the subjugation of Judaea and the
birth of Christ, and similarly between
the crucifixion of Christ and the
fall of the Jewish state.

ἄρχοντα ἀπὸ Ἰουδαίων, ἕως ἂν ἔλθῃ ᾧ ἀπόκειται τὸ βασίλειον. 3. Ἰούδας γὰρ προπάτωρ Ἰουδαίων, ἀφ' οὗ καὶ τὸ Ἰουδαῖοι καλεῖσθαι ἐσχήκασι· καὶ ὑμεῖς μετὰ τὴν γενομένην αὐτοῦ φανέρωσιν καὶ Ἰουδαίων ἐβασιλεύσατε καὶ τῆς ἐκείνων πάσης γῆς ἐκρατήσατε. 4. τὸ δὲ "Αὐτὸς ἔσται προσδοκία ἐθνῶν" μηνυτικὸν ἦν ὅτι ἐκ πάντων τῶν ἐθνῶν προσδοκήσουσιν αὐτὸν πάλιν παραγενησόμενον, ὅπερ ὄψει ὑμῖν πάρεστιν ἰδεῖν καὶ ἔργῳ πεισθῆναι· ἐκ πάντων γὰρ γενῶν ἀνθρώπων προσδοκῶσι τὸν ἐν Ἰουδαίᾳ σταυρωθέντα, μεθ' ὃν εὐθὺς δοριάλωτος ὑμῖν ἡ γῆ Ἰουδαίων παρεδόθη. 5. τὸ δὲ "Δεσμεύων πρὸς ἄμπελον τὸν πῶλον αὐτοῦ καὶ πλύνων τὴν στολὴν αὐτοῦ ἐν αἵματι σταφυλῆς" σύμβολον δηλωτικὸν ἦν τῶν γενησομένων τῷ Χριστῷ καὶ τῶν ὑπ' αὐτοῦ πραχθησομένων. 6. πῶλος γάρ τις ὄνου εἱστήκει ἔν τινι εἰσόδῳ κώμης πρὸς ἄμπελον δεδεμένος, ὃν ἐκέλευσεν ἀγαγεῖν αὐτῷ τότε τοὺς γνωρίμους αὐτοῦ, καὶ ἀχθέντος ἐπιβὰς ἐκάθισε καὶ εἰσελήλυθεν εἰς τὰ Ἱεροσόλυμα, ἔνθα τὸ μέγιστον ἱερὸν ἦν Ἰουδαίων, ὃ ὑφ' ὑμῶν ὕστερον κατεστράφη· καὶ μετὰ ταῦτα ἐσταυρώθη, ὅπως τὸ λεῖπον τῆς προφητείας συντελεσθῇ. 7. τὸ γὰρ "Πλύνων τὴν στολὴν αὐτοῦ ἐν αἵματι σταφυλῆς" προαγγελτικὸν ἦν τοῦ πάθους οὗ πάσχειν ἔμελλε, δι' αἵματος καθαίρων τοὺς πιστεύοντας αὐτῷ. 8. ἡ γὰρ κεκλημένη ὑπὸ τοῦ θείου πνεύματος διὰ τοῦ προφήτου στολὴ οἱ πιστεύοντες αὐτῷ εἰσιν ἄνθρωποι, ἐν οἷς οἰκεῖ τὸ παρὰ τοῦ θεοῦ σπέρμα, ὁ λόγος. 9. τὸ δὲ εἰρημένον αἷμα τῆς σταφυλῆς σημαντικὸν τοῦ ἔχειν μὲν

15. πῶλος γὰρ κτλ.] The reference is plainly to Matt. xxi 1 ff., but the fact recorded in πρὸς ἄμπελον δεδεμένος does not occur in the canonical Gospels, nor does Justin include this particular in *Tryph.* 53, where the same passage of Genesis is similarly interpreted. The detail may be traditional, or may be a gloss of Justin's, suggested to him by the O. T. passage.

20. τὸ λεῖπον] Cf. 52, 2 τὰ λείποντα.

23. δι' αἵματος κτλ.] A reference to the atoning power of Christ's death.

26. τὸ σπέρμα, ὁ λόγος] Cf. 1 John ii 14; iii 9.

αἷμα τὸν φανησόμενον, ἀλλ' οὐκ ἐξ ἀνθρωπείου σπέρματος, ἀλλ' ἐκ θείας δυνάμεως. 10. ἡ δὲ πρώτη δύναμις μετὰ τὸν πατέρα πάντων καὶ δεσπότην θεὸν καὶ υἱὸς ὁ λόγος ἐστίν· ὃς τίνα τρόπον σαρκοποιηθεὶς ἄνθρωπος γέγονεν, ἐν τοῖς ἑξῆς ἐροῦμεν. 11. ὃν τρόπον γὰρ τὸ τῆς ἀμπέλου αἷμα οὐκ ἄνθρωπος πεποίηκεν ἀλλ' ὁ θεός, οὕτως καὶ τοῦτο ἐμηνύετο οὐκ ἐξ ἀνθρωπείου σπέρματος γενήσεσθαι τὸ αἷμα ἀλλ' ἐκ δυνάμεως θεοῦ, ὡς προέφημεν. 12. καὶ Ἠσαίας δέ, ἄλλος προφήτης, τὰ αὐτὰ δι' ἄλλων ῥήσεων προφητεύων οὕτως εἶπεν· Ἀνατελεῖ ἄστρον ἐξ Ἰακώβ, καὶ ἄνθος ἀναβήσεται ἀπὸ τῆς ῥίζης Ἰεσσαί· καὶ ἐπὶ τὸν βραχίονα αὐτοῦ ἔθνη ἐλπιοῦσιν. 13. ἄστρον δὲ φωτεινὸν ἀνέτειλε, καὶ ἄνθος ἀνέβη ἀπὸ τῆς ῥίζης Ἰεσσαί, οὗτος ὁ Χριστός. 14. διὰ γὰρ παρθένου τῆς ἀπὸ τοῦ σπέρματος Ἰακώβ, τοῦ γενομένου πατρὸς Ἰούδα, τοῦ δεδηλωμένου Ἰουδαίων πατρός, διὰ δυνάμεως θεοῦ ἀπεκυήθη· καὶ Ἰεσσαὶ προπάτωρ μὲν κατὰ τὸ λόγιον γεγένηται, τοῦ δὲ Ἰακὼβ καὶ τοῦ Ἰούδα κατὰ γένους διαδοχὴν, υἱὸς ὑπῆρχεν.

33. 1. Καὶ πάλιν ὡς αὐτολεξεὶ διὰ παρθένου μὲν τεχθησόμενος, διὰ τοῦ Ἡσαίου προεφητεύθη, ἀκούσατε. ἐλέχθη δὲ οὕτως· Ἰδοὺ ἡ παρθένος ἐν γαστρὶ ἕξει καὶ τέξεται υἱόν, καὶ ἐροῦσιν ἐπὶ τῷ ὀνόματι αὐτοῦ Μεθ' ἡμῶν ὁ θεός. 2. ἃ γὰρ ἦν ἄπιστα καὶ ἀδύνατα νομιζόμενα παρὰ τοῖς ἀνθρώποις γενήσεσθαι, ταῦτα ὁ θεὸς προεμήνυσε διὰ τοῦ προφητικοῦ πνεύματος μέλλειν γίνεσθαι, ἵνα ὅταν γένηται μὴ ἀπιστηθῇ, ἀλλ' ἐκ τοῦ προειρῆσθαι πιστευθῇ.

2. ἡ πρώτη δύναμις] This is a case of logical precedence. It is unfair to read any Arian idea in it. See *Introd.*, p. xxii.

10. ἀνατελεῖ κτλ.] Cf. Numb. xxiv 17; Isa. xi 1, 10; li 5. Justin has here contaminated a prophecy of Isaiah with a passage from the Pentateuch.

33. *O. T. prophecies of the Virgin-Birth. The Virgin-Birth explained and distinguished from pagan myths.*

22. ἰδού] Cf. Isa. vii 14; Matt. i 23.

26. ἵνα ὅταν κτλ.] Cf. John xiv 29 and above c. 12, 10.

3. ὅπως δὲ μή τινες, μὴ νοήσαντες τὴν δεδηλωμένην προ-
φητείαν, ἐγκαλέσωσιν ἡμῖν ἅπερ ἐνεκαλέσαμεν τοῖς ποιηταῖς, εἰποῦσιν ἀφροδισίων χάριν ἐληλυθέναι ἐπὶ γυναῖκας
τὸν Δία, διασαφῆσαι τοὺς λόγους πειρασόμεθα.   4. τὸ
οὖν "Ἰδοὺ ἡ παρθένος ἐν γαστρὶ ἕξει" σημαίνει οὐ συνου- 5
σιασθεῖσαν τὴν παρθένον συλλαβεῖν· εἰ γὰρ ἐσυνουσιάσθη
ὑπὸ ὁτουοῦν, οὐκ ἔτι ἦν παρθένος· ἀλλὰ δύναμις θεοῦ
ἐπελθοῦσα τῇ παρθένῳ ἐπεσκίασεν αὐτήν, καὶ κυοφορῆσαι
παρθένον οὖσαν πεποίηκε.   5. καὶ ὁ ἀποσταλεὶς δὲ
πρὸς αὐτὴν τὴν παρθένον κατ' ἐκεῖνο τοῦ καιροῦ ἄγγελος 10
θεοῦ εὐηγγελίσατο αὐτὴν εἰπών· "Ἰδοὺ συλλήψῃ ἐν γαστρὶ
ἐκ πνεύματος ἁγίου καὶ τέξῃ υἱόν, καὶ υἱὸς ὑψίστου κληθή-
σεται, καὶ καλέσεις τὸ ὄνομα αὐτοῦ Ἰησοῦν, αὐτὸς γὰρ
σώσει τὸν λαὸν αὐτοῦ ἀπὸ τῶν ἁμαρτιῶν αὐτῶν," ὡς οἱ
ἀπομνημονεύσαντες πάντα τὰ περὶ τοῦ σωτῆρος ἡμῶν 15
Ἰησοῦ Χριστοῦ ἐδίδαξαν, οἷς ἐπιστεύσαμεν, ἐπειδὴ καὶ διὰ
Ἡσαΐου τοῦ προδεδηλωμένου τὸ προφητικὸν πνεῦμα,τοῦτον
γεννησόμενον, ὡς προεμηνύομεν, ἔφη.   6. τὸ πνεῦμα
οὖν καὶ τὴν δύναμιν τὴν παρὰ τοῦ θεοῦ οὐδὲν ἄλλο νοῆσαι θέμις ἢ τὸν λόγον, ὃς καὶ πρωτότοκος τῷ θεῷ ἐστι, 20
Μωϋσῆς ὁ προδεδηλωμένος προφήτης ἐμήνυσε· καὶ τοῦτο

1 ὅπως δὲ μή τινες Thirlb al ὅπως δέ τινες A ‖ 4 πειρασόμεθα Otto
πειρασώμεθα A ‖ 17 τοῦτον γεννησόμενον A τοῦτο γενησόμενον Otto ‖
21 Μωϋσῆς ὁ προδεδηλωμένος edd (Μωσῆς ὁ π. A) ὡς Μωϋσῆς ὁ προδ. Otto
ὡς Ἡσαΐας ὁ προδ. Grab al

6. συλλαβεῖν] A technical word
for '*to conceive*.'
8. ἐπεσκίασεν] Cf. Luke i 35.
11. εὐηγγελίσατο αὐτήν] The
dative of the person preached to is
found in classical Greek; the accusative is common in the N. T., e.g.
Luke iii 18; Acts viii 25, and the
passive, meaning '*to have the Gospel
preached to one*,' occurs in Matt. xi
5; Heb. iv 2, 6.
ib. ἰδοὺ συλλήψῃ] Cf. Luke i
31, 32; Matt. i 20, 21. There is
possibly, but not necessarily, a
reference to the *Protevangel.* ix 14,
where a similar combination is given.
18. γεννησόμενον] used in the
passive sense. Liddell and Scott
refer to a parallel in Diod. xix 2
περὶ τοῦ γεννησομένου βρέφους.
ib. τὸ πνεῦμα] Justin does not
clearly discriminate between the
πνεῦμα and the λόγος. See *Introd.*,
p. xxviii.
20. πρωτότοκος] See above c. 23.
21. Μωϋσῆς] If this reading is
kept, the infinitive εἶναι must be
understood with θέμις indeclinable.

ἐλθὸν ἐπὶ τὴν παρθένον καὶ ἐπισκιάσαν, οὐ διὰ συνουσίας ἀλλὰ διὰ δυνάμεως ἐγκύμονα κατέστησε. 7. τὸ δὲ Ἰησοῦς, ὄνομα τῇ ἑβραΐδι φωνῇ, σωτὴρ τῇ ἑλληνίδι διαλέκτῳ δηλοῖ. 8. ὅθεν καὶ ὁ ἄγγελος πρὸς τὴν παρ-
5 θένον εἶπε· Καὶ καλέσεις τὸ ὄνομα αὐτοῦ Ἰησοῦν· αὐτὸς γὰρ σώσει τὸν λαὸν αὐτοῦ ἀπὸ τῶν ἁμαρτιῶν αὐτῶν. 9. ὅτι δὲ οὐδενὶ ἄλλῳ θεοφοροῦνται οἱ προφητεύοντες εἰ μὴ λόγῳ θείῳ, καὶ ὑμεῖς, ὡς ὑπολαμβάνω, φήσετε.

34. 1. "Ὅπου δὲ καὶ τῆς γῆς γεννᾶσθαι ἔμελλεν, ὡς
10 προεῖπεν ἕτερος προφήτης ὁ Μιχαίας, ἀκούσατε. ἔφη δὲ οὕτως· Καὶ σὺ Βηθλεέμ, γῆ Ἰούδα, οὐδαμῶς ἐλαχίστη εἶ ἐν τοῖς ἡγεμόσιν Ἰούδα· ἐκ σοῦ γὰρ ἐξελεύσεται ἡγούμενος, ὅστις ποιμανεῖ τὸν λαόν μου. 2. κώμη δέ τίς ἐστιν ἐν τῇ χώρᾳ Ἰουδαίων, ἀπέχουσα σταδίους τριάκοντα
15 πέντε Ἱεροσολύμων, ἐν ᾗ ἐγεννήθη Ἰησοῦς Χριστός, ὡς καὶ μαθεῖν δύνασθε ἐκ τῶν ἀπογραφῶν τῶν γενομένων ἐπὶ Κυρηνίου, τοῦ ὑμετέρου ἐν Ἰουδαίᾳ πρώτου γενομένου ἐπιτρόπου.

35. 1. Ὡς δὲ καὶ λήσειν ἔμελλε τοὺς ἄλλους ἀνθρώ-

The reference is to c. 32, 9, 10, where from the Mosaic passage it was inferred that the λόγος was the δύναμις of God (not that he was πρωτότοκος, so that the reading ὡς Μωϋσῆς is incorrect). There is no reference here to the passage of Isaiah, so that there is no need to accept the ingenious suggestion that ὡς ἧς (abbreviated for ἠσαΐας) was the original reading, and was changed into Μωσῆς.

2. τὸ δὲ Ἰησοῦς] Cf. ii 5 (6), 4.
8. λόγῳ θείῳ] In the broad sense of '*God's word*.'

34. *O. T. prophecy as to the place of Christ's birth.*

11. καὶ σὺ Βηθλεέμ] Cf. Mic. v 2; Matt. ii 6. The quotation follows so closely the interpretative form of St Matthew that it cannot be referred to any other source.

13. κώμη δέ τίς ἐστιν] Bethlehem is about five miles south of Jerusalem. Thirty-five stades is about four English miles.

16. ἀπογραφῶν] The ἀπογραφαί are the census returns, which would probably be preserved in the Roman archives.

17. Κυρηνίου] Quirinius was *legatus* of Syria (not *procurator* of Judaea, so that ἐπιτρόπου is not technically correct) in A.D. 6, but had held some post in Syria previously, perhaps B.C. 5–3 or earlier. Cf. Luke ii 2, and Ramsay, *Was Christ born at Bethlehem?*, where the whole subject, which bristles with chronological difficulties, is discussed. The πρώτου looks as if Justin read πρώτου (not πρώτη) ἡγεμονεύοντος in his text of St Luke.

35. *O. T. prophecies about Christ's sufferings.*

πους γεννηθεὶς ὁ Χριστὸς ἄχρις ἀνδρωθῇ, ὅπερ καὶ γέγονεν, ἀκούσατε τῶν προειρημένων εἰς τοῦτο. 2. ἔστι δὲ ταῦτα· Παιδίον ἐγεννήθη ἡμῖν, καὶ νεανίσκος ἡμῖν ἀπεδόθη, οὗ ἡ ἀρχὴ ἐπὶ τῶν ὤμων· μηνυτικὸν τῆς δυνάμεως τοῦ σταυροῦ, ᾧ προσέθηκε τοὺς ὤμους σταυρωθείς, ὡς 5 προϊόντος τοῦ λόγου σαφέστερον δειχθήσεται. 3. καὶ πάλιν ὁ αὐτὸς προφήτης Ἡσαΐας θεοφορούμενος τῷ πνεύματι τῷ προφητικῷ ἔφη· Ἐγὼ ἐξεπέτασα τὰς χεῖράς μου ἐπὶ λαὸν ἀπειθοῦντα καὶ ἀντιλέγοντα, ἐπὶ τοὺς πορευομένους ἐν ὁδῷ οὐ καλῇ. 4. Αἰτοῦσί με νῦν κρίσιν, καὶ 10 ἐγγίζειν θεῷ τολμῶσιν. 5. καὶ πάλιν ἐν ἄλλοις λόγοις δι' ἑτέρου προφήτου λέγει· Αὐτοὶ ὤρυξάν μου πόδας καὶ χεῖρας, καὶ ἔβαλον κλῆρον ἐπὶ τὸν ἱματισμόν μου. 6. καὶ ὁ μὲν Δαυὶδ ὁ βασιλεὺς καὶ προφήτης, ὁ εἰπὼν ταῦτα, οὐδὲν τούτων ἔπαθεν· Ἰησοῦς δὲ Χριστὸς ἐξετάθη 15 τὰς χεῖρας, σταυρωθεὶς ὑπὸ τῶν Ἰουδαίων ἀντιλεγόντων αὐτῷ καὶ φασκόντων μὴ εἶναι αὐτὸν Χριστόν· καὶ γάρ, ὡς εἶπεν ὁ προφήτης, διασύροντες αὐτὸν ἐκάθισαν ἐπὶ βήματος καὶ εἶπον· Κρῖνον ἡμῖν. 7. τὸ δὲ Ὤρυξάν

14 Δαυὶδ edd δᾱδ A

1. ἄχρις ἀνδρωθῇ] 'until He had become a man,' i.e. up to His Crucifixion; not up to His Baptism, for the account of the Crucifixion follows immediately. Ἄχρις ἀνδρωθῇ means 'up to manhood and into it.' It is somewhat strange, however, that the suggestion of λήσειν is not worked out by quoting Isa. liii 1, 2, or similar passages.
3. παιδίον κτλ.] Cf. Isa. ix 6.
8. ἐγὼ ἐξεπέτασα κτλ.] Cf. Isa. lxv 2; lviii 2.
12. δι' ἑτέρου προφ. λέγει] sc. τὸ προφητικὸν πνεῦμα.
ib. αὐτοὶ κτλ.] Cf. Ps. xxi 17, 19 (xxii 16, 18).
14. ὁ μὲν Δαυίδ] Only the last quotation was from 'David.' It is a natural piece of carelessness.
15. ἐξετάθη τὰς χεῖρας] 'had His hands stretched out.'
18. διασύροντες αὐτ. ἐκάθισαν] 'in mockery they set Him on the judgment seat.' This detail is found not in the canonical Gospels but in a fragment of the 'Gospel of Peter' (iii) καὶ ἔλεγον Σύρωμεν τὸν υἱὸν τοῦ θεοῦ...καὶ πορφύραν αὐτὸν περιέβαλλον καὶ ἐκάθισαν αὐτὸν ἐπὶ καθέδραν κρίσεως λέγοντες Δικαίως κρῖνε, βασιλεῦ τοῦ Ἰσραήλ, where see Dr Swete's note, and his discussion on p. xxxiii f. Harnack contends that Justin used this gospel, Krüger (*Early Christ. Lit.* § 16) declares it to be 'quite improbable.' Justin's statement here might be a traditional account, or, if he used the 4th Gospel, might be an interpretation of ἐκάθισεν in John xix 13.

μου χεῖρας καὶ πόδας· ἐξήγησις τῶν ἐν τῷ σταυρῷ παγέντων ἐν ταῖς χερσὶ καὶ τοῖς ποσὶν αὐτοῦ ἥλων ἦν. 8. καὶ μετὰ τὸ σταυρῶσαι αὐτὸν ἔβαλον κλῆρον ἐπὶ τὸν ἱματισμὸν αὐτοῦ, καὶ ἐμερίσαντο ἑαυτοῖς οἱ σταυρώσαντες αὐτόν. 9. καὶ ταῦτα ὅτι γέγονε, δύνασθε μαθεῖν ἐκ τῶν ἐπὶ Ποντίου Πιλάτου γενομένων ἄκτων. 10. καὶ ὅτι ῥητῶς καθεσθησόμενος ἐπὶ πῶλον ὄνου καὶ εἰσελευσόμενος εἰς τὰ Ἱεροσόλυμα προεπεφήτευτο, ἑτέρου προφήτου τοῦ Σοφονίου τὰς τῆς προφητείας λέξεις ἐροῦμεν. 11. εἰσὶ δὲ αὗται· Χαῖρε σφόδρα, θύγατερ Σιών, κήρυσσε, θύγατερ Ἰερουσαλήμ· ἰδοὺ ὁ βασιλεύς σου ἔρχεταί σοι πρᾶος, ἐπιβεβηκὼς ἐπὶ ὄνον καὶ πῶλον υἱὸν ὑποζυγίου.

36. 1. Ὅταν δὲ τὰς λέξεις τῶν προφητῶν λεγομένας ὡς ἀπὸ προσώπου ἀκούητε, μὴ ἀπ' αὐτῶν τῶν ἐμπεπνευσμένων λέγεσθαι νομίσητε, ἀλλ' ἀπὸ τοῦ κινοῦντος αὐτοὺς θείου λόγου. 2. ποτὲ μὲν γὰρ ὡς προαγγελτικῶς τὰ μέλλοντα γενήσεσθαι λέγει, ποτὲ δὲ ὡς ἀπὸ προσώπου τοῦ δεσπότου πάντων καὶ πατρὸς θεοῦ φθέγγεται, ποτὲ δὲ ὡς ἀπὸ προσώπου τοῦ Χριστοῦ, ποτὲ δὲ ὡς ἀπὸ προσώπου

---

8 προεπεφήτευτο Thalemann προεφήτευτο A

1. ἐξήγησις] Cf. Matt. xxvii 35 and parallel passages.
6. ἄκτων] The *Acta* of Pontius Pilate (referred to also in c. 48, 3) would be an official document, probably not seen by Justin, but supposed by him to be in the official archives. It has nothing to do with the apocryphal *Acts of Pilate*. But see the discussion in Stanton *Gosp. as Hist. Docs.* i p. 102.
7. ῥητῶς] 'expressly.'
9. Σοφονίου] The quotation is not from Zephaniah but from Zech. ix 9. Cf. Matt. xxi 5. It is a slip of memory, and the same quotation is rightly ascribed to Zechariah in *Tryph.* 53.
36. *Inspired prophecies are given in different ways. Sometimes the Spirit prophesies in person, sometimes as in God's person, or Christ's, or man's. The Jews failed to recognize this.*

A parenthetic chapter to explain that, though prophecies may differ in the manner of their presentation, they are all the work of the same Spirit, here called ὁ θεῖος λόγος. See *Introd.*, p. xxviii.
14. ὡς ἀπὸ προσώπου] 'as in the person of someone.'
16. προαγγελτικῶς] i.e. prophetic declarations of the Spirit Himself. Cf. c. 39.
17. ἀπὸ προσ. τοῦ θεοῦ] cc. 37, 44.
19. ἀ. π. τ. Χριστοῦ] cc. 38, 49.
ib. ἀ. π. λαῶν] cc. 47, 53.

λαῶν ἀποκρινομένων τῷ κυρίῳ ἢ τῷ πατρὶ αὐτοῦ· ὁποῖον καὶ ἐπὶ τῶν παρ' ὑμῖν συγγραφέων ἰδεῖν ἔστιν, ἕνα μὲν τὸν τὰ πάντα συγγράφοντα ὄντα, πρόσωπα δὲ τὰ διαλεγόμενα παραφέροντα. 3. ὅπερ μὴ νοήσαντες οἱ ἔχοντες τὰς βίβλους τῶν προφητῶν Ἰουδαῖοι οὐκ ἐγνώρισαν οὐδὲ 5 παραγενόμενον τὸν Χριστόν, ἀλλὰ καὶ ἡμᾶς τοὺς λέγοντας παραγεγενῆσθαι αὐτὸν καί, ὡς προεκεκήρυκτο, ἀποδεικνύντας ἐσταυρῶσθαι ὑπ' αὐτῶν μισοῦσιν.

37. 1. Ἵνα δὲ καὶ τοῦτο ὑμῖν φανερὸν γένηται, ἀπὸ προσώπου τοῦ πατρὸς ἐλέχθησαν διὰ Ἡσαΐου τοῦ προ- 10 ειρημένου προφήτου οἵδε οἱ λόγοι· "Ἔγνω βοῦς τὸν κτησάμενον καὶ ὄνος τὴν φάτνην τοῦ κυρίου αὐτοῦ, Ἰσραὴλ δέ με οὐκ ἔγνω καὶ ὁ λαός μου οὐ συνῆκεν. 2. Οὐαὶ ἔθνος ἁμαρτωλόν, λαὸς πλήρης ἁμαρτιῶν, σπέρμα πονηρόν, υἱοὶ ἄνομοι· ἐγκατελίπετε τὸν κύριον." 3. καὶ πάλιν ἀλλα- 15 χοῦ, ὅταν λέγῃ ὁ αὐτὸς προφήτης ὁμοίως ἀπὸ τοῦ πατρός· "Ποῖόν μοι οἶκον οἰκοδομήσετε; λέγει κύριος. 4. ὁ οὐρανός μοι θρόνος, καὶ ἡ γῆ ὑποπόδιον τῶν ποδῶν μου." 5. καὶ πάλιν ἀλλαχοῦ· "Τὰς νουμηνίας ὑμῶν καὶ τὰ σάββατα μισεῖ ἡ ψυχή μου, καὶ μεγάλην ἡμέραν νηστείας 20 καὶ ἀργίαν οὐκ ἀνέχομαι· οὐδ', ἂν ἔρχησθε ὀφθῆναί μοι, εἰσακούσομαι ὑμῶν. 6. πλήρεις αἵματος αἱ χεῖρες ὑμῶν. 7. κἂν φέρητε σεμίδαλιν, θυμίαμα, βδέλυγμά

5 οὐδὲ Thirlb οὔτε A ‖ 16 ὁμοίως ἀπὸ τοῦ πατρός A ὁμοίως ἀπὸ προσώπου τοῦ πατρός Otto Krüger

2. ἕνα μὲν κτλ.] 'The composer of the whole work is one man, but he brings forward characters conversing.'
5. οὐδὲ παραγενόμενον] 'not even after His advent.'
8. μισοῦσιν] Cf. c. 31, 5.
37. *Instances of prophecies spoken by the Logos through a prophet as in the person of God.*
11. ἔγνω κτλ.] Cf. Isaiah i 3, 4.
16. ἀπὸ τοῦ πατρός] The change which Otto suggests is an obvious one, and corruption would have been easy from the homoioteleuton προσώπου τοῦ. But it is not absolutely certain that Justin might not have used ἀπὸ as = ἀπὸ προσώπου, after his first use of ἀπὸ προσώπου in the beginning of the chapter.
17. ποῖον κτλ.] Cf. Isaiah lxvi 1.
19. τὰς νουμηνίας κτλ.] Cf. Isaiah i. 11—15, lviii. 6, 7. Apparently a quotation from memory, in which two passages are combined.
23. σεμίδαλιν] 'fine wheaten flour.'

μοί ἐστι· στέαρ ἀρνῶν καὶ αἷμα ταύρων οὐ βούλομαι. 8. τίς γὰρ ἐξεζήτησε ταῦτα ἐκ τῶν χειρῶν ὑμῶν; ἀλλὰ διάλυε πάντα σύνδεσμον ἀδικίας, διάσπα στραγγαλιὰς βιαίων συναλλαγμάτων, ἄστεγον καὶ γυμνὸν σκέπε, διά-
5 θρυπτε πεινῶντι τὸν ἄρτον σου. 9. ὁποῖα μὲν οὖν ἐστι καὶ τὰ διδασκόμενα διὰ τῶν προφητῶν ἀπὸ τοῦ θεοῦ, νοεῖν δύνασθε.

38. 1. Ὅταν δὲ ἀπὸ προσώπου τοῦ Χριστοῦ λέγῃ τὸ προφητικὸν πνεῦμα, οὕτως φθέγγεται· "Ἐγὼ ἐξεπέτασα
10 τὰς χεῖράς μου ἐπὶ λαὸν ἀπειθοῦντα καὶ ἀντιλέγοντα, ἐπὶ τοὺς πορευομένους ἐν ὁδῷ οὐ καλῇ." 2. καὶ πάλιν· "Τὸν νῶτόν μου τέθεικα εἰς μάστιγας καὶ τὰς σιαγόνας μου εἰς ῥαπίσματα, τὸ δὲ πρόσωπόν μου οὐκ ἀπέστρεψα ἀπὸ αἰσχύνης ἐμπτυσμάτων. 3. καὶ ὁ κύριος βοηθός μου
15 ἐγένετο· διὰ τοῦτο οὐκ ἐνετράπην, ἀλλ' ἔθηκα τὸ πρόσ-ωπόν μου ὡς στερεὰν πέτραν, καὶ ἔγνων ὅτι οὐ μὴ αἰσχυνθῶ, ὅτι ἐγγίζει ὁ δικαιώσας με." 4. καὶ πάλιν ὅταν λέγῃ· "Αὐτοὶ ἔβαλον κλῆρον ἐπὶ τὸν ἱματισμόν μου, καὶ ὤρυξάν μου πόδας καὶ χεῖρας. 5. Ἐγὼ δὲ ἐκοιμήθην
20 καὶ ὕπνωσα, καὶ ἀνέστην, ὅτι κύριος ἀντελάβετό μου." 6. καὶ πάλιν ὅταν λέγῃ· "Ἐλάλησαν ἐν χείλεσιν, ἐκί-νησαν κεφαλὴν λέγοντες· Ῥυσάσθω ἑαυτόν." 7. ἅτινα πάντα ὅτι γέγονεν ὑπὸ τῶν Ἰουδαίων τῷ Χριστῷ, μαθεῖν δύνασθε. 8. σταυρωθέντος γὰρ αὐτοῦ ἐξέστρεφον τὰ

6 ἀπὸ τοῦ θεοῦ A ἀπὸ προσώπου τοῦ θεοῦ Otto Krüger ‖ 23 ὅτι γέγονεν Otto om ὅτι A γεγονέναι Grab

3. στραγγαλιάς] a late form of στραγγαλίς 'a knot,' 'the knots of violent dealings.'
6. ἀπὸ τοῦ θεοῦ] See note above.
38. *Prophecies spoken as in Christ's person.*
9. ἐγὼ κτλ.] Isaiah lxv. 2.
11. τὸν νῶτον κτλ.] Isaiah l. 6—8.

18. αὐτοὶ κτλ.] Ps. xxi. 19, 17 (xxii 18, 16).
19. ἐγὼ δὲ κτλ.] Ps. iii 6 (5).
21. ἐλάλησαν κτλ.] Ps. xxi 8, 9 (xxii 7, 8).
22. ἅτινα πάντα κτλ.] Cf. Matt. xxvii. 39—43.
23. μαθεῖν δύνασθε] Presumably he means from the *Acta* of Pilate.
24. ἐξέστρεφον] 'they twisted.'

χείλη καὶ ἐκίνουν τὰς κεφαλὰς λέγοντες· Ὁ νεκροὺς ἀνεγείρας, ῥυσάσθω ἑαυτόν.

39. 1. Ὅταν δὲ ὡς προφητεῦον τὰ μέλλοντα γίνεσθαι λαλῇ τὸ προφητικὸν πνεῦμα, οὕτως λέγει· Ἐκ γὰρ Σιὼν ἐξελεύσεται νόμος καὶ λόγος κυρίου ἐξ Ἱερουσαλήμ, καὶ κρινεῖ ἀνὰ μέσον ἐθνῶν καὶ ἐλέγξει λαὸν πολύν· καὶ συγκόψουσι τὰς μαχαίρας αὐτῶν εἰς ἄροτρα καὶ τὰς ζιβύνας αὐτῶν εἰς δρέπανα, καὶ οὐ μὴ λήψονται ἔθνος ἐπὶ ἔθνος μάχαιραν καὶ οὐ μὴ μάθωσιν ἔτι πολεμεῖν. 2. καὶ ὅτι οὕτως γέγονε, πεισθῆναι δύνασθε. 3. ἀπὸ γὰρ Ἱερουσαλὴμ ἄνδρες δεκαδύο τὸν ἀριθμὸν ἐξῆλθον εἰς τὸν κόσμον, καὶ οὗτοι ἰδιῶται, λαλεῖν μὴ δυνάμενοι, διὰ δὲ θεοῦ δυνάμεως ἐμήνυσαν παντὶ γένει ἀνθρώπων ὡς ἀπεστάλησαν ὑπὸ τοῦ Χριστοῦ διδάξαι πάντας τὸν τοῦ θεοῦ λόγον· καὶ οἱ πάλαι ἀλληλοφόνται οὐ μόνον οὐ πολεμοῦμεν τοὺς ἐχθρούς, ἀλλ', ὑπὲρ τοῦ μηδὲ ψεύδεσθαι μηδ' ἐξαπατῆσαι τοὺς ἐξετάζοντας, ἡδέως ὁμολογοῦντες τὸν Χριστὸν ἀποθνήσκομεν. 4. δυνατὸν γὰρ ἦν τὸ λεγόμενον

Ἡ γλῶσσ' ὀμώμοκεν, ἡ δὲ φρὴν ἀνώμοτος

19 γλῶσσ' edd. γλῶσσα A

39. *A prophecy of the future, spoken directly by the Spirit Himself, and fulfilled in the spread and influence of Christianity.*

4. ἐκ γὰρ Σιὼν κτλ.] Cf. Isaiah ii 3, 4; Mic. iv 2.

7. ζιβύνας] 'spears.' The ordinary form is σιβύνη.

11. ἄνδρες δεκαδύο] The number is used as an official title for the Twelve, who were the original heads of the Church. The omission of St Paul's name is therefore quite natural; some have explained it by the fact that Justin chiefly used the gospel record; some have supposed that St Paul is tacitly included in the Twelve in place of St James who was killed by Herod; Veil suggests that the early Church was unable to understand the Pauline theology and made little of its author. But these surmises are unnecessary in the case of Justin.

12. ἰδιῶται] Cf. Acts iv 13.

13. ἀπεστάλησαν...πάντας] Cf. Matt. xxviii 19.

14. τὸν τοῦ θεοῦ λόγον] 'The word of God,' meaning the gospel. Cf. Acts vi 2.

15. οἱ πάλαι κτλ.] Cf. c. 14, 2, 3.

16. ὑπὲρ τοῦ μηδὲ κτλ.] 'in order not to utter falsehood or deceive our inquisitors.'

19. ἡ γλῶσσ' ὀμώμοκεν κτλ.] The quotation is from Eur. *Hipp.* 612 (of course the last syllable of ὀμώμοκεν ought to be elided) and the sentiment had already been burlesqued in Aristoph. *Ran.* 101, 1471; *Thesmoph.* 275.

ποιεῖν ἡμᾶς εἰς τοῦτο. 5. γελοῖον ἦν δὴ πρᾶγμα, ὑμῖν μὲν τοὺς συντιθεμένους καὶ καταλεγομένους στρατιώτας καὶ πρὸ τῆς ἑαυτῶν ζωῆς καὶ γονέων καὶ πατρίδος καὶ πάντων τῶν οἰκείων τὴν ὑμετέραν ἀσπάζεσθαι ὁμολογίαν, μηδὲν ἄφθαρτον δυναμένων ὑμῶν αὐτοῖς παρασχεῖν, ἡμᾶς δέ, ἀφθαρσίας ἐρῶντας, μὴ πάνθ᾽ ὑπομεῖναι ὑπὲρ τοῦ τὰ ποθούμενα παρὰ τοῦ δυναμένου δοῦναι λαβεῖν.

40. 1. Ἀκούσατε δὲ πῶς καὶ περὶ τῶν κηρυξάντων τὴν διδαχὴν αὐτοῦ καὶ μηνυσάντων τὴν ἐπιφάνειαν προερρέθη, τοῦ προειρημένου προφήτου καὶ βασιλέως οὕτως εἰπόντος διὰ τοῦ προφητικοῦ πνεύματος· Ἡμέρα τῇ ἡμέρᾳ ἐρεύγεται ῥῆμα, καὶ νὺξ τῇ νυκτὶ ἀναγγέλλει γνῶσιν. 2. οὐκ εἰσὶ λαλιαὶ οὐδὲ λόγοι, ὧν οὐχὶ ἀκούονται αἱ φωναὶ αὐτῶν. 3. εἰς πᾶσαν τὴν γῆν ἐξῆλθεν ὁ φθόγγος αὐτῶν καὶ εἰς τὰ πέρατα τῆς οἰκουμένης τὰ ῥήματα αὐτῶν. 4. ἐν τῷ ἡλίῳ ἔθετο τὸ σκήνωμα αὐτοῦ, καὶ αὐτός, ὡς νυμφίος ἐκπορευόμενος ἐκ παστοῦ αὐτοῦ, ἀγαλλιάσεται ὡς γίγας δραμεῖν ὁδόν. 5. πρὸς τούτοις δὲ καὶ λόγων ἑτέρων τῶν προφητευθέντων δι᾽ αὐτοῦ τοῦ Δαυὶδ καλῶς ἔχον καὶ οἰκείως ἐπιμνησθῆναι, λελογίσμεθα, ἐξ ὧν μαθεῖν ὑμῖν πάρεστι πῶς προτρέπεται ζῆν τοὺς ἀνθρώπους τὸ προφητικὸν πνεῦμα, 6. καὶ πῶς μηνύει τὴν γεγενη-

1 ἦν δὴ Otto ἤδη A

2. τοὺς συντιθεμένους κτλ.] 'covenanted and enrolled.' The reference is to the military *sacramentum*. Cf. Aul. Gell. xvi 4 for the formula. Suet. *Calig.* 15 says Gaius added to the oath 'neque me liberosque meos cariores habebo quam Gaium habeo et sorores eius.' Veil sees here a reminiscence of Socrates' argument in Plat. *Ap.* 28 B, where Socrates draws an analogy between his loyalty to earthly generals and his loyalty to his divine commander.

3. πατρίδος] The word is unexpected and may be wrong. Ashton suggests παίδων.

40. *O.T. prophecies of the preaching of the Apostles. Also a general forecast of certain Christian facts.*

10. τοῦ προειρημένου) in c. 35, 6.

11. ἡμέρα κτλ.] Cf. Ps. xviii 3 (xix 2) ff., Rom. x 18.

13. οὐκ εἰσὶ λαλιαὶ κτλ.] 'There are no languages nor words, in which their voices are not heard.'

17. παστοῦ] 'bridal chamber.'
ib. ὡς γίγας] Similarly quoted in *Tryph.* 64. In *Ap.* i 54, 9 it is ἰσχυρὸς ὡς γίγας. Emendation is uncalled for.

μένην Ἡρώδου τοῦ βασιλέως Ἰουδαίων καὶ αὐτῶν Ἰουδαίων καὶ Πιλάτου τοῦ ὑμετέρου παρ' αὐτοῖς γενομένου ἐπιτρόπου σὺν τοῖς αὐτοῦ στρατιώταις κατὰ τοῦ Χριστοῦ συνέλευσιν, 7. καὶ ὅτι πιστεύεσθαι ἔμελλεν ὑπὸ τῶν ἐκ παντὸς γένους ἀνθρώπων, καὶ ὅτι αὐτὸν υἱὸν καλεῖ ὁ 5 θεὸς καὶ ὑποτάσσειν αὐτῷ πάντας ἐχθροὺς ἐπήγγελται, καὶ πῶς οἱ δαίμονες, ὅσον ἐπ' αὐτοῖς, τήν τε τοῦ πατρὸς πάντων καὶ δεσπότου θεοῦ καὶ τὴν αὐτοῦ τοῦ Χριστοῦ ἐξουσίαν φυγεῖν πειρῶνται, καὶ ὡς εἰς μετάνοιαν καλεῖ πάντας ὁ θεὸς πρὶν ἐλθεῖν τὴν ἡμέραν τῆς κρίσεως. 10
8. εἴρηνται δὲ οὕτως· Μακάριος ἀνὴρ ὃς οὐκ ἐπορεύθη ἐν βουλῇ ἀσεβῶν καὶ ἐν ὁδῷ ἁμαρτωλῶν οὐκ ἔστη καὶ ἐπὶ καθέδραν λοιμῶν οὐκ ἐκάθισεν, ἀλλ' ἢ ἐν τῷ νόμῳ κυρίου τὸ θέλημα αὐτοῦ, καὶ ἐν τῷ νόμῳ αὐτοῦ μελετήσει ἡμέρας καὶ νυκτός. 9. καὶ ἔσται ὡς τὸ ξύλον τὸ πεφυτευ- 15 μένον παρὰ τὰς διεξόδους τῶν ὑδάτων, ὃ τὸν καρπὸν αὐτοῦ δώσει ἐν καιρῷ αὐτοῦ, καὶ τὸ φύλλον αὐτοῦ οὐκ ἀπορρυήσεται, καὶ πάντα ὅσα ἂν ποιῇ κατευοδωθήσεται. 10. οὐχ οὕτως οἱ ἀσεβεῖς, οὐχ οὕτως, ἀλλ' ἢ ὡσεὶ χνοῦς, ὃν ἐκρίπτει ὁ ἄνεμος ἀπὸ προσώπου τῆς γῆς· διὰ τοῦτο 20 οὐκ ἀναστήσονται ἀσεβεῖς ἐν κρίσει οὐδὲ ἁμαρτωλοὶ ἐν βουλῇ δικαίων, ὅτι γινώσκει κύριος ὁδὸν δικαίων, καὶ ὁδὸς ἀσεβῶν ἀπολεῖται. 11. Ἵνα τί ἐφρύαξαν ἔθνη, καὶ

3. ἐπιτρόπου] Cf. c. 13, 3.
4. συνέλευσιν] Cf. Acts iv 27.
ib. τῶν ἐκ παντὸς γένους] Cf. c. 1.
6. ἐπήγγελται] 'has promised.'
7. οἱ δαίμονες] Presumably Justin reads an allusion to them in the ἔθνη, λαοί, βασιλεῖς and ἄρχοντες of the following quotation.
11. μακάριος κτλ.] Cf. Ps. i, ii, which are treated as one Psalm. Cf. Acts xiii 33 and Tischendorf's critical note.
13. λοιμῶν] from the adjective λοιμός = 'pestilent.'

ib. ἀλλ' ἤ] literally 'except'; Liddell and Scott derive it from ἄλλο ἤ, the accent of ἄλλο having been lost. It comes to mean simply 'but,' as here and in § 10 ἀλλ' ἢ ὡσεὶ χνοῦς.
18. κατευοδωθήσεται] 'shall be prospered.'
19. χνοῦς] 'foam,' the 'fine down' on flower or fruit (but also 'dust,' see L. and Sc.).
23. ἐφρύαξαν] Φρυάττομαι is a classical word meaning 'to neigh, to be wanton.' The active is found only in LXX and N.T.

λαοὶ ἐμελέτησαν καινά; παρέστησαν οἱ βασιλεῖς τῆς γῆς, καὶ οἱ ἄρχοντες συνήχθησαν ἐπὶ τὸ αὐτὸ κατὰ τοῦ κυρίου καὶ κατὰ τοῦ χριστοῦ αὐτοῦ, λέγοντες· Διαρρήξωμεν τοὺς δεσμοὺς αὐτῶν καὶ ἀπορρίψωμεν ἀφ᾽ ἡμῶν τὸν ζυγὸν
5 αὐτῶν. 12. ὁ κατοικῶν ἐν οὐρανοῖς ἐκγελάσεται αὐτούς, καὶ ὁ κύριος ἐκμυκτηριεῖ αὐτούς· τότε λαλήσει πρὸς αὐτοὺς ἐν ὀργῇ αὐτοῦ, καὶ ἐν τῷ θυμῷ αὐτοῦ ταράξει αὐτούς. 13. ἐγὼ δὲ κατεστάθην βασιλεὺς ὑπ᾽ αὐτοῦ ἐπὶ Σιὼν ὄρος τὸ ἅγιον αὐτοῦ, διαγγέλλων τὸ πρόσταγμα
10 κυρίου. 14. κύριος εἶπε πρός με· Υἱός μου εἶ σύ, ἐγὼ σήμερον γεγέννηκά σε. 15. αἴτησαι παρ᾽ ἐμοῦ, καὶ δώσω σοι ἔθνη τὴν κληρονομίαν σου, καὶ τὴν κατάσχεσίν σου τὰ πέρατα τῆς γῆς· ποιμανεῖς αὐτοὺς ἐν ῥάβδῳ σιδηρᾷ, ὡς σκεύη κεραμέως συντρίψεις αὐτούς. 16. καὶ
15 νῦν, βασιλεῖς, σύνετε, παιδεύθητε, πάντες οἱ κρίνοντες τὴν γῆν. 17. δουλεύσατε τῷ κυρίῳ ἐν φόβῳ, καὶ ἀγαλλιᾶσθε αὐτῷ ἐν τρόμῳ. 18. δράξασθε παιδείας, μή ποτε ὀργισθῇ κύριος, καὶ ἀπολεῖσθε ἐξ ὁδοῦ δικαίας, ὅταν ἐκκαυθῇ ἐν τάχει ὁ θυμὸς αὐτοῦ. 19. μακάριοι πάντες
20 οἱ πεποιθότες ἐπ᾽ αὐτόν.

41. 1. Καὶ πάλιν δι᾽ ἄλλης προφητείας μηνύον τὸ προφητικὸν πνεῦμα δι᾽ αὐτοῦ Δαυΐδ, ὅτι μετὰ τὸ σταυρωθῆναι βασιλεύσει ὁ Χριστός, οὕτως εἶπεν· Ἄσατε τῷ κυρίῳ πᾶσα ἡ γῆ, καὶ ἀναγγείλατε ἡμέραν ἐξ ἡμέρας τὸ
25 σωτήριον αὐτοῦ· ὅτι μέγας κύριος καὶ αἰνετὸς σφόδρα,

---

1. καινά] The accepted reading is κενά, but eight MSS of the LXX have καινά.

41. *An O. T. prophecy of the reign of Christ.*

23. ᾄσατε κτλ.] Cf. 1 Chron. xvi 23, 25–31 and Ps. xcv (xcvi) 1, 2. 4–10. The psalm is quoted fully in *Tryph.* 73. Justin's text exhibits many variations from the text of 1 Chronicles; thus he has εἴδωλα δαιμονίων for εἴδωλα (the LXX version of the psalm gives δαιμόνια in verse 5), τῷ πατρὶ τῶν αἰώνων for αἱ πατριαὶ τῶν ἐθνῶν, χάριν for δῶρα, and ἀπὸ τοῦ ξύλου is added. Veil considers these differences, especially the last, too significant to be slips of memory, and surmises that an edition of this psalm was used, with these alterations, in Christian worship. It is worth remarking that, according to Eus. *H. E.* iv 18, Justin edited a ψάλτης.

φοβερὸς ὑπὲρ πάντας τοὺς θεούς· ὅτι πάντες οἱ θεοὶ τῶν ἐθνῶν εἴδωλα δαιμονίων εἰσίν, ὁ δὲ θεὸς τοὺς οὐρανοὺς ἐποίησε. 2. δόξα καὶ αἶνος κατὰ πρόσωπον αὐτοῦ, καὶ ἰσχὺς καὶ καύχημα ἐν τόπῳ ἁγιάσματος αὐτοῦ· δότε τῷ κυρίῳ, τῷ πατρὶ τῶν αἰώνων, δόξαν. 3. λάβετε χάριν καὶ εἰσέλθετε κατὰ πρόσωπον αὐτοῦ καὶ προσκυνήσατε ἐν αὐλαῖς ἁγίαις αὐτοῦ· φοβηθήτω ἀπὸ προσώπου αὐτοῦ πᾶσα ἡ γῆ καὶ κατορθωθήτω καὶ μὴ σαλευθήτω. 4. εὐφρανθήτωσαν ἐν τοῖς ἔθνεσιν· ὁ κύριος ἐβασίλευσεν ἀπὸ τοῦ ξύλου.

42. 1. Ὅταν δὲ τὸ προφητικὸν πνεῦμα τὰ μέλλοντα γίνεσθαι ὡς ἤδη γενόμενα λέγῃ, ὡς καὶ ἐν τοῖς προειρημένοις δοξάσαι ἐστίν, ὅπως ἀπολογίαν μὴ παράσχῃ τοῖς ἐντυγχάνουσιν, καὶ τοῦτο διασαφήσομεν. 2. τὰ πάντως ἐγνωσμένα γενησόμενα προλέγει ὡς ἤδη γενόμενα· ὅτι δὲ οὕτως δεῖ ἐκδέχεσθαι, ἐνατενίσατε τῷ νοῒ τοῖς λεγομένοις. 3. Δαυῒδ ἔτεσι χιλίοις καὶ πεντακοσίοις πρὶν ἢ Χριστὸν ἄνθρωπον γενόμενον σταυρωθῆναι τὰ προειρημένα ἔφη, καὶ οὐδεὶς τῶν πρὸ ἐκείνου γενομένων σταυρωθεὶς εὐφροσύνην παρέσχε τοῖς ἔθνεσιν, ἀλλ' οὐδὲ τῶν μετ' ἐκεῖνον. 4. ὁ καθ' ἡμᾶς δὲ Ἰησοῦς Χριστὸς σταυρωθεὶς καὶ ἀποθανὼν

7. φοβηθήτω κτλ.] 'let the whole earth fear before His face and be set right and not be moved.' The verse following in the original, which describes the joy of nature at God's advent, is here omitted; thus the idea becomes ethical, a summons to repentance (κατορθωθήτω) as a condition of not being disturbed.

42. *You note that in some of these passages the future is spoken of in the past tense; but the fulfilment comes only in Christ.* A parenthesis to explain the wording of some prophecies.

13. ἀπολογίαν] 'an excuse' for misunderstanding and therefore disbelieving in Christian teaching. The idea is the same as in c. 3, 4.

15. ἐγνωσμένα γενησόμενα] going together, '*known as future.*'

16. ἐνατενίσατε] '*look carefully.*'

17. ἔτεσι κτλ.] David's reign may roughly be dated 1000 B.C. There may be some mistake in the figures of Justin's text, and some emend πεντακοσίοις to πεντήκοντα. But Justin's chronology is very loose.

19. εὐφροσύνην] referring back to εὐφρανθήτωσαν in c. 41, 4.

20. ὁ καθ' ἡμᾶς] *Noster* (Otto). *In unserer Zeit* (Veil). The latter seems more natural; it is a careless chronological expression, but quite in keeping with Justin's manner.

ἀνέστη, καὶ ἐβασίλευσεν ἀνελθὼν εἰς οὐρανόν, καὶ ἐπὶ τοῖς παρ' αὐτοῦ διὰ τῶν ἀποστόλων ἐν τοῖς πᾶσιν ἔθνεσι κηρυχθεῖσιν εὐφροσύνη ἐστὶ προσδοκώντων τὴν κατηγγελμένην ὑπ' αὐτοῦ ἀφθαρσίαν.

43. 1. Ὅπως δὲ μή τινες ἐκ τῶν προλελεγμένων ὑφ' ἡμῶν δοξάσωσι καθ' εἱμαρμένης ἀνάγκην φάσκειν ἡμᾶς τὰ γινόμενα γίνεσθαι, ἐκ τοῦ προειπεῖν προεγνωσμένα, καὶ τοῦτο διαλύσομεν. 2. τὰς τιμωρίας καὶ τὰς κολάσεις καὶ τὰς ἀγαθὰς ἀμοιβὰς κατ' ἀξίαν τῶν πράξεων ἑκάστου ἀποδίδοσθαι διὰ τῶν προφητῶν μαθόντες καὶ ἀληθὲς ἀποφαινόμεθα· ἐπεὶ εἰ μὴ τοῦτό ἐστιν, ἀλλὰ καθ' εἱμαρμένην πάντα γίνεται, οὔτε τὸ ἐφ' ἡμῖν ἐστιν ὅλως· εἰ γὰρ εἵμαρται τόνδε τινὰ ἀγαθὸν εἶναι καὶ τόνδε φαῦλον, οὔθ' οὗτος ἀπόδεκτος οὐδὲ ἐκεῖνος μεμπτέος. 3. καὶ αὖ εἰ μὴ προαιρέσει ἐλευθέρᾳ πρὸς τὸ φεύγειν τὰ αἰσχρὰ καὶ αἱρεῖσθαι τὰ καλὰ δύναμιν ἔχει τὸ ἀνθρώπειον γένος, ἀναίτιόν ἐστι τῶν ὁπωσδήποτε πραττομένων. 4. ἀλλ'

8 διαλύσομεν Otto διαλύομεν A

43. *Nor does Divine foreknowledge lessen human responsibility or do away with human free-will. We see men acting inconsistently, which is not compatible with the action of fate. And, if all actions were predestined, moral judgments would be a matter of mere convention, which view reason rejects as immoral. The consequences of actions are fated, but the actions themselves are free.*

Justin is led on from c. 42 (ἐκ τῶν προλελεγμένων) to anticipate and refute Fatalistic inferences from the belief in Divine foreknowledge. His arguments may be summed up as follows: (1) Fatalism means the renunciation of all human responsibility, and all moral judgments. (2) Men act inconsistently, which is scarcely possible except by the exercise of free-will. (3) Reason declares an essential distinction between right and wrong. (4) Ineluctable fate decrees the rewards and punishments of actions, not the actions themselves.—Thus Justin scarcely reconciles Divine foreknowledge with human free-will, but confines himself to refuting Fatalism.

7. προειπεῖν προεγνωσμένα] '*foretell things foreknown.*'

8. τιμωρίας...κολάσεις] According to Aristot. *Rhet.* i 10 τιμωρία is vindictive, κόλασις is corrective in idea.

10. μαθόντες καὶ κτλ.] '*We learn from the prophets and assert as true.*'

12. τὸ ἐφ' ἡμῖν] '*free choice.*'
ib. εἰ γὰρ εἵμαρται κτλ.] This is the first of the four arguments enumerated above.

ὅτι ἐλευθέρᾳ προαιρέσει καὶ κατορθοῖ καὶ σφάλλεται, οὕτως ἀποδείκνυμεν. 5. τὸν αὐτὸν ἄνθρωπον τῶν ἐναντίων τὴν μετέλευσιν ποιούμενον ὁρῶμεν. 6. εἰ δὲ εἵμαρτο ἢ φαῦλον ἢ σπουδαῖον εἶναι, οὐκ ἄν ποτε τῶν ἐναντίων δεκτικὸς ἦν καὶ πλειστάκις μετετίθετο· ἀλλ' οὐδ' οἱ μὲν ἦσαν σπουδαῖοι, οἱ δὲ φαῦλοι, ἐπεὶ τὴν εἱμαρμένην αἰτίαν ἀγαθῶν καὶ φαύλων καὶ ἐναντία ἑαυτῇ πράττουσαν ἀποφαινοίμεθα, ἢ ἐκεῖνο τὸ προειρημένον δόξαι ἀληθὲς εἶναι, ὅτι οὐδέν ἐστιν ἀρετὴ οὐδὲ κακία, ἀλλὰ δόξῃ μόνον ἢ ἀγαθὰ ἢ κακὰ νομίζεται· ἥπερ, ὡς δείκνυσιν ὁ ἀληθὴς λόγος, μεγίστη ἀσέβεια καὶ ἀδικία ἐστίν. 7. ἀλλ' εἱμαρμένην φαμὲν ἀπαράβατον ταύτην εἶναι, τοῖς τὰ καλὰ ἐκλεγομένοις τὰ ἄξια ἐπιτίμια, καὶ τοῖς ὁμοίως τὰ ἐναντία τὰ ἄξια ἐπίχειρα. 8. οὐ γὰρ ὥσπερ τὰ ἄλλα, οἷον δένδρα καὶ τετράποδα μηδὲν δυνάμενα προαιρέσει πράττειν, ἐποίησεν ὁ θεὸς τὸν ἄνθρωπον· οὐδὲ γὰρ ἦν ἄξιος ἀμοιβῆς ἢ ἐπαίνου, οὐκ ἀφ' ἑαυτοῦ ἑλόμενος τὸ ἀγαθόν, ἀλλὰ τοῦτο γενόμενος, οὐδ', εἰ κακὸς ὑπῆρχε, δικαίως

7 αἰτίαν ἀγαθῶν καὶ φαύλων Ashton Otto αἰτίαν φαύλων A ‖ 8 ἀποφαινοίμεθα Sylburg ἀποφαινόμεθα A ‖ 14 οὐ γὰρ ὥσπερ κτλ. A οὐχ ὥσπερ τἆλλα οἷον δένδρα τετράποδα μηδένα δυνάμενα προαιρέσει πράττειν ἐποίησεν ὁ θεὸς τὸν ἄνθρωπον· οὐδὲ γὰρ ἦν ἄξιος ἀμοιβῆς ἢ ἐπαίνου οὐκ ἐφ' ἑαυτῷ ἑλόμενος τὸ ἀγαθόν· ἀλλὰ τοῦτο γενόμενος εἰ δὴ κακῶς ὑπάρχει δικαίως κολάσεως ἐτύγχανεν οὐκ ἐφ' ἑαυτοῦ τοιοῦτος ὢν ἀλλ' οὐδὲ δυνάμενος εἶναι ἕτερον παρ' ὃ γεγόνει Sacr Parallel 99.

2. οὕτως ἀποδείκνυμεν] 'we prove as follows.' There follows the second argument, from the inconsistencies of human action.

3. μετέλευσιν] 'pursuit.'

4. οὐκ ἄν ποτε] This deduction is not logical; inconsistency might be predestined, as much as consistency. Δεκτικός = 'capable of,' Lat. capax.

8. ἀποφαινοίμεθα] 'we should have to affirm.' A conditional optative, like δόξαι, below.

ib. ἐκεῖνο τὸ προειρημένον] in c. 28, 4.

11. ὁ ἀληθὴς λόγος] The third argument, an appeal to reason.

12. ἀλλ' εἱμαρμένην κτλ.] The fourth argument.

14. ἐπίχειρα] 'reward,' usually of punishment, as here.

ib. οὐ γάρ] The text here, as quoted in the Sacra Parallela, is given in full in the critical note.

18. τοῦτο γενόμενος] 'having been born so,' i.e. ἀγαθός.

B. 5

κολάσεως ἐτύγχανεν, οὐκ ἀφ' ἑαυτοῦ τοιοῦτος ὤν, ἀλλ' οὐδὲν δυνάμενος εἶναι ἕτερον παρ' ὃ ἐγεγόνει.

44. 1. Ἐδίδαξε δὲ ἡμᾶς ταῦτα τὸ ἅγιον προφητικὸν πνεῦμα, διὰ Μωϋσέως φῆσαν τῷ πρώτῳ πλασθέντι ἀνθρώπῳ εἰρῆσθαι ὑπὸ τοῦ θεοῦ οὕτως· Ἰδοὺ πρὸ προσώπου σου τὸ ἀγαθὸν καὶ τὸ κακόν, ἔκλεξαι τὸ ἀγαθόν. 2. καὶ πάλιν διὰ Ἡσαΐου, τοῦ ἑτέρου προφήτου, ὡς ἀπὸ τοῦ πατρὸς τῶν ὅλων καὶ δεσπότου θεοῦ εἰς τοῦτο λεχθῆναι οὕτως· 3. Λούσασθε, καθαροὶ γένεσθε, ἀφέλετε τὰς πονηρίας ἀπὸ τῶν ψυχῶν ὑμῶν, μάθετε καλὸν ποιεῖν, κρίνατε ὀρφανῷ καὶ δικαιώσατε χήραν, καὶ δεῦτε καὶ διαλεχθῶμεν, λέγει κύριος· καὶ ἐὰν ὦσιν αἱ ἁμαρτίαι ὑμῶν ὡς φοινικοῦν, ὡσεὶ ἔριον λευκανῶ, καὶ ἐὰν ὦσιν ὡς κόκκινον, ὡς χιόνα λευκανῶ. 4. καὶ ἐὰν θέλητε καὶ εἰσακούσητέ μου, τὰ ἀγαθὰ τῆς γῆς φάγεσθε, ἐὰν δὲ μὴ εἰσακούσητέ μου, μάχαιρα ὑμᾶς κατέδεται· τὸ γὰρ στόμα κυρίου ἐλάλησε ταῦτα. 5. τὸ δὲ προειρημένον Μάχαιρα ὑμᾶς κατέδεται οὐ λέγει διὰ μαχαιρῶν φονευθήσεσθαι τοὺς παρακούσαντας, ἀλλ' ἡ μάχαιρα τοῦ θεοῦ ἐστι τὸ πῦρ, οὗ βορὰ γίνονται οἱ τὰ φαῦλα πράττειν αἱρούμενοι. 6. διὰ τοῦτο λέγει· Μάχαιρα ὑμᾶς κατέδεται· τὸ γὰρ στόμα κυρίου ἐλάλησεν. 7. εἰ δὲ καὶ περὶ τεμνούσης καὶ αὐτίκα ἀπαλλασσούσης μαχαίρας

4 Μωϋσέως (et infr Μωϋσέως...Μωϋσῆς) edd Μωσέως...Μωσῆς A ||
8 ἀπὸ τοῦ πατρὸς A ἀπὸ προσώπου τοῦ πατρὸς Otto

44. *Moses and Isaiah each assume the fact of free-will; as does Plato, who, like other Greek philosophers and poets, derived some of his ideas from the Old Testament. The demons have instigated the prohibition to read the books of prophecy. But we Christians read them and try to persuade you by their means.*

5. ἰδοὺ κτλ.] Cf. Deut. xxx 15, 19, but the command is not there addressed to Adam. Possibly Justin is confusing it with Gen. ii. 16, 17.

7. ὡς ἀπὸ τοῦ πατρός] For the reading cf. c. 37, 3 and note.
8. εἰς τοῦτο] 'with this object,' 'in this sense.'
9. λεχθῆναι] Justin has probably forgotten how his sentence began.
ib. λούσασθε κτλ.] Cf. Isaiah i 16—20.
20. τὸ πῦρ] So Clem. Alex. *Protrept.* 95 quotes the passage μάχαιρα ὑμᾶς καὶ πῦρ κατέδεται.
23. ἀπαλλασσούσης] According to Veil the sense is 'which cuts and

ἔλεγεν, οὐκ ἂν εἶπε Κατέδεται. 8. ὥστε καὶ Πλάτων
εἰπών· Αἰτία ἑλομένου, θεὸς δ' ἀναίτιος, παρὰ Μωϋσέως
τοῦ προφήτου λαβὼν εἶπε· πρεσβύτερος γὰρ Μωϋσῆς καὶ
πάντων τῶν ἐν Ἕλλησι συγγραφέων. 9. καὶ πάντα,
ὅσα περὶ ἀθανασίας ψυχῆς ἢ τιμωριῶν τῶν μετὰ θάνατον
ἢ θεωρίας οὐρανίων ἢ τῶν ὁμοίων δογμάτων καὶ φιλόσοφοι
καὶ ποιηταὶ ἔφασαν, παρὰ τῶν προφητῶν τὰς ἀφορμὰς λαβόντες καὶ νοῆσαι δεδύνηνται καὶ ἐξηγήσαντο. 10. ὅθεν,
παρὰ πᾶσι σπέρματα ἀληθείας δοκεῖ εἶναι· ἐλέγχονται δὲ
μὴ ἀκριβῶς νοήσαντες, ὅταν ἐναντία αὐτοὶ ἑαυτοῖς λέγωσιν. 11. ὥστε ὃ φαμεν, πεπροφητεῦσθαι τὰ μέλλοντα γίνεσθαι, οὐ διὰ τὸ εἱμαρμένης ἀνάγκῃ πράττεσθαι
λέγομεν· ἀλλὰ προγνώστου τοῦ θεοῦ ὄντος τῶν μελλόντων
ὑπὸ πάντων ἀνθρώπων πραχθήσεσθαι, καὶ δόγματος ὄντος
παρ' αὐτόν, κατ' ἀξίαν τῶν πράξεων ἕκαστον ἀμείψεσθαι

15 παρ' αὐτόν Otto παρ' αὐτῶν A fortasse παρ' αὐτοῦ

so alters life at once'; according to Maran '*which cuts and then at once lets go.*' The latter is far more natural. The contrast on either rendering is between the quick action of a μάχαιρα and the gradual process implied in κατέδεται.

1. Πλάτων] *Rep.* x 617 E, but without the δ'.

3. λαβὼν εἶπε] This theory had previously been suggested by the Jewish Peripatetic Aristobulus and Philo. In some moods Justin adopts the view of the Spermatic *Logos* existing among the heathen (e.g. ii 10, 2); but he seems unconscious of any inconsistency.

6. θεωρίας οὐρανίων] '*the contemplation of celestial things,*' with special reference to the myth in the *Phaedrus*.

14. δόγματος ὄντος κτλ.] A very awkward sentence. The usual interpretation is '*since it is God's decree, as He intends to reward... that His rewards should be equivalent to the merit of the deeds*'; though Veil suggests that μέλλοντα should go with ἕκαστον, '*each man that is to be.*' But the whole sentence, so taken, seems very unnatural. It may be simpler to read παρ' αὐτοῦ (instead of παρ' αὐτόν) going with what follows, and render '*since it is one of our tenets that each man shall receive from Him according to his deeds.*' The next clause might conceivably mean '*and (that each man shall) meet the things which proceed from himself*' (cf. 2 Cor. v 10), though I can find no parallel to such an accus. with ἀπαντᾶν; or '*that God's awards shall occur according to the merit of the deeds.*' For the absolute use of ἀπαντᾶν in this last rendering cp. Clem. Al. *Strom.* vii p. 870 πρὸς τὸν αὐτὸν ἀπαντᾶν χρόνον. It is not uncommon in Origen; e.g. *Philoc.* xviii 3 (Robinson) τίς γὰρ... ῥίπτει τὰ σπέρματα ἐπὶ τὴν γῆν, μὴ τὰ κρείττονα πιστεύων ἀπαντήσεσθαι; In any case the sentence is somewhat tautologous.

μέλλοντα τῶν ἀνθρώπων, καὶ τὰ παρ' αὐτοῦ κατ' ἀξίαν
τῶν πραττομένων ἀπαντήσεσθαι, διὰ τοῦ προφητικοῦ πνεύματος προλέγει, εἰς ἐπίστασιν καὶ ἀνάμνησιν ἀεὶ ἄγων τὸ
τῶν ἀνθρώπων γένος, δεικνὺς ὅτι καὶ μέλον ἐστὶν αὐτῷ καὶ
5 προνοεῖται αὐτῶν.   12. κατ' ἐνέργειαν δὲ τῶν φαύλων
δαιμόνων θάνατος ὡρίσθη κατὰ τῶν τὰς Ὑστάσπου ἢ
Σιβύλλης ἢ τῶν προφητῶν βίβλους ἀναγινωσκόντων,
ὅπως διὰ τοῦ φόβου ἀποστρέψωσιν ἐντυγχάνοντας τοὺς
ἀνθρώπους, τῶν καλῶν γνῶσιν λαβεῖν, αὐτοῖς δὲ δουλεύ-
10 οντας κατέχωσιν· ὅπερ εἰς τέλος οὐκ ἴσχυσαν πρᾶξαι.
13. ἀφόβως μὲν γὰρ οὐ μόνον ἐντυγχάνομεν αὐταῖς, ἀλλὰ
καὶ ὑμῖν, ὡς ὁρᾶτε, εἰς ἐπίσκεψιν φέρομεν, ἐπιστάμενοι
πᾶσιν εὐάρεστα φανήσεσθαι· κἂν ὀλίγους δὲ πείσωμεν, τὰ
μέγιστα κερδήσαντες ἐσόμεθα· ὡς γεωργοὶ γὰρ ἀγαθοὶ
15 παρὰ τοῦ δεσπόζοντος τὴν ἀμοιβὴν ἕξομεν.

45. 1. Ὅτι δὲ ἀγαγεῖν τὸν Χριστὸν εἰς τὸν οὐρανὸν
ὁ πατὴρ τῶν πάντων θεὸς μετὰ τὸ ἀναστῆσαι ἐκ νεκρῶν
αὐτὸν ἔμελλε, καὶ κατέχειν ἕως ἂν πατάξῃ τοὺς ἐχθραί-
νοντας αὐτῷ δαίμονας, καὶ συντελεσθῇ ὁ ἀριθμὸς τῶν

3 ἐπίστασιν Otto ἐπίτασιν A

3. ἐπίστασιν] 'consideration, thought.' The MS ἐπίτασιν ('tightening') could scarcely mean 'mental attention.'
4. μέλον] Cf. 28, 4.
5. κατ' ἐνέργ.] Cf. ἐνήργησαν, 23, 3.
6. θάνατος ὡρ.] This probably refers to a law of Tiberius' time, which made it a capital crime to consult diviners about the life of Caesar or future history. The *mathematici* were constantly being banished from Rome, but were never extirpated. Cf. Tac. *Ann.* ii. 32, xii 52, *Hist.* i 22, ii 62. Justin seems here to be guilty of some exaggeration of the facts. Veil suggests that after the Judaean war or the revolt of Barcochba Jewish prophecies may have been discouraged.
ib. Ὑστάσπου] c. 20.
7. Σιβύλλης] c. 20. The official Sibylline books, deposited in the Capitol, could be consulted only by the *quindecimuiri*. But the reference here must be to the popular Sibylline prophecies.
8. ἀποστρέψωσιν...λαβεῖν] Τοῦ λαβεῖν would be the normal construction.
ib. ἐντυγχάνοντας] '*reading*.' So in 14, 1; 26, 8.
13. εὐάρεστα] i.e. the contents of the books.
45. *O. T. prophecy of Christ's session in heaven, future triumph and judgment.*
18. κατέχειν] '*keep*' in heaven.

προεγνωσμένων αὐτῷ ἀγαθῶν γινομένων καὶ ἐναρέτων, δι'
οὓς καὶ μηδέπω τὴν ἐπικύρωσιν πεποίηται, ἐπακούσατε
τῶν εἰρημένων διὰ Δαυὶδ τοῦ προφήτου. 2. ἔστι δὲ
ταῦτα· Εἶπεν ὁ κύριος τῷ κυρίῳ μου· Κάθου ἐκ δεξιῶν
μου, ἕως ἂν θῶ τοὺς ἐχθρούς σου ὑποπόδιον τῶν ποδῶν 5
σου. 3. ῥάβδον δυνάμεως ἐξαποστελεῖ σοι κύριος ἐξ
Ἱερουσαλήμ· καὶ κατακυρίευε ἐν μέσῳ τῶν ἐχθρῶν σου.
4. μετὰ σοῦ ἡ ἀρχὴ ἐν ἡμέρᾳ τῆς δυνάμεώς σου ἐν ταῖς
λαμπρότησι τῶν ἁγίων σου· ἐκ γαστρὸς πρὸ ἑωσφόρου
ἐγέννησά σε. 5. τὸ οὖν εἰρημένον Ῥάβδον δυνάμεως 10
ἐξαποστελεῖ σοι ἐξ Ἱερουσαλὴμ προαγγελτικὸν τοῦ λόγου
τοῦ ἰσχυροῦ, ὃν ἀπὸ Ἱερουσαλὴμ οἱ ἀπόστολοι αὐτοῦ
ἐξελθόντες πανταχοῦ ἐκήρυξαν, καί, καίπερ θανάτου
ὁρισθέντος κατὰ τῶν διδασκόντων ἢ ὅλως ὁμολογούντων
τὸ ὄνομα τοῦ Χριστοῦ, ἡμεῖς πανταχοῦ καὶ ἀσπαζόμεθα 15
καὶ διδάσκομεν. 6. εἰ δὲ καὶ ὑμεῖς ὡς ἐχθροὶ ἐντεύξεσθε
τοῖσδε τοῖς λόγοις, οὐ πλέον τι δύνασθε, ὡς προέφημεν, τοῦ
φονεύειν· ὅπερ ἡμῖν μὲν οὐδεμίαν βλάβην φέρει, ὑμῖν δὲ
καὶ πᾶσι τοῖς ἀδίκως ἐχθραίνουσι καὶ μὴ μετατιθεμένοις
κόλασιν διὰ πυρὸς αἰωνίαν ἐργάζεται.

13 καὶ καίπερ Thirlb om καί A

1. δι' οὓς καὶ κτλ.] *'for whose sake He has not consummated His decree'* (of judgment). See above, 28, 2.
4. εἶπεν κτλ.] Cf. Ps. cix (cx) 1—3; Matt. xxii 44; Acts iii 34, 35; 1 Cor. xv 25; Heb. i 13, x 12, 13. Compare also Acts iii 21.
8. μετὰ σοῦ ἡ ἀρχή] *'The rule belongs to thee, on the day of thy power, in the glory of thy saints; I begat thee before the morning star.'* The text has a great place in the history of the Arian controversy. The Latin versions have *principium*, and they represent the usual manner of understanding the text; the rendering given above is an attempt to bring out a sense from the words, but is not necessarily what Justin understood them to mean.
11. τοῦ λόγου τ. ἰσχ.] i.e. the gospel.
12. οἱ ἀπόστολοι] Cf. Mark xvi 20.
16. ἐντεύξεσθε] *'you will read.'* Cf. 44, 13.
17. ὡς προέφημεν] In c. 2, 4; 11, 2.
46. *You may object that those who lived before Christ cannot be considered responsible. But Christ is the Logos and every man has a share of it—those who have lived* μετὰ λόγου *were Christians, those who lived* ἄνευ λόγου *were Christ's enemies.*

46.

1. Ἵνα δὲ μή τινες, ἀλογισταίνοντες εἰς ἀποτροπὴν τῶν δεδιδαγμένων ὑφ' ἡμῶν, εἴπωσι πρὸ ἐτῶν ἑκατὸν πεντήκοντα γεγεννῆσθαι τὸν Χριστὸν λέγειν ἡμᾶς ἐπὶ Κυρηνίου, δεδιδαχέναι δὲ ἅ φαμεν διδάξαι αὐτὸν ὕστερον χρόνοις ἐπὶ Ποντίου Πιλάτου, καὶ ἐπικαλῶσιν ὡς ἀνευθύνων ὄντων τῶν προγεγενημένων πάντων ἀνθρώπων, φθάσαντες τὴν ἀπορίαν λυσόμεθα. 2. τὸν Χριστὸν πρωτότοκον τοῦ θεοῦ εἶναι ἐδιδάχθημεν καὶ προεμηνύσαμεν λόγον ὄντα, οὗ πᾶν γένος ἀνθρώπων μετέσχε. 3. καὶ οἱ μετὰ λόγου βιώσαντες Χριστιανοί εἰσι, κἂν ἄθεοι ἐνομίσθησαν, οἷον ἐν Ἕλλησι μὲν Σωκράτης καὶ Ἡράκλειτος καὶ οἱ ὅμοιοι αὐτοῖς, ἐν βαρβάροις δὲ Ἀβραὰμ καὶ Ἀνανίας καὶ Ἀζαρίας καὶ Μισαὴλ καὶ Ἡλίας καὶ ἄλλοι πολλοί, ὧν τὰς πράξεις ἢ τὰ ὀνόματα καταλέγειν, μακρὸν εἶναι ἐπιστάμενοι, τανῦν παραιτούμεθα. 4. ὥστε καὶ οἱ προγενόμενοι ἄνευ λόγου βιώσαντες ἄχρηστοι καὶ ἐχθροὶ τῷ Χριστῷ ἦσαν καὶ φονεῖς τῶν μετὰ λόγου βιούντων· οἱ δὲ μετὰ λόγου βιώσαντες καὶ βιοῦντες, Χριστιανοὶ καὶ ἄφοβοι καὶ ἀτάραχοι ὑπάρχουσι. 5. δι' ἣν αἰτίαν διὰ δυνάμεως τοῦ λόγου κατὰ τὴν τοῦ πατρὸς πάντων καὶ δεσπότου θεοῦ βουλὴν διὰ παρθένου ἄνθρωπος ἀπεκυήθη

7 λυσόμεθα Otto λυσώμεθα A

1. ἀλογιστ.] 'reasoning absurdly'; not found in classical Greek.
ib. εἰς ἀποτροπήν] 'with a view to refuting.'
2. ἑκατὸν πεντήκοντα] Obviously a round number.
4. ὕστερον χρόνοις] 'somewhat later.' Cf. Lysias 99, 40.
5. ἐπικαλῶσιν] used absolutely, in the sense of 'object,' much like ἐγκαλεῖν = 'to bring in opposition.'
ib. ἀνευθύνων] 'not accountable.'
8. προεμηνύσαμεν] in c. 23.
10. οἱ μετὰ λόγου κτλ.] The possibility of 'Christians before Christ' is definitely allowed for by Justin. See *Introd.* p. xxii.
11. Σωκράτης] Cf. c. 5.
ib. Ἡράκλειτος] Heraclitus attempted to spiritualize religious ideas, whence probably arises Justin's reverence for him.
12. ἐν βαρβάροις] i.e. non-Greeks.
13. Ἀνανίας κ. Ἀζ. κ. Μισ.] The Three Children of Dan. i 7 and its Apocryphal supplement.
15. παραιτούμεθα] 'we forbear.'
16. ἄχρηστοι] There may be a hint of the same play upon words as in c. 4, 1. 5.
21. ἄνθρ. ἀπεκυήθη] Probably ἄνθρ. is to be taken as predicate,

καὶ Ἰησοῦς ἐπωνομάσθη, καὶ σταυρωθεὶς καὶ ἀποθανὼν ἀνέστη καὶ ἀνελήλυθεν εἰς οὐρανόν, ἐκ τῶν διὰ τοσούτων εἰρημένων ὁ νουνεχὴς καταλαβεῖν δυνήσεται. 6. ἡμεῖς δέ, οὐκ ἀναγκαίου ὄντος τανῦν τοῦ περὶ τῆς ἀποδείξεως τούτου λόγου, ἐπὶ τὰς ἐπειγούσας ἀποδείξεις πρὸς τὸ 5 παρὸν χωρήσομεν.

47. 1. Ὅτι οὖν καὶ ἐκπορθηθήσεσθαι ἡ γῆ Ἰουδαίων ἔμελλεν, ἀκούσατε τῶν εἰρημένων ὑπὸ τοῦ προφητικοῦ πνεύματος· εἴρηνται δὲ οἱ λόγοι ὡς ἀπὸ προσώπου λαῶν θαυμαζόντων τὰ γεγενημένα. 2. εἰσὶ δὲ οἵδε· Ἐγενήθη 10 ἔρημος Σιών, ὡς ἔρημος ἐγενήθη Ἱερουσαλήμ, εἰς κατάραν ὁ οἶκος, τὸ ἅγιον ἡμῶν, καὶ ἡ δόξα, ἣν εὐλόγησαν οἱ πατέρες ἡμῶν, ἐγενήθη πυρίκαυστος, καὶ πάντα τὰ ἔνδοξα αὐτῆς συνέπεσε. 3. καὶ ἐπὶ τούτοις ἀνέσχου καὶ ἐσιώπησας καὶ ἐταπείνωσας ἡμᾶς σφόδρα. 4. καὶ ὅτι ἠρήμωτο 15 Ἱερουσαλήμ, ὡς προείρητο γεγενῆσθαι, πεπεισμένοι ἐστέ. 5. εἴρηται δὲ καὶ περὶ τῆς ἐρημώσεως αὐτῆς, καὶ περὶ τοῦ μὴ ἐπιτραπήσεσθαί μηδένα αὐτῶν οἰκεῖν, διὰ Ἡσαΐου τοῦ προφήτου οὕτως· Ἡ γῆ αὐτῶν ἔρημος, ἔμπροσθεν αὐτῶν οἱ ἐχθροὶ αὐτῶν αὐτὴν φάγονται, καὶ οὐκ ἔσται ἐξ 20 αὐτῶν ὁ κατοικῶν ἐν αὐτῇ. 6. ὅτι δὲ φυλάσσεται ὑφ'

1 καὶ ἀποθανὼν Otto om καὶ A ǁ 6 χωρήσομεν Thalem Asht χωρήσωμεν A

and the subject of ἀπεκ. is ὁ λόγος, in spite of διὰ δυν. τ. λόγου.
2. ἐκ τῶν δ. τοσ. εἰρημένων] The reasons so far given for the Incarnation are: to refute the demons (c. 5), to teach the true belief in God (c. 6) and true worship (c. 13), to warn of eternity and judgment (c. 8), to effect a moral regeneration (c. 15), to make atonement for man (c. 32, 7). Δι' ἣν αἰτίαν κτλ. is the object of καταλαβεῖν.
4. τοῦ περὶ κτλ.] 'the argument concerned with the demonstration of this point,' taking τούτου as genitive after ἀποδείξεως (Otto, Maran). Perhaps τούτων should be read.

47. *Prophecies of the fate of Jerusalem.*
10. ἐγενήθη κτλ.] Cf. Isaiah lxiv 10—12.
16. ὡς προείρητο γεγενῆσθαι] 'as it had been foretold to have happened,' i.e. Justin interprets ἐγενήθη as a prophetic past tense (cf. c. 42). The pluperfect ἠρήμωτο is perhaps influenced by προείρητο.
18. μηδένα αὐτῶν] 'none of the people.'
19. ἡ γῆ κτλ.] Cf. Isaiah i 7; Jer. ii 15, l 3.
21. ὅτι δὲ φυλάσσεται] After

ὑμῶν ὅπως μηδεὶς ἐν αὐτῇ γένηται, καὶ θάνατος κατὰ τοῦ καταλαμβανομένου Ἰουδαίου εἰσιόντος ὥρισται, ἀκριβῶς ἐπίστασθε.

48. 1. Ὅτι δὲ καὶ θεραπεύσειν πάσας νόσους καὶ νεκροὺς ἀνεγερεῖν ὁ ἡμέτερος Χριστὸς προεφητεύθη, ἀκούσατε τῶν λελεγμένων. 2. ἔστι δὲ ταῦτα· Τῇ παρουσίᾳ αὐτοῦ ἁλεῖται χωλὸς ὡς ἔλαφος, καὶ τρανὴ ἔσται γλῶσσα μογιλάλων· τυφλοὶ ἀναβλέψουσι καὶ λεπροὶ καθαρισθήσονται καὶ νεκροὶ ἀναστήσονται καὶ περιπατήσουσιν. 3. ὅτι δὲ ταῦτα ἐποίησεν, ἐκ τῶν ἐπὶ Ποντίου Πιλάτου γενομένων ἄκτων μαθεῖν δύνασθε. 4. πῶς τε προμεμήνυται ὑπὸ τοῦ προφητικοῦ πνεύματος ἀναιρεθησόμενος ἅμα τοῖς ἐπ' αὐτὸν ἐλπίζουσιν ἀνθρώποις, ἀκούσατε τῶν λεχθέντων διὰ Ἡσαΐου. 5. ἔστι δὲ ταῦτα· Ἴδε ὡς ὁ δίκαιος ἀπώλετο, καὶ οὐδεὶς ἐκδέχεται τῇ καρδίᾳ· καὶ ἄνδρες δίκαιοι αἴρονται, καὶ οὐδεὶς κατανοεῖ. 6. ἀπὸ προσώπου ἀδικίας ἦρται ὁ δίκαιος καὶ ἔσται ἐν εἰρήνῃ ἡ ταφὴ αὐτοῦ· ἦρται ἐκ τοῦ μέσου.

49. 1. Καὶ πάλιν πῶς δι' αὐτοῦ Ἡσαΐου λέλεκται ὅτι οἱ οὐ προσδοκήσαντες αὐτὸν λαοὶ τῶν ἐθνῶν προσκυνήσουσιν αὐτόν, οἱ δὲ ἀεὶ προσδοκῶντες Ἰουδαῖοι ἀγνοήσουσι

10 ὅτι δὲ ταῦτα Sylb ὅτι τε ταῦτα A ∥ 11 ἄκτων Casaubon edd αὐτῷ A

the rebellion of Barcochba, in which Judaea was almost depopulated, the Jews were forbidden by Hadrian to set foot in Jerusalem, under penalty of death.

48. *Prophecies of Christ's miracles and death.*

6. τῇ παρουσίᾳ κτλ.] Cf. Isaiah xxxv 5, 6; Matt. xi 5.

7. τρανή] Τρανός, -ή, -όν is a later form of τρανής, -ές = 'clear, distinct.'

11. ἄκτων] Cf. 35, 9. Justin probably had not seen them, and is merely surmising that they contained details of Christ's history.

14. ἴδε κτλ.] Cf. Isaiah lvii 1 ff.

17. ἔσται ἐν εἰρ.] In *Tryph.* 97 and 118 ἡ ταφὴ αὐτοῦ ἦρται ἐκ τοῦ μέσου is quoted as a prophecy of Christ's resurrection; and Otto therefore puts here a colon after εἰρήνῃ, removing that after αὐτοῦ. This, however, s not necessary. There is no question here of the resurrection, but only of the death; and Justin frequently quotes passages in different ways.

49. *Prophecies of Christ's rejection by the Jews and acceptance by the Gentiles.*

19. καὶ πάλιν πῶς] sc. ἀκούσατε.

παραγενόμενον αυτόν· ελέχθησαν δε οι λόγοι ως από προσώπου αυτού του Χριστού.   2. εισί δε ούτοι· Ἐμφανὴς ἐγενήθην τοῖς ἐμὲ μὴ ἐπερωτῶσιν, εὑρέθην τοῖς ἐμὲ μὴ ζητοῦσιν· εἶπον· Ἰδού εἰμι, ἔθνει, οἳ οὐκ ἐκάλεσαν τὸ ὄνομά μου.   3. ἐξεπέτασα τὰς χεῖράς μου ἐπὶ λαὸν ἀπειθοῦντα καὶ ἀντιλέγοντα, ἐπὶ τοὺς πορευομένους ἐν ὁδῷ οὐ καλῇ, ἀλλ' ὀπίσω τῶν ἁμαρτιῶν αὐτῶν.   4. ὁ λαὸς ὁ παροξύνων ἐναντίον μου.   5. Ἰουδαῖοι γάρ, ἔχοντες τὰς προφητείας καὶ ἀεὶ προσδοκήσαντες τὸν Χριστὸν παραγενησόμενον, παραγενόμενον ἠγνόησαν, οὐ μόνον δέ, ἀλλὰ καὶ παρεχρήσαντο· οἱ δὲ ἀπὸ τῶν ἐθνῶν μηδέποτε μηδὲν ἀκούσαντες περὶ τοῦ Χριστοῦ, μέχρις οὗ οἱ ἀπὸ Ἱερουσαλὴμ ἐξελθόντες ἀπόστολοι αὐτοῦ ἐμήνυσαν τὰ περὶ αὐτοῦ καὶ τὰς προφητείας παρέδωκαν, πληρωθέντες χαρᾶς καὶ πίστεως τοῖς εἰδώλοις ἀπετάξαντο καὶ τῷ ἀγεννήτῳ θεῷ διὰ τοῦ Χριστοῦ ἑαυτοὺς ἀνέθηκαν.   6. ὅτι δὲ προεγινώσκετο τὰ δύσφημα ταῦτα λεχθησόμενα κατὰ τῶν τὸν Χριστὸν ὁμολογούντων, καὶ ὡς εἶεν τάλανες οἱ δυσφημοῦντες αὐτὸν καὶ τὰ παλαιὰ ἔθη καλὸν εἶναι τηρεῖν λέγοντες, ἀκούσατε τῶν βραχυεπῶς εἰρημένων διὰ Ἡσαΐου. 7. ἔστι δὲ ταῦτα· Οὐαὶ τοῖς λέγουσι τὸ γλυκὺ πικρὸν καὶ τὸ πικρὸν γλυκύ.

50. 1. Ὅτι δὲ καὶ ὑπὲρ ἡμῶν γενόμενος ἄνθρωπος παθεῖν καὶ ἀτιμασθῆναι ὑπέμεινε, καὶ πάλιν μετὰ δόξης παραγενήσεται, ἀκούσατε τῶν εἰρημένων εἰς τοῦτο προφητειῶν.   2. ἔστι δὲ ταῦτα· Ἀνθ' ὧν παρέδωκαν εἰς

4 ἔθνει LXX edd ἔθνη A ‖ 6 ἀπειθοῦντα Grab ἀπιθοῦντα A ‖ 9 χριστὸν παραγενησόμενον, παραγενόμενον Sylb om παραγενόμενον A χριστόν, παραγενόμενον Otto

2. ἐμφανὴς κτλ.] Cf. Isaiah lxv 1—3.
8. Ἰουδαῖοι γάρ] Cf. Acts xiii 27, 48.
11. παρεχρήσαντο] 'misused.'
15. ἀπετάξαντο] 'bade adieu to.'
ib. τῷ ἁγ. θεῷ ἀνέθηκαν] Cf. c. 14, 2.

17. τὰ δύσφημα] The popular charges against Christians.
21. οὐαὶ κτλ.] Cf. Isaiah v 20.
50. Prophecy of Christ's sufferings and death for man.
26. ἀνθ' ὧν κτλ.] Cf. Isaiah lii 12, lii 13—liii 8.

θάνατον τὴν ψυχὴν αὐτοῦ, καὶ μετὰ τῶν ἀνόμων ἐλογίσθη, αὐτὸς ἁμαρτίας πολλῶν εἴληφε καὶ τοῖς ἀνόμοις ἐξιλάσεται. 3. ἴδε γὰρ συνήσει ὁ παῖς μου, καὶ ὑψωθήσεται καὶ δοξασθήσεται σφόδρα. 4. ὃν τρόπον ἐκστήσονται 5 πολλοὶ ἐπὶ σέ, οὕτως ἀδοξήσει ἀπὸ ἀνθρώπων τὸ εἶδός σου καὶ ἡ δόξα σου ἀπὸ τῶν ἀνθρώπων, οὕτως θαυμάσονται ἔθνη πολλά, καὶ συνέξουσι βασιλεῖς τὸ στόμα αὐτῶν· ὅτι οἷς οὐκ ἀνηγγέλη περὶ αὐτοῦ ὄψονται, καὶ οἳ οὐκ ἀκηκόασι συνήσουσι. 5. κύριε, τίς ἐπίστευσε τῇ ἀκοῇ 10 ἡμῶν; καὶ ὁ βραχίων κυρίου τίνι ἀπεκαλύφθη; ἀνηγγείλαμεν ἐνώπιον αὐτοῦ ὡς παιδίον, ὡς ῥίζα ἐν γῇ διψώσῃ. 6. οὐκ ἔστιν εἶδος αὐτῷ οὐδὲ δόξα· καὶ εἴδομεν αὐτόν, καὶ οὐκ εἶχεν εἶδος οὐδὲ κάλλος, ἀλλὰ τὸ εἶδος αὐτοῦ ἄτιμον καὶ ἐκλεῖπον παρὰ τοὺς ἀνθρώπους. 7. ἄνθρωπος ἐν 15 πληγῇ ὢν καὶ εἰδὼς φέρειν μαλακίαν, ὅτι ἀπέστραπται τὸ πρόσωπον αὐτοῦ, ἠτιμάσθη καὶ οὐκ ἐλογίσθη. 8. οὗτος τὰς ἁμαρτίας ἡμῶν φέρει καὶ περὶ ἡμῶν ὀδυνᾶται, καὶ ἡμεῖς ἐλογισάμεθα αὐτὸν εἶναι ἐν πόνῳ καὶ ἐν πληγῇ καὶ ἐν κακώσει. 9. αὐτὸς δὲ ἐτραυματίσθη διὰ τὰς ἀνομίας 20 ἡμῶν καὶ μεμαλάκισται διὰ τὰς ἁμαρτίας ἡμῶν· παιδεία εἰρήνης ἐπ' αὐτόν, τῷ μώλωπι αὐτοῦ ἡμεῖς ἰάθημεν. 10. πάντες ὡς πρόβατα ἐπλανήθημεν, ἄνθρωπος τῇ ὁδῷ αὐτοῦ ἐπλανήθη· καὶ παρέδωκεν αὐτὸν ταῖς ἁμαρτίαις ἡμῶν, καὶ αὐτὸς διὰ τὸ κεκακῶσθαι οὐκ ἀνοίγει τὸ στόμα 25 αὐτοῦ· ὡς πρόβατον ἐπὶ σφαγὴν ἤχθη, καὶ ὡς ἀμνὸς ἐναντίον τοῦ κείροντος αὐτὸν ἄφωνος, οὕτως οὐκ ἀνοίγει τὸ στόμα αὐτοῦ. 11. ἐν τῇ ταπεινώσει αὐτοῦ ἡ κρίσις

8 ὄψονται LXX Otto om A

8. ὄψονται] The insertion of this word from the LXX text is not absolutely necessary, but the homoioteleuton -ται, καὶ makes the omission explicable. Justin quotes the same passage with ὄψονται in *Tryph.* 13, 118.

20. παιδεία εἰρήνης] The LXX text adds ἡμῶν, which perhaps ought to be inserted here.

27. ἡ κρίσις αὐτοῦ ἤρθη] '*His judgment was lifted up,*' perhaps Justin understood it as meaning '*taken away,*' or else '*exalted,*' i.e., His humiliation was His kingly exaltation (on the Cross). Cf. c. 41, 4.

αὐτοῦ ἤρθη. 12. μετὰ οὖν τὸ σταυρωθῆναι αὐτὸν καὶ οἱ γνώριμοι αὐτοῦ πάντες ἀπέστησαν, ἀρνησάμενοι αὐτόν· ὕστερον δέ, ἐκ νεκρῶν ἀναστάντος καὶ ὀφθέντος αὐτοῖς καὶ ταῖς προφητείαις ἐντυχεῖν, ἐν αἷς πάντα ταῦτα προείρητο γενησόμενα, διδάξαντος, καὶ εἰς οὐρανὸν ἀνερχόμενον ἰδόντες καὶ πιστεύσαντες καὶ δύναμιν ἐκεῖθεν αὐτοῖς πεμφθεῖσαν παρ᾽ αὐτοῦ λαβόντες καὶ εἰς πᾶν γένος ἀνθρώπων ἐλθόντες, ταῦτα ἐδίδαξαν καὶ ἀπόστολοι προσηγορεύθησαν.

51. 1. Ἵνα δὲ μηνύσῃ ἡμῖν τὸ προφητικὸν πνεῦμα ὅτι ὁ ταῦτα πάσχων ἀνεκδιήγητον ἔχει τὸ γένος καὶ βασιλεύει τῶν ἐχθρῶν, ἔφη οὕτως· Τὴν γενεὰν αὐτοῦ τίς διηγήσεται; ὅτι αἴρεται ἀπὸ τῆς γῆς ἡ ζωὴ αὐτοῦ, ἀπὸ τῶν ἀνομιῶν αὐτῶν ἥκει εἰς θάνατον. 2. καὶ δώσω τοὺς πονηροὺς ἀντὶ τῆς ταφῆς αὐτοῦ καὶ τοὺς πλουσίους ἀντὶ τοῦ θανάτου αὐτοῦ, ὅτι ἀνομίαν οὐκ ἐποίησεν οὐδὲ εὑρέθη δόλος ἐν τῷ στόματι αὐτοῦ· καὶ κύριος βούλεται καθαρίσαι αὐτὸν τῆς πληγῆς. 3. ἐὰν δῶτε περὶ ἁμαρτίας, ἡ ψυχὴ ὑμῶν ὄψεται σπέρμα μακρόβιον. 4. καὶ βούλεται κύριος ἀφελεῖν ἀπὸ πόνου τὴν ψυχὴν αὐτοῦ, δεῖξαι αὐτῷ φῶς καὶ πλάσαι τῇ συνέσει, δικαιῶσαι δίκαιον εὖ δουλεύοντα πολλοῖς, καὶ τὰς ἁμαρτίας ἡμῶν

1. μετὰ οὖν κτλ.] Cf. Matt. xxvi 31; Zech. xiii 7. In *Tryph.* 53 Justin repeats μετὰ γὰρ τὸ σταυρωθῆναι αὐτὸν οἱ σὺν αὐτῷ ὄντες μαθηταὶ αὐτοῦ διεσκεδάσθησαν μέχρις ὅτε ἀνέστη ἐκ νεκρῶν as a fulfilment of Zechariah. And in *Tryph.* 106 he says that after the Resurrection the disciples μετενόησαν ἐπὶ τῷ ἀφίστασθαι αὐτοῦ ὅτε ἐσταυρώθη. Harnack traces here the influence of the Gospel of Peter vv. 26, 27, 59, where the grief and desertion of the Twelve after the Crucifixion are spoken of. The canonical record, however, gives by itself sufficient ground for Justin's statements,

which are roughly true.

3. ὕστερον δέ] Cf. Luke xxiv 25, 26, 44—46; Acts i 8, 9.

4. ἐντυχεῖν] '*read*,' as previously in many passages.

51. *Prophecies of Christ's generation, triumph, ascension, second advent.*

12. τὴν γενεὰν κτλ.] Isaiah liii 8—12.

15. τοὺς πονηρούς] Referred probably by Justin to the destruction of Jerusalem.

18. ἐὰν δῶτε] sc. αὐτόν, '*if ye give Him.*' The LXX has ἐὰν δῶται = '*if He gives Himself.*'

αὐτὸς ἀνοίσει. 5. διὰ τοῦτο αὐτὸς κληρονομήσει πολλοὺς καὶ τῶν ἰσχυρῶν μεριεῖ σκύλα, ἀνθ᾽ ὧν παρεδόθη εἰς θάνατον ἡ ψυχὴ αὐτοῦ, καὶ ἐν τοῖς ἀνόμοις ἐλογίσθη, καὶ αὐτὸς ἁμαρτίας πολλῶν ἀνήνεγκε καὶ διὰ τὰς ἀνομίας αὐτῶν αὐτὸς παρεδόθη. 6. ὡς δὲ καὶ εἰς τὸν οὐρανὸν ἔμελλεν ἀνιέναι, καθὼς προεφητεύθη, ἀκούσατε. 7. ἐλέχθη δὲ οὕτως· Ἄρατε πύλας οὐρανῶν, ἀνοίχθητε, ἵνα εἰσέλθῃ ὁ βασιλεὺς τῆς δόξης. Τίς ἐστιν οὗτος ὁ βασιλεὺς τῆς δόξης; Κύριος κραταιὸς καὶ κύριος δυνατός. 8. ὡς δὲ καὶ ἐξ οὐρανῶν παραγίνεσθαι μετὰ δόξης μέλλει, ἀκούσατε καὶ τῶν εἰρημένων εἰς τοῦτο διὰ Ἱερεμίου τοῦ προφήτου. 9. ἔστι δὲ ταῦτα· Ἰδοὺ ὡς υἱὸς ἀνθρώπου ἔρχεται ἐπάνω τῶν νεφελῶν τοῦ οὐρανοῦ, καὶ οἱ ἄγγελοι αὐτοῦ σὺν αὐτῷ.

52. 1. Ἐπειδὴ τοίνυν τὰ γενόμενα ἤδη πάντα ἀποδείκνυμεν, πρὶν ἢ γενέσθαι, προκεκηρύχθαι διὰ τῶν προφητῶν, ἀνάγκη καὶ περὶ τῶν ὁμοίως προφητευθέντων, μελλόντων δὲ γίνεσθαι, πίστιν ἔχειν ὡς πάντως γενησομένων. 2. ὃν γὰρ τρόπον τὰ ἤδη γενόμενα προκεκηρυγμένα καὶ ἀγνοούμενα ἀπέβη, τὸν αὐτὸν τρόπον καὶ τὰ λείποντα, κἂν ἀγνοῆται καὶ ἀπιστῆται, ἀποβήσονται. 3. δύο γὰρ αὐτοῦ παρουσίας προεκήρυξαν οἱ προφῆται· μίαν μέν, τὴν ἤδη γενομένην, ὡς ἀτίμου καὶ παθητοῦ ἀνθρώπου, τὴν δὲ

15 ἀποδείκνυμεν A ἀπεδείκνυμεν Otto ‖ 21 ἀπιστῆται B edd ἀπιστεῖται A

7. ἄρατε κτλ.] Ps. xxiii (xxiv) 7, 8.

10. μετὰ δόξης] So in the 'Nicene' Creed. It was not in the Creed adopted at the Council of Nicaea. But the Creed of Caesarea had ἐν δόξῃ; and Epiphanius' version of the Nicene Creed has μετὰ δόξης.

11. Ἱερεμίου] A mistake. The quotation is in the main from Dan. vii 13, but with words from Zech. xiv 5 attached (cf. Matt. xxv 31). It is rightly ascribed in *Tryph.* 76.

52. *The fulfilment of such prophecies leads us to believe that similar prophecies as to the future, the second coming of Christ, and the punishment of the wicked, shall also be fulfilled.*

19. καὶ ἀγνοούμενα] Otto's suggestion κἂν ἀγνοούμενα may be right.

21. ἀποβήσονται] Note the plural with a neuter plural subject, as in 3, 1.

23. παθητοῦ ἀνθρώπου] '*a man of suffering.*'

δευτέραν, ὅταν μετὰ δόξης ἐξ οὐρανῶν μετὰ τῆς ἀγγελικῆς αὐτοῦ στρατιᾶς παραγενήσεσθαι κεκήρυκται, ὅτε καὶ τὰ σώματα ἀνεγερεῖ πάντων τῶν γενομένων ἀνθρώπων, καὶ τῶν μὲν ἀξίων ἐνδύσει ἀφθαρσίαν, τῶν δὲ ἀδίκων ἐν αἰσθήσει αἰωνίᾳ μετὰ τῶν φαύλων δαιμόνων εἰς τὸ αἰώνιον πῦρ πέμψει. 4. ὡς δὲ καὶ ταῦτα προείρηται γενησόμενα, δηλώσομεν. 5. ἐρρέθη δὲ διὰ Ἰεζεκιὴλ τοῦ προφήτου οὕτως· Συναχθήσεται ἁρμονία πρὸς ἁρμονίαν καὶ ὀστέον πρὸς ὀστέον, καὶ σάρκες ἀναφυήσονται. 6. Καὶ πᾶν γόνυ κάμψει τῷ κυρίῳ, καὶ πᾶσα γλῶσσα ἐξομολογήσεται αὐτῷ. 7. ἐν οἵᾳ δὲ αἰσθήσει καὶ κολάσει γενέσθαι μέλλουσιν οἱ ἄδικοι, ἀκούσατε τῶν ὁμοίως εἰς τοῦτο εἰρημένων. 8. ἔστι δὲ ταῦτα· Ὁ σκώληξ αὐτῶν οὐ παυθήσεται, καὶ τὸ πῦρ αὐτῶν οὐ σβεσθήσεται. 9. καὶ τότε μετανοήσουσιν, ὅτε οὐδὲν ὠφελήσουσι. 10. ποῖα δὲ μέλλουσιν οἱ λαοὶ τῶν Ἰουδαίων λέγειν καὶ ποιεῖν, ὅταν ἴδωσιν αὐτὸν ἐν δόξῃ παραγενόμενον, διὰ Ζαχαρίου τοῦ προφήτου προφητευθέντα ἐλέχθη οὕτως· Ἐντελοῦμαι τοῖς τέσσαρσιν ἀνέμοις συνάξαι τὰ ἐσκορπισμένα τέκνα, ἐντε-

4 ἐνδύσει Maran ἐνδύσῃ Α

4. ἐνδύσει ἀφθαρσίαν] 1 Cor. xv 53. So previously ἐνδύσασθαι ἀφθαρσίαν in c. 19, 4. With ἀξίων and ἀδίκων must be understood τὰ σώματα.
ib. ἐν αἰσθήσει αἰωνίᾳ] So in c. 20, 4.
8. συναχθήσεται κτλ.] Ezek. xxxvii 7, 8; Isaiah xlv 23; Rom. xiv 11. 'Αρμονία = '*joint*.'
12. εἰς τοῦτο] '*to this purport.*' Cf. above 44, 2.
13. ὁ σκώληξ κτλ.] Isaiah lxvi 24; Mark ix 48. The LXX text of Isaiah has τελευτήσει, the Greek text of Mark has τελευτᾷ. Justin quotes the passage with τελευτήσει in *Tryph.* 44, with παύσεται in *Tryph.* 140.
14. καὶ τότε κτλ.] This somewhat resembles Prov. i 28, but may not be intended as a quotation at all.
17. Ζαχαρίου] The following quotation is very composite; cf. Zech. ii 6; Isaiah xliii 5, 6, xi 12; Zech. xii 10—12; Joel ii 13; Isaiah lxiii 17, lxiv 11. The LXX reading of Zech. xii 10 is ἐπιβλέψονται πρός με ἀνθ' ὧν κατωρχήσαντο. Justin's version may be derived from John xix 37 ὄψονται εἰς ὃν ἐξεκέντησαν (cf. Revel. i 7), or may be the product of oral tradition. The whole quotation looks like a cento of O.T. passages, somewhat like the exhortation in the Commination Service of the English Prayer-book. Justin in *Tryph.* 14 quotes as from Hosea ὄψεται ὁ λαὸς ὑμῶν καὶ γνωριεῖ εἰς ὃν ἐξεκέντησαν.

λοῦμαι τῷ βορρᾷ φέρειν, καὶ τῷ νότῳ μὴ προσκόπτειν. 11. καὶ τότε ἐν Ἱερουσαλὴμ κοπετὸς μέγας, οὐ κοπετὸς στομάτων ἢ χειλέων, ἀλλὰ κοπετὸς καρδίας, καὶ οὐ μὴ σχίσωσιν αὐτῶν τὰ ἱμάτια, ἀλλὰ τὰς διανοίας. 12. κό-
5 ψονται φυλὴ πρὸς φυλήν, καὶ τότε ὄψονται εἰς ὃν ἐξεκέντησαν, καὶ ἐροῦσι· Τί, κύριε, ἐπλάνησας ἡμᾶς ἀπὸ τῆς ὁδοῦ σου; Ἡ δόξα, ἣν εὐλόγησαν οἱ πατέρες ἡμῶν, ἐγενήθη ἡμῖν εἰς ὄνειδος.

53. 1. Πολλὰς μὲν οὖν καὶ ἑτέρας προφητείας ἔχοντες,
10 εἰπεῖν ἐπαυσάμεθα, αὐτάρκεις καὶ ταύτας εἰς πεισμονὴν τοῖς τὰ ἀκουστικὰ καὶ νοερὰ ὦτα ἔχουσιν εἶναι λογισάμενοι, καὶ νοεῖν δύνασθαι αὐτοὺς ἡγούμενοι ὅτι οὐχ ὁμοίως τοῖς μυθοποιηθεῖσι περὶ τῶν νομισθέντων υἱῶν τοῦ Διὸς καὶ ἡμεῖς μόνον λέγομεν, ἀλλ' οὐκ ἀποδεῖξαι ἔχομεν.
15 2. τίνι γὰρ ἂν λόγῳ ἀνθρώπῳ σταυρωθέντι ἐπειθόμεθα, ὅτι πρωτότοκος τῷ ἀγεννήτῳ θεῷ ἐστι καὶ αὐτὸς τὴν κρίσιν τοῦ παντὸς ἀνθρωπείου γένους ποιήσεται, εἰ μὴ μαρτύρια πρὶν ἢ ἐλθεῖν αὐτὸν ἄνθρωπον γενόμενον κεκηρυγμένα περὶ αὐτοῦ εὕρομεν καὶ οὕτως γενόμενα ἑωρῶμεν, 3. γῆς
20 μὲν Ἰουδαίων ἐρήμωσιν, καὶ τοὺς ἀπὸ παντὸς ἔθνους ἀνθρώπων διὰ τῆς παρὰ τῶν ἀποστόλων αὐτοῦ διδαχῆς πεισθέντας καὶ παραιτησαμένους τὰ παλαιά, ἐν οἷς πλανώμενοι ἀνεστράφησαν, ἔθη, ἑαυτοὺς ἡμᾶς ὁρῶντες, πλείονάς τε καὶ ἀληθεστέρους τοὺς ἐξ ἐθνῶν, τῶν ἀπὸ
25 Ἰουδαίων καὶ Σαμαρέων Χριστιανοὺς εἰδότες; 4. τὰ μὲν γὰρ ἄλλα πάντα γένη ἀνθρώπεια ὑπὸ τοῦ προφητικοῦ

19 ἑωρῶμεν Otto ὁρῶμεν A

53. *This fulfilment of prophecy causes us to believe that Christ is the Son of God. And prophecy also has foretold the belief of the Gentiles and the unbelief of all but a small remnant of the Jews.*
11. ἀκουστικὰ κ. νοερὰ ὦτα] Cf. Matt. xiii 9, 13 ff.
12. οὐχ ὁμ... μόνον λέγομεν] 'we do not...only assert without being able to demonstrate.'
23. ἑαυτοὺς ἡμᾶς ὁρ.] referring to the Gentile Christians. Justin, though born at Flavia Neapolis, cannot have been a Samaritan by descent. It is very remarkable that he should join the Samaritans so closely with the Jews.

πνεύματος καλεῖται ἔθνη, τὸ δὲ ἰουδαϊκὸν καὶ σαμαρειτικὸν φῦλον Ἰσραὴλ καὶ οἶκος Ἰακὼβ κέκληνται. 5. ὡς δὲ προεφητεύθη ὅτι πλείονες οἱ ἀπὸ τῶν ἐθνῶν πιστεύοντες τῶν ἀπὸ Ἰουδαίων καὶ Σαμαρέων, τὰ προφητευθέντα ἀπαγγελοῦμεν. ἐλέχθη δὲ οὕτως· "Εὐφράνθητι, στεῖρα ἡ οὐ τίκτουσα, ῥῆξον καὶ βόησον ἡ οὐκ ὠδίνουσα, ὅτι πολλὰ τὰ τέκνα τῆς ἐρήμου μᾶλλον ἢ τῆς ἐχούσης τὸν ἄνδρα." 6. ἔρημα γὰρ ἦν πάντα τὰ ἔθνη ἀληθινοῦ θεοῦ, χειρῶν ἔργοις λατρεύοντα· Ἰουδαῖοι δὲ καὶ Σαμαρεῖς, ἔχοντες τὸν παρὰ τοῦ θεοῦ λόγον διὰ τῶν προφητῶν παραδοθέντα αὐτοῖς καὶ ἀεὶ προσδοκήσαντες τὸν Χριστόν, παραγενόμενον ἠγνόησαν, πλὴν ὀλίγων τινῶν οὓς προεῖπε τὸ ἅγιον προφητικὸν πνεῦμα διὰ Ἡσαίου σωθήσεσθαι. 7. εἶπε δὲ ὡς ἀπὸ προσώπου αὐτῶν·" Εἰ μὴ κύριος ἐγκατέλιπεν ἡμῖν σπέρμα, ὡς Σόδομα καὶ Γόμορρα ἂν ἐγενήθημεν." 8. Σόδομα γὰρ καὶ Γόμορρα πόλεις τινὲς ἀσεβῶν ἀνδρῶν ἱστοροῦνται ὑπὸ Μωϋσέως γενόμεναι, ἃς πυρὶ καὶ θείῳ καύσας ὁ θεὸς κατέστρεψε, μηδενὸς τῶν ἐν αὐταῖς σωθέντος πλὴν ἀλλοεθνοῦς τινος Χαλδαίου τὸ γένος, ᾧ ὄνομα Λώτ· σὺν ᾧ καὶ θυγατέρες διεσώθησαν. 9. καὶ τὴν πᾶσαν αὐτῶν χώραν ἔρημον καὶ κεκαυμένην οὖσαν καὶ ἄγονον μένουσαν οἱ βουλόμενοι ὁρᾶν ἔχουσιν. 10. ὡς δὲ καὶ ἀληθέστεροι οἱ ἀπὸ τῶν ἐθνῶν καὶ πιστότεροι προεγινώσκοντο, ἀπαγγελοῦμεν τὰ εἰρημένα διὰ Ἡσαίου τοῦ προφήτου. 11. ἔφη δὲ οὕτως· Ἰσραὴλ ἀπερίτμητος τὴν καρδίαν, τὰ δὲ ἔθνη τὴν ἀκροβυστίαν. 12. τὰ τοσαῦτα γοῦν ὁρώμενα πειθὼ καὶ πίστιν τοῖς τἀληθὲς

17 Μωϋσέως edd Μωσέως A

5. εὐφράνθητι κτλ.] Isaiah liv 1.
Cf. Gal. iv 27.
11. προσδοκήσαντες] Cf. above, 49, 1.
14. ὡς ἀπὸ προσώπου αὐτῶν] 'as in the person of the Jews.'
ib. εἰ μὴ κύριος κτλ.] Isaiah i 9.
16. Σόδομα γ. κ. Γόμορρα] Cf. Genes. xix.
25. Ἰσραὴλ κτλ.] Jerem. ix 26. The attribution of the passage to Isaiah is a mistake. Justin quotes it also in *Tryph.* 28, and apparently as from Jeremiah. '*Israel is uncircumcised in heart, but the Gentiles only in the foreskin.*'

ἀσπαζομένοις καὶ μὴ φιλοδοξοῦσι μηδὲ ὑπὸ παθῶν ἀρχομένοις μετὰ λόγου ἐμφορῆσαι δύναται.

54. 1. Οἱ δὲ παραδιδόντες τὰ μυθοποιηθέντα ὑπὸ τῶν ποιητῶν οὐδεμίαν ἀπόδειξιν φέρουσι τοῖς ἐκμανθάνουσι νέοις, καὶ ἐπὶ ἀπάτῃ καὶ ἀπαγωγῇ τοῦ ἀνθρωπείου γένους εἰρῆσθαι ἀποδείκνυμεν κατ' ἐνέργειαν τῶν φαύλων δαιμόνων. 2. ἀκούσαντες γὰρ διὰ τῶν προφητῶν κηρυσσόμενον παραγενησόμενον τὸν Χριστόν, καὶ κολασθησομένους διὰ πυρὸς τοὺς ἀσεβεῖς τῶν ἀνθρώπων, προεβάλλοντο πολλοὺς λεχθῆναι γενομένους υἱοὺς τῷ Διΐ, νομίζοντες δυνήσεσθαι ἐνεργῆσαι τερατολογίαν ἡγήσασθαι τοὺς ἀνθρώπους τὰ περὶ τὸν Χριστόν, καὶ ὅμοια τοῖς ὑπὸ τῶν ποιητῶν λεχθεῖσι. 3. καὶ ταῦτα δ' ἐλέχθη καὶ ἐν Ἕλλησι καὶ ἐν ἔθνεσι πᾶσιν, ὅπου μᾶλλον ἐπήκουον τῶν προφητῶν πιστευθήσεσθαι τὸν Χριστὸν προκηρυσσόντων. 4. ὅτι δὲ καὶ ἀκούοντες τὰ διὰ τῶν προφητῶν λεγόμενα οὐκ ἐνόουν ἀκριβῶς, ἀλλ' ὡς πλανώμενοι ἐμιμήσαντο τὰ περὶ τὸν ἡμέτερον Χριστόν, διασαφήσομεν. 5. Μωϋσῆς οὖν ὁ προφήτης, ὡς προέφημεν, πρεσβύτερος ἦν πάντων συγγραφέων, καὶ δι' αὐτοῦ, ὡς προεμηνύσαμεν, προεφητεύθη οὕτως· "Οὐκ ἐκλείψει ἄρχων

10 λεχθῆναι γενομένους Maran λεχθῆναι λεγομένους A τεχθῆναι λεγομένους Thalemann ‖ 12 ὅμοια Thirlb ὁμοίως A ‖ 19 Μωϋσῆς edd Μωσῆς A

2. ἐμφορῆσαι] '*to implant*.' Sylb. suggests the more usual word ἐμποιῆσαι.

54. *The demons, noticing the prophecies of Christ, tried to forestall them by the heathen myths, but in so doing showed misunderstanding and ignorance of the true meaning of the prophecies.*
Here Justin passes to the third topic forecasted in c. 23, viz., that the heathen myths are due to the demons.

10. προεβάλλοντο πολλ. λεχθ.] '*put forward many to be called,* *caused many to be called.*' Cf. below, τὸν Περσέα λεχθῆναι προεβάλλοντο.

11. νομίζοντες δυνήσ. κτλ.] '*thinking they would be able to cause men to believe that the statements about Christ were fabulous, like the assertions of poets.*'

14. ὅπου μᾶλλον κτλ.] '*where they* (*the demons*) *heard the prophets foretelling that Christ would be especially believed in.*'

19. ὡς προέφημεν] in c. 44, 8.
20. ὡς προεμηνύσαμεν] in c. 32, 1. Genes. xlix 10, 11.

ἐξ Ἰούδα καὶ ἡγούμενος ἐκ τῶν μηρῶν αὐτοῦ, ἕως ἂν ἔλθῃ ᾧ ἀπόκειται· καὶ αὐτὸς ἔσται προσδοκία ἐθνῶν, δεσμεύων πρὸς ἄμπελον τὸν πῶλον αὐτοῦ, πλύνων τὴν στολὴν αὐτοῦ ἐν αἵματι σταφυλῆς." 6. τούτων οὖν τῶν προφητικῶν λόγων ἀκούσαντες οἱ δαίμονες Διόνυσον μὲν ἔφασαν 5 γεγονέναι υἱὸν τοῦ Διός, εὑρετὴν δὲ γενέσθαι ἀμπέλου παρέδωκαν, καὶ οἶνον ἐν τοῖς μυστηρίοις αὐτοῦ ἀναγράφουσι, καὶ διασπαραχθέντα αὐτὸν ἀνεληλυθέναι εἰς οὐρανὸν ἐδίδαξαν. 7. καὶ ἐπειδὴ διὰ τῆς Μωϋσέως προφητείας οὐ ῥητῶς ἐσημαίνετο, εἴτε υἱὸς τοῦ θεοῦ ὁ 10 παραγενησόμενός ἐστι, καὶ εἰ ὀχούμενος ἐπὶ πώλου ἐπὶ γῆς μενεῖ ἢ εἰς οὐρανὸν ἀνελεύσεται, καὶ τὸ τοῦ πώλου ὄνομα καὶ ὄνου πῶλον καὶ ἵππου σημαίνειν ἐδύνατο, μὴ ἐπιστάμενοι εἴτε ὄνου πῶλον ἄγων ἔσται σύμβολον τῆς παρουσίας αὐτοῦ εἴτε ἵππου ὁ προκηρυσσόμενος, καὶ υἱὸς 15

2 ᾧ ἀπόκειται Otto ὃ ἀπόκειται A ‖ 7 οἶνον A ὄνον Sylb alii

3. τὸν πῶλον αὐτοῦ] In *Tryph.* 52 Justin adds the next clause of the quotation καὶ τῇ ἕλικι τὸν πῶλον τῆς ὄνου αὐτοῦ. Here he omits it, perhaps from forgetfulness, and so can continue his argument as if the foal of either horse or ass might equally be intended.

7. οἶνον] The emendation ὄνον is supported by many commentators. Of course wine was sacred to Dionysus, but so was the ass. Grab. quotes Plin. *H. N.* xxiv 1 'Ferulae asinis gratissimo sunt in pabulo, ceteris uero iumentis praesentaneo ueneno; qua de causa id animal Libero Patri assignatur, cui et ferula.' Certainly, if the MS had read ὄνον, the corruption to οἶνον would have been very easy, as Dionysus was the god especially of wine. But in *Tryph.* 69 the same idea recurs, where the MS text reads οἶνον (marg. ὄνον) ἐν τοῖς μυστηρίοις αὐτοῦ παραφέρωσιν; and, as Veil points out, παραφέρωσιν in that passage would go more naturally with οἶνον than with ὄνον. On the whole it may be doubted whether the change to ὄνον in this passage of the Apology carries conviction. Nothing as yet has been said by Justin on the subject of the *foal*; that comes later. And Justin is giving instances in which the demons misunderstood the prophecies; to refer firstly to Dionysus' ass and then to Bellerophon's horse would be merely an admission that the demons provided for either contingency, and not a demonstration that they made a complete mistake.

ib. ἀναγράφουσι] '*ascribe.*' On the myth of Dionysus cf. note on p. 35, line 8.

10. εἴτε υἱός] εἴτε is generally used in the case of alternatives, but not always.

14. σύμβολον] accus. in apposition to πῶλον. The word ἄγων seems to be chosen with reference to the representations of Dionysus; it is inappropriate to Christ.

θεοῦ ἐστιν, ὡς προέφημεν, ἢ ἀνθρώπου, τὸν Βελλεροφόντην καὶ αὐτὸν ἐφ᾽ ἵππου Πηγάσου, ἄνθρωπον ἐξ ἀνθρώπων γενόμενον, εἰς οὐρανὸν ἔφασαν ἀνεληλυθέναι. 8. ὅτε δὲ ἤκουσαν διὰ τοῦ ἄλλου προφήτου Ἡσαΐου λεχθέν, ὅτι 5 διὰ παρθένου τεχθήσεται καὶ δι᾽ ἑαυτοῦ ἀνελεύσεται εἰς τὸν οὐρανόν, τὸν Περσέα λεχθῆναι προεβάλλοντο. 9. καὶ ὅτε ἔγνωσαν εἰρημένον, ὡς προλέλεκται ἐν ταῖς προγεγραμμέναις προφητείαις, Ἰσχυρὸς ὡς γίγας δραμεῖν ὁδόν, τὸν Ἡρακλέα ἰσχυρὸν καὶ ἐκπερινοστήσαντα τὴν πᾶσαν γῆν 10 ἔφασαν. 10. ὅτε δὲ πάλιν ἔμαθον προφητευθέντα, θεραπεύσειν αὐτὸν πᾶσαν νόσον καὶ νεκροὺς ἀνεγερεῖν, τὸν Ἀσκληπιὸν παρήνεγκαν.

55. 1. Ἀλλ᾽ οὐδαμοῦ οὐδ᾽ ἐπί τινος τῶν λεγομένων υἱῶν τοῦ Διὸς τὸ σταυρωθῆναι ἐμιμήσαντο· οὐ γὰρ ἐνοεῖτο 15 αὐτοῖς, συμβολικῶς, ὡς προδεδήλωται, τῶν εἰς τοῦτο εἰρημένων πάντων λελεγμένων. 2. ὅπερ, ὡς προεῖπεν ὁ προφήτης, τὸ μέγιστον σύμβολον τῆς ἰσχύος καὶ ἀρχῆς αὐτοῦ ὑπάρχει, ὡς καὶ ἐκ τῶν ὑπ᾽ ὄψιν πιπτόντων δείκνυται· κατανοήσατε γὰρ πάντα τὰ ἐν τῷ κόσμῳ, εἰ ἄνευ τοῦ

1 ἢ ἀνθρώπου Otto om A || 2 ἐξ ἀνθρώπων Otto ἐξ ἀνθρώπου Α

1. ὡς προέφημεν] Cf. c. 21, 2; 32, 10.
ib. Βελλεροφόντην] Cf. note on p. 35, line 11.
4. Ἡσαΐου] Cf. Isaiah vii 14, quoted in c. 33, 1. The passage in Isaiah has no bearing on the Ascension, but that had been alluded to in cc. 45; 51, 6.
5. δι᾽ ἑαυτοῦ] 'by His own power,' and not on horseback.
6. τὸν Περσέα] 'They caused Perseus to be said' (to have done the same). See notes on p. 35, line 10, and p. 37, line 15.
7. ὡς προλέλεκται] c. 40, 4. Cf. Ps. xviii 6 (xix 5).
10. προφητευθέντα] neuter plural, according to Otto. But it is much better taken with αὐτόν.

11. θεραπεύσειν κτλ.] Cf. 48, 1.
12. Ἀσκληπιόν] c. 21, 2; 22, 6.
55. *But the demons never anticipated the Crucifixion, not grasping the symbolism of prophetic language. The Cross is the symbol of Christ's power, and its form reappears in every circumstance of life.*
15. ὡς προδεδήλωται] in c. 35. The passage of Isaiah (ix 6) there referred to must be intended in ὡς προεῖπεν ὁ προφ.
19. κατανοήσατε γάρ] This argument from the symbolism of the Cross is followed by other writers, e.g. Tertullian *adu. Marc.* iii 18; Minucius *Oct.* 29. Its value is sentimental rather than logical, and it serves as an answer to the ignominy of the Cross, as Maran points

APOLOGIA

σχήματος τούτου διοικεῖται ἢ κοινωνίαν ἔχειν δύναται. 3. θάλασσα μὲν γὰρ οὐ τέμνεται, ἢν μὴ τοῦτο τὸ τρόπαιον, ὃ καλεῖται ἱστίον, ἐν τῇ νηῒ σῶον μείνῃ· γῆ δὲ οὐκ ἀροῦται ἄνευ αὐτοῦ· σκαπανεῖς δὲ τὴν ἐργασίαν οὐ ποιοῦνται οὐδὲ βαναυσουργοὶ ὁμοίως, εἰ μὴ διὰ τῶν τὸ σχῆμα 5 τοῦτο ἐχόντων ἐργαλείων. 4. τὸ δὲ ἀνθρώπειον σχῆμα οὐδενὶ ἄλλῳ τῶν ἀλόγων ζῴων διαφέρει, ἢ τῷ ὀρθόν τε εἶναι καὶ ἔκτασιν χειρῶν ἔχειν καὶ ἐν τῷ προσώπῳ ἀπὸ τοῦ μετωπίου τεταμένον τὸν λεγόμενον μυξωτῆρα φέρειν, δι᾽ οὗ ἥ τε ἀναπνοή ἐστι τῷ ζῴῳ, καὶ οὐδὲν ἄλλο δείκνυσιν 10 ἢ τὸ σχῆμα τοῦ σταυροῦ. 5. καὶ διὰ τοῦ προφήτου δὲ ἐλέχθη οὕτως· Πνεῦμα πρὸ προσώπου ἡμῶν χριστὸς κύριος. 6. καὶ τὰ παρ᾽ ὑμῖν δὲ σύμβολα τὴν τοῦ σχήματος τούτου δύναμιν δηλοῖ, λέγω δὲ τὰ τῶν οὐηξίλλων καὶ τῶν τροπαίων, δι᾽ ὧν αἵ τε πρόοδοι ὑμῶν πανταχοῦ 15 γίνονται, τῆς ἀρχῆς καὶ δυνάμεως τὰ σημεῖα ἐν τούτοις

14 δηλοῖ, λέγω δὲ τὰ τῶν οὐηξίλλων καὶ Otto δηλοῖ * * λλωμεν καὶ A (ad lacunam suppletur υιξι in marg B secunda manu)

out. It is interesting as a literary parallel to the symbolic art of early Christianity.

2. τοῦτο τὸ τρόπαιον] *'this token of victory'* (the Cross). The allusion is to the yards of a ship. The metaphor of τρόπαιον is very frequent in early Christian hymns; from Justin's way of introducing the word it would seem as if the use was already familiar. Cf. Tert. *Apol.* 16.

4. σκαπανεῖς] *'ditchers.'* Βαναυσουργοί = *'craftsmen.'*

6. ἐργαλείων] *'tools.'*

9. μυξωτῆρα]. *'nose,'* rare in singular; used in plural for '*nostrils.*'

11. διὰ τοῦ προφήτου] Lam. iv 20. The LXX text does not read πρό, and the passage is generally quoted elsewhere without it. It is possible that Justin's language was influenced by the memory of Deut. xxviii. 66, a passage which was similarly interpreted. Justin obviously means that as the nose, which is cross-shaped (i.e., at right angles with the brows), is necessary for breath, so the crucified Christ is necessary for the breath of our spirit.

14. λέγω δὲ κτλ.] Otto's emendation is one among many suggestions for completing the lacuna. It is based on the similar passages in Minucius and Tertullian, *l.c.*

ib. τῶν οὐηξίλλων] See *Dict. Antiq.* on *Signa Militaria.* The eagle with outspread wings is not unlike a cross.

15. τροπαίων] The *tropaeum* was a pole with captured weapons hung upon it.

ib. δι᾽ ὧν] *'under which,'* '*to the accompaniment of which.*'

δεικνύντες, εἰ καὶ μὴ νοοῦντες τοῦτο πράττετε. 7. καὶ τῶν παρ' ὑμῖν ἀποθνησκόντων αὐτοκρατόρων τὰς εἰκόνας ἐπὶ τούτῳ τῷ σχήματι ἀνατίθετε, καὶ θεοὺς διὰ γραμμάτων ἐπονομάζετε. 8. καὶ διὰ λόγου οὖν καὶ σχήματος τοῦ φαινομένου, ὅση δύναμις, προτρεψάμενοι ὑμᾶς ἀνεύθυνοι οἴδαμεν λοιπὸν ὄντες, κἂν ὑμεῖς ἀπιστῆτε· τὸ γὰρ ἡμέτερον γέγονε καὶ πεπέρανται.

56. 1. Οὐκ ἠρκέσθησαν δὲ οἱ φαῦλοι δαίμονες πρὸ τῆς φανερώσεως τοῦ Χριστοῦ εἰπεῖν τοὺς λεχθέντας υἱοὺς τῷ Διῒ γεγονέναι, ἀλλ' ἐπειδή, φανερωθέντος αὐτοῦ καὶ γενομένου ἐν ἀνθρώποις, καὶ ὅπως διὰ τῶν προφητῶν προεκεκήρυκτο ἔμαθον καὶ ἐν παντὶ γένει πιστευόμενον καὶ προσδοκώμενον ἔγνωσαν, πάλιν, ὡς προεδηλώσαμεν, προεβάλλοντο ἄλλους, Σίμωνα μὲν καὶ Μένανδρον ἀπὸ Σαμαρείας, οἳ καὶ μαγικὰς δυνάμεις ποιήσαντες πολλοὺς ἐξηπάτησαν καὶ ἔτι ἀπατωμένους ἔχουσι. 2. καὶ γὰρ παρ' ὑμῖν, ὡς προέφημεν, ἐν τῇ βασιλίδι Ῥώμῃ ἐπὶ Κλαυδίου Καίσαρος γενόμενος ὁ Σίμων καὶ τὴν ἱερὰν σύγκλητον καὶ τὸν δῆμον Ῥωμαίων εἰς τοσοῦτο κατεπλήξατο,

6 ἀπιστῆτε Otto ἀπιστεῖτε A

1. δεικνύντες] Used by anacoluthon for δεικνύντων agreeing with ὑμῶν. Cf. c. 11, 1, γινώσκοντες.
2. τὰς εἰκόνας] This may refer to the images of the emperors, which were put, as a sort of medallion, on the eagles of the legions. In this case ἐπὶ τούτῳ τῷ σχήματι would mean practically '*upon a cruciform standard*.' Cavedoni (quoted by Otto) suggests, however, that the reference may be to the pictures of emperors' apotheoses, in which they were represented as being carried to heaven by an eagle or by their genius with outspread wings or arms.
3. διὰ γραμμάτων] '*in inscriptions*.'

4. διὰ λόγου κτλ.] '*we have tried our best to convince you both by argument and by this obvious symbol*.'
5. ὅση δύν.] Cf. c. 13.
ib. ἀνεύθυνοι] For the idea, cf. c. 3, 4.
56. *Even after Christ's coming, the demons tried to deceive mankind by magicians like Simon and Menander*.
11. ὅπως προεκεκήρυκτο] This sentence is the object of ἔμαθον.
13. ὡς προεδηλώσαμεν] in c. 26.
14. προεβάλλοντο] Cf. above, c. 26.
18. τὴν ἱερὰν σύγκλητον] The same phrase as in the dedication, c. 1.

APOLOGIA

ὡς θεὸς νομισθῆναι καὶ ἀνδριάντι, ὡς τοὺς ἄλλους παρ᾽ ὑμῖν τιμωμένους θεούς, τιμηθῆναι. 3. ὅθεν τήν τε ἱερὰν σύγκλητον καὶ τὸν δῆμον τὸν ὑμέτερον συνεπιγνώμονας ταύτης ἡμῶν τῆς ἀξιώσεως παραλαβεῖν αἰτοῦμεν, ἵν᾽, εἴ τις εἴη τοῖς ἀπ᾽ ἐκείνου διδάγμασι κατεχόμενος, τἀληθὲς 5 μαθὼν τὴν πλάνην φυγεῖν δυνηθῇ. 4. καὶ τὸν ἀνδριάντα, εἰ βούλεσθε, καθαιρήσατε.

57. 1. Οὐ γὰρ μὴ γενέσθαι τὴν ἐκπύρωσιν ἐπὶ κολάσει τῶν ἀσεβῶν οἱ φαῦλοι δαίμονες πεῖσαι δύνανται, ὅνπερ τρόπον οὐδὲ λαθεῖν τὸν Χριστὸν παραγενόμενον 10 ἴσχυσαν πρᾶξαι, ἀλλ᾽ ἐκεῖνο μόνον, τοὺς ἀλόγως βιοῦντας καὶ ἐμπαθῶς ἐν ἔθεσι φαύλοις τεθραμμένους καὶ φιλοδοξοῦντας ἀναιρεῖν ἡμᾶς καὶ μισεῖν, δύνανται ποιῆσαι· οὓς οὐ μόνον οὐ μισοῦμεν, ἀλλ᾽, ὡς δείκνυται, ἐλεοῦντες μεταθέσθαι πεῖσαι βουλόμεθα. 2. οὐ γὰρ δεδοίκαμεν 15 θάνατον, τοῦ πάντως ἀποθανεῖν ὁμολογουμένου, καὶ μηδενὸς ἄλλου καινοῦ ἀλλ᾽ ἢ τῶν αὐτῶν ἐν τῇδε τῇ διοικήσει ὄντων· ὧν εἰ μὲν κόρος τοὺς μετασχόντας κἂν ἐνιαυτοῦ ἔχῃ, ἵνα ἀεὶ ὦσι καὶ ἀπαθεῖς καὶ ἀνενδεεῖς, τοῖς ἡμετέροις

1 θεὸς A θεὸν Otto ǁ 18 εἰ μὲν Otto εἰ μὴ A

1. θεός] ὡς θεὸς ν. is correct Greek, and the change to θεὸν is unjustified.

3. συνεπιγνώμονας κτλ.] '*judges with you of our plea.*'

7. εἰ βούλεσθε] Otto cites Theoph. *ad Aut.* I 14, III 30.

57. (*We wish to save you from error and its punishment.*) *For, in spite of the demons, punishment is a certainty. The demons can cause our death, but that is no hardship. All must die and life soon palls; but our faith saves from suffering and lack. And if death is annihilation, it is a boon to kill us, though they do not mean it so.*

This chapter is an appendix to the preceding one, Justin seizing the opportunity to reiterate that his object is really to save those whom he is addressing from error and the certain punishment of error.

8. μὴ γενέσθαι] A timeless aorist, '*that there is not.*'

12. ἐμπαθῶς] '*subject to passions.*' Opposed to ἀπαθεῖς below.

ib. φιλοδοξοῦντας] perhaps in the usual sense of '*vainglorious.*' But more probably (cf. 12, 6) '*deluded*,' '*under illusions.*'

16. τοῦ πάντως κτλ.] Cf. c. 11, 2.

ib. μηδενὸς ἄλλου κτλ.] Cf. Eccles. i 9. On ἀλλ᾽ ἢ cf. note p. 61, l. 13. '*There is nothing new, but everything is the same in this dispensation of life.*'

18. ὧν εἰ μὲν κτλ.] '*And since satiety befalls after only a year's enjoyment of them.*'

διδαγμάσι προσέχειν δεῖ. 3. εἰ δ' ἀπιστοῦσι μηδὲν εἶναι μετὰ θάνατον, ἀλλ' εἰς ἀναισθησίαν χωρεῖν τοὺς ἀποθνήσκοντας ἀποφαίνονται, παθῶν τῶν ἐνταῦθα καὶ χρειῶν ἡμᾶς ῥυόμενοι εὐεργετοῦσιν, ἑαυτοὺς δὲ φαύλους καὶ μισανθρώπους καὶ φιλοδόξους δεικνύουσιν· οὐ γὰρ ὡς ἀπαλλάξοντες ἡμᾶς ἀναιροῦσιν, ἀλλ' ὡς ἀποστεροῦντες ζωῆς καὶ ἡδονῆς φονεύουσι.

58. 1. Καὶ Μαρκίωνα δὲ τὸν ἀπὸ Πόντου, ὡς προέφημεν, προεβάλλοντο οἱ φαῦλοι δαίμονες, ὃς ἀρνεῖσθαι μὲν τὸν ποιητὴν τῶν οὐρανίων καὶ γηΐνων ἁπάντων θεὸν καὶ τὸν προκηρυχθέντα διὰ τῶν προφητῶν Χριστὸν υἱὸν αὐτοῦ καὶ νῦν διδάσκει, ἄλλον δέ τινα καταγγέλλει παρὰ τὸν δημιουργὸν τὸν πάντων θεὸν καὶ ὁμοίως ἕτερον υἱόν· 2. ᾧ πολλοὶ πεισθέντες ὡς μόνῳ τἀληθῆ ἐπισταμένῳ, ἡμῶν καταγελῶσιν, ἀπόδειξιν μηδεμίαν περὶ ὧν λέγουσιν ἔχοντες, ἀλλὰ ἀλόγως (ὡς ὑπὸ λύκου ἄρνες συνηρπασμένοι βορὰ τῶν ἀθέων δογμάτων καὶ δαιμόνων γίνονται. 3. οὐ γὰρ ἄλλο τι ἀγωνίζονται οἱ λεγόμενοι δαίμονες, ἢ ἀπάγειν τοὺς ἀνθρώπους ἀπὸ τοῦ ποιήσαντος θεοῦ καὶ τοῦ πρωτογόνου αὐτοῦ Χριστοῦ· καὶ τοὺς μὲν τῆς γῆς μὴ ἐπαίρεσθαι δυναμένους τοῖς γηΐνοις καὶ χειροποιήτοις προσήλωσαν καὶ προσηλοῦσι, τοὺς δὲ ἐπὶ θεωρίαν θείων

---

3. παθῶν τῶν ἐνταῦθα κτλ.] The same idea is found in Plat., *Ap.* 41 D.

58. *Again, Marcion was inspired by the demons and has caused many to go astray. For the demons wish to lead men away from God and Christ; instead of raising men from earth they impel them to worship earthly things, whilst those who try to contemplate celestial things they try to drive into impiety.*

8. ὡς προέφημεν] in c. 26. Marcion maintained that Christ (non-incarnate) was the son of the First God, and that therefore the Demiurge must have another son.

12. ἄλλον δέ τινα κτλ.] '*He declares that there is another God besides the Maker of all.*'

20. τοὺς μὲν τῆς γῆς κτλ.] '*Those who cannot raise themselves from earth they have pinned and pin to earthly and manufactured things,*' i.e. instead of lifting them up they fix them in degraded servitude. The rendering here given to ἐπαίρεσθαι is possible, as ἐπαίρειν regularly means 'to raise,' and τῆς γῆς could be a genit. of separation. But ἐξαίρεσθαι or (Otto) ἀπαίρεσθαι would certainly be a more satisfactory word.

ὁρμῶντας ὑπεκκρούοντες, ἢν μὴ λογισμὸν σώφρονα καὶ
καθαρὸν καὶ ἀπαθῆ βίον ἔχωσιν, εἰς ἀσέβειαν ἐμβάλ-
λουσιν.

59. 1. Ἵνα δὲ καὶ παρὰ τῶν ἡμετέρων διδασκάλων,
λέγομεν δὲ τοῦ λόγου τοῦ διὰ τῶν προφητῶν, λαβόντα τὸν
Πλάτωνα μάθητε τὸ εἰπεῖν, ὕλην ἄμορφον οὖσαν στρέ-
ψαντα τὸν θεὸν κόσμον ποιῆσαι, ἀκούσατε τῶν αὐτολεξεὶ
εἰρημένων διὰ Μωϋσέως, τοῦ προδεδηλωμένου πρώτου
προφήτου καὶ πρεσβυτέρου τῶν ἐν Ἕλλησι συγγραφέων,
δι' οὗ μηνύον τὸ προφητικὸν πνεῦμα, πῶς (τὴν ἀρχὴν) καὶ
ἐκ τίνων ἐδημιούργησεν ὁ θεὸς τὸν κόσμον, ἔφη οὕτως·
2. Ἐν ἀρχῇ ἐποίησεν ὁ θεὸς τὸν οὐρανὸν καὶ τὴν γῆν.
3. ἡ δὲ γῆ ἦν ἀόρατος καὶ ἀκατασκεύαστος, καὶ σκότος
ἐπάνω τῆς ἀβύσσου· καὶ πνεῦμα θεοῦ ἐπεφέρετο ἐπάνω
τῶν ὑδάτων. 4. καὶ εἶπεν ὁ θεός· Γενηθήτω φῶς.
καὶ ἐγένετο οὕτως. 5. ὥστε λόγῳ θεοῦ ἐκ τῶν ὑποκει-
μένων καὶ προδηλωθέντων διὰ Μωϋσέως γεγενῆσθαι τὸν
πάντα κόσμον, καὶ Πλάτων καὶ οἱ ταῦτα λέγοντες καὶ
ἡμεῖς ἐμάθομεν, καὶ ὑμεῖς πεισθῆναι δύνασθε. 6. καὶ

8 Μωϋσέως edd Μωσέως A (et infra) ‖ 18 ταυτὰ Thirlb Otto ταῦτα A

1. ὑπεκκρούοντες] 'subtly causing to wander' or 'tripping up.'
The word is not elsewhere found;
but ἐκκρούω is a very common word,
and the addition of ὑπό is easily
intelligible. Liddell and Scott mention a use of ὑπέκκρουσις by Irenaeus.
59. Plato and others got their
theories of Creation from our
teachers.
5. τοῦ λόγου τ. δ. τ. προφ.] κη-
ρυχθέντος or some similar word must
be supplied.
6. ὕλην ἄμ. οὖσαν κτλ.] Cf.
c. 10, 2. This is no definite quotation from Plato, but roughly expresses the sense of various passages
in the Timaeus, e.g. 30, 53, 69.
8. τοῦ προδεδηλωμένου] Cf. c.

32, 1; 44, 8.
10. τὴν ἀρχήν] 'originally.'
12. ἐν ἀρχῇ κτλ.] Cf. Genes. i
1—3.
16. ὥστε λόγῳ κτλ.] 'So that
both Plato and his followers and we
ourselves have learnt, and you may
learn, that the whole world came
into being by the word of God out
of the existing subject-matter which
Moses previously spoke of.' Τῶν
ὑποκ. refers to οὐρανός and γῆ, i.e.
unformed heaven and earth. Cf.
I 64, II 5 (6). Justin seems in this
passage to avoid the belief in the
eternity of matter. For he regards
οὐρανός and γῆ as the ὑποκείμενα of
the κόσμος, and these had been
created by God.

τὸ καλούμενον Ἔρεβος παρὰ τοῖς ποιηταῖς εἰρῆσθαι πρότερον ὑπὸ Μωϋσέως οἴδαμεν.

60. 1. Καὶ τὸ ἐν τῷ παρὰ Πλάτωνι Τιμαίῳ φυσιολογούμενον περὶ τοῦ υἱοῦ τοῦ θεοῦ, ὅτε λέγει· Ἐχίασεν αὐτὸν ἐν τῷ παντί, παρὰ Μωϋσέως λαβὼν ὁμοίως εἶπεν. 2. ἐν γὰρ ταῖς Μωϋσέως γραφαῖς ἀναγέγραπται, ὡς κατ' ἐκεῖνο τοῦ καιροῦ, ὅτε ἐξῆλθον ἀπὸ Αἰγύπτου οἱ Ἰσραηλῖται καὶ γεγόνασιν ἐν τῇ ἐρήμῳ, ἀπήντησαν αὐτοῖς ἰοβόλα θηρία, ἔχιδναί τε καὶ ἀσπίδες καὶ ὄφεων πᾶν γένος, ὃ ἐθανάτου τὸν λαόν· 3. καὶ κατ' ἐπίπνοιαν καὶ ἐνέργειαν τὴν παρὰ τοῦ θεοῦ γενομένην, λαβεῖν τὸν Μωϋσέα χαλκὸν καὶ ποιῆσαι τύπον σταυροῦ καὶ τοῦτον στῆσαι

5 Μωϋσέως edd Μωσέως A (ita infra et Μωϋσέα) ‖ 11 γενομένην Otto λεγομένην A

1. Ἔρεβος] Cf. Hes. *Theog.* 123 Ἐκ Χάεος δ' Ἔρεβός τε μέλαινά τε Νὺξ ἐγένοντο. The reference may be to the σκότος of the above quotation, or perhaps to Deut. xxxii 22, quoted in c. 60. It is not impossible, however, that Justin intended to connect the word with the Hebrew *ʿereb*, 'evening,' which occurs in Gen. i 5, etc.

60. *So too Plato has borrowed from Moses (though misunderstanding it) the idea of the Cross and of a Trinity. Thus our doctrines have been the models for others; and the most ignorant among us can teach them, for it is not man's wisdom but God's power which inspires them.*

4. ἐχίασεν κτλ.] This is no verbally accurate quotation; but Plat. *Tim.* 36, 13 has ταύτην οὖν τὴν ξύστασιν πᾶσαν διπλῆν κατὰ μῆκος σχίσας, μέσην πρὸς μέσην ἑκατέραν ἀλλήλαις οἷον χῖ προσβαλὼν κατέκαμψεν εἰς κύκλον, where the idea is of a cruciform distribution of the *anima mundi* throughout the universe. Justin's citation is typically loose. It means 'God set Him (His Son) in the form of a χ in the universe.'

12. ποιῆσαι τύπον σταυροῦ] Justin quotes very loosely and inserts his own commentary. In Numb. xxi 6 ff. we are not told that Moses made a cross, but a brazen serpent, καὶ ἔστησεν αὐτὸν ἐπὶ σημείου. It seems plain that Justin understood σημείου as of a cross. The same idea is found in Barnabas xi 7 Μωσῆς ποιεῖ τύπον τοῦ Ἰησοῦ. Nor are we told that Moses placed the serpent upon the Tabernacle. Again, the quotation ἐὰν προσβλέπητε κτλ. is inexact. The LXX version of the passage in Numbers has ἐγένετο ὅταν ἔδακνεν ὄφις ἄνθρωπον καὶ ἐπέβλεψεν ἐπὶ τὸν ὄφιν τὸν χαλκοῦν καὶ ἔζη. In John iii 14 we read καθὼς Μωϋσῆς ὕψωσεν τὸν ὄφιν ἐν τῇ ἐρήμῳ, οὕτως ὑψωθῆναι δεῖ τὸν υἱὸν τοῦ ἀνθρώπου, ἵνα πᾶς ὁ πιστεύων ἐν αὐτῷ ἔχῃ ζωὴν αἰώνιον. Justin's choice of words may show a knowledge of the text in St John's Gospel, but we can hardly infer it with any confidence. In *Tryph.* 94 he has ἐπὶ σημεῖον ἔστησε, δι' οὗ σημείου ἐσώζοντο οἱ ὀφιόδηκτοι,

ἐπὶ τῇ ἁγίᾳ σκηνῇ καὶ εἰπεῖν τῷ λαῷ· Ἐὰν προσβλέπητε τῷ τύπῳ τούτῳ καὶ πιστεύητε, ἐν αὐτῷ σωθήσεσθε.
4. καὶ γενομένου τούτου τοὺς μὲν ὄφεις ἀποθανεῖν ἀνέγραψε, τὸν δὲ λαὸν ἐκφυγεῖν τὸν θάνατον οὕτως παρέδωκεν.
5. ἃ ἀναγνοὺς Πλάτων καὶ μὴ ἀκριβῶς ἐπιστάμενος, 5
μηδὲ νοήσας τύπον εἶναι σταυροῦ ἀλλὰ χίασμα νοήσας,
τὴν μετὰ τὸν πρῶτον θεὸν δύναμιν κεχιάσθαι ἐν τῷ παντὶ
εἶπε. 6. καὶ τὸ εἰπεῖν αὐτὸν τρίτον, ἐπειδή, ὡς προείπομεν, ἐπάνω τῶν ὑδάτων ἀνέγνω ὑπὸ Μωϋσέως εἰρημένον
ἐπιφέρεσθαι τὸ τοῦ θεοῦ πνεῦμα. 7. δευτέραν μὲν γὰρ 10
χώραν τῷ παρὰ θεοῦ λόγῳ, ὃν κεχιάσθαι ἐν τῷ παντὶ ἔφη,
δίδωσι, τὴν δὲ τρίτην τῷ λεχθέντι ἐπιφέρεσθαι τῷ ὕδατι
πνεύματι, εἰπών· Τὰ δὲ τρίτα περὶ τὸν τρίτον. 8. καὶ
ὡς ἐκπύρωσιν γενήσεσθαι διὰ Μωϋσέως προεμήνυσε τὸ
προφητικὸν πνεῦμα, ἀκούσατε. 9. ἔφη δὲ οὕτως· 15
Καταβήσεται ἀείζωον πῦρ καὶ καταφάγεται μέχρι τῆς
ἀβύσσου κάτω. 10. οὐ τὰ αὐτὰ οὖν ἡμεῖς ἄλλοις
δοξάζομεν, ἀλλ' οἱ πάντες τὰ ἡμέτερα μιμούμενοι λέγουσι.
11. παρ' ἡμῖν οὖν ἔστι ταῦτα ἀκοῦσαι καὶ μαθεῖν παρὰ
τῶν οὐδὲ τοὺς χαρακτῆρας τῶν στοιχείων ἐπισταμένων, 20
ἰδιωτῶν μὲν καὶ βαρβάρων τὸ φθέγμα, σοφῶν δὲ καὶ

4 θάνατον οὕτως παρέδωκεν. ἃ ἀναγνοὺς Otto θάνατον. οὕτως παρέδωκεν ἀναγνοὺς A

and later ἐκήρυσσε σωτηρίαν τοῖς πιστεύουσιν ἐπὶ τούτον τὸν διὰ τοῦ σημείου τούτου τουτέστι τὸν σταυροῦσθαι μέλλοντα (alit. τουτέστι τοῦ σταυροῦ θανατοῦσθαι μέλλοντα), and again καὶ προσβλέπειν αὐτὸν τοὺς δακνομένους ἐκέλευσε.

3. τοὺς μὲν ὅ. ἀποθ.] This again is an addition to the Bible narrative.

6. χίασμα] 'two lines placed cross-wise.' With τὴν μετὰ τὸν πρῶτον θεὸν δύναμιν, cf. c. 32, 10.

8. καὶ τὸ εἰπεῖν κτλ.] 'As to his speaking of a third subsistence (this also he borrowed from Moses) since.' Supply παρὰ Μωϋσέως ἔλαβε, or the like, from the beginning of the chapter.

ib. ὡς προείπομεν] in c. 59, 3.

13. τὰ δὲ τρίτα περὶ τὸν τρίτον] 'third place to the third.' Pseudo-Plat. Epist. ii 312 E has καὶ τρίτον περὶ τὰ τρίτα. Justin's quotation is also found in Proclus Theol. Plat. ii 11. The explanation of the meaning of Plato's phrase is inordinately difficult. Justin, like other Fathers after him, obviously applies it to the Trinitarian theory.

16. καταβήσεται κτλ.] Deut. xxxii 22.

πιστῶν τὸν νοῦν ὄντων, καὶ πηρῶν καὶ χήρων τινῶν τὰς ὄψεις· ὡς συνεῖναι οὐ σοφίᾳ ἀνθρωπείᾳ ταῦτα γεγονέναι, ἀλλὰ δυνάμει θεοῦ λέγεσθαι.

61. 1. Ὃν τρόπον δὲ καὶ ἀνεθήκαμεν ἑαυτοὺς τῷ θεῷ καινοποιηθέντες διὰ τοῦ Χριστοῦ, ἐξηγησόμεθα, ὅπως μὴ τοῦτο παραλιπόντες δόξωμεν πονηρεύειν τι ἐν τῇ ἐξηγήσει. 2. ὅσοι ἂν πεισθῶσι καὶ πιστεύωσιν ἀληθῆ ταῦτα τὰ ὑφ' ἡμῶν διδασκόμενα καὶ λεγόμενα εἶναι, καὶ βιοῦν οὕτως δύνασθαι ὑπισχνῶνται, εὔχεσθαί τε καὶ αἰτεῖν νηστεύοντες παρὰ τοῦ θεοῦ τῶν προημαρτημένων ἄφεσιν διδάσκονται, ἡμῶν συνευχομένων καὶ συννηστευόντων αὐτοῖς. 3. ἔπειτα ἄγονται ὑφ' ἡμῶν ἔνθα ὕδωρ ἐστί, καὶ τρόπον ἀναγεννήσεως, ὃν καὶ ἡμεῖς αὐτοὶ ἀνεγεννήθημεν, ἀναγεννῶνται· ἐπ' ὀνόματος γὰρ τοῦ πατρὸς τῶν ὅλων καὶ δεσπότου θεοῦ καὶ τοῦ σωτῆρος ἡμῶν Ἰησοῦ Χριστοῦ καὶ πνεύματος ἁγίου τὸ ἐν τῷ ὕδατι τότε λουτρὸν

10 νηστεύοντες B νηστεύοντας A

1. πηρῶν] 'maimed,' and so perhaps more generally 'infirm.' Or he may mean 'blind.' Cf. Tryph. 69, and see Robinson Ep. to the Ephesians (referred to in note above, c. 22). Justin seems to be carrying on the idea of οὐδὲ τοὺς χαρακτῆρας κτλ., 'who have lost the power of reading if they once had it.' Being 'maimed' (except in sight) would have no special point.

ib. χήρων τὰς ὄψεις] 'deprived of sight.'

2. συνεῖναι] Cf. 14, 1.
ib. οὐ σοφίᾳ κτλ.] Cf. 1 Cor. ii 5.

61. *An exposition of Christian Baptism.* See Introd. p. xxxvii.

4. ἀνεθήκαμεν ἑ. τ. θ.] Cf. c. 14, 2.

6. πονηρεύειν] 'act wrongly.' The middle form is occasionally found in classical Greek, but not the active; it may be directly transitive 'to falsify something.'

10. νηστεύοντες ... συννηστευόντων] Cf. Didach. 7 πρὸ δὲ τοῦ βαπτίσματος προνηστευσάτω ὁ βαπτίζων καὶ ὁ βαπτιζόμενος καὶ εἴ τινες ἄλλοι δύνανται. Cf. Tert. de Bapt. 20.

12. ἔνθα ὕδωρ ἐ.] This appears to imply that as a rule baptisms took place out of doors, by river, lake, or sea. Cf. Tert. de Bapt. 4. The Didache l.c. prescribes ὕδωρ ζῶν if obtainable.

13. ἀνεγεννήθημεν] 1 Pet. i 3, 23.

14. ἐπ' ὀνόματος κτλ.] Baptism in the threefold Name seems to be the only practice known to Justin, as is the case also in Didach. 7. Cf. Matt. xxviii 19, though in the other N.T. references to Baptism the use of the threefold Name is not explicitly referred to.

16. πν. ἁγίου] The absence of the article (here and below) is a little curious.

ποιοῦνται. 4. καὶ γὰρ ὁ Χριστὸς εἶπεν· Ἂν μὴ ἀναγεννηθῆτε, οὐ μὴ εἰσέλθητε εἰς τὴν βασιλείαν τῶν οὐρανῶν· 5. ὅτι δὲ καὶ ἀδύνατον εἰς τὰς μήτρας τῶν τεκουσῶν τοὺς ἅπαξ γενομένους ἐμβῆναι, φανερὸν πᾶσίν ἐστι. 6. καὶ διὰ Ἡσαΐου τοῦ προφήτου, ὡς προεγράψαμεν, εἴρηται, τίνα τρόπον φεύξονται τὰς ἁμαρτίας οἱ ἁμαρτήσαντες καὶ μετανοοῦντες. 7. ἐλέχθη δὲ οὕτως· Λούσασθε, καθαροὶ γένεσθε, ἀφέλετε τὰς πονηρίας ἀπὸ τῶν ψυχῶν ὑμῶν, μάθετε καλὸν ποιεῖν, κρίνατε ὀρφανῷ καὶ δικαιώσατε χήραν, καὶ δεῦτε καὶ διαλεχθῶμεν, λέγει κύριος· καὶ ἐὰν ὦσιν αἱ ἁμαρτίαι ὑμῶν ὡς φοινικοῦν, ὡσεὶ ἔριον λευκανῶ, καὶ ἐὰν ὦσιν ὡς κόκκινον, ὡς χιόνα λευκανῶ. 8. ἐὰν δὲ μὴ εἰσακούσητέ μου, μάχαιρα ὑμᾶς κατέδεται· τὸ γὰρ στόμα κυρίου ἐλάλησε ταῦτα. 9. καὶ λόγον δὲ εἰς τοῦτο παρὰ τῶν ἀποστόλων ἐμάθομεν τοῦτον. 10. ἐπειδὴ

4 γενομένους A γεννωμένους Otto al

1. ἂν μὴ κτλ.] Cf. John iii 3–5; Matt. xviii 3. (Cod. D in the passage of St John's Gospel reads ἀναγεννηθῆτε. Cf. Westcott *N.T. Canon* p. 154, note 2.) This seems an unquestionable reference to the Fourth Gospel, especially when taken in connexion with the mention of Nicodemus' difficulty. Some commentators compare Ps.-Clem. *Hom.* xi 26 ἀμὴν ὑμῖν λέγω ἐὰν μὴ ἀναγεννηθῆτε ὕδατι ζῶντι εἰς ὄνομα πατρὸς υἱοῦ ἁγίου πνεύματος, οὐ μὴ εἰσέλθητε εἰς τὴν βασιλείαν τῶν οὐρανῶν, and suggest that both citations come from an apocryphal Gospel. But that seems gratuitous. Variation of text, oral tradition, looseness of quotation can all account for Justin's differences from the Gospel version.

5. ὡς προεγράψαμεν] In c. 44, 3. The quotation is from Isaiah i 16—20.

14. λόγον εἰς τοῦτο κτλ.] Referring to the following explanation. Zahn (*Zeitschr. f. Kirchengesch.* viii 1886, 66—84) considers τοῦτον here to be out of place, as not introducing a definite citation. He therefore would excise the word, and see in this sentence (referring back to the exposition of the baptismal ceremonies) a definite acknowledgment of dependence on *Didach.* 7. The reason for such an emendation is inadequate, though it is quite possible that Justin was acquainted with the *Didache*.

15. ἐπειδὴ κτλ.] The following sentences give a synopsis of apostolic teaching on the subject, and give what was doubtless the current doctrine of the Church. Some N.T. passages bearing upon the several points are: Eph. v 8; 1 Pet. i 14 (we are born in ignorance (ἀγνοοῦντες) and become by regeneration τέκνα ἐπιστήμης): Rom. vi 4, viii 2, ix 8; Gal. iv 26, v 1 (we are born κατ' ἀνάγκην and become τέκνα προαιρέσεως); Acts ii 38; xxii 16 (we are born in sin and obtain the remission of sins).

τὴν πρώτην γένεσιν ἡμῶν ἀγνοοῦντες κατ' ἀνάγκην γεγεννήμεθα ἐξ ὑγρᾶς σπορᾶς κατὰ μῖξιν τὴν τῶν γονέων πρὸς ἀλλήλους καὶ ἐν ἔθεσι φαύλοις καὶ πονηραῖς ἀναστροφαῖς γεγόναμεν, ὅπως μὴ ἀνάγκης τέκνα μηδὲ ἀγνοίας
5 μένωμεν ἀλλὰ προαιρέσεως καὶ ἐπιστήμης, ἀφέσεώς τε ἁμαρτιῶν ὧν προημάρτομεν τύχωμεν, ἐν τῷ ὕδατι ἐπονομάζεται τῷ ἑλομένῳ ἀναγεννηθῆναι καὶ μετανοήσαντι ἐπὶ τοῖς ἡμαρτημένοις τὸ τοῦ πατρὸς τῶν ὅλων καὶ δεσπότου θεοῦ ὄνομα, αὐτὸ τοῦτο μόνον ἐπιλέγοντος τοῦ τὸν λουσό-
10 μενον ἄγοντος ἐπὶ τὸ λουτρόν. 11. ὄνομα γὰρ τῷ ἀρρήτῳ θεῷ οὐδεὶς ἔχει εἰπεῖν· εἰ δέ τις τολμήσειεν εἶναι λέγειν, μέμηνε τὴν ἄσωτον μανίαν. 12. καλεῖται δὲ τοῦτο τὸ λουτρὸν φωτισμός, ὡς φωτιζομένων τὴν διάνοιαν τῶν ταῦτα μανθανόντων. 13. καὶ ἐπ' ὀνόματος δὲ
15 Ἰησοῦ Χριστοῦ, τοῦ σταυρωθέντος ἐπὶ Ποντίου Πιλάτου, καὶ ἐπ' ὀνόματος πνεύματος ἁγίου, ὃ διὰ τῶν προφητῶν προεκήρυξε τὰ κατὰ τὸν Ἰησοῦν πάντα, ὁ φωτιζόμενος λούεται.

62. 1. Καὶ τὸ λουτρὸν δὴ τοῦτο ἀκούσαντες οἱ δαί-

6 ἁμαρτιῶν ὧν Otto ἁμαρτιῶν ὑπὲρ ὧν A ‖ 9 ἐπιλέγοντος τοῦ τὸν... ἄγοντος Thirlb ἐπιλέγοντες τοῦτον...ἄγοντες A

9. αὐτὸ τοῦτο μόνον] i.e. no name (for, as Justin immediately goes on to remark, God is ineffable) but only, for the sake of distinction, the title 'Father.'

ib. τοῦ τὸν λ. ἄγοντος] Is this the sponsor, who attests the faith of the candidate? See the difficult passage in Tert. *de Bapt.* 6, with Lupton's note. More probably it is the deacon or other person who superintends and administers the baptism, repeating the threefold Name as he does so. Perhaps the phrase ἄγειν ἐπὶ τ. λ. is used rather than βαπτίζοντος or the like, because, as the word λουσόμενον implies, and as many passages in the N.T. indicate in like manner, the candidate for admission to the Church dipped *himself* in the water; it was his own act, to which others might bring him, but which they did not perform for him.

10. ὄνομα γάρ] Cf. c. 9, 3; ii 5 (6), 1.

11. εἶναι] sc. ὄνομα.

13. φωτισμός] Cf. Heb. vi 4, x 32; and see Suicer s.v. There is an obvious analogy to the mysteries of the heathen, where such a word was used.

14. μανθανόντων] referring to the instruction of catechumens.

62. *The demons have anticipated Christian baptism by heathen sprinklings and lustrations; and the taking-off of shoes is borrowed from Moses' experience.*

μονες διὰ τοῦ προφήτου κεκηρυγμένον ἐνήργησαν καὶ
ῥαντίζειν ἑαυτοὺς τοὺς εἰς τὰ ἱερὰ αὐτῶν ἐπιβαίνοντας καὶ
προσιέναι αὐτοῖς μέλλοντας, λοιβὰς καὶ κνίσας ἀποτε-
λοῦντας· τέλεον δὲ καὶ λούεσθαι ἐπιόντας πρὶν ἐλθεῖν ἐπὶ
τὰ ἱερά, ἔνθα ἵδρυνται, ἐνεργοῦσι. 2. καὶ γὰρ τὸ ὑπο- 5
λύεσθαι ἐπιβαίνοντας τοῖς ἱεροῖς καὶ τοῖς αὐτοῖς τοὺς
θρησκεύοντας κελεύεσθαι ὑπὸ τῶν ἱερατευόντων ἐκ τῶν
συμβάντων Μωϋσεῖ τῷ εἰρημένῳ προφήτῃ μαθόντες οἱ
δαίμονες ἐμιμήσαντο. 3. κατ' ἐκεῖνο γὰρ τοῦ καιροῦ
ὅτε Μωϋσῆς ἐκελεύσθη κατελθὼν εἰς Αἴγυπτον ἐξαγαγεῖν 10
τὸν ἐκεῖ λαὸν τῶν Ἰσραηλιτῶν, ποιμαίνοντος αὐτοῦ ἐν τῇ
ἀρραβικῇ γῇ πρόβατα τοῦ πρὸς μητρὸς θείου, ἐν ἰδέᾳ
πυρὸς ἐκ βάτου προσωμίλησεν αὐτῷ ὁ ἡμέτερος Χριστός,
καὶ εἶπεν· Ὑπόλυσαι τὰ ὑποδήματά σου καὶ προσελθὼν
ἄκουσον. 4. ὁ δὲ ὑπολυσάμενος καὶ προσελθὼν ἀκήκοε 15
κατελθεῖν εἰς Αἴγυπτον καὶ ἐξαγαγεῖν τὸν ἐκεῖ λαὸν τῶν
Ἰσραηλιτῶν, καὶ δύναμιν ἰσχυρὰν ἔλαβε παρὰ τοῦ λαλή-

4 ἐπιόντας Hagen Otto ἀπιόντας A ‖ 6 τοῖς αὐτοῖς τοὺς A τοῖς τοιούτοις Braun αὐτοῖς Pautigny ‖ 8 Μωϋσεῖ edd Μωσεῖ A (ita infra Μωϋσῆς)

1. τοῦ προφήτου] i.e. in Isaiah i 16—20, quoted c. 61, 7.
2. ῥαντίζειν] Sprinklings were common in heathen cultus. Cf. Tert. *de Bapt.* v, with Lupton's and Oehler's notes. For a complete lustration before mysteries (τέλεον λούεσθαι) cf. Paus. xiv 20, 4, who tells us that the women of Tanagra bathed before the orgies of Dionysus.
5. τὸ ὑπολύεσθαι] For the taking-off of shoes cf. Pythagoras' precept ἀνυπόδητος θῦε καὶ προσκύνει. See also Tert. *Apol.* 40; *de Ieiun.* 16.
6. καὶ τοῖς αὐτοῖς κτλ.] The Greek of the MS text is strange. Τοὺς is out of place with θρησκεύοντας, and τοῖς αὐτοῖς seems harsh. If retained it must be translated 'those who serve them (i.e. the demons),' though Maran renders it '*iisdem rebus daemones colunt.*' Liddell and Scott quote a parallel for the use of θρησκεύειν with dative. If emendation be considered necessary, it might be the most simple course to insert an ἐν before τοῖς αὐτοῖς.
12. τοῦ π. μ. θείου] A mistake. Jethro was Moses' father-in-law. It may be a mere slip of memory, or (Thirlb.) Justin may have confused the story of Moses' vision with that of Jacob's, when he was feeding the flocks of his uncle Laban.
14. ὑπόλυσαι κτλ.] Cf. Exod. iii 5. Notice the identification of 'the angel of the Lord,' 'the Lord,' 'God,' with Christ.
15. ἀκήκοε κ.] '*was told to go down.*'

σαντος αὐτῷ ἐν ἰδέᾳ πυρὸς Χριστοῦ, καὶ κατελθὼν ἐξήγαγε
τὸν λαὸν ποιήσας μεγάλα καὶ θαυμάσια, ἃ ͵εἰ βούλεσθε
μαθεῖν, ἐκ τῶν συγγραμμάτων ἐκείνου ἀκριβῶς μαθήσεσθε.
63. 1. Ἰουδαῖοι δὲ πάντες καὶ νῦν διδάσκουσι τὸν
5 ἀνωνόμαστον θεὸν λελαληκέναι τῷ Μωϋσεῖ. 2. ὅθεν
τὸ προφητικὸν πνεῦμα διὰ Ἡσαΐου τοῦ προμεμηνυμένου
προφήτου ἐλέγχον αὐτούς, ὡς προεγράψαμεν, εἶπεν· Ἔγνω
βοῦς τὸν κτησάμενον καὶ ὄνος τὴν φάτνην τοῦ κυρίου
αὐτοῦ, Ἰσραὴλ δέ με οὐκ ἔγνω καὶ ὁ λαός με οὐ συνῆκε.
10 3. καὶ Ἰησοῦς δὲ ὁ Χριστός, ὅτι οὐκ ἔγνωσαν Ἰουδαῖοι τί
πατὴρ καὶ τί υἱός, ὁμοίως ἐλέγχων αὐτοὺς καὶ αὐτὸς εἶπεν·
Οὐδεὶς ἔγνω τὸν πατέρα εἰ μὴ ὁ υἱός, οὐδὲ τὸν υἱὸν εἰ μὴ ὁ
πατὴρ καὶ οἷς ἂν ἀποκαλύψῃ ὁ υἱός. 4. ὁ λόγος δὲ
τοῦ θεοῦ ἐστιν ὁ υἱὸς αὐτοῦ, ὡς προέφημεν. 5. καὶ
15 ἄγγελος δὲ καλεῖται καὶ ἀπόστολος· αὐτὸς γὰρ ἀπαγ-
γέλλει ὅσα δεῖ γνωσθῆναι, καὶ ἀποστέλλεται, μηνύσων ὅσα
ἀγγέλλεται, ὡς καὶ αὐτὸς ὁ κύριος ἡμῶν εἶπεν· Ὁ ἐμοῦ
ἀκούων ἀκούει τοῦ ἀποστείλαντός με. 6. καὶ ἐκ τῶν
τοῦ Μωϋσέως δὲ συγγραμμάτων φανερὸν τοῦτο γενήσεται.

5 Μωϋσεῖ edd Μωσεῖ A (ita infr et Μωϋσέως, Μωϋσῆς)

63. *The Jews suppose it was God who spoke to Moses, but it was really Christ.*

This is a chapter of digression. Justin is anxious to avoid anthropomorphism. The ineffable God needs a medium of communication with men.

4. τὸν ἀνων. θ.] Cf. 61, 11.
7. ὡς προεγράψαμεν] in c. 37, 1. Cf. Isaiah i 3.
12. οὐδεὶς ἔγνω κτλ.] Matt. xi 27; Luke x 22; John viii 19, xvi 3. The quotation appears to come from the Synoptic Gospels, but the comment, with its somewhat curious exegesis (οὐκ ἔγν. τί π. καὶ τί υἱός), seems to betray the influence of St John. Irenaeus iv 6 also quotes the words as forming part of an argument against the Jews. In *Tryph.* 100 the quotation reappears with γινώσκει instead of ἔγνω. As Westcott (*N. T. Canon* p. 137) points out, the variations in the wording of this quotation in our orthodox authorities are striking. Both the use of ἔγνω and the transposition of clauses can be paralleled from writers who admitted the four Canonical Gospels exclusively, e.g. Irenaeus, Origen, Epiphanius.

14. ὡς προέφημεν] in c. 21, 1; 22, 1, 2; 23, 2; 32, 10.
15. ἀπόστολος] Cf. c. 12, 9; Heb. iii 1.
17. ὁ ἐμοῦ ἀκούων κτλ.] Cf. Matt. x 40; Luke x 16; John xiv 24.

7. λέλεκται δὲ ἐν αὐτοῖς οὕτως· Καὶ ἐλάλησε Μωϋσεῖ ἄγγελος θεοῦ ἐν φλογὶ πυρὸς ἐκ τῆς βάτου καὶ εἶπεν· Ἐγώ εἰμι ὁ ὤν, θεὸς Ἀβραάμ, θεὸς Ἰσαάκ, θεὸς Ἰακώβ, ὁ θεὸς τῶν πατέρων σου. 8. κάτελθε εἰς Αἴγυπτον καὶ ἐξάγαγε τὸν λαόν μου. 9. τὰ δ' ἑπόμενα ἐξ ἐκείνων βουλόμενοι μαθεῖν δύνασθε· οὐ γὰρ δυνατὸν ἐν τούτοις ἀναγράψαι πάντα. 10. ἀλλ' εἰς ἀπόδειξιν γεγόνασιν οἵδε οἱ λόγοι ὅτι υἱὸς θεοῦ καὶ ἀπόστολος Ἰησοῦς ὁ Χριστός ἐστι, πρότερον λόγος ὤν, καὶ ἐν ἰδέᾳ πυρὸς ποτὲ φανείς, ποτὲ δὲ καὶ ἐν εἰκόνι ἀσωμάτων· νῦν δὲ διὰ θελήματος θεοῦ ὑπὲρ τοῦ ἀνθρωπείου γένους ἄνθρωπος γενόμενος ὑπέμεινε καὶ παθεῖν ὅσα αὐτὸν ἐνήργησαν οἱ δαίμονες διατεθῆναι ὑπὸ τῶν ἀνοήτων Ἰουδαίων. 11. οἵτινες ἔχοντες ῥητῶς εἰρημένον ἐν τοῖς Μωϋσέως συντάγμασι· Καὶ ἐλάλησεν ἄγγελος τοῦ θεοῦ τῷ Μωϋσεῖ ἐν πυρὶ φλογὸς ἐν βάτῳ καὶ εἶπεν· Ἐγώ εἰμι ὁ ὤν, ὁ θεὸς Ἀβραὰμ καὶ ὁ θεὸς Ἰσαὰκ καὶ ὁ θεὸς Ἰακώβ, | τὸν τῶν ὅλων πατέρα καὶ δημιουργὸν τὸν ταῦτα εἰπόντα λέγουσιν εἶναι. 12. ὅθεν καὶ τὸ προφητικὸν πνεῦμα ἐλέγχον αὐτοὺς εἶπεν· Ἰσραὴλ δέ με οὐκ ἔγνω, καὶ ὁ λαός με οὐ συνῆκε. 13. καὶ πάλιν ὁ Ἰησοῦς, ὡς ἐδηλώσαμεν, παρ' αὐτοῖς ὢν εἶπεν· Οὐδεὶς ἔγνω τὸν πατέρα εἰ μὴ ὁ υἱός, οὐδὲ τὸν υἱὸν εἰ μὴ ὁ πατὴρ καὶ οἷς ἂν ὁ υἱὸς ἀποκαλύψῃ. 14. Ἰουδαῖοι οὖν ἡγησάμενοι ἀεὶ τὸν πατέρα τῶν ὅλων λελαληκέναι τῷ Μωϋσεῖ, τοῦ λαλήσαντος αὐτῷ ὄντος υἱοῦ τοῦ θεοῦ, ὃς καὶ ἄγγελος καὶ ἀπόστολος κέκληται, δικαίως ἐλέγχονται καὶ διὰ τοῦ προφητικοῦ πνεύματος καὶ δι' αὐτοῦ τοῦ Χριστοῦ ὡς οὔτε τὸν πατέρα οὔτε τὸν υἱὸν ἔγνωσαν. 15. οἱ γὰρ τὸν υἱὸν πατέρα φάσκοντες εἶναι ἐλέγχονται

---

1. καὶ ἐλάλησε κτλ.] Exod. iii 2, 6, 10, 14, 15. Justin's argument, though he does not make it quite explicit, turns on the fact that the same speaker who says 'I am the God of Abraham' is described also as 'the angel of the Lord.' Cf. Hil. *de Trin.* iv 32.

5. ἐξ ἐκείνων] i.e. from Moses' writings.

10. ἐν εἰκόνι ἀσωμάτων] i.e. as an angel.

μήτε τὸν πατέρα ἐπιστάμενοι, μηθ' ὅτι ἐστὶν υἱὸς τῷ πατρὶ τῶν ὅλων γινώσκοντες· ὃς λόγος καὶ πρωτότοκος ὢν τοῦ θεοῦ καὶ θεὸς ὑπάρχει. 16. καὶ πρότερον διὰ τῆς τοῦ πυρὸς μορφῆς καὶ εἰκόνος ἀσωμάτου τῷ Μωϋσεῖ καὶ τοῖς ἑτέροις προφήταις ἐφάνη· νῦν δ' ἐν χρόνοις τῆς ὑμετέρας ἀρχῆς, ὡς προείπομεν, διὰ παρθένου ἄνθρωπος γενόμενος κατὰ τὴν τοῦ πατρὸς βουλὴν ὑπὲρ σωτηρίας τῶν πιστευόντων αὐτῷ καὶ ἐξουθενηθῆναι καὶ παθεῖν ὑπέμεινεν, ἵνα ἀποθανὼν καὶ ἀναστὰς νικήσῃ τὸν θάνατον. 17. τὸ δὲ εἰρημένον ἐκ βάτου τῷ Μωϋσεῖ· Ἐγώ εἰμι ὁ ὤν, ὁ θεὸς Ἀβραὰμ καὶ ὁ θεὸς Ἰσαὰκ καὶ ὁ θεὸς Ἰακὼβ καὶ ὁ θεὸς τῶν πατέρων σου, σημαντικὸν τοῦ καὶ ἀποθανόντας ἐκείνους μένειν καὶ εἶναι αὐτοῦ τοῦ Χριστοῦ ἀνθρώπους· καὶ γὰρ πρῶτοι τῶν πάντων ἀνθρώπων ἐκεῖνοι περὶ θεοῦ ζήτησιν ἠσχολήθησαν, Ἀβραὰμ μὲν πατὴρ ὢν τοῦ Ἰσαάκ, Ἰσαὰκ δὲ τοῦ Ἰακώβ, ὡς καὶ Μωϋσῆς ἀνέγραψε.

64. 1. Καὶ τὸ ἀνεγείρειν δὲ τὸ εἴδωλον τῆς λεγομένης Κόρης ἐπὶ ταῖς τῶν ὑδάτων πηγαῖς ἐνεργῆσαι τοὺς δαίμονας, λέγοντας θυγατέρα αὐτὴν εἶναι τοῦ Διός, μιμησαμένους τὸ διὰ Μωϋσέως εἰρημένον, ἐκ τῶν προειρημένων

---

2 ὃς λόγος καὶ Otto ὃς καὶ λόγος A || 20 Μωϋσέως edd Μωσέως A (ita infra Μωϋσῆς)

---

2. ὃς λόγος κτλ.] Cf. John i 1; Phil. ii 6.
4. εἰκόνος ἀσωμάτου] '*image of an incorporeal being*,' or else '*incorporeal form*.'
6. ὡς προείπομεν] in c. 32, 14.
13. μένειν] Cf. Matt. xxii 32.
15. ἠσχολήθησαν] '*busied themselves*.'
64. *The demons anticipated the doctrine of the Spirit in the myth of Koré, and of creation in the myth of Athena.*
17. τὸ ἀνεγείρειν κτλ.] '*to raise an image of Koré over the springs of water*.' It is not easy, in our present state of knowledge, to see the resemblance between the position of Koré and that which is ascribed to the Spirit. In Diod. Sic. v 4 we read τὴν Κόρην λαχεῖν τοὺς περὶ τὴν Ἕνναν λειμῶνας· πηγὴν δὲ μεγάλην αὐτῇ καθιερωθῆναι ἐν τῇ Συρακοσίᾳ, τὴν ὀνομαζομένην Κυάνην. Moreover in the record concerning the mysteries of Andania she is called Ἁγνή and a stream is named after her. (Cf. Farnell *Greek Cults* iii, Demeter-Koré, 246.) There seems to be no other evidence to suggest a connexion between Kore and springs.

νοῆσαι δύνασθε. 2. ἔφη γὰρ ὁ Μωϋσῆς, ὡς προεγράψαμεν· Ἐν ἀρχῇ ἐποίησεν ὁ θεὸς τὸν οὐρανὸν καὶ τὴν γῆν. 3. ἡ δὲ γῆ ἦν ἀόρατος καὶ ἀκατασκεύαστος, καὶ πνεῦμα θεοῦ ἐπεφέρετο ἐπάνω τῶν ὑδάτων. 4. εἰς μίμησιν οὖν τοῦ λεχθέντος ἐπιφερομένου τῷ ὕδατι πνεύματος θεοῦ τὴν Κόρην θυγατέρα τοῦ Διὸς ἔφασαν. 5. καὶ τὴν Ἀθηνᾶν δὲ ὁμοίως πονηρευόμενοι θυγατέρα τοῦ Διὸς ἔφασαν, οὐκ ἀπὸ μίξεως, ἀλλ', ἐπειδὴ ἐννοηθέντα τὸν θεὸν διὰ λόγου τὸν κόσμον ποιῆσαι ἔγνωσαν, ὡς τὴν πρώτην ἔννοιαν ἔφασαν τὴν Ἀθηνᾶν· ὅπερ γελοιότατον ἡγούμεθα εἶναι, τῆς ἐννοίας εἰκόνα παραφέρειν θηλειῶν μορφήν. 6. καὶ ὁμοίως τοὺς ἄλλους λεγομένους υἱοὺς τοῦ Διὸς αἱ πράξεις ἐλέγχουσιν.

65. 1. Ἡμεῖς δὲ μετὰ τὸ οὕτως λοῦσαι τὸν πεπεισμένον καὶ συγκατατεθειμένον ἐπὶ τοὺς λεγομένους ἀδελφοὺς ἄγομεν, ἔνθα συνηγμένοι εἰσί, κοινὰς εὐχὰς ποιησόμενοι ὑπέρ τε ἑαυτῶν καὶ τοῦ φωτισθέντος καὶ ἄλλων πανταχοῦ πάντων εὐτόνως, ὅπως καταξιωθῶμεν τὰ ἀληθῆ μαθόντες καὶ δι' ἔργων ἀγαθοὶ πολιτευταὶ καὶ φύλακες τῶν ἐντεταλμένων εὑρεθῆναι, ὅπως τὴν αἰώνιον σωτηρίαν σωθῶμεν.

5 ἐπιφερομένου A ἐπιφέρεσθαι Otto

1. ὡς προεγράψαμεν] in c. 59, 2.
7. πονηρευόμενοι] '*behaving with trickery*.' Cf. 61, 1.
8. ἐπειδὴ ἐνν. κτλ.] '*Since they knew that God conceived and made the world by the Logos* (or *by Reason*).'
9. τὴν πρώτην ἔννοιαν] Cf. c. 26, 3. The reference here is to the myth of Athena springing fullgrown from the brain of Zeus.
10. γελοιότατον] The absurdity consists in imagining an incorporeal thing in bodily form. Otto quotes Prudent. *c. Symm.* ii 58.
13. αἱ πράξεις] '*their actions*.'
65. *An account of the Christian Eucharist following Baptism.* Cf.

Pliny *Ep.* x 96; *Didach.* 9, 10. This account resembles that in c. 67; but the early part of the service as given in c. 67 is here left out, because Justin is describing only the admission of a convert. Justin's account is very simple and naive, perhaps purposely, on account of his heathen readers.
14. οὕτως] as described in c. 61.
15. συγκατατεθειμένον] '*who has assented*.'
ib. ἀδελφούς] Cf. Matt. xxiii 8. See Tert. *Apol.* 39.
19. ἀγ. πολιτευταί] '*good livers*.' The word is not, so far as I know, found elsewhere in this sense. But cf. πολιτείαν, 4, 20.

2. ἀλλήλους φιλήματι ἀσπαζόμεθα παυσάμενοι τῶν εὐχῶν. 3. ἔπειτα προσφέρεται τῷ προεστῶτι τῶν ἀδελφῶν ἄρτος καὶ ποτήριον ὕδατος καὶ κράματος, καὶ οὗτος λαβὼν αἶνον καὶ δόξαν τῷ πατρὶ τῶν ὅλων διὰ τοῦ ὀνόματος τοῦ υἱοῦ καὶ τοῦ πνεύματος τοῦ ἁγίου ἀναπέμπει καὶ εὐχαριστίαν ὑπὲρ τοῦ κατηξιῶσθαι τούτων παρ' αὐτοῦ ἐπὶ πολὺ ποιεῖται· οὗ συντελέσαντος τὰς εὐχὰς καὶ τὴν εὐχαριστίαν πᾶς ὁ παρὼν λαὸς ἐπευφημεῖ λέγων· Ἀμήν. 4. τὸ δὲ ἀμὴν τῇ ἑβραΐδι φωνῇ τὸ γένοιτο σημαίνει. 5. εὐχαριστήσαντος δὲ τοῦ προεστῶτος καὶ ἐπευφημήσαντος παντὸς τοῦ λαοῦ, οἱ καλούμενοι παρ' ἡμῖν διάκονοι διδόασιν ἑκάστῳ τῶν παρόντων μεταλαβεῖν ἀπὸ τοῦ εὐχαριστηθέντος ἄρτου καὶ οἴνου καὶ ὕδατος καὶ τοῖς οὐ παροῦσιν ἀποφέρουσι.

66. 1. Καὶ ἡ τροφὴ αὕτη καλεῖται παρ' ἡμῖν εὐχαριστία, ἧς οὐδενὶ ἄλλῳ μετασχεῖν ἐξόν ἐστιν ἢ τῷ πιστεύοντι ἀληθῆ εἶναι τὰ δεδιδαγμένα ὑφ' ἡμῶν, καὶ λουσαμένῳ τὸ ὑπὲρ ἀφέσεως ἁμαρτιῶν καὶ εἰς ἀναγέννησιν λουτρόν, καὶ οὕτως βιοῦντι ὡς ὁ Χριστὸς παρέδωκεν. 2. οὐ γὰρ ὡς κοινὸν ἄρτον οὐδὲ κοινὸν πόμα ταῦτα λαμβάνομεν·

1. φιλήματι] Cf. Tert. *de Orat.* 14; Cyr. Jer. *Catech. Myst.* v 3.
2. τῷ προεστῶτι] Cf. 1 Tim. v 17. The word is pagan and not only Christian. The fact that the προεστώς was not present at the actual baptism, and only received the neophyte afterwards, is in accordance with the apostolic practice. Acts xix 5, 6 (cf. 1 Cor. i 14), and x 48.
3. καὶ κράματος] κρᾶμα = '*mixed wine and water*.' On the reading see *Introd.* p. xliii. Could κρᾶμα mean '*wine to mix it with*' or '*wine mixed with it*'?
6. τούτων] i.e. '*these gifts.*'
7. ἐπὶ πολύ] '*at length*.'
8. ἐπευφημεῖ] '*assents*.' So in Homer, *Il.* i 22.

ib. Ἀμήν] Taken from the synagogue worship. Cf. 1 Cor. xiv 16.
11. οἱ διάκονοι] It was apparently not a priestly duty to distribute the sacrament.
13. εὐχαριστηθέντος] '*dedicated with thanks.*' The transitive use recurs in 67, 4. Cf. also Iren. 1 xiii 2 ποτήρια...εὐχαριστεῖν.
66. *Explanation of the term Eucharist and of the belief associated with the elements.*
16. ἧς οὐδενὶ ἄλλῳ κτλ.] The qualifications for admission to the Eucharist are (1) faith, (2) baptism, (3) obedience. Cf. *Didach.* 9.
20. ὡς κοινὸν ἄ.] Cf. Iren. IV xviii 5 (a passage plainly recalling Justin) οὐκέτι κοινὸς ἄρτος ἐστίν, ἀλλ' εὐχαριστία.

ἀλλ' ὃν τρόπον διὰ λόγου θεοῦ σαρκοποιηθεὶς Ἰησοῦς
Χριστὸς ὁ σωτὴρ ἡμῶν καὶ σάρκα καὶ αἷμα ὑπὲρ σωτηρίας
ἡμῶν ἔσχεν, οὕτως καὶ τὴν δι' εὐχῆς λόγου τοῦ παρ' αὐτοῦ
εὐχαριστηθεῖσαν τροφήν, ἐξ ἧς αἷμα καὶ σάρκες κατὰ
μεταβολὴν τρέφονται ἡμῶν, ἐκείνου τοῦ σαρκοποιηθέντος 5
Ἰησοῦ καὶ σάρκα καὶ αἷμα ἐδιδάχθημεν εἶναι. 3. οἱ
γὰρ ἀπόστολοι ἐν τοῖς γενομένοις ὑπ' αὐτῶν ἀπομνημονεύ-
μασιν, ἃ καλεῖται εὐαγγέλια, οὕτως παρέδωκαν ἐντετάλθαι
αὐτοῖς· τὸν Ἰησοῦν λαβόντα ἄρτον εὐχαριστήσαντα εἰ-
πεῖν· Τοῦτο ποιεῖτε εἰς τὴν ἀνάμνησίν μου, τοῦτό ἐστι τὸ 10
σῶμά μου· καὶ τὸ ποτήριον ὁμοίως λαβόντα καὶ εὐχαριστήσαντα εἰπεῖν· Τοῦτό ἐστι τὸ αἷμά μου· καὶ μόνοις
αὐτοῖς μεταδοῦναι. 4. ὅπερ καὶ ἐν τοῖς τοῦ Μίθρα
μυστηρίοις παρέδωκαν γίνεσθαι μιμησάμενοι οἱ πονηροὶ

10 ποιεῖτε Cod Ottob ποιεῖται A || τοῦτό ἐστι τὸ σῶμα Braun Otto τοὐτέστι τ. σ. A

1. ἀλλ' ὃν τρόπον κτλ.] On this passage see *Introd.* p. xli.
ib. διὰ λόγου θεοῦ] Cf. c. 46, 5.
3. δι' εὐχῆς λόγου] A comparison with 13, 1 λόγῳ εὐχῆς καὶ εὐχαριστίας makes it seem improbable that λόγου should depend upon εὐχῆς (*'prayer to the Word'*) instead of εὐχῆς depending upon λόγου. Otto well says 'nempe διὰ λόγου θεοῦ et δι' εὐχῆς λόγου τοῦ παρ' αὐτοῦ (scil. χριστοῦ) sibi inuicem respondent, ita quidem, ut precationis uerbo a Christo profecto Iustinus diuinam uim tribuat, qualis in dei λόγῳ insit.'
8. ἃ καλεῖται εὐαγγ.] There is not the least reason for thinking that these words are a gloss, for the heathen would not have inserted them, and the Christians would not have required them, as they had no gospel that competed with the four of the Canon. Cf. *Tryph.* 10 ὑμῶν δὲ καὶ τὰ ἐν τῷ λεγομένῳ εὐαγγελίῳ παραγγέλματα

and 100 (where also the word ἀπομνημονεύματα for the gospels recurs) καὶ ἐν τῷ εὐαγγελίῳ δὲ γέγραπται. The plural form shows that Justin knew of at least two 'Gospels'; the singular may denote some kind of 'harmony' of them.
9. τὸν Ἰησοῦν κτλ.] Cf. Luke xxii 19 ff.; Mark xiv 22; Matt. xxvi 26; 1 Cor. xi 23.
12. μόνοις] The words prepare for the reference to 'mysteries' in the next sentence; and, like the clause ἧς οὐδενὶ ἄλλῳ κτλ. above, they tacitly meet the objection that the Christian worship was for bad reasons concealed from observation.

13. Μίθρα] Cf. Cumont *Culte de Mithras* p. 176. Tert. *de Praescr. Haer.* 40 says of the Mithras-communicant 'celebrat et panis oblationem.' Justin speaks again of the mysteries of Mithras in *Tryph.* 70.

δαίμονες· ὅτι γὰρ ἄρτος καὶ ποτήριον ὕδατος τίθεται ἐν
ταῖς τοῦ μυουμένου τελεταῖς μετ' ἐπιλόγων τινῶν, ἢ ἐπίστασθε ἢ μαθεῖν δύνασθε.

67. 1. Ἡμεῖς δὲ μετὰ ταῦτα λοιπὸν ἀεὶ τούτων
ἀλλήλους ἀναμιμνήσκομεν· καὶ οἱ ἔχοντες τοῖς λειπομένοις πᾶσιν ἐπικουροῦμεν, καὶ σύνεσμεν ἀλλήλοις ἀεί.
2. ἐπὶ πᾶσί τε οἷς προσφερόμεθα εὐλογοῦμεν τὸν ποιητὴν
τῶν πάντων διὰ τοῦ υἱοῦ αὐτοῦ Ἰησοῦ Χριστοῦ καὶ διὰ
πνεύματος τοῦ ἁγίου. 3. καὶ τῇ τοῦ ἡλίου λεγομένῃ
ἡμέρᾳ πάντων κατὰ πόλεις ἢ ἀγροὺς μενόντων ἐπὶ τὸ
αὐτὸ συνέλευσις γίνεται, καὶ τὰ ἀπομνημονεύματα τῶν
ἀποστόλων ἢ τὰ συγγράμματα τῶν προφητῶν ἀναγινώ-
σκεται, μέχρις ἐγχωρεῖ. 4. εἶτα παυσαμένου τοῦ ἀνα-
γινώσκοντος ὁ προεστὼς διὰ λόγου τὴν νουθεσίαν καὶ
πρόκλησιν τῆς τῶν καλῶν τούτων μιμήσεως ποιεῖται.
5. ἔπειτα ἀνιστάμεθα κοινῇ πάντες καὶ εὐχὰς πέμπομεν·

2. μετ' ἐπιλόγων τινῶν] 'with some words said over them.'
67. *An account of the Sunday Eucharist.*
5. ἀλλήλους ἀναμ.] Cf. Heb. x 24 f.
ib. οἱ ἔχοντες] as in 1 Cor. xi 22.
6. σύνεσμεν] Cf. Tert. *Ap.* 39.
7. προσφερόμεθα] 'we receive.' Cf. 13, 1, and for the custom see 1 Tim. iv 3 f.
9. τῇ τ. ἡλίου λ. ἡ.] The usual Christian term is ἡ κυριακὴ ἡμέρα. On the heathen week and days of the week see *Dict. of Chr. Antiq.* s.v. 'Week.' Cf. also Tert. *Ap.* 16, *ad Nat.* i 13. Clem. Al. *Strom.* vii 12 (p. 877, Potter) refers to the days of Hermes (Wednesday) and Aphrodite (Friday).
10. ἀγρούς] An indication of the spread of Christianity. Cf. Pliny *Ep.* x 96 'neque ciuitates tantum sed uicos etiam atque agros contagio peruagata est.'
11. συνέλευσις] Cf. *Acta S. Justini* 3.
ib. τὰ ἀπομνημ.] The first hint in Christian literature of a liturgical reading of the Gospels. For the public reading of other Christian writings at this period see Dionysius of Corinth ap. Eus. *H. E.* iv 23.
13. μέχρις ἐγχ.] 'as long as there is time for.' Cf. *Tryph.* 118 ὡς ἐγχωρεῖ.
ib. τοῦ ἀναγ.] So the προεστώς did not read.
14. διὰ λόγου] '*in a speech.*'
16. ἀνιστάμεθα] The usual attitude for prayer. Apparently they sat to hear the reading. Were these prayers silent prayers, or private extempore prayers uttered aloud, or fixed prayers that all knew and could join in with their voices? It is perhaps impossible to decide; but from Clem. Rom. *ad Corinth.* 59—61, *Didach.* 9, 10 we see that liturgical prayers may have been in use in the Christian Church by now.

καί, ὡς προέφημεν, παυσαμένων ἡμῶν τῆς εὐχῆς ἄρτος προσφέρεται καὶ οἶνος καὶ ὕδωρ, καὶ ὁ προεστὼς εὐχὰς ὁμοίως καὶ εὐχαριστίας, ὅση δύναμις αὐτῷ, ἀναπέμπει, καὶ ὁ λαὸς ἐπευφημεῖ λέγων τὸ Ἀμήν, καὶ ἡ διάδοσις καὶ ἡ μετάληψις ἀπὸ τῶν εὐχαριστηθέντων ἑκάστῳ γίνεται, καὶ 5 τοῖς οὐ παροῦσι διὰ τῶν διακόνων πέμπεται. 6. οἱ εὐποροῦντες δὲ καὶ βουλόμενοι κατὰ προαίρεσιν ἕκαστος τὴν ἑαυτοῦ ὃ βούλεται δίδωσι, καὶ τὸ συλλεγόμενον παρὰ τῷ προεστῶτι ἀποτίθεται, 7. καὶ αὐτὸς ἐπικουρεῖ ὀρφανοῖς τε καὶ χήραις, καὶ τοῖς διὰ νόσον ἢ δι' ἄλλην 10 αἰτίαν λειπομένοις, καὶ τοῖς ἐν δεσμοῖς οὖσι, καὶ τοῖς παρεπιδήμοις οὖσι ξένοις, καὶ ἁπλῶς πᾶσι τοῖς ἐν χρείᾳ οὖσι κηδεμὼν γίνεται. 8. τὴν δὲ τοῦ ἡλίου ἡμέραν κοινῇ πάντες τὴν συνέλευσιν ποιούμεθα, ἐπειδὴ πρώτη ἐστὶν ἡμέρα, ἐν ᾗ ὁ θεὸς τὸ σκότος καὶ τὴν ὕλην τρέψας κόσμον 15 ἐποίησε, καὶ Ἰησοῦς Χριστὸς ὁ ἡμέτερος σωτὴρ τῇ αὐτῇ ἡμέρᾳ ἐκ νεκρῶν ἀνέστη· τῇ γὰρ πρὸ τῆς κρονικῆς ἐσταύρωσαν αὐτόν, καὶ τῇ μετὰ τὴν κρονικήν, ἥτις ἐστὶν ἡλίου ἡμέρα, φανεὶς τοῖς ἀποστόλοις αὐτοῦ καὶ μαθηταῖς ἐδίδαξε ταῦτα, ἅπερ εἰς ἐπίσκεψιν καὶ ὑμῖν ἀνεδώκαμεν. 20

1. ὡς προέφημεν] in 65, 3.
2. προσφέρεται] i.e. to the president. Cf. 65, 3. It does not refer to an oblation of the elements.
3. ὅση δύν.] Cf. 13, 1; 55, 8; *Tryph.* 80, and the Eucharistic formula in *Const. Apost.* viii 12 εὐχαριστοῦμέν σοι θεὲ παντοκράτορ οὐχ ὅσον ὀφείλομεν ἀλλ' ὅσον δυνάμεθα. See also *Didach.* 10 τοῖς δὲ προφήταις ἐπιτρέπετε εὐχαριστεῖν ὅσα θέλουσιν.
7. κατὰ προαίρεσιν] Cf. 14, 2; Tert. *Ap.* 39 'nemo compellitur sed sponte confert.'
13. κηδεμών] '*curator*' (Otto). Hatch *Organiz.* p. 39 f. makes great use of this passage to support his theory of the origin of the episcopate.

ib. τὴν δὲ τ. ἡλίου ἡ.] Cf. 1 Cor. xvi 2. There is no reference to the fourth commandment.

17. πρὸ τῆς κρονικῆς] Friday was called *dies Veneris*. Some have supposed, perhaps over-fancifully, that this paraphrase is here adopted in order to avoid using the name of Venus.

19. φανεὶς κτλ.] Probably no special discourse is alluded to. The passage need not be understood to mean that Justin knew of no appearance after the first day, though this might be imagined from St Luke's Gospel, if it stood alone. The words τῇ μετὰ τ. κρ. are perhaps to be attached only to φανείς.

68. 1. Καὶ εἰ μὲν δοκεῖ ὑμῖν λόγου καὶ ἀληθείας ἔχεσθαι, τιμήσατε αὐτά· εἰ δὲ λῆρος ὑμῖν δοκεῖ, ὡς ληρωδῶν πραγμάτων καταφρονήσατε, καὶ μὴ ὡς κατ' ἐχθρῶν κατὰ τῶν μηδὲν ἀδικούντων θάνατον ὁρίζετε. 2. προλέγομεν γὰρ ὑμῖν ὅτι οὐκ ἐκφεύξεσθε τὴν ἐσομένην τοῦ θεοῦ κρίσιν, ἐὰν ἐπιμένητε τῇ ἀδικίᾳ· καὶ ἡμεῖς ἐπιβοήσομεν· Ὁ φίλον τῷ θεῷ τοῦτο γενέσθω.

3. καὶ ἐξ ἐπιστολῆς δὲ τοῦ μεγίστου καὶ ἐπιφανεστάτου Καίσαρος Ἀδριανοῦ, τοῦ πατρὸς ὑμῶν, ἔχοντες ἀπαιτεῖν ὑμᾶς, καθὰ ἠξιώσαμεν, κελεῦσαι τὰς κρίσεις γενέσθαι, οὐκ ἐκ τοῦ κεκρῖσθαι τοῦτο ὑπὸ Ἀδριανοῦ μᾶλλον ἠξιώσαμεν, ἀλλ' ἐκ τοῦ ἐπίστασθαι δίκαια ἀξιοῦν τὴν προσφώνησιν καὶ ἐξήγησιν πεποιήμεθα. 4. ὑπετάξαμεν δὲ καὶ τῆς ἐπιστολῆς Ἀδριανοῦ τὸ ἀντίγραφον, ἵνα καὶ κατὰ τοῦτο ἀληθεύειν ἡμᾶς γνωρίζητε. 5. καὶ ἔστι τὸ ἀντίγραφον τοῦτο·

Μινουκίῳ Φουνδανῷ.

Hadrianus Minucio Fundano.

6. ἐπιστολὴν ἐδεξάμην γραφεῖσάν μοι ἀπὸ Σερηνίου

accepi litteras ad me scriptas a decessore tuo

---

7 ὁ φίλον τ. θ. τοῦτο γεν. A ὡς τ. θ. φίλον, ταύτῃ γεν. marg A ‖ 8 ἐπιστολῆς Eus *H E* IV 8 ἀποστολῆς A ‖ 10 γενέσθαι A γίνεσθαι Eus ‖ 11 οὐκ ἐκ τοῦ κεκρ. τοῦτο ὑπ. Ἀδρ. A τοῦτο οὐχ ὡς ὑπὸ Ἀδριανοῦ κελευσθὲν Eus ‖ 12 δίκαια A δικαίαν Eus ‖ 13 καὶ ἐξήγησιν πεποιήμεθα A om Eus ‖ 15 κατὰ A om Eus ‖ 16 ἔστι τὸ ἀντ. τοῦτο A ἔστιν τόδε Eus ‖ 20 Σερηνίου A Σερέννιου Eus *H E* IV 9

68. *If you think our story true, respect it; if not, treat it as nonsense, but do not put to death those who do no ill; for you will be punished by God, if you persist in injustice. There follows Hadrian's rescript to Fundanus.*

2. ἔχεσθαι] used as in Heb. vi 9.
5. τὴν κρίσιν] Cf. Wisd. vi 3 f.
7. ὁ φίλον κτλ.] Cf. Plat. *Crit.* 43 D εἰ ταύτῃ τοῖς θεοῖς φίλον, ταύτῃ ἔστω (the reading of marg. A is nearer to the Platonic form). Καὶ ἡμεῖς seems to imply that the saying had become proverbial. Variant forms of it appear in Plat. *Ap.* 19 A, *Phaedr.* 246 D; Epict. *Enchir.* 50 (79).

9. τοῦ πατρὸς ὑ.] See *Introd.* p. xlvii.
12. τὴν προσφών.] as in c. 1.
17. Μινουκίῳ Φ.] Eus. *H.E.* iv 8 says that Justin αὐτὴν παρατέθεικαι τὴν Ῥωμαϊκὴν ἀντιγραφήν, ἡμεῖς δ'

Γρανιανοῦ, λαμπροτάτου ἀνδρός, ὅντινα σὺ διεδέξω. 7. οὐ δοκεῖ οὖν μοι τὸ πρᾶγμα ἀζήτητον καταλιπεῖν, ἵνα μήτε οἱ ἄνθρωποι ταράττωνται καὶ τοῖς συκοφάνταις χορηγία κακουργίας παρασχεθῇ. 8. ἂν οὖν σαφῶς εἰς ταύτην τὴν ἀξίωσιν οἱ ἐπαρχιῶται δύνωνται διϊσχυρίζεσθαι κατὰ τῶν Χριστιανῶν, ὡς καὶ πρὸ βήματος ἀποκρίνεσθαι, ἐπὶ τοῦτο μόνον τραπῶσιν, ἀλλ' οὐκ ἀξιώσεσιν οὐδὲ μόναις βοαῖς. 9. πολλῷ γὰρ μᾶλλον προσῆκεν, εἴ τις κατηγορεῖν βούλοιτο, τοῦτό σε διαγινώσκειν. 10. εἴ τις οὖν κατηγορεῖ καὶ δείκ-

Serennio Graniano, clarissimo uiro, et non placet mihi relationem silentio praeterire, ne et innoxii perturbentur et calumniatoribus latrocinandi tribuatur occasio. itaque si euidenter prouinciales huic petitioni suae adesse ualent aduersum Christianos, ut pro tribunali eos in aliquo arguant, hoc eis exequi non prohibeo. precibus autem in hoc solis et adclamationibus uti eis non permitto. etenim multo aequius est, si quis uolet accusare, te cognoscere de obiectis. si quis igitur accusat et probat aduersum leges quic-

3 οὖν μοι A μοι οὖν Eus || 8 ἂν...δύνωνται A εἰ ...δύνανται Eus || 13 ἀποκρίνεσθαι A ἀποκρίνασθαι Eus

ἐπὶ τὸ Ἑλληνικὸν κατὰ δύναμιν αὐτὴν μετειλήφαμεν. The MSS of Justin have it in Greek; but what appears to be the Latin original is preserved in Rufinus' translation of Euseb. *Eccl. Hist.* and is inserted above, as it stands in Mommsen's text. On the authenticity of the rescript and the position implied by it see Appendix II. It is to be noted that in some places the Latin seems to be stronger than the Greek, e.g. οἱ ἄνθρωποι represents 'innoxii,' διόριζε 'supplicia statues,' ὅπως ἂν ἐκδικήσειας, 'ut suppliciis seuerioribus uindices'; mistranslation may account for this.
C. Minucius Fundanus was consul

A.D. 107, proconsul of Asia probably about A.D. 125. Q. Licinius Silvanus Granianus was consul A.D. 106, proconsul of Asia about A.D. 123, 124. The mistake Serenius for Silvanus is at least as old as Eusebius, and may be due to a scribe.

3. τὸ πρᾶγμα] i.e. '*the matter referred to me*' (*relationem*).

7. χορηγία κακ.] '*facility for wrongdoing.*'

10. οἱ ἐπαρχ.] '*the provincials.*'

15. μ. βοαῖς] Cf. Tert. *Apol.* 40 'statim Christianos ad leonem acclamatur.'

18. τοῦτό σε διαγ.] '*you must judge*' (and not be led away by mere clamour).

νυσί τι παρὰ τοὺς νόμους
πράττοντας, οὕτως διόριζε
κατὰ τὴν δύναμιν τοῦ ἁμαρ-
τήματος· ὡς μὰ τὸν Ἡρα-
κλέα, εἴ τις συκοφαντίας
χάριν τοῦτο προτείνοι, διαλάμβανε ὑπὲρ τῆς δεινό-
τητος, καὶ φρόντιζε ὅπως
ἂν ἐκδικήσειας.

quam agere memoratos
homines, pro merito pec-
catorum etiam supplicia
statues. illud mehercule
magnopere curabis, ut si
quis calumniae gratia
quemquam horum postu-
lauerit reum, in hunc pro
sui nequitia suppliciis seuerioribus uindices.

1. 1. Καὶ τὰ χθὲς δὲ καὶ πρώην ἐν τῇ πόλει ὑμῶν
γενόμενα ἐπὶ Οὐρβίκου, ὦ Ῥωμαῖοι, καὶ τὰ πανταχοῦ
ὁμοίως ὑπὸ τῶν ἡγουμένων ἀλόγως πραττόμενα ἐξηνάγ-

2 διόριζε A ὅριζε Eus || (Titulus) τοῦ αὐτοῦ ἁγίου ιουστίνου φιλοσόφου
καὶ μάρτυρος ἀπολογία ὑπὲρ χριστιανῶν πρὸς τὴν ῥωμαίων σύγκλητον A

1. παρὰ τοὺς νόμους] The language is quite vague. Christianity
was already illegal, and is not hereby
legalised. See below.
6. διαλάμβανε κτλ.] 'arrest him
for his villainy.' For this use of
διαλαμβάνω cf. Hdt. i 114, Plat. Rep.
615 E.
The four points in this edict,
according to Ramsay (*Ch. in Rom.
Emp.* p. 322), are (1) the desire to
prevent public trouble and to check
the licence of false accusers; (2) the
provincials may prosecute, but must
bring evidence; (3) there must be
proof of illegality; (4) the prose-
cutor who fails must be punished.
The vagueness of the third point is
probably deliberate; it is practically
left open to any governor to consider the mere name of Christian
an offence, if proved (as Trajan's
letter had admitted), or to require
proof of some more definite crime,
according to his own bias in the
matter.
1. *I must for your own sake write
this account. What happened under
Urbicus is only a specimen of what*
*is done to us everywhere. Sinners,
whom Christian friends have reproved, and the demons, who use
judge and magistrate as their tools,
are combined to procure our death.*
On the connexion between this
and the preceding Apology cf. *Introd.*
p. xliv.
11. χθὲς δέ] It has been argued
from this δὲ that these words could
not have formed the beginning of
an independent treatise. But Otto
points out that Xenophon begins
his *Oeconomicus* and his *Apologia
Socratis* (he might have added his
Conuiuium) in a similar manner.
12. Οὐρβίκου] Q. Lollius Urbicus,
a man of distinction; he had been
consul, legatus in Germany and
Britain, and was praefectus Urbi
from A.D. 144 (at the earliest) till
160.
ib. ὦ Ῥωμαῖοι] This may be, as
Veil suggests, an interpolation, inserted after the separation of this
part from the first. But it is not
impossible to regard it as a mere
rhetorical expression.

κασέ με ὑπὲρ ὑμῶν, ὁμοιοπαθῶν ὄντων καὶ ἀδελφῶν, κἂν ἀγνοῆτε καὶ μὴ θέλητε διὰ τὴν δόξαν τῶν νομιζομένων ἀξιωμάτων, τὴν τῶνδε τῶν λόγων σύνταξιν ποιήσασθαι. 2. πανταχοῦ γάρ, ὃς ἂν σωφρονίζηται ὑπὸ πατρὸς ἢ γείτονος ἢ τέκνου ἢ φίλου ἢ ἀδελφοῦ ἢ ἀνδρὸς ἢ γυναικὸς κατ' ἔλλειψιν, χωρὶς τῶν πεισθέντων τοὺς ἀδίκους καὶ ἀκολάστους ἐν αἰωνίῳ πυρὶ κολασθήσεσθαι, τοὺς δ' ἐναρέτους καὶ ὁμοίως Χριστῷ βιώσαντας ἐν ἀπαθείᾳ συγγενέσθαι τῷ θεῷ (λέγομεν δὲ τῶν γενομένων Χριστιανῶν), διὰ τὸ δυσμετάθετον καὶ φιλήδονον καὶ δυσκίνητον πρὸς τὸ καλὸν ὁρμῆσαι, καὶ οἱ φαῦλοι δαίμονες, ἐχθραίνοντες ἡμῖν καὶ τοὺς τοιούτους δικαστὰς ἔχοντες ὑποχειρίους καὶ λατρεύ-

1 ὑμῶν A ἡμῶν Otto ‖ 3 σύνταξιν edd σύναξιν A ‖ 8 συγγενέσθαι A συγγενήσεσθαι Otto Krüger

1. ὑπὲρ ὑμῶν] This is in accordance with Justin's usual idea. Cf. i 3, 4. Otto's emendation is an obvious suggestion, and may be correct.

ib. κἂν ἀγνοῆτε] '(*You are our brothers*), *even if you are ignorant of the fact and repudiate it on account of the splendour of their position*' (i.e. of the ἡγούμενοι above).

3. τῶνδε τ. λόγων σύντ.] Veil suggests that this phrase indicates the two Apologies to be a collection of various λόγοι, and attempts to break them up into three fairly equal parts, supposing the two Apologies (treated as one) to have been written on three rolls. These suppositions are not impossible, but the phrase here is too vague to justify such definiteness; it means either '*the composition of these arguments, of this address,*' or, referring only to what follows, '*the composition of this story*.' Λόγοι is a mere collective plural, and does not imply that the Apologies are a compilation of definitely separable λόγοι.

4. ὃς ἂν κτλ.] A very clumsy sentence. There is a double subject to the verb παρασκευάζουσιν, viz. (1) ὃς ἂν σωφρονίζηται, (2) οἱ φαῦλοι δαίμονες. The enemies of Christianity are therefore (1) any who have been reproved for their sins (ἔλλειψις=*delictum*),—that is, everyone except such as are Christians;—their hostility is caused by their obstinacy and love of pleasure and unreadiness to embrace what is good; (2) the demons, who can control the judges. It should be observed, however, that the MS has left a space before καὶ οἱ φ. δ., as if some words had been lost.

8. συγγενέσθαι] The change to συγγενήσεσθαι marks the parallelism with κολασθήσεσθαι, but is not necessary.

12. τοὺς τοιούτους] i.e. such as Urbicus. 'The judges are their servants and slaves, just as the rulers (or magistrates) are their tools,' i.e. both judicial and administrative officials are under the demons' power.

οντας, ὡς οὖν ἄρχοντας δαιμονιῶντας, φονεύειν ἡμᾶς παρασκευάζουσιν. 3. ὅπως δὲ καὶ ἡ αἰτία τοῦ παντὸς γενομένου ἐπὶ Οὐρβίκου φανερὰ ὑμῖν γένηται, τὰ πεπραγμένα ἀπαγγελῶ.

2. 1. Γυνή τις συνεβίου ἀνδρὶ ἀκολασταίνοντι, ἀκολασταίνουσα καὶ αὐτὴ πρότερον. 2. ἐπεὶ δὲ τὰ τοῦ Χριστοῦ διδάγματα ἔγνω, αὐτὴ < ἐσωφρονίσθη καὶ τὸν ἄνδρα ὁμοίως σωφρονεῖν πείθειν ἐπειρᾶτο, τὰ διδάγματα ἀναφέρουσα, τήν τε μέλλουσαν τοῖς οὐ σωφρόνως καὶ μετὰ λόγου ὀρθοῦ βιοῦσιν ἔσεσθαι ἐν αἰωνίῳ πυρὶ κόλασιν ἀπαγγέλλουσα. 3. ὁ δὲ ταῖς αὐταῖς ἀσελγείαις ἐπιμένων ἀλλοτρίαν διὰ τῶν πράξεων ἐποιεῖτο τὴν γαμετήν. 4. ἀσεβὲς γὰρ ἡγουμένη τὸ λοιπὸν ἡ γυνὴ συγκατακλίνεσθαι ἀνδρί, παρὰ τὸν τῆς φύσεως νόμον καὶ παρὰ τὸ δίκαιον πόρους ἡδονῆς ἐκ παντὸς πειρωμένῳ ποιεῖσθαι, τῆς συζυγίας χωρισθῆναι ἐβουλήθη. 5. καὶ ἐπειδὴ ἐξεδυσωπεῖτο ὑπὸ τῶν αὐτῆς, ἔτι προσμένειν συμβουλευόντων, ὡς εἰς ἐλπίδα μεταβολῆς ἥξοντός ποτε τοῦ ἀνδρός, βιαζομένη ἑαυτὴν ἐπέμενεν. 6. ἐπειδὴ δὲ ὁ ταύτης ἀνὴρ εἰς τὴν Ἀλεξάνδρειαν πορευθεὶς χαλεπώτερα πράττειν ἀπηγγέλθη, ὅπως μὴ κοινωνὸς τῶν ἀδικημάτων καὶ ἀσεβημάτων γένηται, μένουσα ἐν τῇ συζυγίᾳ καὶ ὁμοδίαιτος καὶ ὁμόκοιτος γινομένη, τὸ λεγόμενον παρ' ὑμῖν ῥεπούδιον δοῦσα ἐχωρίσθη. 7. ὁ δὲ καλὸς κἀγαθὸς

6 ἐπεὶ δὲ τὰ Α ἐπειδὴ δὲ τὰ Eus *H E* iv 17 || 7 ἔγνω, αὐτὴ Thirlb ἔγνω αὕτη Α || < ἐσωφρονίσθη—ἐλεγχόμενον > Eus om Α

2. *Story of a Christian martyrdom.*
10. λόγου ὀρθοῦ] a Platonic phrase='*right reason*.' Cf. ii 6 (7), 7; 9, 4.
15. πόρους ἡδονῆς] '*means of pleasure*.'
16. ἐξεδυσωπεῖτο] '*she was intreated earnestly*.' Joseph. *Ant.* xv iv 1.

17. τῶν αὐτῆς] '*her Christian friends.*'
20. Ἀλεξάνδρειαν] Alexandria was a notoriously licentious city.
24. ῥεπούδιον] Lat. *repudium*. Ashton points out that Roman law allowed women to divorce their husbands, whilst Mosaic law only allowed men to divorce their wives. Cf. 1 Cor. vii 13 foll.

ταύτης ἀνήρ, δέον αὐτὸν χαίρειν ὅτι ἃ πάλαι μετὰ τῶν
ὑπηρετῶν καὶ τῶν μισθοφόρων εὐχερῶς ἔπραττε, μέθαις
χαίρουσα καὶ κακίᾳ πάσῃ, τούτων μὲν τῶν πράξεων πέ-
παυτο καὶ αὐτὸν τὰ αὐτὰ παύσασθαι πράττοντα ἐβούλετο,
μὴ βουλομένου ἀπαλλαγείσης κατηγορίαν πεποίηται, λέ- 5
γων αὐτὴν Χριστιανὴν εἶναι. 8. καὶ ἡ μὲν βιβλίδιόν
σοι τῷ αὐτοκράτορι ἀνέδωκεν πρότερον συγχωρηθῆναι
αὐτῇ διοικήσασθαι τὰ ἑαυτῆς ἀξιοῦσα, ἔπειτα ἀπολογή-
σασθαι περὶ τοῦ κατηγορήματος μετὰ τὴν τῶν πραγμάτων
αὐτῆς διοίκησιν· καὶ συνεχώρησας τοῦτο. 9. ὁ δὲ 10
ταύτης ποτὲ ἀνήρ, πρὸς ἐκείνην μὲν μὴ δυνάμενος τανῦν
ἔτι λέγειν, πρὸς Πτολεμαῖόν τινα, [ὃν Οὔρβικος ἐκολά-
σατο], διδάσκαλον ἐκείνης τῶν Χριστιανῶν μαθημάτων
γενόμενον, ἐτράπετο διὰ τοῦδε τοῦ τρόπου. 10. ἑκα-
τόνταρχον [εἰς δεσμὰ ἐμβαλόντα τὸν Πτολεμαῖον,] φίλον 15
αὐτῷ ὑπάρχοντα, ἔπεισε λαβέσθαι τοῦ Πτολεμαίου καὶ
ἀνερωτῆσαι εἰ, αὐτὸ τοῦτο μόνον, Χριστιανός ἐστι.
11. καὶ τὸν Πτολεμαῖον, φιλαλήθη ἀλλ' οὐκ ἀπατηλὸν
οὐδὲ ψευδολόγον τὴν γνώμην ὄντα, ὁμολογήσαντα ἑαυτὸν
εἶναι Χριστιανόν, ἐν δεσμοῖς γενέσθαι ὁ ἑκατόνταρχος 20
πεποίηκε, καὶ ἐπὶ πολὺν χρόνον ἐν τῷ δεσμωτηρίῳ ἐκολά-
σατο. 12. τελευταῖον δέ, ὅτε ἐπὶ Οὔρβικον ἤχθη ὁ

12 Οὔρβικος edd Οὐρβίκιος Eus (ita infra Οὔρβικον, Οὐρβίκου, Οὔρβικον,
Οὔρβικε) ‖ 17 εἰ, αὐτὸ τοῦτο μόνον Eus αὐτὸ τοῦτο μόνον, εἰ Steph Otto

5. μὴ βουλομένου] Genitive of
separation after ἀπαλλαγείσης, agreeing with αὐτοῦ understood. ' When
she had separated from him since
he refused to alter his ways.'
6. βιβλίδιον] Lat. libellus.
7. σοι τῷ αὐτοκράτορι] There
is apparently only one αὐτοκράτωρ
concerned. See *Introd.* p. li.
12. ὃν Οὔρβ. ἐκολ.] These words
certainly look like a gloss, though
they were probably already inserted
in Justin's text by the time of
Eusebius.

14. ἑκατόνταρχον] On the question how 'centurions' came to do such
duty, see Le Blant *Les Persécuteurs
et les Martyrs* ch. xxv, esp. p. 300 f.
15. εἰς δεσμὰ ἐμβ. τ. Πτολ.]
These words may be retained, the
sense being ' *to imprison Ptolemy
and, arresting him, to ask.*' But
they read like a gloss to explain
λαβέσθαι. They are found in
Eusebius' version.
17. αὐτὸ τοῦτο μόνον] Cf. i 4.
Eusebius' text may quite well stand.

ἄνθρωπος, ὁμοίως αὐτὸ τοῦτο μόνον ἐξητάσθη, εἰ εἴη Χριστιανός. 13. καὶ πάλιν, τὰ καλὰ ἑαυτῷ συνεπιστάμενος διὰ τὴν ἀπὸ τοῦ Χριστοῦ διδαχήν, τὸ διδασκαλεῖον τῆς θείας ἀρετῆς ὡμολόγησεν. 14. ὁ γὰρ 5 ἀρνούμενος ὁτιοῦν ἢ κατεγνωκὼς τοῦ πράγματος ἔξαρνος γίνεται, ἢ ἑαυτὸν ἀνάξιον ἐπιστάμενος καὶ ἀλλότριον τοῦ πράγματος τὴν ὁμολογίαν φεύγει· ὧν οὐδὲν πρόσεστι τῷ ἀληθινῷ Χριστιανῷ. 15. καὶ τοῦ Οὐρβίκου κελεύσαντος αὐτὸν ἀπαχθῆναι Λούκιός τις, καὶ αὐτὸς ὢν 10 Χριστιανός, ὁρῶν τὴν ἀλόγως οὕτω γενομένην κρίσιν, πρὸς τὸν Οὔρβικον ἔφη· 16. Τίς ἡ αἰτία; τοῦ μήτε μοιχὸν μήτε πόρνον μήτε ἀνδροφόνον μήτε λωποδύτην μήτε ἅρπαγα μήτε ἁπλῶς ἀδίκημά τι πράξαντα ἐλεγχόμενον >, ὀνόματος δὲ Χριστιανοῦ προσωνυμίαν ὁμολογοῦντα τὸν 15 ἄνθρωπον τοῦτον ἐκολάσω; οὐ πρέποντα εὐσεβεῖ αὐτοκράτορι οὐδὲ φιλοσόφῳ Καίσαρος παιδὶ οὐδὲ τῇ ἱερᾷ συγκλήτῳ κρίνεις, ὦ Οὔρβικε. 17. καὶ ὃς οὐδὲν ἄλλο ἀποκρινάμενος καὶ πρὸς τὸν Λούκιον ἔφη· Δοκεῖς μοι καὶ σὺ εἶναι τοιοῦτος. 18. καὶ τοῦ Λουκίου φήσαντος· 20 Μάλιστα, πάλιν καὶ αὐτὸν ἀπαχθῆναι ἐκέλευσεν. 19. ὁ δὲ καὶ χάριν εἰδέναι ὡμολόγει, πονηρῶν δεσποτῶν τῶν

11 αἰτία; τοῦ Braun Otto αἰτία τοῦ Eus ‖ 14 ὀνόματος δὲ Χριστιανοῦ Eus παθήματος δὲ χριστοῦ A ‖ 16 φιλοσόφῳ Eus φιλοσόφου A ‖ τῇ ἱερᾷ A ἱερᾷ Eus ‖ 19 τοῦ Λουκίου Eus Λουκίου A ‖ 21 καὶ χάριν A χάριν Eus ‖ πονηρῶν κτλ A πονηρῶν γὰρ δ. τ. τ. ἀπ. ἐπεῖπε καὶ παρὰ ἀγαθῶν πατέρα καὶ βασιλέα τὸν θεὸν πορ. Eus

2. τὰ καλὰ ἑαυτῷ συνεπιστ.] 'conscious of the good which he owed to the teaching which proceeded from Christ, he confessed the doctrine of divine virtue.'
4. ὁ γὰρ ἀρνούμενος κτλ.] 'For he who denies anything either denies it because he has condemned it, or shrinks from confessing it, because he knows himself to be unworthy of and alien to it.'
7. ὧν οὐδὲν κτλ.] Cf. Plin. Ep. x

96 'quorum nihil posse cogi dicuntur qui sunt re uera Christiani.'
9. ἀπαχθῆναι] Lat. duci, as in Pliny l.c. Cf. Acts xii 19.
11. τίς ἡ αἰτία; τοῦ] Τοῦ stands for τίνος (χάριν). Cf. Tryph. 20, τοῦ μὴ ἀκούσεσθε;
15. εὐσεβεῖ κτλ.] The omission of Verus' name seems strange. See Introd. p. li.
16. ἱερᾷ συγκλήτῳ] Cf. i 1.

τοιούτων ἀπηλλάχθαι γινώσκων καὶ πρὸς τὸν πατέρα καὶ βασιλέα τῶν οὐρανῶν πορεύεσθαι. 20. καὶ ἄλλος δὲ τρίτος ἐπελθὼν κολασθῆναι προσετιμήθη.

3 (4). 1. "Οπως δὲ μή τις εἴπῃ· Πάντες οὖν ἑαυτοὺς

3 ἐπελθών Eus ἀπελθών A

3. κ. προσετιμήθη] 'was also sentenced to be punished.'

3 (4). *You may ask 'why do you not all commit suicide and so go at once to heaven?' The answer is that to commit suicide is to shirk our duty to man and is therefore contrary to God's will; and we do not deny our Christianity, when accused, because to do so would be untrue, and because we wish to free you from your prejudices against Christianity.*

In the text the order of chapters as it stands in the MSS has been preserved. In most editions (e.g. Maran, Otto, Braun, Krüger) c. viii has been taken out of its place and put after c. ii, and this chapter appears therefore as c. iv. The reasons for this transposition are twofold; (1) Euseb. *H. E.* iv 17, after quoting the second chapter of this Apology, adds τούτοις ὁ Ἰουστῖνος εἰκότως καὶ ἀκολούθως ἃς προεμνημονεύσαμεν (in *H. E.* iv 16) αὐτοῦ φωνὰς ἐπάγει λέγων Κἀγὼ οὖν προσδοκῶ ὑπό τινος τῶν ὠνομασμένων ἐπιβουλευθῆναι, καὶ τὰ λοιπά. But Eusebius is so inaccurate in his quotations that such words can scarcely entitle us to neglect the MS order; nor need ἀκολούθως mean 'immediately following,' though certainly that is the more natural meaning to assign to it. (2) It is said that the transposition gives a better consecutiveness of ideas, that c. viii interferes with the sequence of cc. vii and ix. This argument, even if true, is hardly convincing in the case of a thinker so inconsecutive as Justin. But it may even be doubted whether the argument is true. (*a*) Chapter iii certainly seems to follow c. ii very naturally; the heathen opponent wishes the Christians would all do like the τρίτος just mentioned, and πορεύεσθε in c. iv § 1 picks up the idea in πορεύεσθαι c. iii § 19. (*b*) Chapter viii follows very naturally on c. vii. In c. vii Justin shows how the demons have caused attacks upon philosophers. In c. viii he adds that himself (a philosopher) expects the same fate ὑπό τινος τῶν ὠνομασμένων (i.e. one of the demons' servants). If c. viii followed on c. ii it would not be very clear who were referred to in τῶν ὠνομασμένων. We should have to hark back to c. i and find the reference there. (*c*) In c. ix Justin takes up the idea that eternal fire is a vain threat. This perhaps would follow better on c. vii than c. viii would. But it is to be noted that in c. ix he is definitely turning to a new objection in the words ἵνα δὲ μή τις εἴπῃ. And c. viii is a sort of parenthesis, Justin taking the opportunity for a hit at Crescens and for a personal explanation.

It seems therefore that the reasons for the transposition are scarcely strong enough to justify so entire a desertion of the MS order. There is no possible explanation of the way in which the chapters could have been altered to the order in which they now stand in the MSS, except the improbable theory of sheer error. The transposition would never have been suggested but for Eusebius' words. And his statement is not decisive enough, nor is his authority sufficiently strong, to entitle us to make the change.

4. πάντες οὖν] All editors quote Tert. *ad Scap.* 5 'Arrius

φονεύσαντες πορεύεσθε ἤδη παρὰ τὸν θεὸν καὶ ἡμῖν
πράγματα μὴ παρέχετε· — ἐρῶ δι' ἣν αἰτίαν τοῦτο οὐ
πράττομεν, καὶ δι' ἣν ἐξεταζόμενοι ἀφόβως ὁμολογοῦμεν.
2. οὐκ εἰκῆ τὸν κόσμον πεποιηκέναι τὸν θεὸν δεδιδάγμεθα,
5 ἀλλ' ἢ διὰ τὸ ἀνθρώπειον γένος· χαίρειν τε τοῖς τὰ
προσόντα αὐτῷ μιμουμένοις προέφημεν, ἀπαρέσκεσθαι δὲ
τοῖς τὰ φαῦλα ἀσπαζομένοις ἢ λόγῳ ἢ ἔργῳ. 3. εἰ
οὖν πάντες ἑαυτοὺς φονεύσομεν, τοῦ μὴ γεννηθῆναί τινα
καὶ μαθητευθῆναι εἰς τὰ θεῖα διδάγματα, ἢ καὶ μὴ εἶναι τὸ
10 ἀνθρώπειον γένος, ὅσον ἐφ' ἡμῖν, αἴτιοι ἐσόμεθα, ἐναντίον
τῇ τοῦ θεοῦ βουλῇ καὶ αὐτοὶ ποιοῦντες, ἐὰν τοῦτο πράξω-
μεν. 4. ἐξεταζόμενοι δὲ οὐκ ἀρνούμεθα διὰ τὸ συνεπίστα-
σθαι ἑαυτοῖς μηδὲν φαῦλον, ἀσεβὲς δὲ ἡγούμενοι μὴ κατὰ
πάντα ἀληθεύειν, ὃ καὶ φίλον τῷ θεῷ γινώσκομεν, ὑμᾶς
15 δὲ καὶ τῆς ἀδίκου προλήψεως ἀπαλλάξαι νῦν σπεύδοντες.

4 (5). 1. Εἰ δέ τινα ὑπέλθοι καὶ ἡ ἔννοια αὕτη ὅτι, εἰ
θεὸν ὡμολογοῦμεν βοηθόν, οὐκ ἄν, ὡς λέγομεν, ὑπὸ ἀδίκων ἐκρατούμεθα καὶ ἐτιμωρούμεθα, καὶ τοῦτο διαλύσω.
2. ὁ θεὸς τὸν πάντα κόσμον ποιήσας καὶ τὰ ἐπίγεια

8 τοῦ μὴ Perion Sylburg τοῦ καὶ A

Antoninus in Asia cum persequeretur instanter, omnes illius ciuitatis Christiani ante tribunalia eius se manu facta obtulerunt. Tum ille, paucis duci iussis, reliquis ait ὦ δειλοί, εἰ θέλετε ἀποθνήσκειν, κρημνοὺς ἢ βρόχους ἔχετε.' To court martyrdom in fanatical zeal, or presumption, or morbid ambition, was not unknown in the days of Christian persecution, and is censured by many Church fathers.

6. προέφημεν] Cf. i 10, 1. Some editors suspect προέφημεν here to be a gloss, and certainly it might easily have been inserted. But no one would have suspected it except on *a priori* grounds.

ib. ἀπαρέσκεσθαι] The middle is used by classical writers in the sense of '*to be displeased*'; but this may be passive.

7. εἰ οὖν κτλ.] Justin's view of suicide is that it is a shirking of the responsibility belonging to a member of corporate humanity, and as such contrary to the will of God.

15. προλήψεως] '*prejudice.*'

4 (5). *You ask why God allows us to be persecuted. The answer is that God intrusted the government of the world to angels; these by unnatural union with women produced the demons who enslaved mankind. Poets and mythologists ignorantly ascribe this result to their God and the sons and brothers of their God.*

16. ἡ ἔννοια αὕτη] This was a common argument against Christianity. Maran quotes Clem. *Strom.* iv 11 § 80 διὰ τί δὲ οὐ βοηθεῖσθε διωκόμενοι; φασί.

APOLOGIA

ἀνθρώποις ὑποτάξας καὶ τὰ οὐράνια στοιχεῖα εἰς αὔξησιν
καρπῶν καὶ ὡρῶν μεταβολὰς κοσμήσας καὶ θεῖον τούτοις
νόμον τάξας, ἃ καὶ αὐτὰ δι' ἀνθρώπους φαίνεται πεποιη-
κὼς τὴν μὲν τῶν ἀνθρώπων καὶ τῶν ὑπὸ τὸν οὐρανὸν
πρόνοιαν ἀγγέλοις, οὓς ἐπὶ τούτοις ἔταξε, παρέδωκεν. 5
3. οἱ δ' ἄγγελοι, παραβάντες τήνδε τὴν τάξιν, γυναικῶν
μίξεσιν ἡττήθησαν καὶ παῖδας ἐτέκνωσαν, οἵ εἰσιν οἱ λεγόμενοι δαίμονες. 4. καὶ προσέτι λοιπὸν τὸ ἀνθρώπειον
γένος ἑαυτοῖς ἐδούλωσαν· τὰ μὲν διὰ μαγικῶν γραφῶν,
τὰ δὲ διὰ φόβων καὶ τιμωριῶν, ὧν ἐπέφερον, τὰ δὲ διὰ 10
διδαχῆς θυμάτων καὶ θυμιαμάτων καὶ σπονδῶν, ὧν ἐνδεεῖς
γεγόνασι μετὰ τὸ πάθεσιν ἐπιθυμιῶν δουλωθῆναι· καὶ εἰς
ἀνθρώπους φόνους, πολέμους, μοιχείας, ἀκολασίας καὶ
πᾶσαν κακίαν ἔσπειραν. 5. ὅθεν καὶ ποιηταὶ καὶ
μυθολόγοι, ἀγνοοῦντες τοὺς ἀγγέλους καὶ τοὺς ἐξ αὐτῶν 15
γεννηθέντας δαίμονας ταῦτα πρᾶξαι εἰς ἄρρενας καὶ
θηλείας καὶ πόλεις καὶ ἔθνη, ἅπερ συνέγραψαν, εἰς αὐτὸν
τὸν θεὸν καὶ τοὺς ὡς ἀπ' αὐτοῦ σπορᾷ γενομένους υἱοὺς

2 μεταβολὰς edd μεταβολαῖς A ‖ τούτοις νόμον Thirlb τοῦτον νόμον A ‖
10 ὧν ἐπέφερον Thirlb ἐπέφερον A

1. τὰ οὐράνια στοιχεῖα] 'The celestial elements' i.e. the sun, moon, and stars (object of κοσμήσας). They are called τὰ στοιχεῖα in *Tryph.* 23, *Ep. ad Diogn.* 7, Theoph. *ad Autol.* i 4.
2. ὡρῶν μετ.] Cf. i 13, 2.
6. οἱ δ' ἄγγελοι] Cf. Gen. vi 1—4, a piece of 'unassimilated mythology' (Delitzsch) intended to explain a legendary race of giants. The oldest interpretation treated the phrase there used, 'the sons of God,' as referring to semi-divine beings. (So the LXX and the book of Enoch vi 2; cf. Jude 6.) The Targums supposed it to denote the young men of the upper classes, who married maidens of the lower classes. Many Christian expositors have taken it to mean a union be-tween sons of Seth and daughters of Cain. See Driver *Genesis ad loc.* Justin's theory reappears in many Church fathers (the list is given in Turmel *Hist. de la théologie positive* c. 9) but is rejected by Origen and others. Cf. also Joseph. *Ant.* i 3.

ib. γυναικῶν μίξεσιν] Cf. i 5, 2 δαίμονες φαῦλοι γυναῖκας ἐμοίχευσαν. But here he speaks of the *fathers* of the δαίμονες.

11. ἐνδεεῖς γεγόν.] i.e. the demons. Thirlb. quotes Porphyry *de Abstin.* ii p. 204 to a similar effect. Οὗτοι οἱ χαίροντες λοιβῇ τε κνίσσῃ τε, δι' ὧν αὐτῶν τὸ πνευματικὸν πιαίνεται.

14. π. καὶ μυθ.] Cf. above i 23, 54.

17. εἰς αὐτὸν τὸν θεὸν κτλ.] '*in ipsum Deum* (i.e. Zeus) *ac in eos qui*

καὶ τῶν λεχθέντων ἐκείνου ἀδελφῶν καὶ τέκνων ὁμοίως τῶν ἀπ' ἐκείνων, Ποσειδῶνος καὶ Πλούτωνος, ἀνήνεγκαν. 6. ὀνόματι γὰρ ἕκαστον, ὅπερ ἕκαστος ἑαυτῷ τῶν ἀγγέλων καὶ τοῖς τέκνοις ἔθετο, προσηγόρευσαν.

5 (6). 1. Ὄνομα δὲ τῷ πάντων πατρὶ θετόν, ἀγεννήτῳ ὄντι, οὐκ ἔστιν· ᾧ γὰρ ἂν καὶ ὄνομά τι προσαγορεύεται, πρεσβύτερον ἔχει τὸν θέμενον τὸ ὄνομα. 2. τὸ δὲ πατὴρ καὶ θεὸς καὶ κτίστης καὶ κύριος καὶ δεσπότης οὐκ ὀνόματά ἐστιν, ἀλλ' ἐκ τῶν εὐποιῶν καὶ τῶν ἔργων προσρήσεις. 3. ὁ δὲ υἱὸς ἐκείνου, ὁ μόνος λεγόμενος

6 ὀνομά τι Otto ὀνόματι A

tum ipsius satu geniti, tum ex eius fratribus Neptuno et Plutone eorumque filiis procreati ferebantur, ea transtulere' (Maran). Ἀδελφῶν and τέκνων are parallel to αὐτοῦ, governed by ἀπό, but the whole sentence is decidedly clumsy.

3. ὀνόματι γὰρ κτλ.] Cf. i 5, 2, where it is said that the 'demons' (the word is probably used in the wider sense, including fallen angels as well as their offspring) call themselves by name.

5 (6). *God has no name, but only a title. The Son has no name before the Incarnation, but only the title Christ, as agent in Creation; at the Incarnation He is named Jesus, which means Saviour; and His power is still to be seen in miraculous cures.*

5. ὄνομα δέ] Cf. i 10, 1. The same idea is found in Plat. *Tim.* 28 c.

ib. θετόν] explained by τὸν θέμενον below.

10. ὁ δ. υἱὸς κτλ.] For a discussion of this passage see *Introd.* p. xxiv. 'But His Son, who is alone properly called Son, the Word who is with God and is (not γεννηθείς) begotten before the Creation, when in the beginning God created and set in order everything through Him, is called Christ...the name Christ also containing an incomprehensible meaning, just as the title "God" is not a name, but the opinion, innate in human nature, of an inexpressible reality.' Cf. Col. i 15 ff. and John i 1—3. Justin takes the title Christ as referring not merely to the Messianic office, but to the office of agent in Creation. The words κατὰ τὸ κεχρῖσθαι κτλ. are translated by Otto 'quia unctus est et per eum deus omnia ornauit.' But the construction of the Greek, so rendered, is very awkward; and the sense is not good; Christ's being anointed has nothing obvious to do with His part in Creation. It is possible that Grabe and others are right in making κεχρῖσθαι here active in meaning (like πεποιῆσθαι and other words), though I know of no parallel use of this word. There is a close connexion between χρίειν and κοσμεῖν. Κοσμεῖν clearly bears, along with the thought of order, the notion of adornment; and for the use of χρίειν in this sense cf. Theoph. *ad Autol.* i 12, a passage which also suggests that etymological exactness is not to be expected in such cases. And this use of κεχρῖσθαι is the more possible, because the active form κεχρικέναι would be a clumsy word. If this theory be rejected, Scaliger's emendation or something like it seems very possible.

APOLOGIA

κυρίως υἱός, ὁ λόγος πρὸ τῶν ποιημάτων καὶ συνὼν καὶ γεννώμενος, ὅτε τὴν ἀρχὴν δι' αὐτοῦ πάντα ἔκτισε καὶ ἐκόσμησε, Χριστὸς μὲν κατὰ τὸ κεχρῖσθαι καὶ κοσμῆσαι τὰ πάντα δι' αὐτοῦ τὸν θεὸν λέγεται, ὄνομα καὶ αὐτὸ περιέχον ἄγνωστον σημασίαν, ὃν τρόπον καὶ τὸ θεὸς προσ- 5 αγόρευμα οὐκ ὄνομά ἐστιν, ἀλλὰ πράγματος δυσεξηγήτου ἔμφυτος τῇ φύσει τῶν ἀνθρώπων δόξα. 4. Ἰησοῦς δὲ καὶ ἀνθρώπου καὶ σωτῆρος ὄνομα καὶ σημασίαν ἔχει. 5. καὶ γὰρ καὶ ἄνθρωπος, ὡς προέφημεν, γέγονε κατὰ τὴν τοῦ θεοῦ καὶ πατρὸς βουλὴν ἀποκυηθεὶς ὑπὲρ τῶν 10 πιστευόντων ἀνθρώπων καὶ ἐπὶ καταλύσει τῶν δαιμόνων· καὶ νῦν ἐκ τῶν ὑπ' ὄψιν γινομένων μαθεῖν δύνασθε. 6. δαιμονιολήπτους γὰρ πολλοὺς κατὰ πάντα τὸν κόσμον καὶ ἐν τῇ ὑμετέρᾳ πόλει πολλοὶ τῶν ἡμετέρων ἀνθρώπων, τῶν Χριστιανῶν, ἐπορκίζοντες κατὰ τοῦ ὀνόματος Ἰησοῦ 15 Χριστοῦ, τοῦ σταυρωθέντος ἐπὶ Ποντίου Πιλάτου, ὑπὸ τῶν ἄλλων πάντων ἐπορκιστῶν καὶ ἐπαστῶν καὶ φαρμακευτῶν μὴ ἰαθέντας, ἰάσαντο καὶ ἔτι νῦν ἰῶνται, καταργοῦντες καὶ ἐκδιώκοντες τοὺς κατέχοντας τοὺς ἀνθρώπους δαίμονας.

3 κατὰ τὸ κεχρῖσθαι A κατὰ τὸ καὶ χρῖσαι Scalig || 11 ἐπὶ καταλύσει Perion Otto καταλύσει A || 12 καὶ νῦν A ὡς καὶ νῦν Otto

7. Ἰησοῦς] Cf. i 33, 7, Matt. i 21. Possibly also there is a play upon the resemblance between Ἰησοῦς and ἰάομαι, such as is found in Clem. *Paedag.* iii 12 § 98, Eus. *Dem. Eu.* iv 10 § 19, Cyr. Jer. *Catech.* x 4 and 13 (Otto).

9. ὡς προέφημεν] Cf. i 23, 2; 63, 10, 16.

12. καὶ νῦν κτλ.] Cf. *Tryph.* 85.

18. ἰάσαντο κτλ.] This phenomenon of the expulsion of demons by Christian exorcism is frequently referred to by the Church fathers. (See *Tryph.* 30, 49, 76, 85 and Otto's note at the last-mentioned passage, as well as here. Otto also refers to Tert. *Ap.* 23, 27, 32, 37,

Iren. *c. Haer.* ii 32, 4 ff., Cypr. *ad Demetr.* 15, Orig. *Cels.* i 46, 67, August. *de Ciu. Dei* xxii 8.) It seems antecedently probable that the power of exorcism, if it ever existed in apostolic times, continued for some time in the Church; and the consensus of patristic opinion is general. But it is not denied that the fact of exorcism can be explained scientifically.

6 (7). *It is for the Christians' sake that God delays the end of the world; which however will happen, though not by necessity, as the Stoics assert; nor is human conduct fated, but men have free-will and responsibility. The Stoic ethic allows for*

6 (7). 1. Ὅθεν καὶ ἐπιμένει ὁ θεὸς τὴν σύγχυσιν καὶ κατάλυσιν τοῦ παντὸς κόσμου μὴ ποιῆσαι, ἵνα καὶ οἱ φαῦλοι ἄγγελοι καὶ δαίμονες καὶ ἄνθρωποι μηκέτι ὦσι, διὰ τὸ σπέρμα τῶν Χριστιανῶν ὃ γινώσκει ἐν τῇ φύσει, ὅτι
5 αἴτιόν ἐστιν. 2. ἐπεὶ εἰ μὴ τοῦτο ἦν, οὐκ ἂν οὐδὲ ὑμῖν ταῦτα ἔτι ποιεῖν καὶ ἐνεργεῖσθαι ὑπὸ τῶν φαύλων δαιμόνων δυνατὸν ἦν, ἀλλὰ τὸ πῦρ τὸ τῆς κρίσεως κατελθὸν ἀνέδην πάντα διέκρινεν, ὡς καὶ πρότερον ὁ κατακλυσμὸς μηδένα λιπὼν ἀλλ' ἢ τὸν μόνον σὺν τοῖς ἰδίοις παρ' ἡμῖν
10 καλούμενον Νῶε, παρ' ὑμῖν δὲ Δευκαλίωνα, ἐξ οὗ πάλιν οἱ τοσοῦτοι γεγόνασιν, ὧν οἱ μὲν φαῦλοι, οἱ δὲ σπουδαῖοι. 3. οὕτω γὰρ ἡμεῖς τὴν ἐκπύρωσίν φαμεν γενήσεσθαι, ἀλλ' οὐχ, ὡς οἱ Στωϊκοί, κατὰ τὸν τῆς εἰς ἄλληλα πάντων μεταβολῆς λόγον, ὃ αἴσχιστον ἐφάνη· ἀλλ' οὐδὲ καθ'
15 εἱμαρμένην πράττειν τοὺς ἀνθρώπους ἢ πάσχειν τὰ γινόμενα, ἀλλὰ κατὰ μὲν τὴν προαίρεσιν ἕκαστον κατορθοῦν ἢ

this, but their metaphysic does away either with God or with the distinction between virtue and vice.

1. ὅθεν] A vague term, pointing back to the beginning of 4 (5) εἰ δέ τινα, and subsequently explained in διὰ τὸ σπ. τ. Χ. For the idea cf. i 28 and 45.

4. ὃ γινώσκει κτλ.] an ambiguous phrase. It might mean 'which He (God) knows is the reason in nature' i.e. 'is the reason why nature is not destroyed'; but this explanation of Otto's seems feeble. Duncker (quoted by Veil) explains it 'which He recognizes as the cause in nature,' i.e. as the efficient cause of all true life. This is not convincing; and possibly a better explanation is to be found in taking γινώσκει (by comparison with i 28 and 45) to include the idea of προγινώσκει. The object of γινώσκει will then be not ὅτι but directly ὃ = τὸ σπέρμα τ. Χρ. The verb would be used in the same kind of sense as in 1 Cor. viii 3; Gal. iv 9; Matt. vii 23; God 'knows' the seed of the Christians ἐν τῇ φύσει, which might mean 'in the race' or 'in its place in nature.' Because of the place which it occupies in history or in nature, God delays the end. After this ὅτι might be taken as = 'because' or as secondary object to γινώσκει.

6. ταῦτα ἔτι κτλ.] 'to do and be impelled to these things.'

7. κατελθόν] Probably based on Gen. xix 24.

10. Νῶε] Identified with Deucalion by Philo (*de Praem. et Poen.* p. 412, Mangey), Theophilus (*ad Autol.* ii 30) and others.

12. οὕτω] 'in the manner just described,' including God's will.

13. οἱ Στωϊκοί] Cf. i. 20.
ib. κατὰ τὸν κτλ.] 'by a law of the permutation of all things into one another.'

16. κατορθοῦν] a favourite word with the Stoics.

ἁμαρτάνειν, καὶ κατὰ τὴν τῶν φαύλων δαιμόνων ἐνέργειαν τοὺς σπουδαίους, οἷον Σωκράτην καὶ τοὺς ὁμοίους, διώκεσθαι καὶ ἐν δεσμοῖς εἶναι, Σαρδανάπαλον δὲ καὶ Ἐπίκουρον καὶ τοὺς ὁμοίους ἐν ἀφθονίᾳ καὶ δόξῃ δοκεῖν εὐδαιμονεῖν. 4. ὃ μὴ νοήσαντες οἱ Στωϊκοὶ καθ᾽ εἱμαρμένης ἀνάγκην πάντα γίνεσθαι ἀπεφήναντο. 5. ἀλλ᾽ ὅτι αὐτεξούσιον τό τε τῶν ἀγγέλων γένος καὶ τῶν ἀνθρώπων τὴν ἀρχὴν ἐποίησεν ὁ θεός, δικαίως ὑπὲρ ὧν ἂν πλημμελήσωσι τὴν τιμωρίαν ἐν αἰωνίῳ πυρὶ κομίσονται. 6. γενητοῦ δὲ παντὸς ἥδε ἡ φύσις, κακίας καὶ ἀρετῆς δεκτικὸν εἶναι· οὐ γὰρ ἂν ἦν ἐπαινετὸν οὐδὲν αὐτῶν, εἰ οὐκ ἂν ἐπ᾽ ἀμφότερα τρέπεσθαι καὶ δύναμιν εἶχε. 7. δεικνύουσι δὲ τοῦτο καὶ οἱ πανταχοῦ κατὰ λόγον τὸν ὀρθὸν νομοθετήσαντες καὶ φιλοσοφήσαντες ἄνθρωποι ἐκ τοῦ ὑπαγορεύειν τάδε μὲν πράττειν, τῶνδε δὲ ἀπέχεσθαι. 8. καὶ οἱ Στωϊκοὶ φιλόσοφοι ἐν τῷ περὶ ἠθῶν λόγῳ τὰ αὐτὰ τιμῶσι καρτερῶς, ὡς δηλοῦσθαι ἐν τῷ περὶ ἀρχῶν καὶ ἀσωμάτων λόγῳ οὐκ εὐοδοῦν αὐτούς. 9. εἴτε γὰρ

10 γενητοῦ Asht γεννητοῦ A ‖ 12 εἰ οὐκ ἂν Goez Otto εἰ οὐκ ἦν A ‖ 15 τάδε μὲν Thirlb τόδε μὲν A

2. Σωκράτην] Cf. i 5, 46.
3. Σαρδανάπαλον] A king of Assyria, celebrated for his effeminacy, who at last burnt himself with his treasures.
6. ἀλλ᾽ ὅτι κτλ.] The theory of free-will alone justifies the punishment of the wicked. Cf. i 28.
12. καὶ δύναμιν] The καὶ 'also' is curiously out of its place.
16. ἐν τῷ περὶ ἠθῶν λόγῳ] The Stoic ethic is inconsistent with the Fatalism of the Stoic metaphysic.
17. ἀρχῶν καὶ ἀσ.] i.e. that σώματα are the ἀρχαί of everything, by necessity, and that there are no such things as ἀσώματα. Ashton cites Plut. *Plac. Phil.* i 28 and 11; *Laert.* 7, 149 and 134; Orig. *Cels.* p. 325; Eus. *Praep. Eu.* 15, 14 and 15.

18. εὐοδοῦν] 'to be right.' In classical Greek the passive is more usual in this sense.
ib. εἴτε γὰρ κτλ.] Maran supposes the apodosis to begin at ἢ μηδὲν εἶναι θεὸν, and inserts καὶ before φθαρτῶν. 'If human actions are due to fate, either there is no God except transitory matter, and so the Stoics only acknowledge corruptible things and involve God with evil, or there is no virtue and vice.' This makes good sense, but it not only requires the insertion of καί, but also treats εἴτε as if it were simply εἰ. It would indeed be in some cases possible to understand the alternative to εἴτε—'or (if they deny this, understood).' But it would be harsh to do this when there are alternatives expressed, as

8—2

καθ' εἱμαρμένην φήσουσι τὰ γινόμενα πρὸς ἀνθρώπων γίνεσθαι, ἢ μηδὲν εἶναι θεὸν παρὰ τρεπόμενα καὶ ἀλλοιούμενα καὶ ἀναλυόμενα εἰς τὰ αὐτὰ ἀεί, φθαρτῶν μόνων φανήσονται κατάληψιν ἐσχηκέναι καὶ αὐτὸν τὸν θεὸν διά
5 τε τῶν μερῶν καὶ διὰ τοῦ ὅλου ἐν πάσῃ κακίᾳ γινόμενον ἢ μηδὲν εἶναι κακίαν μηδ' ἀρετήν· ὅπερ καὶ παρὰ πᾶσαν σώφρονα ἔννοιαν καὶ λόγον καὶ νοῦν ἐστι.

7 (8). 1. Καὶ τοὺς ἀπὸ τῶν Στωϊκῶν δὲ δογμάτων, ἐπειδὴ κἂν τὸν ἠθικὸν λόγον κόσμιοι γεγόνασιν, ὡς καὶ ἔν
10 τισιν οἱ ποιηταί, διὰ τὸ ἔμφυτον παντὶ γένει ἀνθρώπων σπέρμα τοῦ λόγου, μεμισῆσθαι καὶ πεφονεῦσθαι οἴδαμεν· Ἡράκλειτον μέν, ὡς προέφημεν, καὶ Μουσώνιον δὲ ἐν τοῖς καθ' ἡμᾶς καὶ ἄλλους οἴδαμεν. 2. ὡς γὰρ ἐσημάναμεν,

here. According to the existing text, the apodosis begins at φθαρτῶν 'whether they will say that human actions are due to fate, or whether they say that God is nothing but transitory matter, the Stoics will either be found to acknowledge only corruptible things and to teach that God, etc.' On Maran's interpretation ἀνάγκη or φήσουσι must be understood with μηδὲν εἶναι θεὸν and μηδὲν εἶναι κακίαν; on the other interpretation we must understand φήσουσι or ἀνάγκη with καὶ αὐτὸν τὸν θεὸν κτλ. and with μηδὲν εἶναι κακίαν. The similar passage in i 43, 6 should be compared.

7 (8). *The nobility of the Stoic ethic, which is due to the Logos, caused the persecution of men like Heraclitus and Musonius, at the instigation of the demons; and the persecution of Christians is a piece of the same policy. But the day of punishment will come.*

9. κἄν] See note p. 17 line 4: 'because they were honourable, at any rate in their ethical teaching.'

11. σπέρμα τοῦ λόγου] See *Introd.* p. xxii.

ib. πεφονεῦσθαι] Justin is in error. Heraclitus (ob. circ. 470 B.C.) was not a Stoic, but a predecessor of Zeno, the founder of the Stoic school; there is, however, a relation of thought between them. He was banished from Ephesus on political grounds, not executed. Musonius Rufus, a Stoic, was banished by Nero in A.D. 65 (Tac. *Ann.* xv 71), but returned after his death (Tac. *Hist.* iii 81), and apparently lived to be known to Pliny (*Ep.* iii 11). Πεφονεῦσθαι is therefore an exaggeration so far as these two men are concerned. But it is scarcely necessary to emend the text to πεφυγαδεῦσθαι, as suggested by Veil.

12. ὡς προέφημεν] Cf. i 46, though there is there but the vaguest of hints that Heraclitus suffered for his philosophy, in κἂν ἄθεοι ἐνομίσθησαν (§ 3) and φονεῖς τῶν μετὰ λόγου βιούντων (§ 4, cf. οἱ μετὰ λόγου βιώσαντες...οἷον...Ἡράκλειτος § 3). The words ὡς προέφημεν here have therefore been suspected of being a gloss; but the case is hardly strong enough to justify their excision.

13. ὡς γ. ἐσημήναμεν] Cf. i 5, ii 6 (7) among many other passages.

πάντας τοὺς κἂν ὁπωσδήποτε κατὰ λόγον βιοῦν σπουδάζοντας καὶ κακίαν φεύγειν μισεῖσθαι ἀεὶ ἐνήργησαν οἱ δαίμονες. 3. οὐδὲν δὲ θαυμαστόν, εἰ τοὺς οὐ κατὰ σπερματικοῦ λόγου μέρος, ἀλλὰ κατὰ τὴν τοῦ παντὸς λόγου, ὅ ἐστι Χριστοῦ, γνῶσιν καὶ θεωρίαν πολὺ μᾶλλον 5 μισεῖσθαι οἱ δαίμονες ἐλεγχόμενοι ἐνεργοῦσιν· οἳ τὴν ἀξίαν κόλασιν καὶ τιμωρίαν κομίσονται ἐν αἰωνίῳ πυρὶ ἐγκλεισθέντες. 4. εἰ γὰρ ὑπὸ τῶν ἀνθρώπων ἤδη διὰ τοῦ ὀνόματος Ἰησοῦ Χριστοῦ ἡττῶνται, δίδαγμά ἐστι τῆς καὶ μελλούσης αὐτοῖς καὶ τοῖς λατρεύουσιν αὐτοῖς ἐσο- 10 μένης ἐν πυρὶ αἰωνίῳ κολάσεως. 5. οὕτως γὰρ καὶ οἱ προφῆται πάντες προεκήρυξαν γενήσεσθαι, καὶ Ἰησοῦς ὁ ἡμέτερος διδάσκαλος ἐδίδαξε.

8 (3). 1. Κἀγὼ οὖν προσδοκῶ ὑπό τινος τῶν ὠνομασμένων ἐπιβουλευθῆναι καὶ ξύλῳ ἐμπαγῆναι, ἢ κἂν ὑπὸ 15 Κρίσκεντος τοῦ φιλοψόφου καὶ φιλοκόμπου. 2. οὐ γὰρ φιλόσοφον εἰπεῖν ἄξιον τὸν ἄνδρα, ὅς γε περὶ ἡμῶν ἃ μὴ ἐπίσταται δημοσίᾳ καταμαρτυρεῖ, ὡς ἀθέων καὶ ἀσεβῶν Χριστιανῶν ὄντων, πρὸς χάριν καὶ ἡδονὴν τῶν πολλῶν τῶν πεπλανημένων ταῦτα πράττων. 3. εἴτε γὰρ μὴ ἐν- 20 τυχὼν τοῖς τοῦ Χριστοῦ διδάγμασι κατατρέχει ἡμῶν, παμπόνηρός ἐστι καὶ ἰδιωτῶν πολὺ χείρων, οἳ φυλάτ-

3 εἰ τοὺς οὐ Otto εἰ τοὺς A ‖ 14 ὠνομασμένων Eus *H E* iv 16 ὀνομασμένων A ‖ 15 ἐμπαγῆναι A ἐντιναγῆναι Eus ‖ 16 φιλοψόφου A ἀφιλοσόφου Eus ‖ 17 περὶ ἡμῶν ἃ A περὶ ὧν Eus ‖ 20 ταῦτα πράττων A τοῦτο πράττων Eus

8. εἰ γὰρ ὑπὸ κτλ.] i.e. in cures of demoniacs. Cf. ii 5 (6), 6.

10. ἐσομένης] A slip for ἔσεσθαι.

8 (3). *I am expecting similar persecution, perhaps from Crescens, whom I have already confuted and am ready to confute again publicly before you.*

14. τῶν ὠνομασμένων] i.e. one of those whom the demons instigate.

15. ξύλῳ] Unless there is something in the context to determine otherwise, ξ. seems always to =

neruus, 'stocks' of various kinds; Le Blant *Les Persécuteurs* p. 282; Allard *Dix Leçons sur le Martyre* p. 243.

16. Κρίσκεντος] Tatian *Or.* 19 also has a very bad opinion of Crescens, who was a leading Cynic in Justin's time. See *Introd.* p. x.

21. κατατρέχει] 'inveighs against,' 'runs us down.'

22. ἰδιωτῶν] '*inexperienced people*,' as contrasted with experts.

τονται πολλάκις περὶ ὧν οὐκ ἐπίστανται διαλέγεσθαι καὶ
ψευδομαρτυρεῖν· ἢ εἰ ἐντυχὼν μὴ συνῆκε τὸ ἐν αὐτοῖς
μεγαλεῖον, ἢ συνεὶς πρὸς τὸ μὴ ὑποπτευθῆναι τοιοῦτος
ταῦτα ποιεῖ, πολὺ μᾶλλον ἀγεννὴς καὶ παμπόνηρος, ἰδιω-
5 τικῆς καὶ ἀλόγου δόξης καὶ φόβου ἐλάττων ὤν. 4. καὶ
γὰρ προθέντα με καὶ ἐρωτήσαντα αὐτὸν ἐρωτήσεις τινὰς
τοιαύτας καὶ μαθεῖν καὶ ἐλέγξαι, ὅτι ἀληθῶς μηδὲν ἐπίσταται, εἰδέναι ὑμᾶς βούλομαι.   5. καὶ ὅτι ἀληθῆ λέγω,
εἰ μὴ ἀνηνέχθησαν ὑμῖν αἱ κοινωνίαι τῶν λόγων, ἕτοιμος
10 καὶ ἐφ' ὑμῶν κοινωνεῖν τῶν ἐρωτήσεων πάλιν· βασιλικὸν
δ' ἂν καὶ τοῦτο ἔργον εἴη.   6. εἰ δὲ καὶ ἐγνώσθησαν
ὑμῖν αἱ ἐρωτήσεις μου καὶ αἱ ἐκείνου ἀποκρίσεις, φανερὸν
ὑμῖν ἐστιν ὅτι οὐδὲν τῶν ἡμετέρων ἐπίσταται· ἢ εἰ καὶ
ἐπίσταται, διὰ τοὺς ἀκούοντας δὲ οὐ τολμᾷ λέγειν, ὁμοίως
15 Σωκράτει, ὡς προέφην, οὐ φιλόσοφος ἀλλὰ φιλόδοξος ἀνὴρ
δείκνυται, ὅς γε μηδὲ τὸ σωκρατικὸν ἀξιέραστον ὂν τιμᾷ·
Ἀλλ' οὔτι γε πρὸ τῆς ἀληθείας τιμητέος ἀνήρ.   7. ἀδύ-

2 ἢ εἰ ἐντυχὼν A καὶ εἰ ἐντυχὼν Eus ‖ μὴ συνῆκε τὸ ἐν αὐτοῖς μεγαλεῖον
Eus τῷ ἐν αὐτοῖς μεγαλείῳ A ‖ 6 προθέντα Eus προτεθέντα A ‖ 7 καὶ
μαθεῖν A μαθεῖν Eus ‖ 13 τῶν ἡμετέρων Eus om A ‖ ἢ εἰ καὶ A ἢ
εἰ Eus ‖ 14 ὁμοίως Σωκράτει A om Eus ‖ 15 προέφην A πρότερον ἔφην
Eus

2. ἢ εἰ ἐντυχὼν κτλ.] Otto
holds that κατατρέχει ἡμῶν is here
understood, and that therefore μὴ
συνῆκε κτλ. is an apodosis. This
is possible, but the sentence seems
to run stiffly. It is perhaps better
to take συνῆκε with εἰ, and make
πολὺ μᾶλλον κτλ. the only apodosis.
In that case the apodosis only refers
directly to the second alternative;
but that is no serious objection to
this method of taking the sentence.

3. μεγαλεῖον] 'magnitude, majesty.'

ib. τοιοῦτος] i.e. a Christian.

4. ἰδιωτικῆς] 'popular,' 'vulgar.'

6. ἐρωτήσεις] In later times a
tract called *Quaestiones et Responsiones* was attributed to Justin.

7. καὶ μαθεῖν καὶ ἐλέγξαι] The
infinitives depend on εἰδέναι, and
go with με.

ib. μηδὲν ἐπίσταται] Cf. note
p. 39, line 13.

10. βασιλικὸν δ'] Cf. i. 14, 4.

14. ὁμοίως Σωκράτει] 'as Socrates did dare' i. 5.

15. ὡς προέφην] in the beginning
of the chapter.

ib. φιλόδοξος] Cf. i 57.

16. τὸ σωκρατικὸν ἀξ. ὂν] 'the
admirable saying of Socrates.' Cf.
Plat. *Rep.* 595 C.

νατον δὲ Κυνικῷ, ἀδιάφορον τὸ τέλος προθεμένῳ, τὸ ἀγαθὸν εἰδέναι πλὴν ἀδιαφορίας.

9. 1. Ἵνα δὲ μή τις εἴπῃ τὸ λεγόμενον ὑπὸ τῶν νομιζομένων φιλοσόφων, ὅτι κόμποι καὶ φόβητρά ἐστι τὰ λεγόμενα ὑφ' ἡμῶν ὅτι κολάζονται ἐν αἰωνίῳ πυρὶ οἱ ἄδικοι, καὶ διὰ φόβον ἀλλ' οὐ διὰ τὸ καλὸν εἶναι καὶ ἀρεστὸν ἐναρέτως βιοῦν τοὺς ἀνθρώπους ἀξιοῦμεν, βραχυεπῶς πρὸς τοῦτο ἀποκρινοῦμαι, ὅτι, εἰ μὴ τοῦτό ἐστιν, οὔτε ἔστι θεός, ἤ, εἰ ἔστιν, οὐ μέλει αὐτῷ τῶν ἀνθρώπων, καὶ οὐδέν ἐστιν ἀρετὴ οὐδὲ κακία, καί, ὡς προέφημεν, ἀδίκως τιμωροῦσιν οἱ νομοθέται τοὺς παραβαίνοντας τὰ διατεταγμένα καλά. 2. ἀλλ' ἐπεὶ οὐκ ἄδικοι ἐκεῖνοι καὶ ὁ αὐτῶν πατήρ, τὰ αὐτὰ αὐτοῖς πράττειν διὰ τοῦ λόγου διδάσκων, οἱ τούτοις συντιθέμενοι οὐκ ἄδικοι. 3. ἐὰν δέ τις τοὺς διαφόρους νόμους τῶν ἀνθρώπων προ-

1 προθεμένῳ Otto προεμένῳ A ‖ 7 βραχυεπῶς Otto βραχυεποῖς A ‖ 13 τὰ αὐτὰ αὐτοῖς Sylburg Krüger τὰ αὐτὰ αὐτῷ A Otto

1. ἀδιάφορον] '*indifferent*.' The Cynic philosophy considered the *summum bonum* to be ἀδιάφορον, i.e. not to be absolute, but to be merely relative to circumstances.

9. *Some so-called philosophers call our threats of punishment degrading terrors. But if there is no punishment, there is no God who cares for men, and no right or wrong, and the punishments of human law are unjust. It may be urged that laws differ in various places; but this is due to the demons, and right reason by itself speaks decisively about right and wrong in general.*

6. διὰ φόβον κτλ.] A common accusation, made even nowadays, that Christians are good from mere fear of hell, a charge not entirely unjustified by some popular theology and homiletics. Justin does not go deeply into the matter, but simply reasserts the truth of punishment.

10. ὡς προέφημεν] Cf. i 28, 4, ii 6 (7), 5.

12. ἀλλ' ἐπεὶ κτλ.] '*But since lawgivers are not unjust* (in inflicting punishments), *nor their father* (i.e. God), *who teaches by reason* (or *by the Logos) the same conduct as they require, those who agree with them are not unjust either*,' i.e. the Christians are not unjust in proclaiming eternal punishment. So Veil explains the sense. The other explanation, which Otto gives, is 'those who listen to them are not unjust'; but this seems very weak. Otto's text must be translated '*who teaches even by reason that they ought to act like Him*' (cf. Matt. v 48). For Justin's use of συντ. cf. *Tryph.* 123, 130 and elsewhere.

13. ὁ αὐτῶν πατήρ] Maran quotes Philo *de Sacrif. Abel* 152 νομοθέτης γὰρ καὶ πηγὴ νόμων αὐτός, ὑφ' οὗ πάντες οἱ κατὰ μέρος νομοθέται.

15. ἐὰν δέ τις κτλ.] This is the argument from the variations of the moral code. Cf. Plat. *de Legg.* ii 661 D.

βάληται, λέγων ὅτι παρ' οἷς μὲν ἀνθρώποις τάδε καλά, τὰ δὲ αἰσχρὰ νενόμισται, παρ' ἄλλοις δὲ τὰ παρ' ἐκείνοις αἰσχρὰ καλά, καὶ τὰ καλὰ αἰσχρὰ νομίζεται, ἀκουέτω καὶ τῶν εἰς τοῦτο λεγομένων. 4. καὶ νόμους διατάξασθαι
5 τῇ ἑαυτῶν κακίᾳ ὁμοίους τοὺς πονηροὺς ἀγγέλους ἐπιστάμεθα, οἷς χαίρουσιν οἱ ὅμοιοι γενόμενοι ἄνθρωποι, καὶ ὀρθὸς λόγος παρελθὼν οὐ πάσας δόξας οὐδὲ πάντα δόγματα καλὰ ἀποδείκνυσιν, ἀλλὰ τὰ μὲν φαῦλα, τὰ δὲ ἀγαθά· ὥστε μοι καὶ πρὸς τοὺς τοιούτους τὰ αὐτὰ καὶ τὰ ὅμοια
10 εἰρήσεται, καὶ λεχθήσεται διὰ πλειόνων, ἐὰν χρεία ᾖ. 5. τανῦν δὲ ἐπὶ τὸ προκείμενον ἀνέρχομαι.

10. 1. Μεγαλειότερα μὲν οὖν πάσης ἀνθρωπείου διδασκαλίας φαίνεται τὰ ἡμέτερα διὰ τοῦ τὸ λογικὸν τὸ ὅλον τὸν φανέντα δι' ἡμᾶς Χριστὸν γεγονέναι, καὶ σῶμα

13 διὰ τοῦτο λογικὸν A διὰ τὸ λογικὸν Otto

7. ὀρθὸς λόγος] Maran understands this to refer to the Incarnate *Logos*. It seems a possible inference from the use of the word παρελθών, but it is not unavoidable. It may be a mere appeal to the moral reason of mankind. '*When the truth* (incarnate or not) *comes to men* (undisturbed by the demons).'

10. *Our teaching surpasses all other, because in Christ the whole Logos became incarnate, which had previously been known only fragmentarily; and those who then used it were punished. But they persuaded none to die for their belief; Christ persuades not only philosophers, but all classes of men, to do so.*

13. διὰ τοῦ τὸ λογικὸν κτλ.] Otto translates '*quia totus logos exstitit Christus, qui propter nos apparuit, nempe corpus et logos et anima*,' i.e. '*because Christ was, etc.*' The notion then is that the Incarnate Christ was the whole *Logos*. If, however, γεγονέναι be taken to mean '*became*' or '*was made*,' the rendering of Dorner (*Person of Christ* Per. i Ep. 2 § 1) and Veil must be right; 'because the whole of the rational principle (of the universe) became the Christ who appeared for our sakes, body, logos, and soul.' Otto's omission of an article with the infinitive γεγονέναι is surely wrong. Διὰ τοῦ τὸ must be read. Dorner (*loc. cit.*) discusses the question whether Justin conceived of Christ as having a human soul. Since ψυχή means '*the animal principle*,' it would seem as if λόγον meant the Divine *Logos* in place of a human πνεῦμα. But it is a mistake thus to read back the subject-matter of later controversy into Justin's words. Σῶμα, λόγος, ψυχή, are the three departments in which the ἐνανθρώπησις took place. The division is in the main a dichotomy; the words are not all three in the ascending scale. In the invisible half Justin begins with 'reason,' the rational soul, and then adds the animal soul. All that he means is that τὸ λογικὸν became wholly man.

καὶ λόγον καὶ ψυχήν. 2. ὅσα γὰρ καλῶς ἀεὶ ἐφθέγξαντο καὶ εὗρον οἱ φιλοσοφήσαντες ἢ νομοθετήσαντες, κατὰ λόγου μέρος δι' εὑρέσεως καὶ θεωρίας ἐστὶ πονηθέντα αὐτοῖς. 3. ἐπειδὴ δὲ οὐ πάντα τὰ τοῦ λόγου ἐγνώρισαν, ὅς ἐστι Χριστός, καὶ ἐναντία ἑαυτοῖς πολλάκις 5 εἶπον. 4. καὶ οἱ προγεγενημένοι τοῦ Χριστοῦ κατὰ τὸ ἀνθρώπινον λόγῳ πειραθέντες τὰ πράγματα θεωρῆσαι καὶ ἐλέγξαι, ὡς ἀσεβεῖς καὶ περίεργοι εἰς δικαστήρια ἤχθησαν. 5. ὁ πάντων δὲ αὐτῶν εὐτονώτερος πρὸς τοῦτο γενόμενος Σωκράτης τὰ αὐτὰ ἡμῖν ἐνεκλήθη· καὶ γὰρ 10 ἔφασαν αὐτὸν καινὰ δαιμόνια εἰσφέρειν, καὶ οὓς ἡ πόλις νομίζει θεοὺς μὴ ἡγεῖσθαι αὐτόν. 6. ὁ δὲ δαίμονας μὲν τοὺς φαύλους καὶ τοὺς πράξαντας ἃ ἔφασαν οἱ ποιηταί, ἐκβαλὼν τῆς πολιτείας καὶ Ὅμηρον καὶ τοὺς ἄλλους ποιητάς, παραιτεῖσθαι τοὺς ἀνθρώπους ἐδίδαξε, πρὸς θεοῦ δὲ 15 τοῦ ἀγνώστου αὐτοῖς διὰ λόγου ζητήσεως ἐπίγνωσιν προὐτρέπετο, εἰπών· Τὸν δὲ πατέρα καὶ δημιουργὸν πάντων οὔθ' εὑρεῖν ῥᾴδιον, οὔθ' εὑρόντα εἰς πάντας εἰπεῖν ἀσφαλές. 7. ἃ ὁ ἡμέτερος Χριστὸς διὰ τῆς ἑαυτοῦ δυνάμεως ἔπραξε. 8. Σωκράτει μὲν γὰρ οὐδεὶς ἐπείσθη ὑπὲρ τούτου τοῦ 20 δόγματος ἀποθνῄσκειν· Χριστῷ δέ, τῷ καὶ ὑπὸ Σωκράτους ἀπὸ μέρους γνωσθέντι (λόγος γὰρ ἦν καὶ ἔστιν ὁ ἐν παντὶ ὤν, καὶ διὰ τῶν προφητῶν προειπὼν τὰ μέλλοντα γίνεσθαι καὶ δι' ἑαυτοῦ ὁμοιοπαθοῦς γενομένου καὶ διδάξαντος

3 δι' εὑρέσεως Otto εὑρέσεως A ‖ 6 οἱ προγεγενημένοι Otto οἱ προγεγραμμένοι A ‖ 20 ἐπείσθη Otto ἐπιστεύθη A

3. πονηθέντα] 'elaborated.'
9. εὐτονώτερος] 'more firm, forcible.'
10. ἐνεκλήθη] 'was accused.' Cf. Plat. *Apol.* 24 B, and see above i 5.
12. ὁ δὲ κτλ.] '*But he, by ejecting Homer and other poets from his ideal state* (cf. Plat. *Rep.* Bks ii and x), *taught men to renounce the evil demons, who had done the deeds of which the poets spoke, and urged them to know the God, whom they did not know, by rational inquiry.*' Cf. note p. 8, line 11.
16. τοῦ ἀγν.] Acts xvii 23.
17. τὸν δὲ πατέρα κτλ.] A verbally incorrect quotation from Plat. *Tim.* 28 C.
22. λόγος γὰρ ἦν κτλ.] '*For He was and is the Logos, who is in everybody, and who foretold the future by the prophets and in person when He became, etc.*' The last clause καὶ δι' ἑ. is not regularly logical.

ταῦτα), οὐ φιλόσοφοι οὐδὲ φιλόλογοι μόνον ἐπείσθησαν,
ἀλλὰ καὶ χειροτέχναι καὶ παντελῶς ἰδιῶται, καὶ δόξης
καὶ φόβου καὶ θανάτου καταφρονήσαντες· ἐπειδὴ δύναμίς
ἐστι τοῦ ἀρρήτου πατρὸς καὶ οὐχὶ ἀνθρωπείου λόγου
5 κατασκευή.

11. 1. Οὐκ ἂν δὲ οὐδὲ ἐφονευόμεθα οὐδὲ δυνατώ-
τεροι ἡμῶν ἦσαν οἵ τε ἄδικοι ἄνθρωποι καὶ δαίμονες, εἰ
μὴ πάντως παντὶ γεννωμένῳ ἀνθρώπῳ καὶ θανεῖν ὠφεί-
λετο· ὅθεν καὶ τὸ ὄφλημα ἀποδιδόντες εὐχαριστοῦμεν.
10 2. καίτοι γε καὶ τὸ ξενοφώντειον ἐκεῖνο νῦν πρός τε
Κρίσκεντα καὶ τοὺς ὁμοίως αὐτῷ ἀφραίνοντας καλὸν καὶ
εὔκαιρον εἰπεῖν ἡγούμεθα. 3. τὸν Ἡρακλέα ἐπὶ
τρίοδόν τινα ἔφη ὁ Ξενοφῶν βαδίζοντα εὑρεῖν τήν τε
ἀρετὴν καὶ τὴν κακίαν, ἐν γυναικῶν μορφαῖς φαινομένας.
15 4. καὶ τὴν μὲν κακίαν, ἁβρᾷ ἐσθῆτι καὶ ἐρωτοπεποιημένῳ καὶ ἀνθοῦντι ἐκ τῶν τοιούτων προσώπῳ, θελκτικήν
τε εὐθὺς πρὸς τὰς ὄψεις οὖσαν, εἰπεῖν πρὸς τὸν Ἡρακλέα
ὅτι, ἢν αὐτῇ ἔπηται, ἡδόμενόν τε καὶ κεκοσμημένον τῷ
λαμπροτάτῳ καὶ ὁμοίῳ τῷ περὶ αὐτὴν κόσμῳ διαιτήσειν
20 ἀεὶ ποιήσει. 5. καὶ τὴν ἀρετὴν ἐν αὐχμηρῷ μὲν τῷ

4 ἀνθρωπείου edd ἀνθρωπίου A ∥ 5 κατασκευή Thalem τὰ σκεύη A ∥
10 ξενοφώντειον Thirlb ξενοφώτειον A

3. ἐπειδὴ κτλ.] 'Since it (namely, the doctrine of Christ, implied in διδάξαντος ταῦτα) is the power of the ineffable Father, and not an artifice of human reason.' See above 14, 5; 60, 11. Cf. *Ep. ad Diogn.* 7 ταῦτα ἀνθρώπου οὐ δοκεῖ τὰ ἔργα, ταῦτα δύναμίς ἐστι θεοῦ. Cf. also 1 Cor. i 18; Rom. i 16. Another rendering is '*since He was the power, etc.*,' but in this case the word κατασκευή would be unsuitable.

11. *Death is the debt of nature, and we do not mind paying the debt. But we are like all who follow virtue, in that we despise pleasure and have no fear of death.*

8. καὶ θανεῖν] Cf. note, p, 16, line 1. Otto suggests that κατθανεῖν may be the right reading.

10. ξενοφώντειον] Cf. Xen. *Mem.* ii 1.

11. ἀφραίνοντας] A poetic word, used later as a philosophic term.

15. ἐρωτοπεποιημένῳ κτλ.] I know of no other instance of this word. Its formation is very curious. 'Ad amorem eliciendum apto et florescente ex illis ornamentis uultu.' (Otto.)

16. θελκτικὴν κτλ.] '*immediately seductive to the eyes.*'

προσώπῳ καὶ τῇ περιβολῇ οὖσαν εἰπεῖν· Ἀλλ' ἢν ἐμοὶ
πείθῃ, οὐ κόσμῳ οὐδὲ κάλλει τῷ ῥέοντι καὶ φθειρομένῳ
ἑαυτὸν κοσμήσεις ἀλλὰ τοῖς ἀϊδίοις καὶ καλοῖς κόσμοις.
6. καὶ πάνθ' ὁντινοῦν πεπείσμεθα, φεύγοντα τὰ δοκοῦντα
καλά, τὰ δὲ νομιζόμενα σκληρὰ καὶ ἄλογα μετερχόμενον, 5
εὐδαιμονίαν ἐκδέχεσθαι. 7. ἡ γὰρ κακία, πρόβλημα
ἑαυτῆς τῶν πράξεων τὰ προσόντα τῇ ἀρετῇ καὶ ὄντως
ὄντα καλὰ διὰ μιμήσεως ἀφθάρτων περιβαλλομένη (ἄ-
φθαρτον γὰρ οὐδὲν ἔχει οὐδὲ ποιῆσαι δύναται), δουλαγωγεῖ
τοὺς χαμαιπετεῖς τῶν ἀνθρώπων, τὰ προσόντα αὐτῇ φαῦλα 10
τῇ ἀρετῇ περιθεῖσα. 8. οἱ δὲ νενοηκότες τὰ πρόσοντα

8 μιμ. ἀφθάρτων Maran Goez Otto μιμ. φθαρτῶν A Sacr Par Holl 101
Veil ‖ 11 οἱ δὲ νενοηκότες κτλ. A ὧν καταπτύουσιν οἱ κατανενοηκότες τὰ
προσόντα τῷ ὄντι καλὰ καὶ ἄφθαρτα τῇ ἀρετῇ Sacr Par ib

1. τῇ περιβολῇ] 'vesture.'
2. τῷ ῥέοντι] 'transitory.'
4. καὶ πάνθ' ὁντ.] 'And we are persuaded that everyone, who flees what is superficially fair and follows what is thought hard and foolish, finds happiness awaiting him (εὐδαιμονίαν is the subject of ἐκδέχ.). For Vice, veiling her actions in the beauties which properly belong to Virtue and are genuine (though only by imitation of incorruptible things, for she possesses and can produce nothing which is incorruptible) enslaves grovelling men, clothing Virtue in the ugliness which properly belongs to herself.' The idea is that Vice offers all the attractions which properly belong to Virtue, and deceives men into seeing Virtue clad in all the unattractiveness which properly belongs to Vice. But her assumed attractions are a mere copy of the true attractions of Virtue, and are impermanent. Justin's thought may be influenced by passages like Plat. Rep. ii 361 and ix 591, where the question of the benefits of Virtue, apart from rewards, is considered. Veil retains μιμήσεως φθαρτῶν, supposing Justin to distinguish between the corruptible and the incorruptible attractions of Virtue (e.g. practical advantages on the one hand and spiritual blessings on the other); Vice assumes the former but not the latter. This is possible, but seems somewhat too subtle. And could it be said that Vice veiled herself with τὰ ὄντως ὄντα καλά, if she merely assumed corruptible attractions? The point surely is, that Vice makes a show of giving all the blessings, which Virtue really can give, but that her attractions are delusive and transitory, whilst those of Virtue are permanent.

11. οἱ δὲ νενοηκότες κτλ.] 'But they who perceive the true beauties that belong to Virtue are also incorruptible through her help.' Perhaps, however, it is simpler to make τῷ ὄντι the direct dat. after προσόντα. We are now a long way from τὰ πρ. τῇ ἀρετῇ, and another τὰ πρ. has occurred meanwhile. It would also suit the argument, 'Those who have caught the beauties belonging to true existence become themselves incorruptible by means of virtue.'

τῷ ὄντι καλὰ καὶ ἄφθαρτοι τῇ ἀρετῇ· ὃ καὶ περὶ Χριστιανῶν καὶ τῶν ἀπὸ τοῦ ἄθλου καὶ τῶν ἀνθρώπων τῶν τοιαῦτα πραξάντων, ὁποῖα ἔφασαν οἱ ποιηταὶ περὶ τῶν νομιζομένων θεῶν, ὑπολαβεῖν δεῖ πάντα νουνεχῆ, ἐκ τοῦ
5 καὶ τοῦ φευκτοῦ καταφρονεῖν ἡμᾶς θανάτου λογισμὸν ἕλκοντα.

12. 1. Καὶ γὰρ αὐτὸς ἐγώ, τοῖς Πλάτωνος χαίρων διδάγμασι, διαβαλλομένους ἀκούων Χριστιανούς, ὁρῶν δὲ ἀφόβους πρὸς θάνατον καὶ πάντα τὰ ἄλλα νομιζόμενα
10 φοβερά, ἐνενόουν ἀδύνατον εἶναι ἐν κακίᾳ καὶ φιληδονίᾳ ὑπάρχειν αὐτούς. 2. τίς γὰρ φιλήδονος ἢ ἀκρατὴς καὶ ἀνθρωπίνων σαρκῶν βορὰν ἀγαθὸν ἡγούμενος δύναιτο ἂν θάνατον ἀσπάζεσθαι, ὅπως τῶν αὐτοῦ ἀγαθῶν στερηθῇ, ἀλλ' οὐκ ἐκ παντὸς ζῆν μὲν ἀεὶ τὴν ἐνθάδε βιοτὴν καὶ
15 λανθάνειν τοὺς ἄρχοντας ἐπειρᾶτο, οὐχ ὅτι γε ἑαυτὸν κατήγγελλε φονευθησόμενον; 3. ἤδη καὶ τοῦτο ἐνήρ-

2 τῶν ἀνθρώπων τῶν Otto τῶν ἀνθρ. καὶ τῶν A ‖ 3 ἔφασαν Perion ἔφθασαν A ‖ 4 πάντα νουνεχῆ Thirlb πάντα οὖν ἔχει A ‖ 8 ὁρῶν δὲ A ὁρῶν δὲ καὶ Eus *H E* IV 8 ‖ 9 πάντα τὰ ἄλλα A πάντα τὰ Eus ‖ 12 ἀνθρωπίνων A ἀνθρωπείων Eus ‖ ἀγαθὸν ἡγούμενος A ἡγούμενος ἀγαθὸν Eus ‖ 13 αὐτοῦ ἀγαθῶν στερηθῇ A ἑαυτοῦ στερηθείη ἐπιθυμιῶν Eus ‖ 14 ζῆν μὲν A ζῆν Eus ‖ 15 γε ἑαυτὸν A ἑαυτὸν Eus ‖ 16 κατήγγελλε Eus κατήγγειλε A

2. τῶν ἀπὸ τοῦ ἄθλου] 'athletes,' as types of men who choose labour, without caring for death, and renounce pleasure. The Greek phrase is a curious one. It looks as if ἄθλου must be used in the sense of 'arena,' from ἆθλος, not ἆθλον.
ib. τῶν ἀνθρώπων κτλ.] i.e. heroes, like Hercules, not those demigods of another character, referred to in i 21.
5. λογισμὸν ἕλκ.] 'arguing from the fact, etc.'; going with πάντα νουνεχῆ.
12. *Even when I was a Platonist, I used to disbelieve the popular charges against Christians, because their lives and their readiness for* death *seemed inconsistent with those accusations. But, if Christians did the acts alleged against them, they might call them mysteries of Cronos or Jupiter, and show that their conduct was only like to what is done openly by pagans.*
12. ἀνθρωπίνων σαρκῶν βορὰν] Cf. i 26, 7.
13. τῶν αὐτοῦ ἀγ.] Cf. Luke xvi 25.
15. οὐχ ὅτι γε] 'nedum.' The Christian does this when he confesses himself to be a Christian.
16. ἤδη καὶ τοῦτο] τοῦτο refers to what follows. Διά τινων πονηρῶν ἀνθρώπων refers probably to the anti-Christian agitators, like Cres-

γησαν οἱ φαῦλοι δαίμονες διά τινων πονηρῶν ἀνθρώπων πραχθῆναι. 4. φονεύοντες γὰρ αὐτοί τινας ἐπὶ συκοφαντίᾳ τῇ εἰς ἡμᾶς καὶ εἰς βασάνους εἵλκυσαν οἰκέτας τῶν ἡμετέρων ἢ παῖδας ἢ γύναια, καὶ δι' αἰκισμῶν φοβερῶν ἐξαναγκάζουσι κατειπεῖν ταῦτα τὰ μυθολογούμενα, 5 ἃ αὐτοὶ φανερῶς πράττουσιν· ὧν ἐπειδὴ οὐδὲν πρόσεστιν ἡμῖν, οὐ φροντίζομεν, θεὸν τὸν ἀγέννητον καὶ ἄρρητον μάρτυρα ἔχοντες τῶν τε λογισμῶν καὶ τῶν πράξεων. 5. τίνος γὰρ χάριν οὐχὶ καὶ ταῦτα δημοσίᾳ ὡμολογοῦμεν ἀγαθὰ καὶ φιλοσοφίαν θείαν αὐτὰ ἀπεδείκνυμεν, φά- 10 σκοντες Κρόνου μὲν μυστήρια τελεῖν ἐν τῷ ἀνδροφονεῖν, καὶ ἐν τῷ αἵματος ἐμπίπλασθαι, ὡς λέγεται, τὰ ἴσα τῷ

cens. Αὐτοί must refer to the πονηροὶ ἄνθρωποι, though grammatically it should refer to the δαίμονες. Veil suspects the whole passage ἤδη καὶ...πράττουσιν to be a gloss of a later writer, who was influenced by a reminiscence of the *Epist. Vienn. et Lugd.* (ap. Eus. *H.E.* v 1), where it is said συνελαμβάνοντο δὲ καὶ ἐθνικοί τινες οἰκέται τῶν ἡμετέρων,...οἵ...φοβηθέντες τὰς βασάνους ...κατεψεύσαντο ἡμῶν Θυέστεια δεῖπνα καὶ Οἰδιποδείους μίξεις. Veil's reasons for suspicion are partly that ἃ αὐτοὶ φανερῶς πράττουσιν is impossibly rude, being an insult to the rulers, to whom the Apology is addressed; but I see no reason for thinking that the rulers are meant by αὐτοί; and partly that Athenagoras (*Leg.* 25) definitely says δοῦλοί εἰσιν ἡμῖν...οὓς οὐκ ἔστι λαθεῖν· ἀλλὰ καὶ τούτων οὐδεὶς καθ' ἡμῶν τὰ τηλικαῦτα οὐδὲ κατεψεύσατο. The contradiction with Athenagoras seems strange; there is nothing to show (as Ashton suggests) that Athenagoras is referring only to Christian slaves, whilst Justin is speaking of Gentile slaves (whom the Epistle quoted above definitely specifies). But Athenagoras may quite well have been ignorant of facts which were known to Justin; or he may be exaggerating his case. The case for treating the passage as a gloss is really frivolous; and if a gloss is to be discovered, it should be carried down to πράξεων; for, if it be cut short at πράττουσιν, it is not easy to see what ὧν οὐδὲν refers to; presumably it would have to be to φιλήδονος κτλ.

11. Κρόνου μυστήρια] The evidence for human sacrifice in the cult of *Cronos* is strong; for that reason he was later identified with Moloch. The Latin *Saturnus* corresponds to the Greek Cronos. For the authorities cf. Farnell *Greek Cults* vol. i c. 3.

12. τὰ ἴσα] governed by τελεῖν. This is a reference to the worship of Jupiter Latiaris; many Christian writers allude to the practice of human sacrifice as existing in this cult, e.g. Tert. *Apol.* 9, but Wissowa (*Religion der Römer* p. 109 n. 3) is emphatically sceptical on the point. It is not mentioned by any heathen writer, except Porphyry (*de Abstin.* ii 56) ἀλλὰ ἔτι καὶ νῦν τίς ἀγνοεῖ κατὰ τὴν μεγάλην πόλιν τῇ τοῦ Λατιαρίου Διὸς ἑορτῇ σφαζόμενον ἄνθρωπον;

παρ' ὑμῖν τιμωμένῳ εἰδώλῳ, ᾧ οὐ μόνον ἀλόγων ζώων
αἵματα προσραίνεται ἀλλὰ καὶ ἀνθρώπεια, διὰ τοῦ παρ'
ὑμῖν ἐπισημοτάτου καὶ εὐγενεστάτου ἀνδρὸς τὴν πρόσ-
χυσιν τοῦ τῶν φονευθέντων αἵματος ποιούμενοι, Διὸς δὲ
5 καὶ τῶν ἄλλων θεῶν μιμηταὶ γενόμενοι ἐν τῷ ἀνδροβατεῖν
καὶ γυναιξὶν ἀδεῶς μίγνυσθαι, Ἐπικούρου μὲν καὶ τὰ τῶν
ποιητῶν συγγράμματα ἀπολογίαν φέροντες; 6. ἐπειδὴ
δὲ ταῦτα τὰ μαθήματα καὶ τοὺς ταῦτα πράξαντας καὶ
μιμουμένους φεύγειν πείθομεν, ὡς καὶ νῦν διὰ τῶνδε
10 τῶν λόγων ἠγωνίσμεθα, ποικίλως πολεμούμεθα· ἀλλ' οὐ
φροντίζομεν, ἐπεὶ θεὸν τῶν πάντων ἐπόπτην δίκαιον οἴδαμεν. 7. εἴθε καὶ νῦν τις ἂν τραγικῇ φωνῇ ἀνεβό-
ησεν ἐπί τι βῆμα ὑψηλὸν ἀναβάς· Αἰδέσθητε, αἰδέσθητε
ἃ φανερῶς πράττετε εἰς ἀναιτίους ἀναφέροντες, καὶ τὰ
15 προσόντα καὶ ἑαυτοῖς καὶ τοῖς ὑμετέροις θεοῖς περιβάλ-
λοντες τούτοις, ὧν οὐδὲν οὐδ' ἐπὶ ποσὸν μετουσία ἐστί.
5. μετάθεσθε, σωφρονίσθητε.

13. 1. Καὶ γὰρ ἐγώ, μαθὼν περίβλημα πονηρὸν εἰς

2 προσραίνεται A προσραίνετε Thirlb Otto ‖ 12 εἴθε καὶ νῦν τις ἂν Otto
εἰ δὲ καὶ νῦν τις ἦν A

3. ἐπισ...ἀνδρὸς] i.e. consul or prefect.
4. τῶν φονευθέντων] i.e. the fighters with wild beasts, as we learn from Tert. *Apol.* 9.
11. θεὸν...δίκ. οἴδ.] Cf. 1 Pet. ii 23.
12. εἴθε καὶ νῦν κτλ.] The text here is uncertain. The use of ἂν in a wish is not normal, and possibly εἴθε ἦν ἀναβοήσων would be better. Veil prefers a suggestion of Buecheler, who reads εἰ δὲ...ἦν (according to the MS) and ἂν ἐβόησεν, translating 'but if there were one (some ἐπόπτης δίκαιος), he would, etc.,' thus making the sentence a covert appeal to the rulers. But this expansion of τις seems harsh, and possibly Otto's text is open to least objection. Otto compares Plat. *Clitoph.* 407 A, where Socrates is represented ὥσπερ ἐπὶ μηχανῆς τραγικῆς θεός, exclaiming ποῖ φέρεσθε, ἄνθρωποι, καὶ ἀγνοεῖτε οὐδὲν τῶν δεόντων πράττοντες κτλ.
15. περιβάλλοντες] Cf. above ii 11, 7.
16. τούτοις ὦν] 'to these, who have no part in them.' Certainly, as Veil suggests, οἷς τούτων would be more natural.
13. *I think scorn of the demons' falsehoods about us. I declare that in Christianity all past truth is summed up. Previous thinkers had only a seed of the Logos; we have in Christ the whole Logos.*
18. μαθὼν κτλ.] 'perceiving that discredit had been cast by the demons over the Divine doctrines of Christianity, in order to avert other men

ἀποστροφὴν τῶν ἄλλων ἀνθρώπων περιτεθειμένον ὑπὸ τῶν φαύλων δαιμόνων τοῖς Χριστιανῶν θείοις διδάγμασι, καὶ ψευδολογουμένων ταῦτα καὶ τοῦ περιβλήματος κατεγέλασα καὶ τῆς παρὰ τοῖς πολλοῖς δόξης. 2. Χριστιανὸς εὑρεθῆναι καὶ εὐχόμενος καὶ παμμάχως ἀγωνιζόμενος ὁμολογῶ, οὐχ ὅτι ἀλλότριά ἐστι τὰ Πλάτωνος διδάγματα τοῦ Χριστοῦ, ἀλλ' ὅτι οὐκ ἔστι πάντη ὅμοια, ὥσπερ οὐδὲ τὰ τῶν ἄλλων, Στωϊκῶν τε καὶ ποιητῶν καὶ συγγραφέων. 3. ἕκαστος γάρ τις ἀπὸ μέρους τοῦ σπερματικοῦ θείου λόγου τὸ συγγενὲς ὁρῶν καλῶς ἐφθέγξατο· οἱ δὲ τἀναντία ἑαυτοῖς ἐν κυριωτέροις εἰρηκότες οὐκ ἐπιστήμην τὴν ἄποπτον καὶ γνῶσιν τὴν ἀνέλεγκτον φαίνονται ἐσχηκέναι. 4. ὅσα οὖν παρὰ πᾶσι καλῶς εἴρηται, ἡμῶν τῶν Χριστιανῶν ἐστί· τὸν γὰρ ἀπὸ ἀγεννήτου καὶ ἀρρήτου θεοῦ λόγον μετὰ τὸν θεὸν προσκυνοῦμεν καὶ ἀγαπῶμεν, ἐπειδὴ καὶ δι' ἡμᾶς ἄνθρωπος γέγονεν, ὅπως καὶ τῶν παθῶν τῶν

3 ψευδολογουμένων Otto ψευδολογούμενον A ‖ 11 ἑαυτοῖς Otto αὐτοῖς A ‖ ἄποπτον edd ἄπωπτον A

from them.' For περίβλημα cf. ii 11, 7.
3. ψευδολογουμένων] governed by κατεγέλασα.
4. Χριστιανὸς κτλ.] Εὔχομαι may mean '*boast*' or '*declare*' as in i 15, 6, and this suits the sense well. But here, being joined by the double καὶ with ἀγωνιζόμενος, it may be more naturally taken to mean '*pray*.' For the sentiment cf. Phil. iii 9 f. Ign. *Eph.* 1 ἵνα δυνηθῶ μαθητὴς εἶναι with Lightfoot's note.
7. οὐκ ἔστι π. ὅμ.] '*they are not altogether the same*,' i.e. as Christ's teaching.
9. ἕκαστος γάρ τις κτλ.] '*for each, by having a share in the Divine Logos, spoke well, whenever he saw what was congruous to it.*' Or could τὸ συγγενὲς here mean '*homogeneous*' (as in Aristotle), as contrasted with what follows? For the idea cf. ii 8 and 10. Note that

grammatically ἀπὸ μ. belongs to ὁρῶν.
10. τἀναντία ἑ.] Cf. i 44, 10; ii 10, 3.
11. ἄποπτον] probably means '*hidden.*'
13. ὅσα οὖν κτλ.] A fine claim of the summing up of all things in Christ. Cf. 1 Cor. iii 21 f. Aubé (*S. Justin* p. 100) points out that Seneca makes similar claims; 'Quidquid bene dictum est ab ullo, meum est' (*Epist. ad Lucil.* xvi sub fin.); 'quod uerum est, meum est' (*Epist.* xii). But Seneca only claims all discovered truth as his heritage. The Christian claim is that all truth is actually his possession, as being the revelation of the *Logos*, and so that all truth is Christian truth.
15. μετὰ τὸν θεὸν] The *Logos* is second in liturgical precedence. See *Introd.* p. xxii.

ἡμετέρων συμμέτοχος γενόμενος καὶ ἴασιν ποιήσηται.
5. οἱ γὰρ συγγραφεῖς πάντες διὰ τῆς ἐνούσης ἐμφύτου τοῦ λόγου σπορᾶς ἀμυδρῶς ἐδύναντο ὁρᾶν τὰ ὄντα. 6. ἕτερον γάρ ἐστι σπέρμα τινὸς καὶ μίμημα κατὰ δύναμιν δοθέν, καὶ ἕτερον αὐτὸ οὗ κατὰ χάριν τὴν ἀπ' ἐκείνου ἡ μετουσία καὶ μίμησις γίνεται.

14. 1. Καὶ ὑμᾶς οὖν ἀξιοῦμεν ὑπογράψαντας τὸ ὑμῖν δοκοῦν προθεῖναι τουτὶ τὸ βιβλίδιον, ὅπως καὶ τοῖς ἄλλοις τὰ ἡμέτερα γνωσθῇ καὶ δύνωνται τῆς ψευδοδοξίας
10 καὶ ἀγνοίας τῶν καλῶν ἀπαλλαγῆναι, οἳ παρὰ τὴν ἑαυτῶν αἰτίαν ὑπεύθυνοι ταῖς τιμωρίαις γίνονται [εἰς τὸ γνωσθῆναι τοῖς ἀνθρώποις ταῦτα], 2. διὰ τὸ ἐν τῇ φύσει τῇ τῶν ἀνθρώπων εἶναι τὸ γνωριστικὸν καλοῦ καὶ αἰσχροῦ, καὶ διὰ τὸ ἡμῶν, οὓς οὐκ ἐπίστανται τοιαῦτα ὁποῖα λέ-

11 εἰς τ. γνωσθῆναι τ. ἀ. ταῦτα A ‖ 12 διὰ τὸ ἐν τῇ φύσει Perion διὸ ἐν τῇ φύσει A ‖ 13 γνωριστικὸν Sylb Otto γνωριστὸν A

2. διὰ τῆς ἐνούσης κτλ.] Does ἐμφ. belong to λόγου or to σπορᾶς? A comparison with James i 21 might favour the former view, and it may be correct, though above ii 8, 1 we find διὰ τὸ ἔμφυτον παντὶ γένει ἀνθρώπων σπέρμα τοῦ λόγου. In this passage the addition of ἐνούσης somewhat alters the turn of the phrase.

3. ἀμυδρῶς] 'dimly.'
4. ἕτερον γὰρ κτλ.] explaining ἀμυδρῶς. 'It is one thing to have the seed of a thing and to be enabled to imitate it according to one's capacity; the thing itself, so partaken in and imitated by virtue of its own favour, is quite another.' The principle is stated in general terms; but of course the point is that there is a difference between the σπέρμα of the Logos and the Logos itself, i.e. Christ sums up all the truth of past times.

14. We ask you to publish this address, that others may know our doctrines and be saved from the punishment, to which their persecution of us makes them liable.

7. ὑπογράψαντας] A libellus was presented to the rulers, who, if they wished, placed a comment at the end and had it published, cf. i 29, 3. See e.g. the libelli from the Decian persecution.

10. παρὰ τὴν ἑαυτῶν αἰτίαν] 'through their own fault.' Cf. Tryph. 88.

11. εἰς τὸ γνωσθῆναι κτλ.] These words are intolerably tautologous.

12. διὰ τὸ κτλ.] The reasons why the persecutors are liable to punishment (from God) are : (1) There is in man a capacity for recognizing right and wrong; (2) They condemn men on mere suspicion without knowledge; (3) They worship gods who commit and permit, nay demand (ἀπαιτοῦσι) the immoralities which are charged against Christians.

APOLOGIA

γουσιν αἰσχρὰ πράττειν, καταψηφίζεσθαι, καὶ διὰ τὸ
χαίρειν τοιαῦτα πράξασι θεοῖς καὶ ἔτι νῦν ἀπαιτοῦσι
παρὰ ἀνθρώπων τὰ ὅμοια, ὡς ἐκ τοῦ καὶ ἡμῖν, ὡς τοιαῦτα
πράττουσι, θάνατον ἢ δεσμὰ ἢ ἄλλο τι τοιοῦτον προστιμᾶν ἑαυτοὺς κατακρίνειν, ὡς μὴ δέεσθαι ἄλλων δικαστῶν. 5
15. 1. [Καὶ τοῦ ἐν τῷ ἐμῷ ἔθνει ἀσεβοῦς καὶ πλά-
νου σιμωνιανοῦ διδάγματος κατεφρόνησα.] 2. ἐὰν δὲ
ὑμεῖς τοῦτο προγράψητε, ἡμεῖς τοῖς πᾶσι φανερὸν ἂν ποι-
ήσαιμεν, ἵνα εἰ δύναιντο μεταθῶνται· τούτου γε μόνου
χάριν τούσδε τοὺς λόγους συνετάξαμεν. 3. οὐκ ἔστι 10
δὲ ἡμῶν τὰ διδάγματα κατὰ κρίσιν σώφρονα αἰσχρά,
ἀλλὰ πάσης μὲν φιλοσοφίας ἀνθρωπείου ὑπέρτερα· εἰ δὲ
μή, κἂν σωταδείοις καὶ φιλαινιδείοις καὶ ἀρχεστρατείοις
καὶ ἐπικουρείοις καὶ τοῖς ἄλλοις τοῖς τοιούτοις ποιητι-
κοῖς διδάγμασιν οὐχ ὅμοια, οἷς ἐντυγχάνειν πᾶσι, καὶ 15

1 πράττειν καταψηφίζεσθαι Asht καταψηφιζομένους A ‖ 3 ὡς ἐκ τοῦ Thirlb ἐκ τοῦ A ‖ 4 προστιμᾶν Thirlb πρόστιμον A ‖ 8 φανερὸν ἂν π. nos φανερὸν π. A φ. ποιήσομεν Perion ‖ 13 ἀρχεστρατείοις Leutsch ὀρχηστικοῖς A

3. ὡς ἐκ τοῦ κτλ.] Since Christians are punished on suspicion of doing deeds which the heathen themselves commit, the heathen are condemning themselves.

15. *We pray that our apology may become known; for our teaching is better than any human philosophy, or, at least, than the poems which you allow anyone to read.*

6. καὶ τοῦ κτλ.] These words are obviously out of place, and must be a marginal note which has strayed into the text. Their proper place seems to be in ii 13, after τῆς παρὰ τ. π. δόξης. Cf. *Tryph.* 120.

8. προγράψητε] either '*to publish*,' in the sense that the emperors put it forth officially; or else '*to proscribe.*' The latter fits the context, which contrasts the ὑμεῖς with the ἡμεῖς.

ib. ποιήσαιμεν] without ἂν must be a wish, which would be very strange in this place. Otto translates (without inserting ἂν) '*nos ut in omnium notitiam ueniat curabimus,*' which is a paraphrase, scarcely justified by the MS reading.

13. σωταδείοις] Sotades of Maronea was the author of obscene verses.

ib. φιλαινιδείοις] Philaenis of Leucadia was the authoress of a poem περὶ ἀφροδισίων.

ib. ἀρχεστρατείοις] Archestratus of Gela wrote a gastronomic poem called Ἡδυπάθεια. Some prefer to retain here the MS ὀρχηστικοῖς as referring to *ballets*, and γενομένοις, meaning '*acted.*' But evidently a proper name was wanted.

14. ἐπικουρείοις] the teachings of Epicurus.

B.

λεγομένοις καὶ γεγραμμένοις, συγκεχώρηται. 4. καὶ
παυσόμεθα λοιπόν, ὅσον ἐφ᾽ ἡμῖν ἦν πράξαντες, καὶ
προσεπευξάμενοι τῆς ἀληθείας καταξιωθῆναι τοὺς πάντη
πάντας ἀνθρώπους. 5. εἴη οὖν καὶ ὑμᾶς ἀξίως εὐσε-
5 βείας καὶ φιλοσοφίας τὰ δίκαια ὑπὲρ ἑαυτῶν κρῖναι.

1 λεγομένοις Otto γενομένοις A || 4 εἴη οὖν καὶ ὑμᾶς Sylb εἴη οὖν καὶ ἡμᾶς A

1. λεγομένοις] It is, of course, only by a kind of zeugma that this can go with ἐντυγχάνειν 'to read.'
2. ὅσον ἐφ᾽ ἡμ.] Cf. i 55, 8.
3. τοὺς πάντη π. ἀ.] Cf. 1 Tim. ii 4.
4. ἀξίως κτλ.] refers back to the epithets of the dedication i 1.

5. ἑαυτῶν] This is in accordance with Justin's general idea, that the rulers' own case, i.e. the case of their own salvation, is in question. Cf. i 8, 1, Tert. *ad Scap.* 1 'Hunc libellum non nobis timentes misimus, sed uobis et omnibus inimicis nostris.'

APPENDIX I.

The following letters appear in the MSS after i 68. But there is every reason to doubt their authenticity. The first appears in Eus. *H. E.* iv 13 in a very different version, as written by Marcus Aurelius. It cannot have been extant in Justin's time, though it may have been added to the Apology before the time of Eusebius. It is needless to discuss whether it proceeds from Pius or Aurelius, as it is almost certainly a forgery. It is not referred to by Melito in Eus. *H. E.* iv 26 (though he enumerates the rescripts of Hadrian and Pius on the subject of the Christians), and it is quite an unsuitable and unconvincing composition. The view which it takes of the gods is wholly frivolous and unbecoming to Pius or Aurelius, its laudation of the Christians as innocent models of religious fidelity and zeal, and the facts suggested in μηδὲν ὀχλεῖν κτλ., are unhistorical and untrue.

The second letter cannot have been inserted by Justin, who was long dead, since it refers to events that must have taken place about A.D. 174. It is an obvious forgery. Eus. *H. E.* v 5 only knows of its existence from Tertullian[1]. The Greek is barbarous, and the circumstances a palpable absurdity. The fact referred to seems to be the deliverance of the Roman army in Hungary, during the campaign against the Quadi, by a sudden shower, as pictured in a sculpture on the column of Aurelius. This was attributed by the heathen to the gods of Rome, to an Egyptian sorcerer, or to the Emperor's own prayers. The Christian legend of the *Legio Fulminata* is a mere fiction. The name was an old one, being known in Augustus' time, and, though the event related in the legend

---

[1] But Eusebius also quotes, with reference to the alleged miracle, the testimony of Apollinaris. See Allard *Histoire des Persécutions* i 391 foll.

was said to have diverted Aurelius from his purposes of cruelty towards the Christians, the Gallic persecution of A.D. 177 is a proof that such a supposition was equally fictitious[1].

The text of the subjoined epistles is that of Otto.

Ἀντωνίνου Ἐπιστολὴ πρὸς τὸ κοινὸν τῆς Ἀσίας.

Αὐτοκράτωρ Καῖσαρ Τίτος Αἴλιος Ἀδριανὸς Ἀντωνῖνος Σεβαστὸς Εὐσεβής, Ἀρχιερεὺς Μέγιστος, δημαρχικῆς ἐξουσίας τὸ καʹ, ὕπατος τὸ δʹ, πατὴρ πατρίδος, τῷ κοινῷ τῆς Ἀσίας χαίρειν. ἐγὼ
5 ᾤμην ὅτι καὶ τοὺς θεοὺς ἐπιμελεῖς ἔσεσθαι μὴ λανθάνειν τοὺς τοιούτους. πολὺ γὰρ μᾶλλον ἐκείνους κολάσοιεν, εἴπερ δύναιντο, τοὺς μὴ βουλομένους αὐτοῖς προσκυνεῖν. οἷς ταραχὴν ὑμεῖς ἐμβάλλετε, καὶ τὴν γνώμην αὐτῶν ἥνπερ ἔχουσιν, ὡς ἀθέων κατηγορεῖτε, καὶ ἕτερά τινα ἐμβάλλετε, ἅτινα οὐ δυνάμεθα ἀποδεῖξαι. εἴη δʼ ἂν
10 ἐκείνοις χρήσιμον τὸ δοκεῖν ἐπὶ τῷ κατηγορουμένῳ τεθνάναι· καὶ νικῶσιν ὑμᾶς προϊέμενοι τὰς ἑαυτῶν ψυχάς, ἤπερ πειθόμενοι οἷς ἀξιοῦτε πράσσειν αὐτούς. περὶ δὲ τῶν σεισμῶν τῶν γεγονότων καὶ τῶν γινομένων οὐκ εἰκὸς ὑπομνῆσαι ὑμᾶς ἀθυμοῦντας, ὅταν περ ὦσι, παραβάλλοντας τὰ ὑμέτερα πρὸς τὰ ἐκείνων, ὅτι εὐπαρρησιαστό-
15 τεροι ὑμῶν γίνονται πρὸς τὸν θεόν. καὶ ὑμεῖς μὲν ἀγνοεῖν δοκεῖτε παρʼ ἐκεῖνον τὸν χρόνον τοὺς θεούς, καὶ τῶν ἱερῶν ἀμελεῖτε, θρησκείαν δὲ τὴν περὶ τὸν θεὸν οὐκ ἐπίστασθε. ὅθεν καὶ τοὺς θρησκεύοντας ἐζηλώκατε, καὶ διώκετε ἕως θανάτου. ὑπὲρ τῶν τοιούτων καὶ ἄλλοι τινὲς τῶν περὶ τὰς ἐπαρχίας ἡγεμόνων τῷ θειοτάτῳ μου
20 πατρὶ ἔγραψαν· οἷς καὶ ἀντέγραψε μηδὲν ὀχλεῖν τοῖς τοιούτοις, εἰ μὴ φαίνοιντό τι ἐπὶ τὴν ἡγεμονίαν Ῥωμαίων ἐγχειροῦντες· καὶ ἐμοὶ δὲ περὶ τῶν τοιούτων πολλοὶ ἐσήμαναν· οἷς δὴ καὶ ἀντέγραψα, τῇ

1. κοινόν] The common council of Asia, which supervised the provincial affairs and the cult of Caesar.

3. δημαρχικῆς ἐξ. τὸ καʹ, ὑπ. τὸ δʹ, π. πατρίδος] Mommsen (=A.D. 158). δημ. ἐξ. ὕπατος πδʹ, πατ. πατρίδος τὸ καʹ A.

5. ὅτι...ἔσεσθαι] A similar anacoluthon in *Tryph.* 45 is pointed out by Otto.

ib. τοὺς τοιούτους] i.e. the Christians.

14. παραβάλλοντας] edd. παραβάλλοντες A.

20. μηδὲν ὀχλεῖν] See Hadrian's rescript at the end of i 68. The provisions of that rescript are not at all as here stated.

[1] See the discussion of the whole subject in Lightfoot *Ignatius* i 465 foll. (ed. 1).

APPENDIX I

τοῦ πατρός μου κατακολουθῶν γνώμῃ. εἰ δέ τις ἔχει πρός τινα τῶν τοιούτων πρᾶγμα καταφέρειν ὡς τοιούτου, ἐκεῖνος ὁ καταφερόμενος ἀπολελύσθω τοῦ ἐγκλήματος, κἂν φαίνηται τοιοῦτος ὤν, ἐκεῖνος δὲ ὁ καταφέρων ἔνοχος ἔσται τῇ δίκῃ.

Μάρκου βασιλέως Ἐπιστολὴ πρὸς τὴν Σύγκλητον, ἐν ᾗ μαρτυρεῖ 5
Χριστιανοὺς αἰτίους γεγενῆσθαι τῆς νίκης αὐτῶν.

Αὐτοκράτωρ Καῖσαρ Μάρκος Αὐρήλιος Ἀντωνῖνος Γερμανικὸς Παρθικὸς Σαρματικὸς Δήμῳ Ῥωμαίων καὶ τῇ ἱερᾷ Συγκλήτῳ χαίρειν. φανερὰ ὑμῖν ἐποίησα τὰ τοῦ ἐμοῦ σκοποῦ μεγέθη, ὁποῖα ἐν τῇ Γερμανίᾳ ἐκ περιστάσεως διὰ περιβολῆς ἐπακολουθήματα 10
ἐποίησα ἐν τῇ μεθορίᾳ καμὼν καὶ παθών, ἐν Καρνούντῳ καταλαμβανομένου μου ὑπὸ δρακόντων ἑβδομήκοντα τεσσάρων ἀπὸ μιλίων ἐννέα. γενομένων δὲ αὐτῶν ἐγγὺς ἡμῶν ἐξπλωράτωρες ἐμήνυσαν ἡμῖν καὶ Πομπηϊανὸς ὁ ἡμέτερος πολέμαρχυς ἐδήλωσεν ἡμῖν ἅτινα εἴδομεν (καταλαμβανόμενος δὲ ἤμην ἐν μεγέθει πλήθους 15
ἀμίκτου, καὶ στρατευμάτων λεγεῶνος πρίμας, δεκάτης, γεμίνας, φρεντησίας μίγμα κατηριθμημένον) πλήθη παρεῖναι παμμίκτου ὄχλου χιλιάδων ἐνακοσίων ἑβδομήκοντα ἑπτά. ἐξετάσας οὖν ἐμαυτὸν καὶ τὸ πλῆθος τὸ ἐμὸν πρὸς τὸ μέγεθος τῶν βαρβάρων καὶ πολεμίων, κατέδραμον εἰς τὸ θεοῖς εὔχεσθαι πατρῴοις. ἀμελού- 20
μενος δὲ ὑπ' αὐτῶν καὶ τὴν στενοχωρίαν μου θεωρήσας τῆς δυνάμεως παρεκάλεσα τοὺς παρ' ἡμῖν λεγομένους Χριστιανούς· καὶ ἐπερωτήσας εὗρον πλῆθος καὶ μέγεθος αὐτῶν, καὶ ἐμβριμησάμενος εἰς αὐτούς, ὅπερ οὐκ ἔπρεπε διὰ τὸ ὕστερον ἐπεγνωκέναι με τὴν δύναμιν αὐτῶν. ὅθεν ἀρξάμενοι οὐ βελῶν παράρτησιν οὔτε ὅπλων οὔτε 25

---

9. σκοποῦ μεγέθη] i.e. his plans against Marcomannia and Sarmatia.

ib. ὁποῖα ἐν τῇ κτλ.] 'such advantages as I won out of the danger of being surrounded.'

11. καμὼν καὶ παθών] Scalig. καμ. καὶ σπαθών A.

ib. Καρνούντῳ] Otto, κοτίνῳ A. Aurelius had his headquarters for three years at Carnuntum during the Marcomannic war.

12. δρακόντων] Mythical, unless it refers figuratively to the enemy. Or the idea may be of 7 legions, each with 10 standards with dragons thereon (Salmasius). Scaliger suggests δρούγκων, *drungus* being a late Latin name for a barbarian cohort.

14. Πομπηϊανός] Son-in-law of Aurelius and his general in Rhaetia and Noricum.

16. γεμίνας, φρεντησίας Otto, γεμιναφρεντησίᾳ A. φρεντήσιον = *fretense*.

25. ὅθεν ἀρξάμενοι] As it stands, the sentence is evidently defective.

134   APPENDIX I

σαλπίγγων, διὰ τὸ ἐχθρὸν εἶναι τὸ τοιοῦτο αὐτοῖς διὰ τὸν θεόν, ὃν
φοροῦσι κατὰ συνείδησιν. εἰκὸς οὖν ἐστιν, οὓς ὑπολαμβάνομεν
ἀθέους εἶναι, ὅτι θεὸν ἔχουσιν αὐτόματον ἐν τῇ συνειδήσει τετει-
χισμένον. ῥίψαντες γὰρ ἑαυτοὺς ἐπὶ τὴν γῆν οὐχ ὑπὲρ ἐμοῦ μόνον
5 ἐδεήθησαν ἀλλὰ καὶ ὑπὲρ τοῦ παρόντος στρατεύματος, παρήγορον
γενέσθαι δίψης καὶ λιμοῦ τῆς παρούσης. πεμπταῖοι γὰρ ὕδωρ οὐκ
εἰλήφειμεν διὰ τὸ μὴ παρεῖναι· ἦμεν γὰρ ἐν τῷ μεσομφάλῳ τῆς
Γερμανίας καὶ τοῖς ὅροις αὐτῶν. ἅμα δὲ τῷ τούτους ῥίψαι ἐπὶ τὴν
γῆν ἑαυτοὺς καὶ εὔχεσθαι θεῷ, ᾧ ἐγὼ ἠγνόουν, εὐθέως ὕδωρ ἠκο-
10 λούθει οὐρανόθεν, ἐπὶ μὲν ἡμᾶς ψυχρότατον, ἐπὶ δὲ τοὺς Ῥωμαίων
ἐπιβούλους χάλαζα πυρώδης. ἀλλὰ καὶ εὐθὺ θεοῦ παρουσίαν ἐν
εὐχῇ γινομένῃν παραυτίκα ὡς ἀνυπερβλήτου καὶ ἀκαταλύτου. αὐ-
τόθεν οὖν ἀρξάμενοι συγχωρήσωμεν τοῖς τοιούτοις εἶναι Χριστιανοῖς,
ἵνα μὴ καθ' ἡμῶν τι τοιοῦτον αἰτησάμενοι ὅπλον ἐπιτύχωσι. τὸν
15 δὲ τοιοῦτον συμβουλεύω, διὰ τὸ τοιοῦτον εἶναι Χριστιανόν, μὴ
ἐγκαλεῖσθαι. εἰ δὲ εὑρεθείη τις ἐγκαλῶν τῷ Χριστιανῷ ὅτι Χριστιανός ἐστι, τὸν μὲν προσαγόμενον Χριστιανὸν πρόδηλον εἶναι
βούλομαι, γίνεσθαι ὁμολογήσαντα τοῦτο, ἄλλο ἕτερον μηδὲν ἐγκα-
λούμενον ἢ ὅτι Χριστιανός ἐστι μόνον, τὸν προσάγοντα δὲ τοῦτον
20 ζῶντα καίεσθαι· τὸν δὲ Χριστιανὸν ὁμολογήσαντα καὶ συνασφα-
λισάμενον περὶ τοῦ τοιούτου, τὸν πεπιστευμένον τὴν ἐπαρχίαν εἰς
μετάνοιαν καὶ ἀνελευθερίαν τὸν τοιοῦτον μὴ μετάγειν. ταῦτα δὲ
καὶ τῆς συγκλήτου δόγματι κυρωθῆναι βούλομαι, καὶ κελεύω τοῦτό
μου τὸ διάταγμα ἐν τῷ φόρῳ τοῦ Τραϊανοῦ προτεθῆναι πρὸς τὸ
25 δύνασθαι ἀναγινώσκεσθαι. φροντίσει ὁ πραίφεκτος Βιτράσιος Πολ-
λίων εἰς τὰς πέριξ ἐπαρχίας πεμφθῆναι· πάντα δὲ τὸν βουλόμενον
χρῆσθαι καὶ ἔχειν μὴ κωλύεσθαι λαμβάνειν ἐκ τῶν προτεθέντων
παρ' ἡμῶν.

Perhaps the original verb is concealed in παράρτησιν, or ἐποίησαν is lost after it.
8. ἅμα δὲ τῷ τούτους] Otto, ἅμα δὲ τῷ τούτοις A.
11. ἀλλὰ καὶ εὐθὺ κτλ.] sc. συνείδομεν, or some such verb.
17. πρόδηλον κτλ.] 'become clear that he is accused for no other cause.'
19. τὸν προσάγοντα δέ] Cf. Dan. iii 29, vi 24.

20. συνασφαλισάμενον] 'proving.'
22. ἀνελευθερίαν] either 'loss of freedom' or 'dishonesty' (by abjuring his faith).
25. Βιτράσιος] Brisson, Otto. Βηράσιος A. Vitrasius Pollio was prefect of the praetorians from A.D. 172.
27. χρῆσθαι καὶ ἔχειν] sc. a copy of the decree.

APPENDIX II.

HADRIAN'S RESCRIPT TO MINUCIUS FUNDANUS. (i 68.)

The genuineness of this rescript has been much disputed, e.g. by Baur, Keim, Aubé, Veil, Lipsius, Overbeck, by whom it is regarded as a Christian forgery of a later generation. On the other hand Neander, Wieseler, Funk, Renan, Mommsen, Lightfoot, Ramsay defend its authenticity without hesitation; and it seems open to question whether the doubts about it are not due to a false view of the Roman government's relations to Christianity. The arguments may be summarized as follows:

(1) It is maintained that the rescript is an anti-climax in its present position, and that the appeal to it is unworthy of Justin. But this seems over-fanciful. There is no unworthiness involved in quoting it, as Justin does, with the statement that the Christians might claim a fair trial as their legal right in accordance with it, but preferred to base their plea on considerations of abstract justice.

(2) It is pointed out that Tatian, Athenagoras, Minucius Felix, and Tertullian make no reference to it. But this argument is quite inconclusive. Neither Justin nor Athenagoras quotes Trajan's earlier and undoubtedly authentic rescript; and Melito (A.D. 172) mentions Hadrian's rescript (Eus. *H. E.* iv 26).

(3) It is said to be out of accord with Hadrian's character. But that is quite untrue. Hadrian was a thorough sceptic, and this rescript, as Ramsay says (*Ch. in Rom. Emp.* p. 324), 'was a sarcasm.' Trajan's principle, that the Name of Christianity is a crime, is neither asserted nor rescinded by him; the State religion is left unaltered, but the practical application in the case of Christianity is left to the personal

bias of individual governors by the studied vagueness of the language, e.g. εἴ τις δείκνυσί τι παρὰ τοὺς νόμους πράττοντας might be interpreted either to include the mere proof of being a Christian or to include only definite crimes.

(4) The heading is said to be informal. But, as Allard points out (*Hist. des perséc.* p. 249), Trajan's letters to Pliny are headed simply *Traianus Plinio S.*

(5) It is said that there was no need for a change of administration; that Trajan's letter had fixed the procedure. But the situation was now changed. In Trajan's time the Christians were subject to anonymous denunciations; now they are the objects of popular clamour; and this rescript is an ordinance to protect public order.

(6) It is pointed out that the Latin text is more severe than the Greek, and it is argued that the Christians would not have weakened the Latin in a Greek translation; but that a Christian translator into Latin of a Christian forgery in Greek might colour the phrases. But the differences are after all very slight, and may be due to mere ignorance or carelessness. On the whole the rescript seems quite in the line of Roman State policy. Christianity was always a *religio illicita*, and so Pliny assumed it to be; the Christians disturbed the public peace and denied the State religion, and as such could be put to death. But their numbers caused anxiety as to the expediency of a general persecution of Christianity. Trajan therefore prescribed mildness in the exercise of administrative power against them. Hadrian's rescript is on similar lines. But that in no way justifies a theory that this rescript was a forgery, imitated from Trajan's. And it is very dangerous to reject not only this quotation of Justin, but also Melito's and Eusebius' quite distinct and unequivocal statements, as due to forgery or ignorance. No doubt the rescript was originally private, but it would soon have become known, like other official rescripts.

INDEX I.

SUBJECTS.

A

Abraham, a Christian before Christ, 70, 12
Achilles, story of, 41, 3
Acta of Pilate, see Pontius Pilate
Adonis, myth of, 40, 8
Agapé, possible allusion to, 100, 6
Amphilochus, oracle of, 30, 5
Ananias, Azarias, and Misael, Christians before Christ, 70, 13
Angels, xxix sq.; 9, 13; 111, 5; fall of, xxxi; 111, 6
Antinous, deification of, 47, 13
Antiope, myth of, 40, 13
Antoninus Pius, adoption of, xlvii; character of, xvii; 2, 8; rescript of, 131
Aphrodite, 40, 8
Apollo, 40, 6
Apologies, characteristics of Justin's, xi; date of, xlvii; editions of, liii; MSS of, lii; number of, xlix
Archestratus, 129, 13
Ariadne, myth of, 35, 12
Arianism, possible, in Apologies, xxii; 52, 2
Asclepius, myth of, 35, 7; 38, 3; 40, 10; 82, 10
Athena, birth of, 97, 7
Aurelius, M., adoption of, xlvii; character of, xvii; 2, 8; letter of, 131

B

Baptism, Justin's account of, xxxvii; 23, 6; 90, 3; fasting before, 90, 10
Barcochba, ill-treatment of Christians by, 49, 17

Bellerophon, myth of, 35, 11; 82, 1
Bethlehem, 54, 11
Body, Resurrection of, 31, 2; 32, 3; 77, 2; see Eschatology
Briareus, Thetis and, 41, 1
Briseis, Achilles and, 41, 3

C

Canon, Justin's evidence to, xxxiii; see Non-canonical books
Carnuntum, Aurelius at, 133, 11
Christ, name of, 5, 8; 113, 3
Christians, popular charges against, 9, 8; 15, 5, 10; 44, 1; 73, 17; 117, 18; 124, 11; before Christ, 70, 10
Church organization, Justin's evidence on, xxxvi
Crescens, x; li; 117, 16
Cronos, cult of, 125, 11; myth of, 36, 9
Cross, symbolism of, 55, 4; 82, 16; 88, 12
Cynics, views of, 119, 1

D

David, date of, 63, 17
Demonology, Justin's, xxix and references
Deucalion identified with Noah, 114, 10
Dionysus, myth of, 35, 8; 40, 6; 81, 5
Dioscuri, 35, 10
Divorce, Justin's views on, 22, 15
Dodona, oracle at, 30, 6

E

Elias, a Christian before Christ, 70, 13
Empedocles, eschatology of, 30, 7
Emperors, apotheosis of, 36, 1; 84, 1
Epicurus, Justin's views on, xiii; 115, 3; 126, 6; 129, 14
Erebus, 88, 1
Eschatology, Justin's, xxxii and references; causes of a delay of end of world, 46, 5; 114, 1; see Body, Resurrection of
Ethics, Justin's views on, xxxi; 16, 3; 21, 4; 22, 19; 26, 6; 44, 8; 59, 15
Eucharist, Justin's evidence on, xxxix; 98, 2, 15; 100, 10; wine or water in, xlii
Eusebius, evidence of, about Apologies, xlv
Exorcisms, Christian, 113, 18
Exposure of children, Justin's views on, 44, 8; 47, 1

F

Fasting before Baptism, 90, 10
Felix, Munatius, xlix; 47, 7
Free-will, Justin's views on, xxxii; 14, 13; 46, 9; 64, 8; 114, 15; and Divine foreknowledge, 63, 14; 67, 11

G

Ganymede, 36, 11; 40, 14
Gehenna, 33, 4
Gitta, Simon of; see Simon
God, Justin's doctrine of, xix sq.; 9, 10; 11, 17; 13, 7; 14, 2; 20, 9; 21, 4; 34, 2; 112, 8
Gospels, 99, 6; Justin's quotations from, xxxv; knowledge of Fourth Gospel, xxi; xxxv; 91, 1; use of, in Eucharistic service, 100, 11
Granianus, 102, 20

H

Hadrian, character of, 135; rescript of, 102, 15; 135
Helena, Marcion and, 42, 6

Heraclitus, a Christian before Christ, 70, 11; fate of, 116, 12
Herakles, choice of, 122, 12; story of, 35, 9; 82, 8
Hermes, myth of, 35, 6; 37, 5
Herod, 49, 4; 61, 1
Holy Ghost, Justin's doctrine of, xxvii and references
Homer, referred to, 30, 8; 41, 1
Hystaspes, eschatology of, 33, 7; forbidden to be read, 68, 6

I

Idolatry, Justin's views on, 12, 17
Incarnation, Justin's doctrine of, xxii; xxvi; 38, 12; 71, 2; 96, 6; 113, 9; 127, 16; Virgin-Birth, 37, 14; 51, 26; 52, 20

J

Jerusalem, fate of, 71, 21
Jesus, name of, 54, 2; 113, 7
Judah, 51, 2
Junius Rusticus, ix
Jupiter Latiaris, cult of, 125, 12
Justin, life of, ix; 124, 7; martyrdom of, ix; methods of quotation of, xxxv; 24, 1, 3; 26, 10, 13; 27, 9; 62, 23; origin of, ix; 1, 7; place in history of, xii sq.; style of, xi; Apologies; Demonology; doctrine of Angels, God, Holy Ghost, Incarnation, Logos; Eschatology; Ethics; evidence on Baptism, Canon, Church organization, Eucharist, Sunday; knowledge of Fourth Gospel, non-canonical books; possible Arianism in, Subordinationism in; possible belief in eternity of matter; relation to Plato; views on Free-will, see separate headings

K

Koré, myth of, 96, 18

L

Legio fulminata, 131
Logos, Justin's doctrine of, xx and references

Lot, 79, 19
Lucius, a Christian martyr, 108, 9

M

Marcion, xlix; 43, 4; 86, 8
Marriage, Justin's views on, 47, 3; see Divorce
Matter, Justin's views on eternity of, xix; 14, 5; 87, 16
Menander the poet, 34, 14
Menander the heretic, 42, 9; 84, 14
Minos, 12, 7
Minucius Fundanus, 102, 17
Mithras, mysteries of, 99, 13
Moses, first of prophets, 50, 12; 67, 3; 80, 19; 87, 8; and Brazen Serpent, 88, 6
Musonius, fate of, 116, 12

N

Noah, 114, 10
Non-canonical books, Justin's knowledge of, xxxiii; 53, 11; 55, 18; 75, 1; 91, 1

O

Oracles, pagan, 30, 1

P

Paganism under Empire, 7, 8; 29, 9; 39, 8; 40, 9; 45, 10; analogies to Christianity, 34, 7; 35, 3; 36, 18; 81, 7; 92, 19; 96, 17; 99, 13; 114, 10
Persephone, myth of, 40, 8
Perseus, myth of, 35, 10; 37, 15; 82, 6
Philaenis, 129, 13
Philo, Justin and, xxi
Philosophy, Christianity regarded as, xiv; 7, 4; 11, 4
Pius, see Antoninus
Plato, borrowings of, from Moses, 67, 3; 87, 4; 88, 3; Justin's relation to, xiii, xix; quoted, 4, 7; 12, 6; 30, 8; 34, 8; 67, 2; 88, 4; 118, 17; 121, 10, 12, 17; teaching of, compared to Christ's, 127, 6
Pompeianus, 133, 14

Pontius Pilate, 20, 4; 61, 2; 70, 5; Acta of, 56, 5; 72, 10
Prophecy, argument from, 48, 8; methods of, 56, 13; 63, 11
Ptolemaeus, a Christian martyr, 107, 12
Ptolemy and the Septuagint, 48, 18
Pythagoras, 30, 8
Pytho, oracle of, 30, 6

Q

Quirinius, 54, 17; 70, 3

R

Reservation, xl
Resurrection of body, see Body
Rhadamanthys, 12, 7
Rusticus, see Junius

S

Sardanapalus, 115, 3
Satan, xxxi; 45, 18
Sects, immoral Christian, 7, 1
Semo Sancus, statue of, 42, 3
Septuagint, 49, 7
Serpent, brazen, 88, 6
Sibyl, eschatology of, 33, 7; forbidden to be read, 68, 7
Simon of Gitta, 41, 11; 84, 14
Socrates, Justin's view of, 8, 11; 30, 8; 70, 11; 115, 2; 118, 14; 121, 9
Sodom and Gomorrah, 79, 16
Sotades, 129, 13
Spirit, Holy, see Holy Ghost
State, relations of Christianity to, xvi; 5, 5; 11, 6; 15, 9; 28, 1; 68, 5; 107, 6; 125, 2; 136; relations of Judaism to, xvi
Stoicism, Justin's views on, xiii; 32, 7; 33, 9; 114, 13; 116, 8
Subordinationism, possible, in Justin, xxii; 18, 2; 20, 6
Sunday, xxxix; 101, 13

T

Thetis, 41, 1
Tiberius Caesar, 20, 5
Trajan, 5, 5; 136

U

Urbicus, l; 104, 12

V

Verissimus, name of Aurelius, xlviii
Virgin-Birth, see Incarnation
Vitrasius Pollio, 134, 25

W

Worship, Christian, 13, 17; 19, 4, 10

X

Xenophon, quoted, 122, 10

Z

Zeus, myth of, and Cronos, 36, 9

INDEX II.

SCRIPTURE REFERENCES.

GENESIS

i. 1–3	87, 12
2	14, 5 (n.)
5	88, 1 (n.)
ii. 16, 17	66, 5 (n.)
iii. 1	46, 1 (n.)
vi.	8, 5 (n.)
1–4	111, 6
xix.	79, 16
xlix. 10, 11	50, 13; 80, 20

EXODUS

iii. 2, 6, 10, 14, 15	95, 1
5	93, 14

NUMBERS

xxi. 6 ff.	88, 12
xxiv. 17	52, 10

DEUTERONOMY

xxviii. 66	83, 11 (n.)
xxx. 15, 19	66, 5
xxxii. 22	88, 1 (n.); 89, 16

1 CHRONICLES

xvi. 23, 25–31	62, 23

PSALMS

i. ii.	61, 11
iii. 5	58, 19
xix. 2 ff.	60, 11
5	82, 7
xxii. 7, 8	58, 21
16, 18	55, 12; 58, 18
xxiv. 7, 8	76, 7
xcvi. 1, 2, 4–10	62, 23
cx. 1–3	69, 4

PROVERBS

i. 28	77, 14 (n.)

ECCLESIASTES

i. 9	85, 16 (n.)

ISAIAH

i. 3	94, 7
3, 4	57, 11
7	71, 19
9	79, 14
11–15	57, 19
16–20	66, 9; 91, 5; 93, 1 (n.)
ii. 3, 4	59, 4
v. 20	73, 21
vii. 14	52, 22; 82, 4
ix. 6	55, 3; 82, 15 (n.)
xi. 1, 10	52, 10
12	77, 17
xxxv. 5, 6	72, 6
xli. 22	18, 13 (n.)
xliii. 5, 6	77, 17
xliv. 9–17	12, 15 (n.)
xlv. 23	77, 8
l. 6–8	58, 11
li. 5	52, 10
lii. 13–liii. 8	73, 26
liii. 1, 2	55, 1 (n.)
8–12	75, 12
12	73, 26
liv. 1	79, 5
lvii. 1 ff.	72, 14
lviii. 2	55, 8
6, 7	57, 19
lxiii. 17	77, 17
lxiv. 10–12	71, 10
11	77, 17
lxv. 1–3	73, 2
2	55, 8; 58, 9

lxvi. 1 .... 57, 17
    24 .... 77, 13

JEREMIAH

ii. 15 .... 71, 19
ix. 26 .... 79, 25
l. 3 .... 71, 19

LAMENTATIONS

iv. 20 .... 83, 11

EZEKIEL

xviii. 23 .... 24, 1 (n.)
xxxiii. 11 .... 24, 1 (n.)
xxxvii. 7, 8 .... 77, 8

DANIEL

i. 7 .... 70, 13 (n.)
iii. 29 .... 134, 19 (n.)
vi. 24 .... 134, 19 (n.)
vii. 13 .... 76, 12

JOEL

ii. 13 .... 77, 17

MICAH

iv. 2 .... 59, 4
v. 2 .... 54, 11

ZECHARIAH

ii. 6 .... 77, 17
ix. 9 .... 56, 9
xii. 10–12 .... 77, 17
xiii. 7 .... 75, 1 (n.)
xiv. 5 .... 76, 12

WISDOM

ii. 24 .... 46, 1 (n.)
vi. 3 .... 102, 5 (n.)

MATTHEW

i. 20, 21 .... 53, 11
    21 .... 113, 7 (n.)
    23 .... 52, 22
ii. 2, 11 .... 34, 14 (n.)
    6 .... 54, 11
iv. 23 .... 49, 22
v. 16 .... 25, 18
    22 .... 25, 16
    28 .... 22, 10

v. 29, 30 .... 22, 11
    32 .... 22, 15
    34, 37 .... 26, 10
    39 .... 25, 14; 25, 20
    41 .... 25, 17
    42 .... 24, 9
    44 .... 24, 5
    45, 48 .... 24, 20
    46 .... 24, 9
    46, 47 .... 24, 3
    48 .... 119, 12 (n.)
vi. 1 .... 25, 10
    19, 20 .... 24, 13
    20 .... 24, 16
    21 .... 25, 2
    25 ff., 31–33 .... 25, 2
vii. 15, 16, 19 .... 27, 16
    21 .... 27, 7
    22, 23 .... 27, 11
    23 .... 114, 4 (n.)
    24 .... 27, 9 (n.)
    29 .... 22, 8 (n.)
ix. 13 .... 23, 13
    35 .... 49, 22
x. 1 .... 49, 22
    22 .... 1, 5 (n.)
    26 .... 18, 7 (n.)
    28 .... 33, 1
    33 .... 6, 19
    40 .... 27, 9 (n.); 94, 17
xi. 5 .... 53, 11 (n.); 72, 6
    27 .... 94, 12
xiii. 9, 13 ff. .... 78, 11 (n.)
    42, 43 .... 27, 11
xvi. 26 .... 24, 16
xviii. 3 .... 91, 1 (n.)
    9 .... 22, 11
xix. 11, 12 .... 22, 16
    17 .... 26, 16
    26 .... 32, 15
xxi. 1 ff. 51, 15
    5 .... 56, 9
xxii. 17–21 .... 28, 3
    32 .... 96, 13 (n.)
    44 .... 69, 4 (n.)
xxiii. 8 .... 97, 15 (n.)
xxiv. 5 .... 27, 16
    9 .... 18, 7 (n.)
    25 .... 18, 11 (n.)
xxv. 15 .... 28, 16 (n.)
    31 .... 76, 12
    41 .... 46, 5
xxvi. 26 .... 99, 9
    31 .... 75, 1 (n.)

SCRIPTURE REFERENCES

xxvii. 35 .... 56, 1
    39–43 .... 58, 22
xxviii. 19 ... 59, 13 (n.); 90, 14 (n.)

MARK

ii. 17 .... 23, 13
vi. 14 .... 39, 3 (n.)
    33 .... 38, 6 (n.)
viii. 38 .... 6, 19
ix. 47 .... 22, 11
    48 .... 77, 13
x. 17, 18 .... 26, 16
    27 .... 32, 15
xii. 29, 30 .... 26, 13
xiv. 22 .... 99, 9
xvi. 20 .... 69, 12 (n.)

LUKE

i. 31, 32 .... 53, 11
    35 .... 53, 8
ii. 2 .... 54, 17
iii. 1 .... 20, 5 (n.)
    18 .... 53, 11 (n.)
v. 32 .... 23, 13
vi. 27, 28 .... 1, 6 (n.); 24, 5
    29 .... 25, 14
    30 .... 24, 9
    32 .... 24, 3
    34 .... 24, 9
    35, 36 .... 24, 20
ix. 26 .... 6, 19
x. 16 .... 27, 9 (n.); 94, 17
    22 .... 94, 12
    27 .... 26, 13
xii. 4 .... 17, 15 (n.)
    4, 5 .... 33, 1
    22 ff., 29–31, 34 ..... 25, 2
    48 .... 29, 1
xiii. 26–28 .... 27, 11
xiv. 18 .... 2, 3 (n.)
xvi. 18 .... 22, 15
    25 .... 124, 13 (n.)
xviii. 18, 19 .... 26, 16
    27 .... 32, 15
xx. 21–25 .... 28, 3
xxii. 19 .... 99, 9
xxiv. 25, 26, 44–46 .... 75, 3 (n.)

JOHN

i. 1 .... 96, 2 (n.)
    1–3 .... 112, 10 (n.)
    15 .... 18, 2 (n.)
iii. 3–5 .... 91, 1
    14 .... 88, 12 (n.)
iv. 23 .... 34, 14 (n.)
    24 .... 10, 2 (n.)
v. 23 .... 10, 2 (n.)
viii. 19 .... 94, 12 (n.)
xiv. 24 .... 27, 9 (n.); 94, 17 (n.)
    29 .... 52, 26 (n.)
xvi. 3 .... 94, 12 (n.)
    4 .... 18, 11 (n.)
xviii. 36 .... 15, 12 (n.)
xix. 13 .... 55, 18 (n.)
    37 .... 77, 17 (n.)

ACTS

i. 8, 9 .... 75, 3 (n.)
ii. 34, 35 .... 69, 4 (n.)
    38 .... 91, 15 (n.)
iii. 21 .... 69, 4 (n.)
iv. 13 .... 59, 12 (n.)
    27 .... 61, 4 (n.)
vi. 2 .... 59, 14 (n.)
viii. 4 ff. .... 41, 11 (n.)
    25 .... 53, 11 (n.)
x. 48 .... 98, 2 (n.)
xii. 19 .... 108, 9 (n.)
xiii. 27, 48 .... 73, 8 (n.)
    33 .... 61, 11 (n.)
xvii. 23 .... 121, 16 (n.)
    24, 25 .... 12, 15 (n.)
    25 ..... 13, 18 (n.); 19, 4 (n.)
xix. 5, 6 .... 98, 2 (n.)
xxii. 16 .... 91, 15 (n.)
xxv. 11 .... 2, 3 (n.)

ROMANS

i. 16 .... 122, 3 (n.)
    20, 21 .... 46, 11 (n.)
vi. 4 .... 91, 15 (n.)
viii. 2 .... 91, 15 (n.)
    3 .... 15, 4 (n.)
ix. 8 .... 91, 15 (n.)
    21 .... 13, 4 (n.)
x. 18 .... 60, 11
xiii. 1–7 .... 28, 3 (n.)
xiv. 11 .... 77, 8

I CORINTHIANS

i. 14 .... 98, 2 (n.)
    18 .... 122, 3 (n.)
    24 .... 22, 8 (n.); 38, 12 (n.)

ii. 5 .... 90, 2 (n.)
iii. 21 .... 127, 13 (n.)
vi. 1 .... 3, 14 (n.)
vii. 13 .... 106, 24 (n.)
viii. 3 .... 114, 4 (n.)
xi. 22 .... 100, 5 (n.)
   23 .... 99, 9
xii. 6, 11 .... 39, 3 (n.)
xiv. 16 .... 98, 8 (n.)
xv. 25 .... 69, 4 (n.)
   53 .... 32, 5; 77, 4
xvi. 2 .... 101, 13 (n.)

II CORINTHIANS

v. 10 .... 67, 14 (n.)
xi. 16 .... 30, 11 (n.)

GALATIANS

iv. 9 .... 114, 4 (n.)
   26 .... 91, 15 (n.)
   27 .... 79, 5
v. 1 .... 91, 15 (n.)

EPHESIANS

v. 8 .... 91, 15 (n.)

PHILIPPIANS

ii. 6 .... 12, 18 (n.); 96, 2 (n.)
iii. 9 .... 127, 4 (n.)

COLOSSIANS

i. 15 ff. ...... 38, 12 (n.); 112, 10 (n.)

I TIMOTHY

ii. 1, 2 .... 28, 11 (n.)
   4 .... 24, 1 (n.); 130, 3 (n.)
   10 .... 7, 5 (n.)
iv. 3 ff. .... 100, 7 (n.)
v. 17 .... 98, 2 (n.)

II TIMOTHY

ii. 12 .... 14, 8 (n.)

HEBREWS

i. 13 .... 69, 4 (n.)
iii. 1 .... 18, 9; 94, 15
iv. 2, 6 .... 53, 11 (n.)
   12 .... 23, 5 (n.)
vi. 4 .... 92, 13 (n.)
   9 .... 102, 2 (n.)
x. 12, 13 .... 69, 4 (n.)
   24 .... 100, 5 (n.)
   32 .... 92, 13 (n.)
xii. 19 .... 2, 3 (n.)

JAMES

i. 21 .... 128, 2 (n.)
v. 12 .... 26, 10

I PETER

i. 3, 23 .... 90, 13 (n.)
   14 .... 91, 15 (n.)
ii. 23 .... 126, 11 (n.)
iv. 14–16 .... 5, 5 (n.)
   15 .... 3, 4 (n.)

II PETER

iii. 9 .... 24, 1 (n.)

I JOHN

ii. 14 .... 51, 26 (n.)
iii. 9 .... 51, 26 (n.)

JUDE

6 .... 111, 6 (n.)

REVELATION

i. 7 .... 77, 17 (n.)
xii. 9 .... 46, 1
xx. 2 .... 46, 1

INDEX III.

GREEK WORDS.

ἄβυσσος 87, 14; 89, 17
ἀγαλλιάομαι 60, 17; 62, 17
ἀγαπάω 24, 3, 4, 6; 127, 15
ἀγγαρεύω 25, 17
ἀγγελικός 77, 1
ἄγγελος 10, 1; 53, 10; 54, 4; 76, 13; 95, 2, 15; 111, 5, 6, 15; 112, 3; 114, 3; 115, 7; 120, 5; (of Christ) 94, 15; 95, 26
ἀγγελτικός 37, 6
ἀγεννής 118, 4
ἀγέννητος 21, 4, 7; 40, 12; 73, 15; 78, 16; 112, 5; 125, 7; 127, 14
ἁγίασμα 63, 4
ἅγιον πνεῦμα 50, 21; 53, 12; 66, 3; 79, 12; 90, 16; 98, 5; 100, 9
ἄγνωστος 113, 5; 121, 16
ἀγωνιάω 6, 4
ἀγωνίζομαι 20, 16; 21, 2; 86, 18; 126, 10; 127, 5
ἀδελφοί (of the Christians) 97, 15; 98, 3
ἀδιαφορία 119, 2
ἀδιάφορος 119, 1
ἀδιάφθορος 29, 9
ἀδοξέω 74, 5
ἀείζωος 89, 16
ἀθανασία 67, 5
ἀθέμιτος 13, 15
ἄθεος 8, 1; 8, 15; 9, 8; 9, 9; 15, 5; 19, 3; 45, 7; 70, 10; 86, 17; 117, 18
ἀθεότης 7, 8
ἄθλον 7, 11; 124, 2
ἀΐδιος 123, 3
αἵρεσις 44, 6
αἴσθησις 29, 6; 30, 2; 34, 10; 77, 5, 11
αἴτησις 20, 1
αἰών (ἀπέραντος) 46, 5

αἰώνιος 11, 15; 12, 10; 16, 6, 10, 22, 14; 27, 16; 28, 16; 29, 7; 36, 17; 69, 20; 77, 5; 97, 20; 105, 7; 106, 10; 115, 9; 117, 7, 11; 119, 5
ἀκατασκεύαστος 87, 13; 97, 3
ἀκουστικός 78, 11
ἀκρίτως 8, 3; 15, 10
ἀκροβυστία 79, 26
ἄκτα 56, 6; 72, 11
ἄληπτος 4, 3
ἀλλαγή 38, 13
ἀλλάττω 13, 5
ἀλλ' ἤ 61, 13, 19
ἀλληλοφόνος 21, 10
ἀλληλοφόντης 59, 15
ἀλλοεθνής 79, 19
ἀλλοιόω 116, 2
ἄλλως 7, 2
ἀλογισταίνω 70, 1
ἄλογος 3, 1, 7; 8, 2; 13, 6; 17, 10, 12; 83, 7; 85, 11; 86, 16; 104, 13; 108, 10; 118, 5; 123, 5; 126, 1
ἁμαρτία 53, 14; 54, 6; 57, 14; 66, 13; 73, 7; 74, 2, 17, 20, 23; 75, 18, 22; 76, 4; 91, 6, 11; 92, 6; 98, 18
ἁμαρτωλός 22, 20; 23, 13; 24, 2; 25, 2; 39, 8; 57, 14; 61, 12, 21
'Αμήν 98, 8, 9; 101, 4
ἄμορφος 14, 5; 87, 6
ἀμυδρῶς 128, 3
ἀναγγέλλω 60, 12; 62, 24; 74, 8, 10
ἀναγεννάω 90, 13, 14; 91, 1; 92, 7
ἀναγέννησις 90, 13; 98, 18
ἀναγράφω 45, 13; 81, 7; 88, 6; 89, 3; 95, 7; 96, 16

B.

10

ἀναδίδωμι 47, 6; 101, 20; 107, 7
ἀναιρέω 15, 15, 17; 33, 1; 39, 8;
    49, 14; 72, 12; 85, 13; 86, 6
ἀναισθησία 29, 5; 86, 2
ἀναλαμβάνω 47, 1
ἀναλογία 28, 16
ἀναλύω 34, 1; 116, 3
ἀνάλωσις 33, 8
ἀνάμνησις 68, 3; 99, 10
ἀναπέμπω 98, 5; 101, 3
ἀναπνοή 83, 10
ἀναπολόγητος 5, 3; 46, 11
ἀναστροφή 14, 7; 92, 3
ἀνατίθημι 13, 14; 21, 7; 40, 13; 73,
    16; 84, 3; 90, 4
ἀνατροπή 44, 2
ἀνατροφή 47, 3
ἀναφέρω 45, 11; 76, 4; 106, 9; 112,
    2; 118, 9; 126, 14
ἀναφύω 77, 9
ἀνδροβατέω 126, 5
ἀνδροφονέω 125, 11
ἀνδροφόνος 47, 2; 108, 12
ἀνδρόω 49, 22; 55, 1
ἀνεγείρω 38, 2; 42, 1; 50, 1, 3; 59,
    1; 72, 5; 77, 3; 82, 11; 96, 17
ἀνέδην 44, 3; 47, 6; 114, 8
ἀνεκδιήγητος 75, 11
ἀνέλεγκτος 11, 9; 127, 12
ἀνέλευσις 41, 6
ἀνενδεής 19, 4; 85, 19
ἀνεξίκακος 25, 13
ἀνεπίμικτος 9, 11
ἀνέρχομαι 35, 2, 8; 36, 2; 50, 4;
    64, 1; 71, 2; 75, 5; 81, 8, 12;
    82, 3, 5; 120, 11
ἀνετάζομαι 15, 11
ἀνεύθυνος 70, 5; 84, 5
ἀνθρωπαρεσκεία 2, 14
ἄνειμι 76, 6
ἀνίστημι 31, 13; 32, 5; 35, 2; 58,
    20; 61, 21; 64, 1; 68, 17; 71, 2;
    72, 9; 75, 3; 96, 9; 100, 16;
    101, 17
ἀνομία 27, 14; 74, 19; 75, 14, 16;
    76, 4
ἀνταίρω 26, 1
ἀντάλλαγμα 24, 18
ἀντίγραφον 102, 14, 16
ἀντιποιοῦμαι 11, 17
ἀντιτίθημι 48, 3
ἀντιτυπέω 12, 4
ἀνωνόμαστος 94, 5
ἀξιέραστος 118, 16

ἄξιος (w. dative) 14, 6
ἀξίωσις 85, 4; 103, 10, 15
ἀόρατος 87, 13; 97, 3
ἀόργητος 25, 14
ἀπάγω 8, 13; 49, 20; 86, 19; 108,
    9, 20
ἀπαγωγή 80, 5
ἀπαθανατίζομαι 35, 14; 36, 14
ἀπάθεια 105, 8
ἀπαθής 14, 9; 40, 12; 85, 19; 87, 2
ἀπαλλάττω 16, 12; 34, 11; 45, 15;
    66, 23; 86, 6; 109, 1; 110, 15;
    128, 10
ἀπαντάω 68, 2; 88, 8
ἀπαράβατος 65, 12
ἀπαρέσκω 110, 6
ἀπέραντος 46, 5
ἀπερίτμητος 79, 25
ἀπιστέω 32, 14; 46, 13; 52, 27; 76,
    21; 84, 6; 86, 1
ἀπιστία 31, 13
ἄπιστος 12, 12; 31, 3; 52, 24
ἀπογραφή 54, 16
ἀπόδειξις 22, 4; 34, 6; 39, 4; 48,
    6, 10; 71, 4, 5; 80, 4; 86, 15;
    95, 7
ἀπόδεκτος 64, 14
ἀποκαλύπτω 74, 10; 94, 13; 95,
    23
ἀποκόπτομαι 45, 10
ἀπόκρισις 118, 12
ἀποκυέω 52, 16; 70, 21; 113, 10
ἀπολογία 63, 13; 126, 7
ἀπολύω 11, 9
ἀπομνημόνευμα 99, 7; 100, 11
ἀπομνημονεύω 53, 15
ἄποπτος 127, 11
ἀπόστολος (of Christ) 18, 9; 94, 15;
    95, 8, 26; (of the Apostles) 64, 2;
    69, 12; 73, 13; 75, 8; 78, 21;
    91, 15; 99, 7; 100, 12; 101,
    19
ἀποστροφή 127, 1
ἀποτάσσομαι 73, 15
ἀποτελέω 93, 3
ἀποτροπή 70, 1
ἀρεστός 11, 2; 14, 11; 119, 7
ἁρμονία 77, 8
ἀρρητοποιός 45, 3
ἄρρητος 13, 7; 122, 4; 125, 7; 127,
    14
ἀρχηγέτης 45, 18; 49, 17
ἀρχὴν (τὴν) 14, 4, 10, 13; 46, 9;
    47, 2; 87, 10; 113, 1; 115, 8

GREEK WORDS

ἀσχολέω 96, 15
ἀσώματος 95, 10; 96, 4; 115, 18
ἄσωτος 92, 12
ἄτρεπτος 20, 9
αὔξησις 111, 1
αὐτεξούσιος 115, 7
αὐτοκράτωρ 1, 1; 35, 14; 84, 2; 107, 7; 108, 15
αὐτολεξεί 50, 13; 52, 20; 87, 7
ἄφεσις 90, 10; 92, 5; 98, 18
ἀφθαρσία 14, 12; 19, 13; 32, 5; 60, 6; 64, 4; 77, 4
ἄφθαρτος 14, 9; 60, 5; 123, 8; 124, 1
ἄφθορος 23, 7
ἀφραίνω 122, 11
ἀφροντιστέω 28, 14
ἄψυχος 12, 17

βαναυσουργός 83, 5
βάρβαροι 9, 2; 11, 4; 70, 12
βασιλεία 15, 9, 14; (of heaven) 22, 13, 18; 25, 7; 27, 8; 91, 2
βασιλεύς (τῶν οὐρανῶν) 109, 2
βδέλυγμα 57, 23
βιβλίδιον 47, 6; 107, 6; 128, 8
βιβλιοθήκη 49, 1
βλασφημέω 49, 19
βλασφημία 37, 7
βόθρος 30, 9
βούλευμα 14, 6
βραχυεπῶς 73, 20; 119, 7
βρυγμός 27, 14
βρῶσις 24, 14, 16

γαμετή 106, 12
γέεννα 33, 3, 4
γένεσις 37, 4; 92, 1
γενετή 38, 1
γενητός 115, 10
γεννάω (of Christ) 20, 3; 37, 14; 38, 11; 49, 21; 53, 18; 54, 9, 15; 55, 1; 70, 3; (of the *Logos*) 18, 3; 34, 18; 37, 4; 113, 2
γέννημα 34, 17
γεννήτωρ 20, 10; 36, 8
γήϊνος 86, 10, 21
γινώσκω 114, 4
γνώριμος 49, 8; 51, 17; 75, 2
γνωριστικός 128, 13
γράμμα 2, 11; 84, 3

δαιμονιάω 106, 1
δαιμονιόληπτος 30, 4; 113, 13

δαίμων 8, 2; 5, 9, 11, 13; 9, 5, 6; 13, 1; 15, 5; 17, 9; 20, 14; 36, 14; 39, 1; 41, 5, 7, 12; 43, 7; 46, 1; 61, 7; 68, 6, 19; 77, 5; 80, 7; 81, 5; 84, 8; 85, 9; 86, 9, 17, 18; 92, 19; 93, 9; 95, 12; 96, 19; 100, 1; 105, 11; 111, 8, 16; 113, 11, 20; 114, 3, 6; 115, 1; 117, 3, 6; 121, 12; 122, 7; 125, 1; 127, 2
δεινότης 104, 8
δεισιδαίμων 3, 1
δεκτικός 65, 5; 115, 11
δεσπόζω 22, 1; 68, 15
δεσπότης (θεός) 18, 9; 52, 3; 56, 18; 61, 8; 66, 8; 70, 21; 90, 15; 92, 8; 112, 8
δηλωτικός 51, 13
δημιουργέω 14, 5; 87, 11
δημιουργός 11, 17; 19, 3; 34, 15; 43, 6; 86, 13; 95, 18; 121, 17
διαβεβαιοῦμαι 31, 10
διάβολος 46, 1
διαγγέλλω 62, 9
διάγω 34, 12
διαγωγή 11, 17; 12, 3
διαδέχομαι 18, 4; 103, 2
διάδοσις 101, 4
διαθρύπτω 58, 4
διάκονοι 98, 11; 101, 6
διακρίνω 114, 8
διασαφέω 53, 4; 63, 14; 80, 18
διασπάω 58, 3
διασύρω 55, 18
διατίθημι 13, 2; 95, 13
διατροφή 19, 8
διαφορά 36, 5
διγαμία 22, 20
δίδαγμα 7, 10; 22, 3; 27, 5, 21; 30, 7; 85, 5; 86, 1; 106, 7, 8; 110, 9; 117, 9, 21; 124, 8; 127, 6; 129, 7, 11, 15
διδασκαλεῖον 108, 4
διδασκαλία 120, 13
διδάσκαλος 18, 8; 20, 2; 23, 1; 27, 1; 32, 15; 35, 1, 6; 50, 20; 87, 4; 107, 13; 117, 13
διδαχή 60, 9; 78, 21; 108, 3; 111, 11
διέξοδος 61, 16
διηγοῦμαι 75, 13
δικαιοπραγέω 17, 6
δικαιόω 58, 17; 75, 21; 91, 9
διοίκησις 85, 17; 107, 10

δόγμα 11, 3; 34, 9; 43, 12; 44, 5;
  67, 6, 14; 86, 17; 116, 8; 120,
  7; 121, 21
δογματίζω 2, 5; 7, 7; 11, 2
δοξάζω 7, 6; 8, 1; 16, 4; 63, 13;
  64, 6; 74, 4; 89, 18
δοριάλωτος 51, 10
δουλαγωγέω 123, 9
δράσσομαι 62, 17
δύναμις ('*miracle*') 27, 12; 41, 12;
  48, 5; 84, 15; (applied to λόγος)
  22, 8; 38, 12; 52, 2; 53, 19; 89,
  7; 122, 3; (plur. 'faculties') 14,
  15; 28, 17
δυσεξήγητος 113, 6
δυσκίνητος 105, 10
δυσμετάθετος 105, 10
δυσφημέω 73, 19
δύσφημος 39, 3; 44, 1; 73, 17

ἐγκαταλείπω 57, 15; 79, 14
ἐγκρατεύομαι 47, 4
ἐγκύμων 54, 2
ἔθος 17, 14; 21, 11; 73, 19; 78, 23;
  85, 12; 92, 3
εἴδωλον 96, 17; 126, 1
εἰκονοποιέω 31, 6
εἱμαρμένη 64, 6, 11; 65, 7, 12;
  67, 12; 114, 15; 115, 5; 116,
  1
εἰσποιητός 1, 4
ἑκατόνταρχος 107, 14, 20
ἑκατοντάχειρ 41, 2
ἐκβάλλω 23, 3; 121, 14
ἐκγελάω 62, 5
ἐκδέχομαι 72, 15; 123, 6
ἐκδυσωπέω 106, 16
ἐκκεντέω 78, 5
ἐκμανθάνω 80, 4
ἐκμυκτηρίζω 62, 6
ἐκ παντός 11, 2
ἐκπαιδεύω 36, 5
ἐκπερινοστέω 82, 9
ἐκπύρωσις 34, 9; 85, 8; 89, 14;
  114, 12
ἐκστρέφω 58, 24
ἔκτασις 83, 8
ἐκτίθημι 44, 9; 47, 1
ἔλλειψις 105, 6
ἐμβροντησία 13, 12
ἐμπαθῶς 85, 12
ἐμπήγνυμι 117, 15
ἐμπνέω 56, 14
ἔμπτυσμα 58, 14

ἐμφορέω 80, 2
ἐνάρετος 6, 7; 16, 5; 69, 1; 105,
  7, (-ως) 36, 15; 119, 7
ἐνατενίζω 63, 16
ἐνέργεια 68, 5; 80, 6; 88, 10; 115,
  1
ἐνεργέω 8, 14; 9, 1; 17, 11; 39, 3;
  41, 11; 42, 10; 80, 11; 93, 1, 5;
  95, 12; 96, 18; 114, 6; 117, 2, 6;
  124, 16
ἐνθύμημα 23, 5
ἔννοια 36, 7; 42, 8; 97, 10, 11; 110,
  16; 116, 7
ἐντελοῦμαι 77, 18, 19
ἔντευξις 1, 9
ἐντολή 26, 13
ἐντυγχάνω 20, 15; 44, 7; 63, 14;
  68, 8, 11; 69, 16; 75, 4; 117, 20;
  118, 2; 129, 15
ἐξακολουθέω 2, 3; 14, 13
ἐξαναγκάζω 104, 13; 125, 5
ἐξεταστικός 2, 13; (-ῶς) 8, 12
ἐξήγησις 56, 1; 90, 6; 102, 13
ἐξηγητής 50, 21
ἐξηγοῦμαι 20, 12; 67, 8; 90, 5
ἐξιλάσκομαι 74, 2
ἐξίστημι 74, 4
ἐξομοιόω 10, 1
ἐξομολογοῦμαι 77, 10
ἐξουθενέω 96, 8
ἐξουσία 61, 9
ἐπαγγέλλω 61, 6
ἐπαίρω 86, 21
ἐπακούω 80, 15
ἐπαναγωγή 38, 13
ἐπαρχιώτης 103, 10
ἐπαστής 113, 17
ἐπείγω 71, 5
ἐπερωτάω 73, 3
ἐπευφημέω 98, 8, 10; 101, 4
ἐπηρεάζω 1, 6; 24, 8
ἐπίγειος 110, 19
ἐπιγινώσκομαι 27, 19
ἐπίγνωσις 121, 16
ἐπιγραφή 42, 2
ἐπιγράφομαι 7, 5
ἐπικαλέω 70, 5
ἐπικατηγορέω 11, 5; 43, 13
ἐπικουρέω 100, 6; 101, 9
ἐπικύρωσις 69, 2
ἐπιλέγω 92, 9
ἐπίλογος 100, 2
ἐπιμιξία 34, 18
ἐπιμονή 46, 6

GREEK WORDS

ἐπίπνοια 88, 10
ἐπίσκεψις 4, 10; 30, 10; 68, 12; 101, 20
ἐπισκιάζω 53, 8; 54, 1
ἐπίστασις 68, 3
ἐπιτίμιον 65, 13
ἐπιτροπή 47, 9
ἐπίτροπος 20, 5; 54, 18; 61, 3
ἐπιφάνεια 8, 5; 20, 17; 21, 12; 60, 9
ἐπίχειρον 65, 14
ἐπονομάζω 13, 5, 8; 18, 10; 71, 1; 84, 4; 92, 5
ἐπόπτευσις 29, 10
ἐπόπτης 126, 11
ἐπορκίζω 113, 15
ἐπορκιστής 113, 17
ἐραστής 1, 4; 2, 9
ἐργαλεῖον 83, 6
ἐργασία 83, 4
ἐργάτης 3, 4; 27, 13
Ἔρεβος 88, 1
ἐρεύγομαι 60, 12
ἐρημόω 71, 15
ἐρήμωσις 71, 17; 78, 20
ἕρμαιον 29, 5
ἑρμηνευτικός 35, 6
ἐρώτησις 118, 6, 10, 12
ἐρωτοπεποιημένος 122, 15
εὐαγγέλια 99, 8
εὐαγγελίζομαι 53; 11
εὐδαιμονέω 4, 9; 115, 5
εὐεργετέω 86, 4
εὐθύνη 4, 2
εὐθύνω 6, 17
εὐλογέω 24, 7; 71, 12; 78, 7; 100, 7
εὐλόγως 6, 6
εὐνουχίζω 22, 16, 18
εὐοδόω 115, 18
εὐποιΐα 112, 9
εὑρετής 81, 6
εὐρωστία 19, 11
εὔτονος 97, 18; 121, 9
εὐφροσύνη 63, 19; 64, 3
εὐφώνως 7, 12
εὐχαριστέω 98, 10, 13; 99, 4, 9, 11; 101, 5; 122, 9
εὐχαριστία 19, 6; 98, 6, 7, 15; 101, 3
εὐχάριστος 19, 10
εὐχή 19, 5; 97, 16; 98, 2, 7; 99, 3; 100, 16; 101, 1, 2
εὔχομαι 21, 13; 23, 7; 24, 5, 7; 28, 11, 13; 90, 9; 127, 5

ἐχθραίνω 105, 11
ἑωσφόρος 69, 9

ζιβύνη 59, 7

ἡγεμονεύω 47, 7
ἡγεμών 36, 8; 47, 8; 54, 12

θανατόω 47, 2; 88, 10
θεῖος 108, 4; 110, 9; 111, 2; 125, 10; 127, 2; (θ. λόγος) 15, 4; 54, 8; 56, 16; 127, 9; see πνεῦμα
θείως 34, 6
θέλημα 27, 9; 61, 14; 95, 10
θελκτικός 122, 16
θεοφορέω 54, 7; 55, 7
θεραπεία 13, 8; 17, 10
θεραπευτής 35, 7
θεραπεύω 49, 22; 72, 4; 82, 11
θετός 14, 4; 112, 5
θεωρητικός 46, 12
θησαυρίζω 24, 13, 14, 18
θησαυρός 25, 9
θρησκεύω 93, 7

ἴασις 128, 1
ἰδίως 37, 3
ἰδιώτης 89, 21; 117, 22; 122, 2
ἰδιωτικός 118, 4
ἱερατεύω 93, 7
ἰοβόλος 88, 8

καθαίρω 51, 23
καθαρίζω 72, 8; 75, 18
καθαρός 11, 16; 66, 9; 87, 2
καθέδρα 61, 13
καινοποιέω 90, 5
κακία 3, 4; 8, 14; 9, 11; 12, 4; 13, 10; 16, 9; 46, 14, 15; 65, 9; 107, 3; 111, 14; 115, 10; 116, 5, 6; 117, 2; 119, 10; 120, 5; 122, 14, 15; 123, 6; 124, 10
κακόω 74, 24
κάκωσις 74, 19
καλλιερέω 18, 2
κἄν 17, 4; 30, 11; 44, 5
καταγγέλλω 7, 10; 11, 7; 64, 3; 86, 12; 124, 16
καταδίκη 16, 10
κατακλυσμός 114, 8
κατακυριεύω 69, 7
καταλέγω 7, 2; 60, 2
κατάληψις 116, 4
κατάλυσις 113, 11; 114, 2

κατάρα 71, 11
καταρῶμαι 24, 7
καταργέω 113, 18
καταριθμέω 13, 10
κατασκευή 122, 5
καταστερίζω 35, 13
κατάσχεσις 62, 12
κατατρέχω 117, 21
καταφαίνομαι 20, 8
κατευοδόω 61, 18
κατορθόω 65, 1; 114, 16
καύχημα 63, 4
κηδεμών 101, 13
κιναιδία 45, 10
κλαυθμός 27, 14
κληρονομέω 76, 1
κληρονομία 62, 12
κλῆσις 29, 10
κοινωνέω 21, 10; 24, 8; 43, 12; 118, 10
κοινωνία 83, 1; 118, 9
κοινῶς 37, 1
κόλασις 6, 5, 6; 12, 10; 16, 6; 17, 1; 24, 2; 29, 7; 64, 8; 66, 1; 69, 20; 77, 11; 85, 8; 106, 10; 117, 7, 11
κολαστήριος 16, 12
κοπετός 78, 2, 3
κόπτομαι 78, 4
κοσμέω 34, 8; 111, 2; 113, 3; 122, 18; 123, 3
κρᾶμα 98, 3
κρίσις 2, 13; 3, 13; 8, 2; 55, 10; 61, 10, 21; 74, 27; 78, 16; 102, 6, 10; 108, 10; 114, 7; 129, 11
κρονική 101, 17, 18
κτίζω 113, 2
κτίστης 112, 8
κυοφορέω 53, 8
κύριος ('the Lord') 26, 13, 15; 27, 7, 11; 57, 1, 15, 17; 58, 14, 20; 59, 5; 61, 13, 22; 62, 2, 6, 10, 16, 18, 24, 25; 63, 5, 9; 66, 12, 17, 22; 69, 4, 6; 74, 9, 10; 75, 17, 20; 77, 10; 78, 6; 79, 14; 91, 10, 14; 94, 17; 112, 8
κυρίως 113, 1

λαλιά 60, 13
λαμπρότης 69, 9
λάμπω 27, 15
λατρεύω 26, 14; 79, 9; 105, 12; 117, 10
λογικός 14, 15; 46, 12; 120, 13

λόγιον 52, 17
λογισμός 87, 1; 124, 5; 125, 8
λόγος ('*word*,' '*argument*,' '*reckoning*,' '*law*,' '*doctrine*') 2, 13; 4, 3; 19, 5, 10; 28, 17; 37, 12; 53, 4; 55, 6, 11; 57, 11; 60, 13, 18; 69, 17; 71, 5, 9; 81, 5; 84, 4; 87, 5; 91, 14; 95, 8; 99, 3; 100, 14; 110, 7; 114, 14; 115, 16; 116, 9; 118, 9; 126, 10; 129, 10; (λ. of Christ) 22, 7, 8; (θεῖος, of God) 37, 6; 54, 8; 79, 10; 87, 16; 99, 1; (κυρίου) 59, 5; (of the Gospel) 69, 11; (reason) 2, 2; 5, 2; 8, 7; 9, 2; 10, 2; 20, 7; 78, 15; 80, 2; 102, 1; 116, 7; 117, 1; 121, 16; 122, 4; (σώφρων λ.) 2, 5; (ἀληθὴς λ.) 3, 11; 8, 11; 65, 11; (ὀρθὸς λ.) 106, 10; 115, 13; 120, 7; ('*reason*' or '*the Logos*') 15, 4; 18, 6; 21, 3; 70, 10, 16, 17, 18; 97, 9; 119, 14; 121, 7; ('*the Logos*') 9, 3; 18, 2; 34, 17; 37, 4; 38, 11; 51, 26; 52, 3; 53, 20; 70, 9, 20; 89, 11; 94, 13; 95, 9; 96, 2; 113, 1; 116, 11; 117, 4, 5; 121, 1, 3, 4, 22; 127, 9, 15; 128, 3
λοιμός 61, 13
λουτρόν 90, 16; 92, 10, 13, 19; 98, 18
λούω 66, 9; 91, 7; 92, 9, 18; 93, 4; 97, 14; 98, 17
λυχνία 44, 2

μαγικός 20, 17; 21, 6; 41, 12; 43, 1; 48, 5; 84, 15; 111, 9
μάγος 29, 11
μάθημα 4, 10; 107, 13; 126, 8
μαθητεύω 23, 6; 110, 9
μαθητής 101, 19
μακρόβιος 75, 19
μαλακία 50, 1; 74, 15
μαλακίζω 74, 20
μάστιξ 8, 2
μεγαλεῖος 118, 3; 120, 12
μεμπτέος 64, 14
μεταβάλλω 18, 18; 23, 9; 26, 5; 34, 3; 36, 16; 49, 9
μεταβολή 19, 12; 34, 1; 99, 5; 106, 18; 111, 2; 114, 14
μετάληψις 101, 5
μετανοέω 77, 15; 91, 7; 92, 7
μετάνοια 23, 11; 24, 1; 46, 8; 61, 9

GREEK WORDS

μεταποιέω 13, 14
μετατίθημι 69, 19; 85, 15; 126, 17; 129, 9
μετέλευσις 65, 3
μετέρχομαι 7, 11; 123, 5
μηνυτικός 51, 6; 55, 4
μήτρα 91, 3
μίλιον 25, 18
μισάλληλος 21, 10
μισάνθρωπος 86, 5
μογιλάλος 72, 8
μονόφθαλμος 22, 13
μορφή 12, 18, 19; 13, 7
μορφοποιέω 13, 5
μορφόω 9, 3; 12, 16
μυθολόγος 111, 15
μυθοποιέω 39, 2; 78, 13; 80, 3
μυξωτήρ 83, 9
μυστήριον 20, 11; 40, 9; 45, 11, 13; 47, 6; 81, 7; 99, 14; 125, 11
μώλωψ 74, 21

νεκρόω 30, 12
νεκυομαντεῖαι 29, 9
νηστεία 57, 20
νηστεύω 90, 10
νοερός 46, 9; 78, 11
νουθεσία 100, 14
νουμηνία 57, 19
νουνεχής 18, 6; 71, 3; 124, 4

ξύλον ('cross') 63, 10; ('stocks') 117, 15

ὀδυνάομαι 74, 17
ὁμιλέω 2, 12
ὁμογνώμων 47, 12
ὁμοδίαιτος 21, 12; 106, 22
ὁμόζυγος 45, 9
ὁμοιοπαθής 105, 1; 121, 24
ὁμόκοιτος 106, 23
ὁμολογία 6, 16; 60, 4; 108, 7
ὁμόφυλος 21, 11
ὀνειροπομπός 29, 11
ὄνομα (referring to God) 14, 4; 90, 14; 92, 9, 10; 112, 5; 113, 6; (of Christ) 27. 12, 17; 39, 7; 52, 23; 69, 15; 92, 14; 98, 5; 113, 4, 15; 117, 9; (of Jesus) 53, 13; 54, 3, 5; 113, 8; (of the Spirit) 92, 16; (of Christian) 5, 7; 6, 1, 3, 6, 10, 11; 11, 5; 108, 14
ὄντως 20, 6
ὀρύσσω 55, 12, 19; 58, 19

οὐήξιλλον 83, 14
οὐράνιος 24, 1; 25, 6; 67, 6; 86, 10; 111, 1
οὐρανός 24, 19; 25, 12; 35, 3; 36, 2; 41, 7; 50, 4; 57, 17; 62, 5; 63, 2; 64, 1; 68, 16; 71, 2; 75, 5; 76, 5, 7, 10, 13; 77, 1; 81, 8; 82, 3, 6; 87, 12; 97, 2; 111, 4; see βασιλεία, βασιλεύς
ὄφις 45, 12; 46, 1; 88, 9; 89, 3

παθητός 76, 23
πάθος 3, 13; 8, 2; 18, 5; 37, 9, 11; 51, 22; 80, 1; 86, 3; 111, 12; 127, 16
παιδεία 1, 4; 2, 9; 62, 17; 74, 20
παμμάχως 127, 5
παραγίνομαι 49, 21; 51, 7; 57, 6, 7; 73, 1, 10, 25; 76, 10; 77, 2, 17; 79, 11; 80, 8; 81, 11; 85, 10
παραιτοῦμαι 2, 3; 47, 3; 70, 15; 78, 22; 121, 15
παρακελεύομαι 6, 20; 26, 9
παρακολουθέω 26, 6
παρακούω 66, 19
παραλυτικός 38, 1
παραφέρω 82, 12; 97, 11
παραχράομαι 73, 11
πάρεδρος 29, 11
παρεπίδημος 101, 12
πάρθενος 37, 14; 49, 21; 52, 14, 20, 22; 53, 5, 6, 7, 8, 9, 10; 54, 1, 4; 70, 21; 82, 5; 96, 6
παρουσία 72, 6; 76, 22; 81, 15
παστός 60, 17
πατήρ (of God) 57, 10, 16; 94, 11; 95, 28; 96, 1, 7; 109, 1; 112, 8; 122, 4; (ἀρετῶν) 9, 10; (οὐράνιος) 24, 1; 25, 6; (πάντων) 11, 17; 18, 8; 52, 3; 56, 18; 61, 7; 68, 17; 70, 20; 112, 5; 121, 17; (τῶν αἰώνων) 63, 5; (τῶν νομοθέτων) 119, 13; (τῶν ὅλων) 66, 8; 90, 14; 92, 8; 95, 17, 24; 96, 1; 98, 4; (ὑμῶν) 24, 20; 25, 11, 20; (τοῦ Χριστοῦ) 27, 9; 57, 1; 113, 10
πατροφόντης 36, 9
πεισμονή 78, 10
περίβλημα 126, 18; 127, 3
περιβολή 123, 1
περιέπω 48, 18
περινοστέω 42, 6
περίοδος 12, 11

πιστεύω 31, 11; 32, 1; 10, 12; 33, 5; 36, 17; 48, 7; 52, 27; 61, 4; 74, 9; 75, 6; 79, 3; 89, 2; 98, 16; 113, 11; (w. πείθομαι) 12, 1; 14, 1; 28, 14; 29, 8; 90, 7; (w. God, Christ, etc.) 30, 12; 50, 7; 51, 23, 25; 53, 16; 80, 15; 84, 12; 96, 7
πίστις 14, 15; 19, 13; 73, 15; 76, 18; 79, 27
πιστός 79, 23; 90, 1
πλάνη 12, 13; 85, 6
πλημμελέω 5, 1; 115, 9
πνεῦμα 83, 12; (τὸ) 53, 18; (θεῖον) 50, 21; 51, 24; (θεοῦ) 87, 14; 89, 10, 13; 97, 4, 5; see ἅγιον πνεῦμα, προφητικός
ποίημα 113, 1
ποιητής ('maker') 34, 3; 43, 8; 86, 10; 100, 7
ποιότης 19, 12
πολιτεία 6, 3
πολιτευτής 97, 19
πομπή 19, 10
πονέω 121, 3
πονηρεύω 90, 6; 97, 7
πονηρία 11, 12; 66, 10; 91, 8
πονηρός 3, 5, 12; 25, 2; 26, 11; 38, 1; 44, 9; 57, 14; 75, 15; 92, 3; 99, 14; 108, 21; 120, 5; 125, 2; 126, 18
πράγματα ἐπάγω 3, 13
πραότης 26, 2
προαγγελτικός 51, 22; 69, 11; (-ῶς) 56, 16
προάγω 44, 11
προαγωγεύομαι 45, 9
προαίρεσις 64, 15; 65, 1, 15; 92, 5; 101, 7; 114, 16
προαμαρτάνω 90, 10; 92, 6
πρόβλημα 123, 6
προγνώστης 67, 13
προγράφω 91, 5; 94, 7; 97, 1; 129, 8
προδιαβάλλω 20, 14
προελέγχω 10, 8
προεστώς (ὁ) 98, 2, 10; 100, 14; 101, 2, 9
προκαταριθμέω 37, 8
προκατέχω 3, 2
προκηρύσσω 48, 13; 49, 21; 57, 7; 76, 16, 19, 22; 80, 16; 81, 15; 84, 12; 86, 11; 92, 17; 117, 12
πρόκλησις 4, 1; 100, 15

πρόληψις 2, 14; 110, 15
προμηνύω 46, 5; 52, 25; 53, 18; 70, 8; 72, 11; 80, 21; 89, 14; 94, 6
πρόνοια 111, 5
προπάτωρ 51, 2; 52, 17
προσαγόρευμα 113, 5
προσγράφω 45, 15
προσδέχομαι 13, 19
προσδοκία 50, 15; 51, 6; 81, 2
προσεπεύχομαι 130, 3
προσηγορία 6, 2
προσηλόω 86, 22
προσκόπτω 78, 1
προσομιλέω 93, 13
προσονομάζω 8, 9
προσραίνω 126, 2
πρόσρησις 112, 10
πρόσταγμα 62, 9
πρόσταξις 32, 5
προστιμάω 109, 3; 129, 4
προσφέρω 19, 6, 9; 98, 2; 100, 7; 101, 2
προσφορά 13, 18
προσφώνησις 1, 9; 102, 13
πρόσχυσις 126, 3
προσωνυμία 5, 5; 108, 14
προσώπου (ἀπὸ) 56, 14, 17, 19; 57, 9; 58, 8; 71, 9; 73, 1; 79, 14
προτρέπω 15, 2; 20, 12; 26, 3; 60, 21; 84, 5; 121, 16
προτροπή 36, 6
προφητεία 48, 15; 49, 3, 5; 50, 21; 51, 20; 53, 1; 56, 9; 62, 21; 73, 9, 14, 25; 75, 4; 78, 9; 81, 10; 82, 8
προφητεύω 48, 8, 9, 16; 50, 7; 52, 10, 21; 54, 7; 56, 8; 59, 3; 60, 19; 67, 11; 72, 5; 76, 6, 17; 77, 18; 79, 3, 4; 80, 21; 82, 10
προφήτης 38, 7; 48, 13, 17; 49, 20; 50, 11, 12; 51, 25; 52, 9; 53, 21; 54, 10; 55, 7, 12, 14, 17; 56, 8, 13; 57, 5, 11, 16; 58, 6; 60, 10; 64, 10; 66, 7; 67, 3, 7; 68, 7; 69, 3; 71, 19; 76, 12, 16, 22; 77, 7, 18; 79, 10, 25; 80, 7, 15, 17, 19; 82, 4, 17; 83, 11; 84, 11; 86, 11; 87, 5, 9; 91, 5; 92, 16; 93, 1, 8; 94, 7; 96, 5; 100, 12; 117, 12; 121, 23
προφητικός 10, 2; 20, 7; 48, 13; 50, 22; 52, 26; 53, 17; 55, 8;

GREEK WORDS

58, 9; 59, 4; 60, 11, 22; 62, 22; 63, 11; 66, 3; 68, 2; 71, 8; 72, 12; 75, 10; 78, 26; 79, 13; 81, 4; 87, 10; 89, 15; 94, 6; 95, 19, 27
πρωτόγονος 86, 20
πρωτότοκος 38, 12; 53, 20; 70, 8; 78, 16; 96, 2
πῦρ (of Hell) 16, 10; 22, 14; 27, 16; 28, 16; 36, 17; 46, 3; 66, 20; 69, 20; 77, 6; 80, 9; 105, 7; 106, 10; 115, 9; 117, 7, 11; 119, 5
πυρίκαυστος 71, 13

ῥανίς 31, 5; 32, 1
ῥᾷον 18, 17
ῥάπισμα 58, 13'
ῥεπούδιον 106, 24
ῥῆσις 52, 9
ῥητῶς 56, 7; 81, 10; 95, 14
ῥιπτέω 30, 3

σάββατον 57, 20
σαλεύω 63, 8
σαρκοποιέω 52, 4; 99, 1, 5
σατανᾶς 46, 1
σεμίδαλις 57, 23
σημαντικός 51, 27; 96, 12
σημασία 113, 5, 8
σής 24, 14, 15
σιαγών 25, 15; 58, 12
σκανδαλίζω 22, 12
σκαπανεύς 83, 4
σκέπω 58, 4
σκευάζω 34, 16
σκεῦος 13, 4
σκηνή 89, 1
σκήνωμα 60, 16
σκορπίζω 77, 19
σκώληξ 77, 13
σοφίζομαι 22, 2
σπερματικός 117, 4; 127, 9
σταυρός 55, 5; 56, 1; 83, 11; 88, 12; 89, 6
σταυρόω 20, 3, 10; 35, 1; 37, 7; 50, 2; 51, 10, 20; 55, 5, 16; 56, 3, 4; 57, 8; 58, 24; 62, 22; 63, 18, 19, 21; 71, 1; 75, 1; 78, 15; 82, 14; 92, 15; 101, 17; 113, 16
στέαρ 58, 1
στεῖρα 79, 5
στολή 50, 17; 51, 12, 25; 81, 3
στραγγαλιά 58, 3

στροφή 21, 1
συγγενής 127, 10
σύγγραμμα 46, 2; 49, 2; 94, 3, 19; 100, 12; 126, 7
συγκατατίθημι 97, 15
σύγκλητος 1, 4; 84, 18; 85, 3; 108, 16
συγκόπτω 59, 7
σύγχυσις 114, 1
συζυγία 106, 16, 22
συλλαμβάνω 53, 6, 11
σύλληψις 43, 7
συμβασιλεύω 14, 8
συμβολικῶς 82, 15
σύμβολον 45, 12; 51, 13; 81, 14; 82, 17; 83, 13
συμμέτοχος 128, 1
συμπραγματεύομαι 26, 8
συνάλλαγμα 58, 4
συναρπάζω 8, 8; 86, 16
σύνδεσμος 58, 3
συνείδησις 47, 12
συνέλευσις 61, 4; 100, 11; 101, 14
συνεπιγνώμων 85, 3
συνεπίσταμαι 108, 2; 110, 12
σύνεσις 75, 21
συνεύχομαι 90, 11
συζῆ 20, 15; 49, 13; 57, 13; 62, 15; 74, 3, 9; 90, 2; 118, 2, 3
συννηστεύω 90, 11
συνοδοιπόρος 26, 7
συνουσία 14, 12; 54, 1
συνουσιάζω 53, 5, 6
σύνταγμα 44, 6; 95, 14
σύνταξις 105, 3
συντελέω 51, 20; 98, 7
συντίθεμαι 60, 2; 68, 19; 119, 14
συντόμως 18, 18
συνών 113, 1
σχῆμα 7, 5; 13, 1, 4; 83, 1, 5, 6, 11, 13; 84, 3, 4
σώζω 27, 6; 46, 8; 53, 14; 54, 6; 79, 13, 18; 89, 2; 97, 20
σωτήρ 53, 15; 54, 3; 90, 15; 99, 2; 101, 16; 113, 8
σωτηρία 16, 7; 21, 2; 96, 7; 97, 20; 99, 2
σωτήριον 62, 25

τάξις 20, 7; 111, 6
ταπεινόω 71, 15
ταπείνωσις 74, 27
τεκνόω 111, 7
τέλος 29, 3; 45, 5; 68, 10

τελώνης 24, 12
τερατολογία 80, 11
τεχνίτης 13, 29
τρανός 72, 7
τρόπαιον 83, 2, 15
τυραννίς 4, 4
τυφλώττω 5, 1

υἱός (referring to Christ; of God) 9, 12; 18, 9; 20, 5; 21, 4; 36, 18; 37, 1; 38, 11; 48, 6; 50, 4; 52, 3; 86, 11; 94, 14; 95, 8, 25; 100, 8; 112, 10; (ὑψίστου) 53, 12; (ἀνθρώπου) 76, 12
ὕλη 13, 2; 14, 5; 87, 6; 101, 15
ὑλικός 13, 17
ὕμνος 19, 10
ὑπαγορεύω 2, 2; 3, 11; 18, 6; 115, 15
ὑπεκκρούω 87, 1
ὑπέρχομαι 110, 16
ὑπεύθυνος 128, 11
ὑπηρετικός 25, 13
ὑπνόω 58, 20
ὑπογράφω 47, 10; 128, 7
ὑποθημοσύνη 21, 15
ὑπολύομαι 93, 5, 14, 15
ὑπομονή 26, 2, 7
ὑποπίπτω 5, 6
ὑπόσχεσις 7, 5
ὑποτάσσω 61, 6; 102, 13; 111, 1
ὑφαιροῦμαι 18, 5
ὑψόω 74, 3

φανερόω 84, 10
φανέρωσις 50, 19; 51, 4; 84, 9
φαρμακευτής 113, 17
φευκτός 124, 5

φθαρτός 13, 8; 33, 8; 116, 3
φιλαλήθης 2; 6; 18, 18; 107, 18
φιλανθρωπία 14, 3
φιληδονία 124, 10
φιλήδονος 105, 10; 124, 11
φίλημα 98, 1
φιλοδοξέω 80, 1; 85, 12
φιλόδοξος 86, 5; 118, 15
φιλόκομπος 117, 16
φιλόλογος 122, 1
φιλόψοφος 117, 16
φόβητρον 8, 6; 119, 4
φρυάσσω 61, 23
φῦλον 79, 2
φυσιολογέω 88, 3
φωτίζω 92, 13; 97, 17
φωτισμός 92, 13, 17

χαμαιπετής 123, 10
χειροποίητος 86, 21
χειροῦμαι 21, 1
χιάζω 88, 4; 89, 7, 11
χίασμα 89, 6
χιλιονταετής 12, 11
χνοῦς 61, 19
χορηγία 103, 7
χρηστός 5, 8; 6, 12; 24, 20; 25, 1
χρίω 113, 3
χωλός 38, 1
χωνεύω 13, 3
χώρα 20, 6, 9; 89, 11
χωρέω 22, 19; 32, 7; 71, 6; 86, 2

ψευδοδοξία 128, 9
ψευδολογέω 11, 15; 127, 3
ψευδολόγος 107, 19
ψευδομαρτυρέω 45, 17; 118, 2

www.ingramcontent.com/pod-product-compliance
Lightning Source LLC
Chambersburg PA
CBHW060608230426
43670CB00011B/2019